FOXES AND LIONS

FOXES AND LIONS

Machiavelli's Confidence Men

Wayne A. Rebhorn

Cornell University Press

Ithaca and London

*Cornell University Press gratefully acknowledges
a grant from the Andrew W. Mellon Foundation
that aided in bringing this book to publication.*

First published 1988 by Cornell University Press.

International Standard Book Number 0-8014-2095-4
Library of Congress Catalog Card Number 87-47824
Printed in the United States of America
*Librarians: Library of Congress cataloging information
appears on the last page of the book.*

*The paper in this book is acid-free and meets the guidelines for
permanence and durability of the Committee on Production Guidelines
for Book Longevity of the Council on Library Resources.*

For Marlette, Matthew, and Rebecca

Contents

Preface

My primary aim in writing this book has been to show how Machiavelli saw the world through the lens of literature. I have based my analysis on the assumption that all human beings construct the reality they see — certainly the reality they write — primarily by means of inherited schemes and models that they acquire in reading, viewing, and listening to literary works. I have furthermore assumed that those works are perceived not as isolated entities but as instances of larger categories, of genres and subgenres, and that those categories are then replicated, extended, modified, combined, even subverted in their applications. To put the matter in a nutshell: I have operated on the assumption that genre is a means for people — and for Machiavelli — to think the world. Such an approach reverses the more usual tendency among readers of Machiavelli to see him as a proto-political scientist, a "realist" who faced without prejudices and preconceptions a world of historical facts. It insists instead that for all his fascination with power politics, Machiavelli's political vision is mediated by literature, that it partakes as much of myth and story as of raw events, and that its power and enduring interest derive in good measure from that literary shaping. Students of Machiavelli have long been bothered by the mythical or literary quality they noted in his nonfictional writings, because that quality seemed to impede the claims so many wished to make for him as an empirical "scientist." By recognizing that even scientists, when they write the world, do so through the inherited schemas and models of literature, I not only account for the literariness of Machiavelli's nonfictional writing but undo the opposition between myth and science which has troubled so much criticism of his works.

The second aim of this book is an extension of the first: to place Machiavelli's writings within their literary context, primarily that of the late Middle Ages and Renaissance in Italy and throughout Europe, and secondarily that of antiquity, which was so important for Renaissance authors. More specifically, my book relates Machiavelli's works to the host of Renaissance texts, to the stories, plays, and novels of such writers as Boccaccio and Sacchetti, Shakespeare and Jonson, Quevedo and Molière, who wrote about trickster figures, ranging from clever servants and wandering rogues to conniving merchants, enterprising gentlemen, and calculating princes—in short, foxes of every species. This disparate band of characters, whom Renaissance Italians usually called *beffatori*, I have labeled "confidence men" in what should be interpreted as a genealogical gesture, an insistence that the tricky characters who proliferate in the works of Machiavelli and other Renaissance writers are originary figures for the later confidence men of the nineteenth and twentieth centuries. My analysis also places those characters in their own tradition, which stretches back to Boccaccio, the medieval *fabliau* and farce, and the Italian *novella* on the one hand, and to classical, particularly Roman, comedy on the other. Furthermore, I argue that Renaissance writers, Machiavelli included, turned to such figures to produce works shaped generically as confidence tricks because in that way they could clarify, reflect on, and respond to concerns of enormous significance for their culture, specifically the issues of self-fashioning and social mobility and the perceived fragility, contingency, and transformability of the social order. Like his contemporaries, then, Machiavelli was drawn to the confidence man and the generic form of the confidence trick as a means to make sense of the world he lived in, to deal with the problem of identity, and to diagnose what he saw as the singular transformation—the historical crisis—of contemporary Italy as well as to propose remedies for it.

It would not be an exaggeration to say that Machiavelli was obsessed by confidence men, and this obsession serves my third interest in writing this book: the desire to see Machiavelli whole, to connect his literary works with his political and historical ones, and to relate all of them to his biography, his concerns with power and degradation, and his characteristic modes of self-representation. After defining the confidence man and the literary genre of the confidence trick which Machiavelli shared with his culture, I have ordered my book so that it traces the various shapes the figure assumed in his writings, moving from the literary through the political and historical to the personal and autobiographical. Thus, in order to unfold as fully as possible the model of the confidence trick as Machiavelli conceived it, I begin with an analysis of his great comedy, *La mandragola*, in which he creates his most fully literary and traditional, though not unproblematic, versions of the confidence man. The two following chapters are concerned with the reshaping of the figure as a player on the grim stage of history in such works as *Il principe*, the *Discorsi*, and the *Istorie fiorentine*. In these works his ethos is darkened and deepened as he is made a redeemer for Renaissance Italy in its moment of historical crisis. Here the confidence man is amalgamated with the figure of the epic hero to become a warrior as well as a cunning deceiver, a lion as well as a fox. Finally, I offer a pair of chapters focused on Machiavelli's representation of himself as a confidence man throughout his writings — and as a particularly carnivalesque one in his personal letters — arguing that he adopted that guise not just as a means to render his experience comprehensible, as a way to think the world, but as an instrument of power to enable him to deal with a life marked by frustration, disappointment, defeat, and degradation. It was an instrument that ultimately failed him, as it always did his heroes, and thus exposed him to the ridicule he reserved for the dupe. From such a fate, however, as I argue in my last chapter, he did manage an escape, at least in one incident in his life: he rose above his dialectic of confidence man and dupe not by some futile attempt to abandon it but by turning to literature once more and shaping his experience as brilliant, ironic comedy.

I incurred a series of debts in the writing of this book. The essay that serves as the basis for Chapter 6 appeared in another form in *Italian Quarterly* 24 (1983). A substantial debt of gratitude is owed to the Research Institute of the University of Texas for a Faculty Research Assignment that provided a semester for uninterrupted work and a grant that enabled me to have much of the manuscript transferred to a computer disk. I also thank Thomas M. Greene, Stephen Greenblatt, and Robert Turner for their invaluable support. Perhaps my greatest debt of this sort is owed to William Sutherland, chairman of the Department of English at the University of Texas, and Robert King, dean of the College of Liberal Arts at the University of Texas, who made it possible for me to have free time in the summer of 1985 to finish much of the writing of this book.

I cannot begin to thank all the students and colleagues who have suffered through endless discussions and readings of my work on Machiavelli and Renaissance confidence men; certain names, however, must be mentioned. William Scheick and Peter Bondanella graciously read an early draft of the book and provided much-needed encouragement and many valuable suggestions. Douglass Parker helped with the classical materials in Chapter 2, and Mark Hulliung, Jack D'Amico, John Rumrich, Dolora Wojciehowski, and Frank Whigham read various portions of the finished work and provided extremely useful commentary. Thanks also are due to Barbara H. Salazar and Trudie Calvert for their careful editing of my manuscript, and to Bernhard Kendler, my editor at Cornell University Press, for his help and encouragement. Without doubt my greatest debt is owed to my wife, Marlette, who read the entire manuscript many times, provided both sharp conceptual challenges and invaluable stylistic recommendations, and went beyond the call of love and duty, interrupting her own work, to transfer a portion of it for me to a computer disk at a crucial stage in the writing. That my book is clear and relatively free of jargon may be credited to her; whatever infelicities remain are my own responsibility. The greatest debt I owe to her and to my children concerns a less tangible matter: they provided the cooperation, firm support, and affectionate encouragement that enabled me to bring this project to completion and without which my doing so would have counted for very little. My dedication of it to them is hardly adequate repayment for all they have given me.

WAYNE A. REBHORN

Austin, Texas

Abbreviations and Editions
of Machiavelli's Works

Arte   *Arte della guerra*. In the *Arte della guerra e scritti politici minori*, ed. Sergio Bertelli. Milan: Feltrinelli, 1961. References will supply book and page number in the following form: 1, 1.

CC   *La vita di Castruccio Castracani da Lucca*. In *Istorie fiorentine*, ed. Franco Gaeta. Milan: Feltrinelli, 1962. References will supply the page number.

Disc   *Discorsi sopra la prima deca di Tito Livio*. In *Il principe e Discorsi*, ed. Sergio Bertelli. Milan: Feltrinelli, 1960. References will supply book, chapter, and page number in the following form: 1, i, 1.

Ist   *Istorie fiorentine*. See the edition listed under *CC*. References will supply book, chapter, and page number in the following form: 1, i, 1.

Let   *Lettere*, ed. Franco Gaeta. 2d ed. Milan: Feltrinelli, 1981. References will supply the number of the letter and the page number in the following form: #1, 1.

La mandragola   In *Il teatro e tutti gli scritti letterari*, ed. Franco Gaeta. Milan: Feltrinelli, 1965. References will supply act, scene, and page number in the following form: 1.i.1.

Pr   *Il principe*. See the edition listed under *Disc*. References will supply chapter and page number in the following form: 1, 1.

SL   *Scritti letterari*. See the edition listed under *La mandragola*. References will supply the page number.

SP   *Scritti politici minori*. See the edition listed under *Arte*. References will supply the page number.

All translations are my own.

FOXES AND LIONS

Machiavelli and the
Renaissance Confidence Man

When Giuliano de' Medici and the Signoria sent Machiavelli to the small town of Carpi in the late spring of 1521, and the Arte della lana (Wool Guild) asked him to seek out a Lenten preacher for Florence, the irreverent and anticlerical writer must have laughed inwardly at the absurdity and incongruity of his mission. Once in Carpi, he wrote to his friend Francesco Guicciardini that if he had his way, he would find for the Florentines exactly the opposite of what they wanted—someone who would teach them not the way to Paradise (*Let, #184*, 403: "insegnasse loro la via del Paradiso") but the way to the devil ("la via di andare a casa il diavolo"). Convinced of the depravity and wickedness of most friars, Machiavelli declared, with tongue deep in cheek, that instead of seeking out a prudent and honest man, he would find one who was "più pazzo che il Ponzo, più versuto che fra Girolamo, più ippocrito che frate Alberto" (ibid.: "madder than il Ponzo [one of Savonarola's opponents], wilier than fra Girolamo [Savonarola], more hypocritical than frate Alberto"). Always the realist, however, Machiavelli restrained his desires and negotiated with a conventional, pious, albeit rather parochial friar, rather than follow his fancy and visit someone "more hypocritical than frate Alberto" upon his fellow citizens.

Striking here is Machiavelli's revelation of the deep, and deeply ambivalent, attraction he felt toward confidence men. As he lets his imagination (ibid.: "la mia fantasia") range freely and dreams up a preacher in his own manner (ibid.: "a mio modo"), he instinctively produces a grotesque creature who is one-third clown (the mad Ponzo) and two-thirds clever rogue and charlatan. Machiavelli makes it clear that he disapproves of friars who hide their wickedness "sotto il mantello della religione" (ibid.: "under the cloak of religion"), instead of steadfastly following the traces of Saint Francis, and he patriotically asserts his willingness to serve Florence in any capacity. Yet at the same time the letter reveals a Machiavelli who glories in his stubbornness and contrariness, who is distant from and critical of the city he serves, and who is clearly taken with the equally recalcitrant, highly individualistic scoundrels he labels his sort of preacher. In short, the letter betrays a complex attraction to and repulsion from those wily friars even as it ambivalently unfurls a devotion to Florence, which is simultaneously undercut by Machiavelli's gay contempt for the opinions of his fellow citizens. As we shall see, the ambivalent though instinctive engagement with confidence men and charlatans by Machiavelli's "fantasia" is not limited to this letter from Carpi or to his reactions to friars.

Equally striking is the list of three candidates Machiavelli produces for model preacher. All three men are conniving friars, and if Machiavelli is silent elsewhere in his works about the first and the last, he does devote considerable space to fra Girolamo in his writings, scorning his folly of lacking arms in *Il principe* (VI, 32) and, in an early letter, mingling contempt for his "bugie" (*Let*, #3, 33: "lies") with marvel at his rhetorical ability to shift public opinion from one extreme to another practically overnight.[1] As Machiavelli's imagination moves from il Ponzo through fra Girolamo to frate Alberto, it goes from a lesser-known public figure through one with a significant historical, even mythic, identity to one who was a widely known though purely literary character.[2] In other words, as his mind ranges, Machiavelli makes no hard-and-fast distinction between historical individuals and literary characters, be-

[1] Il Ponzo was fra Domenico da Ponzo, a Franciscan friar prominent in Florence, who made various prophecies in 1492. When they did not come true, the Signoria expelled him from the city. Then, despite his early support for Savonarola, he was persuaded to speak out against the man in 1495 and was miserably defeated in the ensuing verbal duel, although he did live to see Savonarola's final destruction in 1498. See Roberto Ridolfi, *The Life of Girolamo Savonarola*, trans. Cecil Grayson (London: Routledge & Kegan Paul, 1959), pp. 47, 107–8, 113. Machiavelli may have lumped him together with other confidence men because of the man's false prophecies and his obvious opportunism. *Pazzo* may be a reference to his foolhardy and clownish decision to go head-to-head with Savonarola in an oratorical contest.

[2] Gaeta's edition of the *Lettere* argues in n. 3, p. 403, that if il Ponzo and fra Girolamo are historical characters, frate Alberto must be one as well, and it identifies him with a maestro Alberto da Orvieto, whom the pope sent to Florence as his ambassador in 1495, in connection with Savonarola. Yet this identification seems forced in view of the relative obscurity of maestro Alberto (in comparison with the well-known Ponzo and Savonarola, at least in Florentine circles), and its logic is less than compelling. Moreover, as frate Alberto was one of Boccaccio's most famous literary creations and Machiavelli was certainly well acquainted with the *Decameron*, the identification of Machiavelli's reference with the literary character is at least as probable as Gaeta's identification of him with a historical one. Allan Gilbert in his translation of this letter simply identifies frate Alberto with the character in the *Decameron*; see Niccolò Machiavelli, *The Chief Works and Others*, trans. Allan Gilbert (Durham, N.C.: Duke University Press, 1965), p. 972, n. 1.

tween actual swindlers operating on the stage of Florentine politics and an entirely fictional character out of Boccaccio, between the stuff of life and the stuff of art. Confidence men do not live exclusively in one domain or the other for him, but circulate freely between them. Moreover, if one notes that the modifiers attached to the three names gradually lengthen and become more linguistically elevated ("pazzo," "versuto," "ippocrito"), then one may detect here less a series of equivalent terms than a progression in which the supreme position is occupied by a confidence man from the realm of art, not that of history. No matter how one reads the sequence, however, the interpenetration of art and life in Machiavelli's imagination remains unmistakable.

To say that these two realms interpenetrate in Machiavelli's imagination and its creations is, in a sense, to reconfirm two observations that have frequently been made about him: first, that he often injects his personal experiences, aspirations, and irritations into his nonpersonal writings, and second, that his literary as well as his political creations evince a deep engagement with the historical world and a persistent preoccupation with politics and power. One need only recall here Machiavelli's obsession with mercenaries, his presentation of himself, albeit in a deformed fashion, in the figure of the ridiculous old man Nicomaco in *Clizia,* or his direct revelation of his feelings of resentment in the prologue to *La mandragola,* to see how he allows his personal life to enter into his works. And his deep involvement with politics and history throughout his opus surely needs no documentation. Machiavelli's obsessions have led some readers to conclude that his imagination was determined primarily by facts, by questions of history and biography, and by an overwhelming interest in power politics. In its most extreme form, this reading has led to a vision of him as a rationalistic "scientist," dispassionately dissecting the political environment in which he lived.[3] One of the most dramatic expressions of this tendency has been the attempt to see his greatest literary creation, *La mandragola,* as a disguised political allegory, either by identifying its "meaning" with the issues and themes it shares with his political writings or, more specifically, by arguing that Lucrezia signifies Florence, Callimaco the ideal

[3]For classic expressions of the view of Machiavelli as a "scientific" analyst of politics and history, a precursor of modern empirical political science, see Herbert Butterfield, *The Statecraft of Machiavelli* (London, G. Bell, 1940); Ernst Cassirer, *The Myth of the State* (New Haven: Yale University Press, 1946); and Leonard Olschki, *Machiavelli the Scientist* (Berkeley: University of California Press, 1945). To say that Machiavelli views reality by means of schemata such as those provided by literature is not to deny the value of his observations or his importance historically to a discipline such as political science. It is, however, to deny a naive empiricism in connection with him.

prince, and so on.[4] Such an interpretation, however, ignores the fact that the organization of *La mandragola* is determined not by politics or history but by the typical characters and plotting of comedy, Machiavelli's legacies from Boccaccio, Plautus, and Terence, rather than the outcome of "scientific" observation. In fact, the "allegory" discovered in the play and derived from his political works resembles the plot of a comedy more than the product of factual analysis—Florence is barren like Lucrezia and desperate; her leaders, embodied in Nicia, have failed her; but her new prince, Callimaco, defeats those leaders and saves her so that she may be reborn. In short, Machiavelli is not a dispassionate "scientist" slavishly following facts; he always structures what he observes; and to do so he turns instinctively to the shapes he is familiar with from works of art.

The preceding statement could be usefully rephrased along the following lines: his works reveal that Machiavelli essentially responds to the world through literary genres. This is not surprising, for genres are, as Rosalie Colie and others have argued, not merely ways of shaping works of art but basic ways of organizing experience so that human beings can understand themselves and their world. Genres provide both a means of forming an identity and the source of the schemata that enable people to see reality.[5] Thus one can go beyond Mark Hulliung's argument about the literary importance of genres for Machiavelli, which suggests that he links historical eras together by seeing them through the various genres of Roman literature which prescribed behaviors and ordered them hierarchically.[6] Artistic forms fundamentally conditioned, indeed rendered possible, not just Machiavelli's writing of literature and history but his perception of reality.

Machiavelli's writings amply demonstrate that he imagined the world of experience through literary genres. To be sure, not every detail of his

[4]For examples of the first, more general form of allegorical reading, in which *La mandragola* is seen through the lens provided by Machiavelli's political works, see Luigi Vanossi, "Situazione e sviluppo del teatro machiavelliano," in *Lingua e strutture del teatro italiano del Rinascimento: Machiavelli, Ruzzante, Aretino, Guarini, Commedia dell'arte*, ed. G. Folena (Padua: Liviana, 1970), pp. 3–57; Guilio Ferroni, *"Mutazione" e "riscontro" nel teatro di Machiavelli, e altri saggi sulla commedia del Cinquecento* (Rome: Bulzoni, 1972), pp. 22–26; and Martin Fleisher, "Trust and Deceit in Machiavelli's Comedies," *Journal of the History of Ideas* 27 (1966): 365–67, 376–80. For the more specific allegory, see Theodore A. Sumberg, "*La mandragola*: An Interpretation," *Journal of Politics* 2 (1940): 320–40; and Antonio Parronchi, "La prima rappresentazione della *Mandragola*. Il modello dell'apparato. L'allegoria," *La Bibliofilia* 64 (1962): 59–69.

[5]Rosalie L. Colie, *The Resources of Kind: Genre-Theory in the Renaissance*, ed. Barbara K. Lewalski (Berkeley: University of California Press, 1973). See also Stephen Orgel, "Shakespeare and the Kinds of Drama," *Critical Inquiry* 6 (1979): 107–33.

[6]Mark Hulliung, *Citizen Machiavelli* (Princeton: Princeton University Press, 1983), pp. 182–83.

personal biography or every isolated historical fact can be assigned a generic affiliation. Nevertheless, the overarching shape of his works and
many of their constituent elements can be accounted for in that way.
Various scholarly studies have revealed that the *Istorie fiorentine* was
shaped largely by the principles of Renaissance historiography and the
Vita di Castruccio Castracani by those of Renaissance biography.[7]
Moreover, as I noted above, Machiavelli's hopeful vision of an ideal redeemer prince for Florence and Italy is connected to the plot of comedy, or perhaps to something closer to that of epic or chivalric romance.
Revealingly, in a letter to Francesco Guicciardini, Machiavelli self-
consciously characterizes his vision of the contemporary political scene
and his personal experience of it as a "commedia" (#228, 496), and he
says in the same letter that the Spaniards in the army of Charles V
"hanno potuto qualche volta farci di gran natta" (495: "could have
sometimes played great tricks on us"). The operative term here is *natta*,
a word that means both trick, in the sense of practical joke or prank,
and the literary genre that recounted such tricks and was otherwise labeled *beffa*. The line between the two meanings is obviously a fine one
here, just as it is in the letter Machiavelli wrote describing a comparable
trick played by the sodomite Giuliano Brancacci on Filippo di Casa-
vecchia (#147, 327-30). In this last letter Machiavelli stresses the literariness of his account of an actual incident: he covertly alludes to Ovid
at the start, calling the trick a "metamorfosi ridicola" (327: "ridiculous
metamorphosis"); he later cites a verse from that ancient Roman poet
which identifies the tale as a "fabula" (330), a fable or story; finally, he
invokes Boccaccio as a writer about love in order to encourage his correspondent to pursue his amatory interests. Thus it should be clear that
if reality and history offered Machiavelli the raw material for his writings, he shaped that material according to the literary principles and
conventions of history, biography, comedy, and romance. In the broad-
est sense of the term, for Machiavelli, history was indeed story.[8]

[7]See, for example, Felix Gilbert, "Machiavelli's 'Istorie fiorentine': An Essay in Interpretation," in *Studies on Machiavelli*, ed. Myron P. Gilmore (Florence: Sansoni, 1972),
pp. 73-99; Peter E. Bondanella, *Machiavelli and the Art of Renaissance History* (Detroit:
Wayne State University Press, 1973); and the Introduction to the *Vita di Castruccio Castracani*, 3-7.
[8]That Machiavelli's correspondent Francesco Guicciardini also saw experience through
generic forms is revealed in a letter he wrote to Machiavelli in 1526: "Machiavello
carissimo. Ho la vostra de' 5. La novella del Borgo a S. Donnino fu commedia schietta,
quella di Modana tenne della tragedia, la vostra di Roma ha tenuto di cantafavola" (*Let*,
#230, 498: "Dearest Machiavelli. I have your letter of the fifth. The story of Borgo a San
Donnino was pure comedy, that of Modena a bit of a tragedy, yours of Rome something
of a tall tale").

One cannot always be certain, of course, whether Machiavelli was consciously selecting literary genres in order to shape his vision of experience or was simply responding unconsciously in that way to the world, past and present. Nevertheless, since his works do evince a generic organization, their characters and plots can be fruitfully examined through the lens of the literatures of ancient Rome and of medieval and Renaissance Italy which Machiavelli knew so well. And that is what I propose to do. Whereas scholars have traditionally read Machiavelli's works as a "realistic" exploration of politics and history, albeit one animated by what they sometimes see as a zeal for republican liberty and the redemption of Italy, and have accordingly turned even a literary masterpiece such as *La mandragola* into a political allegory, I am going to turn the tables and read those works from the opposite direction. I will approach such political characters as the new prince of *Il principe*, the Castruccio Castracani of Machiavelli's *Vita,* the clever rulers and condottieri described in the *Istorie fiorentine,* and the tricky consuls and generals from Roman history celebrated in the *Discorsi* as though they were all so many politic Callimacos. And I will view the organization of all those works and of incidents within them, their "plots," as being shaped by literary genres as well. In short, I will demonstrate that for Machiavelli art was not merely the handmaiden of history but something closer to its mistress.

More specifically, I will read Machiavelli's works, whether literary, historical, political, or personal, by focusing on a particular pair of literary characters toward which his imagination repeatedly gravitates. Throughout his writings he reveals an obsession with confidence men and their dupes and with the characteristic generic plots—the confidence tricks or games—associated with them. That obsession is unmistakable in his literary production and especially in his two most original works, *La mandragola* and the short story usually called "Belfagor arcidiavolo." But, as we shall see, it is equally clear in *Il principe,* whose central character may be read as a confidence man, and in Machiavelli's political and historical works generally, which consistently split the human race into statesmen, generals, ecclesiastical potentates, and rulers, all of whom behave like confidence men, and the vast mass of humanity who serve as their prey. Indeed, as one scholar has noted, even the state of Rome at some points in the *Discorsi* assumes the role of confidence man—or woman—in relation to the weaker city-states around it.[9] Finally, Machiavelli structured his persona in his political

[9]On Rome as trickster (the term *confidence man* is not used), see Martin Fleisher, "A Passion for Politics: The Vital Core of the World of Machiavelli," in *Machiavelli and the Nature of Political Thought,* ed. Martin Fleisher (New York: Atheneum, 1972), p. 137.

writings so that he could play the confidence man with his readers, and he adopted the role of confidence man in his personal life so as to gain and maintain the power and dignity his socially inferior position denied him. Thus it should not be surprising that when Machiavelli at Carpi tried to imagine a preacher for Florence "a mio modo," he should have instinctively thought of a confidence man, not just because friars in particular elicited such a response but because confidence men dominated the great stage of his imagined world.

Before exploring some of the ways in which the confidence man engaged Machiavelli's energies as a writer, that character must be defined in some detail. For although, as Luigi Russo has observed, Machiavelli focuses on trickery and deception throughout his works, it is not sufficient to define the confidence man merely as someone who tricks others.[10] Any definition of the confidence man must, at the very least, distinguish the behavior he displays and define the typical "plot" he is involved in as well as his character. Moreover, since Machiavelli's vision of life was profoundly shaped by the literary genre of the confidence trick, I will indicate the literary sources that nourished his imagination and explain the ways he adapted and transformed that material. In other words, I will define the distinctive conception of the confidence man which appears in Machiavelli's writings and separates him from his predecessors. Once the defining features of the Machiavellian confidence man are clear, it should be possible to understand why that conception had the seminal place it did in the literature and culture of the European Renaissance.

To speak of confidence men in the Italian and European Renaissance is admittedly to indulge in an anachronism, for the term originated in an editorial of the *New York Herald* written in 1849 and was later popularized by Herman Melville's *Confidence-Man* of 1857.[11] Critics of Italian Renaissance literature prefer to speak of the *beffatore* and the *beffa* (and use such related terms as *beffare* or *sbeffare* and *beffato* or *sbeffato*), especially since those words were employed by Boccaccio and the *novella* writers who came after him as well as by Machiavelli.[12] *Beffa*

---

[10] Luigi Russo, *Machiavelli*, 3d ed. (Bari: Laterza, 1949), p. 106.

[11] On the origin of the term *confidence man*, see Johannes D. Bergmann, "The Original Confidence Man," *American Quarterly* 21 (1969): 560-77.

[12] The Centre de Recherche sur la Renaissance Italienne of the Université de la Sorbonne Nouvelle dedicated two entire volumes to the place of the *beffa* in Italian Renaissance literature. In André Rochon, ed., *Formes et significations de la "beffa" dans la littérature italienne de la Renaissance* (Paris: Université de la Sorbonne Nouvelle, 1972), see especially the studies of Mireille Celse, "La *beffa* chez Machiavel, dramaturge et conteur," pp. 99-110, and Marina Marietti, "Aspects de la *beffa* dans les *Istorie fiorentine* de Machiavel," pp. 111-19.

identifies both a collection of related behaviors and a set of attitudes: it could mean antisocial trickery, roguery, and deceit as well as indulgence in sometimes crude and cruel practical joking; and it also served as the label for violent satirical attacks on others and a mocking, cynical, skeptical attitude toward human affairs. Sometimes the *beffatore* resembles the clown and engages in farcical antics that make him, as well as his prey, look ridiculous. Boccaccio's Martellino of *Decameron* II, I, exemplifies these characteristics when he fakes a "miraculous" cure at the altar of a saint and trembles in fright before a vicious judge. So does messer Dolcibene, a professional buffoon who is described as making a comic spectacle of himself in the fourteenth-century "Paradiso degli Alberti" as well as in many of Franco Sacchetti's *Trecentonovelle* (10, 24, 25, 33, 117, 145, 153, 156, 157). Playing the clown, the *beffatore* is comparable to the folkloric and mythic figure called the "trickster." This term has enjoyed great popularity since Paul Radin used it to translate the Amerindian name *Wakdjunkaga* in his book *The Trickster* of 1956.[13] Thus one might well be content to label as *beffatori*, or "tricksters," a wide array of Renaissance characters: many of Boccaccio's protagonists, the main figures of countless Italian *novelle* and comedies, such characters as Shakespeare's Falstaff and Autolycus, Ben Jonson's Face and Subtle, and, of course, Machiavelli's Callimaco and Gianmatteo in "Belfagor."

Those terms do not seem appropriate, however, to describe a host of related characters: Boccaccio's clever gentlemen and ladies who trick others usually to obtain sexual pleasure, the almost demonic scholar of *Decameron* VIII, 7, and the marquis who torments Griselda in X, 10; Shakespeare's Richard III, Prince Hal, and Iago; Jonson's Volpone and the gentlemen heroes of *Epicoene*; Molière's Tartuffe and Don Juan; and, of course, Machiavelli's Cesare Borgia and Castruccio Castracani, Cosimo de' Medici and Francesco Sforza. All of these figures have a clear affinity to the *beffatore,* in that they all shamelessly use deceit and trickery to gain morally dubious ends, but unlike him, they seldom make ridiculous spectacles of themselves, they possess important positions in the social and political order, and in general they are far more serious,

---

[13] *Wakdjunkaga* actually means *the tricky one* in the language of the Winnebago. In related Indian languages, the equivalent word is *isktinike* (Ponca), *itsike* (Osage), and *ikto-mi* (Dakota Sioux). All of these names Paul Radin and others translate as "trickster," although Radin admits that the meanings of the first two are unknown and that of the third is "spider." Even their etymology is unknown, and it is likely that the names actually precede ascribed meanings, so that *wakdjunkaga* means essentially "one who acts like Wakdjunkaga," and the idea of trickiness became attached to the name because of Wakdjunkaga's activities. See Paul Radin, *The Trickster: A Study in American Indian Mythology* (1956; rpt. New York: Schocken, 1972), p. 132.

indeed often sinister and threatening. Consequently, I will identify all these characters, from the most lowly, clownish peasants, friars, and jesters through self-possessed gentlemen and merchants to the most elevated princes and popes, by the somewhat more open term *confidence man.*

I have, to be sure, more compelling reasons for using this term as a translation for *beffatore,* despite its anachronistic flavor.[14] First—and perhaps least important—is its inherent suggestion of the betrayal, or at least manipulation, of confidence—a central issue, if not *the* central issue, in tales and plays from Boccaccio to Molière. More important are the associations of the confidence man with a complex, capitalistic urban culture. But most important is the recognition by writers, practically from the time *confidence man* was coined, that the character type predated the term, a recognition that typically led them to locate its most remote antecedents in the literature of the Renaissance.[15] Thus, although I do not wish to dismiss important differences between nineteenth- and twentieth-century confidence men and such Renaissance figures as Ciappelletto, Ligurio, Falstaff, and Tartuffe, I do insist on the connections between them. In some ways, those five-hundred-year-old characters are indeed our contemporaries. Let us consider two of those connections briefly.

In the first place, the goals pursued by Renaissance and modern confidence men are not absolutely different. Admittedly, whereas Renaissance figures aim at a fairly wide variety of goals, modern ones seem primarily to pursue money, possibly because in the world of the nineteenth and twentieth centuries money is crucial for the acquisition of status and power. Renaissance confidence men, by contrast, pursue food and sex and political and religious power and authority as well as

[14]On scholars' identification of the confidence man with the trickster of folklore, see the work of Barbara Babcock (or Babcock-Abrahams): "'A Tolerated Margin of Mess': The Trickster and His Tales Reconsidered," *Journal of the Folklore Institute* 11 (1975): 147–86; and "'Liberty's a Whore': Inversions, Marginalia, and Picaresque Narrative," in *The Reversible World: Symbolic Inversion in Art and Society,* ed. Barbara Babcock (Ithaca: Cornell University Press, 1978), pp. 95–116. For the American confidence man as folk trickster, see Warwick Wadlington, *The Confidence Game in American Literature* (Princeton: Princeton University Press, 1975). And for an identification of two exemplary Renaissance confidence men as tricksters, see Phillip Mallett, "Shakespeare's Trickster-Kings: Richard III and Henry V," in *The Fool and the Trickster; Studies in Honor of Enid Welsford,* ed. Paul V. A. Williams (Cambridge: D. S. Brewer, 1979), pp. 64–82.

[15]On the Renaissance antecedents of the American confidence man, see John G. Blair, *The Confidence Man in Modern Fiction* (New York: Barnes & Noble, 1979), pp. 13–14; and Susan Kuhlmann, *Knave, Fool, and Genius: The Confidence Man as He Appears in Nineteenth-Century American Fiction* (Chapel Hill: University of North Carolina Press, 1973), pp. 3–6.

wealth, in part because wealth did not so completely determine class standing and status as it was to do later. Nevertheless, although the obsession of Melville's confidence man with money may be typical of such figures in more recent literature, a desire for wealth does not exhaust the range of possible motives for modern authors: Thomas Mann's Felix Krull, for instance, pursues sex among other things, and Mann's story "Mario and the Magician" is basically concerned with politics as a confidence game. Moreover, many Renaissance characters seek wealth just like their modern counterparts. Thus the differences between Renaissance and latter-day confidence men flow from a narrowing of motives rather than from a replacement of one set by another. Ciappelletto, Ligurio, and Falstaff, then, are clearly the ancestors of Melville's nameless hero, not members of some other family.

Second, there are important affinities between the conceptions of mobility and identity at issue in confidence-man works of the Renaissance and the nineteenth and twentieth centuries. Modern confidence men are mobile both spatially and socially. They emerge out of nowhere, as Melville's confidence man always seems to do, and in random encounters they deceive people who have never seen them before and will never see them again. They play an enormous variety of roles, from beggar to businessman to aristocrat back to beggar again. Their behavior thus seems related both to the overwhelming size of modern society, with its attendant anonymity, and to the modern ideology of individualism, which sees people creating their own identities in a world imagined as a competitive arena, a marketplace that generates a free-floating social hierarchy in which one's position supposedly corresponds to one's personal merit. By contrast, although some Renaissance confidence men — the peripatetic friars in Boccaccio's stories, the picaros, and coney-catchers such as Shakespeare's Autolycus — are wanderers, few manage the almost total anonymity of their modern counterparts, and their role-playing is somewhat more restrained than that found in Melville's or Mann's works. Nevertheless, Renaissance figures do wander from town to town just like later confidence men, and they do create identities for themselves by playing roles. The two sets of characters behave similarly, in essence, because both are complicated, parodic responses to related social environments and ideologies. After all, both the Renaissance and the nineteenth century saw significant growth in urban centers and a dramatic increase in the number of marginal wanderers. More important, such Renaissance thinkers as Giovanni Pico della Mirandola and Erasmus defined in their writings an emergent ideology of self-fashioning, which ran counter to the period's dominant ideology of fixed selves and a fixed social order. This new ideology may be seen as the germ of the modern notion of individualism, of the "self-made man." Thus, while recognizing differences of degree and emphasis, one understands why Melville sought the ancestors of his confidence man in characters from the Renaissance.

In choosing *confidence man* over *trickster* as a label for Renaissance characters from Boccaccio's Ciappelletto to Molière's Tartuffe, then, I am insisting on a genealogy, validating the investigations of scholars who have traced the heritage of Melville's confidence man beyond the newspaper story in which the term first appeared or the Yankee peddlers of nineteenth-century America, back to literary figures, and especially to those of the English Renaissance, such as Iago and Milton's Satan. In pushing further back to Machiavelli and his Italian antecedents, I am completing a process already begun. Strikingly, Melville himself suggests such a connection by identifying his nameless hero with Machiavelli in the twenty-third and forty-fifth chapters of his novel and by having his narrator, in an extremely ironic passage, explicitly link the tricky, diabolically treacherous Indian Mocmohoc to Cesare Borgia, recalling in Mocmohoc's dealings with his enemies Borgia's betrayal of Oliverotto da Fermo. The direct literary model for Melville's confidence man, to be sure, is not Machiavelli and his characters but Milton's Satan. But because Satan may be traced back to the Machiavels of the Renaissance English stage, to such figures as Iago and Richard III, and they in turn are refractions of Machiavelli's princes, one arrives at the same starting point. Machiavelli's princes are thus seminal figures for a wide array of characters. As much as a minor swindler operating his scam on the streets of New York, they are the true source of Melville's confidence man and his descendants.

A reader might argue that it is illegitimate and reductive to subsume under a single term all the disparate Renaissance figures mentioned above. But if so, then writers from Boccaccio to Molière stand guilty of the charge. In the eighth day of the *Decameron*, for instance, which is explicitly concerned with *beffe*, and hence with *beffatori*, Boccaccio not only gives us the lower-class Bruno and Buffalmacco, who play the clown to some extent in tricking maestro Simone (VIII, 9), but the scholar Rinieri, who misogynistically torments Elena (VIII, 7). Boccaccio also takes pains to link the wit, or "ingegno," of frate Cipolla to that of a Cavalcanti or a Giotto, thus suggesting a definite connection between marginal rogues and the elite of Florentine society. Similarly, Shakespeare brings the future Henry V into Falstaff's tavern and underscores the profound affinities between the prince and the déclassé knight. Moreover, it should be recalled that scholars of the English Renaissance drama have traced both Falstaff's and Iago's ancestry back to the figure of the

Vice in the morality play.[16] Ben Jonson ironically identifies his two male swindlers at the start of *The Alchemist* as a sovereign and a lord general, thus suggesting connections between them and the ruling powers of England as well as linking them to the more sinister political tricksters who appear in *Sejanus* and *Catiline*. Christopher Marlowe's Dr. Faustus starts out as a self-made man, a genius with all but godlike power and knowledge, but he behaves in ways that identify him with the clowns of the play before it is done. Finally, if Molière's Tartuffe is ridiculous in his sexual pursuit of Elmire, he is also a seriously threatening and destructive character not unlike Shakespeare's Iago, and there is nothing clownish about Tirso de Molina's Don Juan, even if he is considered a *burlador* or trickster. In short, to yoke together Ciappelletto and Prince Hal, Falstaff and Don Juan, and label them all confidence men is merely to do what Renaissance writers themselves did; it is to validate their implicit perception that wandering rogues and rascally friars share important traits with deceiving courtiers and merchants, gentlemen and ladies, princes and popes. Machiavelli's good friend Francesco Vettori makes that implicit perception explicit in his *Viaggo in Alemagna* when he meditates on the scam a phony beggar performed before an inn:

> . . . pensai tra me medesimo con quanti modi, con quante astuzie, con quante varie arti, con quale industria un uomo s'ingegna ingannar l'altro, e per questa variazione il mondo si fa piú bello, il cervello di questo si fa acuto a trovare arte nuova per fraudare, e quello d'un altro si fa sottile per guardarsene, ed in effetto tutto il mondo è ciurmeria, e comincia ai religiosi e va discorrendo ne' giureconsulti, ne' medici, negli astrologi, ne' principi secolari, in quelli che sono loro intorno, in tutte l'arti ed esercizii, e di giorno in giorno ogni cosa piú s'assottiglia ed affina.[17]

> I thought to myself with what means, with what deceptions, with how many varied arts, with what industry a man sharpens his wits to deceive another, and through these variations the world is made more beautiful. The mind of this one is made more acute in order to find a new art to deceive, and that of another is made more subtle in order to protect itself. In effect, all the world is a confidence game [*ciurmeria*], and it begins with the religious and continues on to the lawyers, the doctors, the astrologers, the temporal princes and all those about them, to all the arts

---

[16]On the relationship of Iago and Falstaff to Vice, see the classic study of Bernard Spivack, *Shakespeare and the Allegory of Evil* (New York: Columbia University Press, 1958).

[17]Quoted in Ezio Raimondi, *Politica e commedia: Dal Beroaldo al Machiavelli* (Bologna: Il Mulino, 1972), p. 142.

and disciplines. And from day to day, everything becomes more subtle and refined.

This half-facetious, half-serious passage must be read as a mock-encomium not unlike Erasmus's *Praise of Folly* and Mosca's praise of parasites in Act III, scene ii, of *Volpone*. Vettori's key term here is *ciurmeria*, a word I define as *confidence game*, which identified the art of street vendors and hucksters who told fortunes and sold, among other things, magical remedies against snakebite. That normally pejorative term here becomes ironically a term of praise, and its range of reference is extended until confidence men or *ciurmatori* appear to be lodged in every nook and cranny of the social order. Vettori, as all those other Renaissance writers were suggesting more indirectly in their works, is showing that individuals of every rank in society could be considered potential confidence men; the whole of human life is a confidence game.

Machiavelli fully embraces such a vision. His major literary works all center on trickery and the abuse of confidence. Thus, although he never calls *La mandragola* a *beffa,* he does say that Ligurio "uccella" (1.i.63: "gulls") Nicia and he calls Nicia a ridiculous "uccellaccio" (II.iv.73: "great gull").[18] Like Vettori, Machiavelli also refers occasionally to *ciurmatori* in his works, writing at one point an obscene carnival song to be sung by *ciurmadori* as they entice women into their clutches, and using the word in one of his letters to identify a friar selling bogus salvation.[19] In that letter he labels Florence the "calamita di tutti i ciurmatori del mondo" (#141, 308: "lodestone of all the confidence men in the world"), either because his native city attracted so many friars of that sort or because he saw Florentine society as being open to confidence men at every conceivable level. More clearly indicative of Machiavelli's vision of the world as a confidence game is his use of the verb *beffare* or *sbeffare* in his historical writings to describe how a clever individual outwits and humiliates a rival. Thus he describes how the *condottiere*

---

[18]See "Belfagor," *SL*, 176: "Le quali cose tutte da Roderigo erano uccellate" ("All these things were mocked by Roderigo"). Here *uccellare* means to poke fun at or mock superstitions (the "cose" referred to in the quotation). Thus the term seems to be practically identical with *beffare* in Machiavelli's mind.

[19]The poem is the sixth of the *Canti carnascialeschi*, "De' ciurmadori" (see *SL*, 338–39). The word *ciurmare* derives ultimately from the Latin *carmen* (poem or charm) with some influence from *ciurma*, a slightly pejorative term for the rowers of a galley and, by extension, a confused multitude or mob. At least as early as Sacchetti, *ciurmare* meant to deceive or enchant someone with words. See the relevant entries in the *Grande dizionario della lingua italiana*, ed. Salvatore Battaglia (Turin: Unione Tipografico-Editrice Torinese, n.d.).

Niccolò Piccinino outmaneuvered the pope and easily took twenty cit-adels from him in the spring of 1438: "Né gli bastò con questa ingiuria avere offeso il pontefice, che lo volle ancora con le parole, come egli aveva fatto con i fatti, sbeffare" (*Ist*, v, xvii, 354: "Nor did it suffice that he offended the pope with this injury whom he wanted to mock [*sbeffare*] with words as he had done with deeds"). Similarly, Cosimo de' Medici defeats a political rival, Donato Cocchi, by having the man publicly humiliated by his partisans (*Ist*, vii, iii, 455: "lo fece . . . sbeffare"). Although Machiavelli does not speak of *beffe* in *Il principe* or the *Discorsi*, he does refer repeatedly to *inganno* or deception, and sees his ideal princes as well as his Roman consuls and generals as crafty deceivers, those they deceive as fools and simpletons. At one point, for instance, he praises his ideal prince as a "gran simulatore e dissimula-tore" ("great feigner and dissembler"), then concludes: "e sono tanto semplici li uomini, e tanto obediscano alle necessità presenti, che colui che inganna troverrà sempre chi si lascerà ingannare" (*Pr*, xviii, 73: "and men are so simple and so obedient to present necessities, that he who deceives will always find someone who will let himself be de-ceived"). Who could fail to see that his ideal prince and those he de-ceives are here playing the roles of *beffatore* and *beffato*, confidence man and dupe? Thus, from the *uccellatori* in *La mandragola* through the *ciurmatori* who have inundated Florence in Machiavelli's letter and the *beffatori* who outwit their political enemies in the *Istorie fiorentine* down to the *ingannatori* who abound in the political writings, Machia-velli's world is saturated with confidence men. He detects them at every level of the social hierarchy, just as other Renaissance writers did. Of course, Machiavelli, like those other writers, also knew that not all con-fidence men are alike, and he did discriminate between the slightly clownish Callimaco and the consistently serious Cesare Borgia, just as Shakespeare did between the comic Falstaff and the sinister Iago. I shall return to those important discriminations later in this chapter. At this point, however, if one takes Machiavelli's vision of society as seriously as one takes the comparable views of Boccaccio and Shakespeare, Jonson and Molière, then what we are dealing with looks more like a contin-uum of characters, an immense family of confidence men and women, ranging from tricky peasants to brutal princes, than a series of discrete and unrelated types. Before we begin to discriminate among them, we must recognize, as so many Renaissance writers did, their profound similarity. Hence we must define just what constituted a confidence man for them and explain why they were so fascinated by the figure they placed at the center of so many vital literary works, from the *Decam-eron* through *Henry iv* to *Tartuffe*.

How can these Renaissance confidence men be defined? Perhaps their most important trait is the fundamental ambiguity, and especially the moral ambiguity, of their trickery.[20] They elicit admiration, envy, or identification because of their incredible cleverness, wit, facility with language, and improvisational skill as actors. Their energy, courage and daring, and willingness to gamble also produce a sympathetic response, as does their relentless pursuit of physical pleasure, wealth, social position, and power. All of these traits speak to similar desires in most people, to that basic bit of unabashed individualism, hedonism, and lust for domination in everyone. Finally, Renaissance confidence men are attractive because they are profoundly creative as they carry out their schemes, inventing tricks, making up speeches, stories, and plays, and ultimately generating entire worlds for their dupes to inhabit. Thus, from one perspective, these confidence men are ideal versions of what most people wish to be: absolutely free, egocentric individuals who possess immense talent, energy, courage, and creativity and who frankly rejoice in their pleasures and their triumphs over others.

At the same time, however, the Renaissance confidence man dramatically separates himself from his audience, causing dismay or offense as his egocentric, self-serving drives lead him to ignore or defy moral and social norms. Generally, the confidence man in the Renaissance has no respect for conventions and proprieties, little concern for the public interest when it differs from his own, and scarcely a drop of altruism in his veins. He pursues personal wealth at the expense of religion (Boccaccio's frate Cipolla), sexual satisfaction in defiance of marriage (Tirso's and Molière's Don Juan), political power no matter what it costs the common good (Shakespeare's Richard III). To be sure, the actions of some confidence men, such as Machiavelli's Moses, Cyrus, Romulus, and Theseus and Shakespeare's Henry IV and Henry V, are presented as being beneficial for the peoples they lead, but it is striking that neither set of princes is ever described as acting explicitly for that purpose. Rather, Machiavelli offers his figures as models for the new prince who wants to acquire a state, thus suggesting that the pursuit of personal power and glory, rather than the good of the state, is the prime issue. And although Shakespeare's kings may brood in the most intimate soliloquies, their subject matter is their tactics for obtaining power, the illegitimacy of their rule and their guilt over it, and their weariness

---

[20]For the moral and other ambiguities of tricksters and confidence men, see Babcock, "'A Tolerated Margin of Mess,'" 159–61; and David M. Abrams and Brian Sutton-Smith, "The Development of the Trickster in Children's Narrative," *Journal of American Folklore* 90 (1977): 32–35.

in the role of king, not what is best for England; nor do they ever argue explicitly that unified rule under them would be better for the country than the fragmentation that would result if their enemies were victorious. Thus, although a few figures may seem to act for some noble end beyond themselves, closer inspection reveals their "altruistic" behavior to be virtually indistinguishable from the self-serving individualism that animates their fellow confidence men.

Machiavelli's heroes, from Gianmatteo through Ligurio and Callimaco down to the ideal princes Cesare Borgia and Castruccio Castracani, share the fundamental ambiguity of other Renaissance confidence men. All are brilliant actors and rhetoricians, egocentric individualists who pursue pleasure, status, and power with enormous energy and daring and who willingly violate moral principles and social rules when they must. Like other confidence men, if they connive at the destruction of all orthodoxies, they are also profoundly creative as they produce speeches, put on shows and plays, and invent tricks and stratagems to achieve their ends. Indeed, if the actions of the more political among them often lead to the loss of human life and the savaging of states, Machiavelli also assigns those individuals the lofty tasks of founding new states, inventing new constitutions and sets of laws, and reforming the moribund social order by taking it back to the vitality of its beginnings. Like the folk trickster, Machiavelli's political confidence men come close to being both demonically destructive and divinely creative at the same time.

The deep moral ambiguity of Machiavelli's confidence men needs to be stressed precisely because so many commentators on his works have wished to remove it either by a simple, direct identification of those men as figures of evil or by arguing that their evil deeds are merely means and can be justified by the higher end they serve. The first alternative is the response of many writers throughout the Renaissance, and it has recently been powerfully reformulated, though from a less hostile viewpoint, by Leo Strauss.[21] The problem with such a view is that it assumes Judaeo-Christian morality as a norm, ignores the positive value Machiavelli assigns to power, conquest, and glory, or both. His celebration of power is evident, for instance, in the passage from the *Discorsi* in which he faults Giovampagolo Baglioni of Perugia for not having killed his enemy Pope Julius II when he could easily have done so, for Baglioni would have done a deed "la cui grandezza avesse superato ogni infamia, ogni pericolo che da quella potesse dependere" (I, xxvii, 196: "whose grandeur would have conquered any infamy, any danger that could have re-

[21] Leo Strauss, *Thoughts on Machiavelli* (Chicago: University of Chicago Press, 1978).

sulted from it"). As Mark Hulliung has argued, Machiavelli is intensely hostile to Christianity and rejects its ethical teachings, espousing instead a pagan morality of heroic, glorious violence.[22] Hulliung is oversimplifying, however, for Machiavelli does not ignore Christian morality, as the idea of rejection might imply; in fact, he repeatedly goes out of his way to remind his readers of its existence. In *La mandragola,* for example, he has Callimaco offer to marry Lucrezia after he has seduced her, thereby recalling the very Christian morality he is violating. And throughout *Il principe* Machiavelli recalls traditional moral and social norms by stressing the need to violate them if his prince is to succeed. He directs the reader's attention to the ambiguous moral status of the prince's action in the following passage, in which he tries to explain how Agathocles of Syracuse managed to maintain control over his state despite his excessive cruelty and violence:

> Credo che questo avvenga dalle crudeltà male usate o bene usate. Bene usate si possono chiamare quelle (se del male è licito dire bene) che si fanno ad un tratto, per necessità dello assicurarsi, e di poi non vi si insiste dentro, ma si convertiscono in piú utilità de' sudditi che si può. [VIII, 44]

> I believe that this results from cruelties used badly or used well. Those can be called well used (if it is permissible to speak well of evil) which are done at one stroke, out of the necessity of securing oneself, and from that point on are not insisted upon, but are converted into as much utility for one's subjects as possible.

For someone who supposedly espouses a full-blown pagan morality or embraces evil with open arms, such moral nervousness should be inconceivable, just as it should be inconceivable for Machiavelli to declare, as he does at one point in the *Discorsi,* that fraud, except in war and to save one's *patria,* is detestable, and that one can acquire no true glory by breaking treaties or failing to keep one's word (III, xl-xli, 493-95). In short, it may be better to conclude that Machiavelli entertains at least two distinct value systems — the traditional Christian one he would like to reject but cannot fully free himself of and the pagan one that Hulliung has analyzed — and that he never completely resolves the dissonances.

Very few scholars and critics argue for a pagan or an evil Machiavelli, however. Most prefer to save him for post-Enlightenment liberalism, as

---

[22]Hulliung, *Citizen Machiavelli,* pp. 219-51 and passim. Although Hulliung's book is powerfully argued and serves as a useful corrective for those who would "save" Machiavelli for what Hulliung calls the "liberal tradition," it ignores Machiavelli's moral hesitations. On its limitations, see J. G. A. Pocock, "Machiavelli in the Liberal Cosmos," *Political Theory* 13 (1985): 559-74.

Mark Hulliung has shown, by claiming that he espoused one version or another of the "end justifies the means" argument. Some assert that Machiavelli is a republican, valuing freedom over tyranny and seeing the highest function of a prince as the institution of a free state; others say that he has his princes violate traditional morality for the ultimate benefit of their subjects and the security and survival of the state. But, as Hulliung has demonstrated, the Roman republic that Machiavelli sets up as a model is very different from the republic later advocated by George Washington and Thomas Jefferson. He imagines a fundamentally predatory state that values freedom because it results in constant internal strife and produces a high level of energy, which in turn allows it to expand and thereby acquire glory. The ultimate ends of Machiavelli's ideal republic are conquest and glory; the freedom and security of its citizens turn out to be merely means. Consequently, those Roman consuls and generals who use deception and violence on the Roman people in the service of the state may appear to honor traditional morality despite their questionable behavior, but their character is rendered deeply ambiguous because the state they serve pursues immoral ends. The second argument advanced in an attempt to reclaim some sort of traditional morality for Machiavelli's princes seems to be based on passages like the one cited above, in which even excessive cruelties are justified if a prince converts them to the benefit of his subjects. As the passage continues, however, it becomes clear that the ultimate end envisaged is the prince's acquisition and maintenance of his personal power, not the good of the state or its people. Again, the argument of means and ends leads to the conclusion that Machiavelli's princely confidence men essentially act in defiance of traditional morality. If they cannot be simply labeled evil, neither can they be redefined as paragons of virtue. Instead, they remain suspended between the two, intensely, consistently ambiguous.

Since Machiavelli's confidence men, along with those created by writers from Boccaccio to Molière, are morally ambiguous, they must be distinguished from the many other characters in Renaissance literature who also use deception and disguise but for more acceptable, publicly approved goals, as do the heroes and heroines of countless romantic comedies—Boccaccio's Gilletta di Nerbona (*Decameron*, III, 9), the young Lucentio in Shakespeare's Italianate *Taming of the Shrew*, the young couples and their accomplices who hoodwink oppressive fathers in Molière's comedies. In this camp may be numbered Machiavelli's own heroine Sofronia in *Clizia*, who, although she employs a clever stratagem that leads to her husband's painful public humiliation and thus might be considered a classic example of a *beffa*, is not really a *beffa-*

trice because her motives and her trick are socially respectable: she acts not against public ethics or to satisfy egocentric desire but to free her husband from a debilitating madness and to restore his dignity as a householder and citizen. Sofronia is, as a result, a moral paragon, whereas most confidence men in the Renaissance are, to say the least, shameless, amoral deceivers. Machiavelli's innovating princes who found republics or reform states and return them to their origins may appear to resemble Sofronia, but that appearance is misleading, for their acts of foundation or reformation always involve violent breaks with the past, the destruction of human life, and the violation of traditional morality. Moreover, the state they seek to found or reform is intended to resemble Rome and hence will be predatory and imperialistic. Most important, Machiavelli makes it clear that such princes aim at the well-being of their subjects only as a means to help them achieve personal security as rulers and, after their deaths, to enjoy "la gloria del mondo" (*Disc*, I, x, 159: "the glory of the world").

Such characters are amoral, not immoral. Although they flout social conventions and violate moral taboos, they are not presented as unmitigatedly wicked villains. Indeed, even when they behave as despicably as Shakespeare's Richard III and Iago — and some of Machiavelli's princes — they always retain an element of moral ambiguity that makes it difficult to condemn them definitively. Thus, although Boccaccio's ser Ciappelletto violates the sacraments, deceives a representative of God, and courts eternal damnation, the reader is led to marvel at his energy, inventiveness, and skill as an actor rather than simply to dismiss him as depraved. Similarly, Richard III's bravado and strength of will in his final scenes qualify substantially one's horror at his murders and treachery, just as the aura of sexual vitality and the daring of Don Juan produce an attraction that mitigates his villainy. Comparable qualities in Machiavelli's heroes — their ingeniousness and energy, their skill as actors and rhetoricians, their daring and defiance of conventional pieties and even of death itself, their fundamental creativity — all help to place them in a moral limbo despite their treachery, violence, and murder. Consider, by way of contrast, the legions of the fraudulent who are unambiguously condemned to the lowest reaches of Dante's Hell or such melodramatic villains as Don John in Shakespeare's *Much Ado About Nothing* and Sir Giles Overreach in Thomas Middleton's *A New Way to Pay Old Debts*, violent men who lack any redeeming qualities. Works about true confidence men never encourage readers or audiences to visit such harsh, dismissive judgments on their protagonists.

Machiavelli's works are most problematic on this score, for although he does occasionally condemn some forms of deceit and violence as evil, his condemnation is never pure and unqualified. In *Il principe*, for instance, he declares that Oliverotto da Fermo and Agathocles of Syracuse, despite their success, were so brutal, cruel, and inhuman that they deserve no glory and cannot be celebrated "infra li eccellentissimi uomini" (VIII, 42: "among the most excellent men"). Nevertheless, it is extremely difficult to keep such figures distinct from characters whom Machiavelli holds up for imitation, such as Cesare Borgia and Castruccio Castracani, who unhesitatingly kill the innocent, betray friends and dependents, and savage cities. Moreover, although Machiavelli explicitly condemns Julius Caesar as a tyrant in the *Discorsi* (I, x, 156-59), he faults Caesar less for depriving human beings of liberty than for sealing the doom of the gloriously predatory and imperialistic Roman Republic. Finally, although Machiavelli generally faults the Medici and other Italian rulers in the *Istorie fiorentine* for having encouraged the partisan politics and factionalism that he considered responsible for the decadence of his city-state and country, in individual cases his indignation yields to admiration for the ability of such figures as Francesco Sforza and Cosimo and Lorenzo de' Medici to play the confidence man.[23] In fact, Machiavelli is so attracted to the confidence man and so closely identifies with him that he can seldom refrain from presenting him in a positive light, no matter how much his politics opposed Machiavelli's own: witness, in the *Discorsi* (I, xl-xlv, 224-33), the Roman consul Appius Claudius, who used trickery and deceit in an attempt to destroy the republic Machiavelli cherished.[24] Even the few confidence men whom he seems to condemn retain a fundamental ambiguity; they never stray far outside the no-man's-land of the moral universe.

The ambiguity of Renaissance confidence men usually depends less on their actions, which are often immoral or at least antisocial, than on their author's manipulation of the audience's response. In general, writers adopt one or more of three aesthetic strategies to keep their heroes in a sphere beyond any simple judgment. The first is to present them as denizens of a world inhabited exclusively by scoundrels, so that the work devolves into a pure contest of wits rather than a moral confrontation between the wicked and the innocent. The hero is distinguished not by his moral depravity (everyone in his world is equally depraved) but by his greater cunning, daring, and ruthlessness. In a universe peopled only

[23]For Machiavelli's ambiguous view of the Medici, see John M. Najemy, "Machiavelli and the Medici: The Lessons of Florentine History," *Renaissance Quarterly* 35 (1982): 551-76.
[24]For Machiavelli's personal attraction to the figure I have been labeling the confidence man, see Chapters 5 and 6. See also Hanna F. Pitkin, *Fortune Is a Woman: Gender and Politics in the Thought of Niccolò Machiavelli* (Berkeley: University of California Press, 1984), pp. 40-47.

by rascals, an audience cannot distinguish among them on moral grounds and thus will feel free to side with the one who outfoxes the others and make off with the loot. This strategy appears in some of the *beffe* presented by Boccaccio during the eighth and ninth days of the *Decameron*, such as the famous tale of the scholar and the widow (VIII, 7), and it is a favorite with English writers of "city comedy" such as Jonson and Middleton. It is the strategy Machiavelli adopts in his "Belfagor," in which the peasant Gianmatteo and the devil Roderigo collaborate as confidence men in swindling others, but the peasant finally shows himself to be the verier rogue of the two. Machiavelli employs the same strategy in *Il principe* and his other political and historical writings insofar as he argues that all men are evil, all potential confidence men, and the game of politics is played not by saints and devils but by sharpers and would-be sharpers distinguished from one another only by degrees of cunning and ruthlessness. In such a world, admiration for the likes of Cesare Borgia, Castruccio Castracani, and Francesco Sforza seems inevitable.

A second authorial strategy for preserving the moral neutrality of the confidence man is closely related to the first and shades into it. In this one, the world is not composed of a collection of more or less gifted sharpers but split between confidence men and dupes, between those who are relentlessly cunning and those who are pitifully stupid. The latter, however, are as morally compromised as their deceivers, and for this reason, as well as for their damning mental opacity, they appear to deserve the gulling visited upon them. Since most of these dupes are would-be confidence men, proud of their presumed ability to swindle others, the distinction between this strategy and the first one appears to break down. The first case, however, involves a world in which people are distinguished only by degrees of cunning, whereas in the second the characters have qualitatively different mental capacities, linguistic skills, and abilities to understand the nature of society. As an example of this opposition, consider Boccaccio's sharpers Bruno and Buffalmacco in contrast to their victim, the archgull Calandrino. The former are clever, fairly sophisticated, inventive with language, and good at role-playing; their prey is utterly ignorant of the world, of the implications and subtleties of language, and of the potentional deceptiveness of men. He is also morally compromised: he is vain and pretentious, gluttonous, ready to cheat on his wife, and willing to steal once he is protected by the cloak of invisibility supposedly granted by the magical heliotrope. Calandrino is an innocent, but only in his lack of moral self-awareness, experience with men, and social sophistication; his duping, although cruel and sadistic at moments, seems thoroughly justified. A similar case could

be made for the duping of other "innocents" in Renaissance texts, from
Boccaccio's *Decameron,* through the *novelle* of Sacchetti, Giovanni
Sercambi, and others that follow, down to such works as *Henry IV,* Part
2, The Alchemist, and *Tartuffe.* Machiavelli provides one of the greatest examples of this strategy in *La mandragola,* in which Nicia's paro-
chialism, linguistic ignorance, lack of moral self-awareness, and
pretentiousness combine to invite—and justify—the cuckolding he willingly participates in. Ironically, Nicia, like Calandrino and some other
dupes, fancies himself an adroit confidence artist, but he is really only
a pathetic caricature of one.

   The third and final authorial strategy for preserving the amoral status of the confidence man depends on manipulation of the audience's
or reader's distance from the characters, especially when the protagonist is juxtaposed not to other confidence men or contemptible gulls but
to genuine, morally attractive innocents. To keep the confidence man
from becoming a monster, the writer must deflect sympathy from the
dupe, and he does so in several ways: the dupe's appearances—his presence—in the work are reduced to a minimum, and it is difficult to focus
on a pain one cannot see; he is presented almost entirely from the outside, more as an object than as a person, so that one cannot enter into
his feelings and identify with him in his defeat and humiliation; and the
swindle is often made to benefit the dupe in some way, perhaps increasing his feelings of security and power or his domestic and marital happiness, even if they are all based on illusion.[25] Shakespeare keeps offstage
the suffering of Richard III's innocent victims, the little princes; ser
Ciappelletto's confession actually aids the friars and people of Burgundy, who acquire as a result the spiritual protection and solid income
associated with the shrine of a saint; the elder Touchwood's impregna-
tion of Kix's wife in Middleton's *A Chaste Maid in Cheapside* satisfies
the barren couple's desire for a child. Although Machiavelli's vision of
a world filled with sharpers and morally compromised dupes, a world
in which all men are perceived as wicked, little inclines him to have recourse to such a strategy, he nevertheless turns to it in *La mandragola.*
There he presents Callimaco's cuckolding of Nicia as a source of satisfaction for Nicia because it guarantees him an heir and hence is the key
to the domestic and marital tranquillity on which the curtain falls.
Moreover, to preserve the moral neutrality of his hero, which is threatened by the resistance of the chaste, morally conscious heroine,
Machiavelli first elects to keep her largely offstage to minimize the au-

[25]For a discussion of how a writer blunts criticism of the trickster's amoral, if not
immoral, actions, see Orrin E. Klapp, "The Clever Hero," *Journal of American Folklore*
67 (1954): 21-34.

dience's identification with her and then has her "convert" at a crucial moment, switching her allegiance from her husband to Callimaco and becoming a confidence woman alongside him. Thus, using the strategy of distancing the audience from the gull, Machiavelli, like many other Renaissance writers, ensures the amoral status of his hero.

This emphasis on the amoral character of the confidence man would be misleading if it were allowed to suggest that his actions were essentially negative, defined exclusively as opposition to something, or that they were evil and their evil was merely made palatable by means of artistic subterfuge. The confidence man is not a villain *manqué* but a truly ambiguous character who is both good and evil, attractive and repulsive, possessing traits both socially advantageous and socially dangerous. If he infringes on moral codes or disregards the proprieties in his relentless pursuit of personal advantage, his deeds are not simply destructive. For the appetites informing them are universal; the individualism at the core of his being is shared in good measure by everyone; and both are absolutely necessary if social life is to be carried on. In other words, although the confidence man's actions threaten society by denying its rules, hierarchies, and static structures, they also involve qualities essential to its ongoing life. The confidence man has an energy, ingenuity, and creativity that society needs and that emerges most dramatically and most purely only when normal social boundaries are transgressed. If by nature confidence men, like folk tricksters, break rules, their rule-breaking is paradoxical: it constitutes a threat to society, but it also allows society to come to a recognition of itself, of the ordering principle that has been violated, and it manifests the creativity needed for society's continued existence. Morally ambiguous confidence men thus bear eloquent witness to their creators' recognition that societies need limits as well as free spirits that transcend them, orderly structures as well as the animating though chaos-threatening energies embodied in individuals.[26] They also need, as Machiavelli and other Re-

[26]My interpretation of the confidence man as a rule-breaker is indebted to the social analysis of such anthropologists as Victor Turner, Mary Douglas, and Clifford Geertz. For all of them, human cultures constitute themselves and mediate experience for the individual by providing categories for perception and structures for social interaction. This patterning is never complete, nor is it desirable that it should be, for a totally structured society would be cold, unchanging, and dead. There are always spaces in the structure, if only because structure depends on distance and discontinuity to create itself, because all semiotic systems depend on negations to define themselves. Thus there will always be the anomalous, the peripheral, and the disorderly, what Turner has labeled "anti-structure" and identified both as a rejection of the social structure and as the generative source of that structure. The confidence man is, of course, an example of the anomalous and disorderly. For a detailed treatment of these issues, see Victor Turner, *Dramas, Fields, and Metaphors: Symbolic Action in Human Society* (Ithaca: Cornell

naissance writers recognized fully, the profound creativity of the confidence man, which may lead him to violate social norms but is essential if societies are ever to escape the stultification and decadence produced by moribund structures and habits.

Renaissance confidence men are also defined by their manipulation and abuse of confidence; works about them are really concerned with the precariousness of the belief or trust on which normal human intercourse is founded. In Renaissance literature, unlike folk tales about tricksters, that trust is not merely a simple faith in the supposed veracity of another individual who pledges friendship, comfort, or support; it is an all-encompassing trust in the appearance he maintains, the social role he plays, the authority he embodies, and the language and rhetoric he employs. In a sense, confidence men from Boccaccio's frate Cipolla through Jonson's alchemist Subtle to Molière's Tartuffe do not ask others merely to trust them—although they do do that—but to believe in them and what they represent, to depend on them as authorities for action and even for the very order of the world. This distinction can be made clearer through an example: Boccaccio's Cipolla is not a friar who also happens to be a swindler, as though being a friar and a swindler were entirely separate activities; rather, he is a friar who uses his religious role to gain the trust of his victims, to establish his authority over them, and to deceive them precisely because they repose their full confidence in the role he plays and order their world on the basis of the authority he enshrines. Similarly, Shakespeare's Henry IV and Prince Hal are both confidence men—kings adept at gaining and maintaining political power by manipulating the faith others place in the roles they play self-consciously as monarchs. And Machiavelli is acutely aware of the issue of *credito,* the trust that is virtually identical to religious faith and that people must be brought to place in their prince (see *Il principe,* IV, 27). He dramatizes the religious character of that *credito* most strikingly in *La mandragola* when he has Callimaco ask Nicia for his "fede" and the latter swears he is ready "per credervi più che al mio confessoro" (II.vi.75: "to believe in you more than in my confessor"). In this play Machiavelli not only illuminates the faith and trust at the heart of all social intercourse and all confidence games; he also shows how one individual, through language, costumes, and other marks of social po-

University Press, 1974), pp. 237, 273, 293; Mary Douglas, *Purity and Danger: An Analysis of the Concepts of Pollution and Taboo* (Harmondsworth: Penguin, 1966), pp. 52-53, 114-18, 191-92; and Clifford Geertz, *The Interpretation of Cultures* (New York: Basic Books, 1973), pp. 44-49. For a synthesis of these views, to which my analysis is indebted, see Babcock, "'A Tolerated Margin of Mess,'" 147-52. See also Laura Makarius, "Le Mythe du 'Trickster,'" *Revue de l'histoire des religions* 175 (1969): 19-25, and "Ritual Clowns and Symbolic Behaviour," *Diogenes* 69 (1970): 56.

sition, can bring another to accept him as nothing less than a substitute for religion, the supreme authority in his world, and thereby to submit willingly, if unwittingly, to his abuse and domination.

To play the game of confidence in this way, one must implicitly accept a radical, unstabilizing view of both self and society. In this view, personal identity becomes a malleable fiction, and the social order and its authorities are rendered contingent, deprived of any absolute status, and made potentially transformable at the impulse of the human will. In the literature of the confidence man in the Renaissance, human life is treated as theater, a play in which all men are actors. Parts become interchangeable; no necessary connection exists between the individual and the role he plays; institutions are reduced to movable scenery; and the plot of social life becomes a purely human fabrication without divine sanction. From Boccaccio to Molière, the confidence man is repeatedly presented as an actor, a performer or masquerader, who conceives of life in histrionic terms and uses the role he plays, whether frate Alberto's Angel Gabriel, Prince Hal's "legitimate" king, or Subtle's learned alchemist, to work his will on others. Moreover, as we have noted, Renaissance writers do not relegate confidence men to marginal positions as rogues and petty sharpers but spot them in every nook and cranny of the social order. For Renaissance writers, all the world's truly a stage, and all the men and women at least potential confidence artists.

That Machiavelli, like others in the Renaissance, saw the world as a theater and the confidence man as its chief actor will be demonstrated fully later; here it should suffice to recall his emphasis on the necessity for the ideal prince to play a role, to maintain the appearance of magnanimity, religiosity, and the like, even while engaging in the most improper behavior. Machiavelli builds the entirety of *La mandragola* around the successful playing of roles and execution of a "plot." Like other writers, Machiavelli sees people as fashioning their own identities through calculated role-playing, and like them he views life as a struggle to command the faith of others in and through the roles one plays. Finally, Machiavelli recognizes that his heroes will win that struggle primarily because they correctly assess the nature of reality as a shadow-play, and that the vast majority of people will lose because they foolishly take appearances for realities, see roles as fixed and intrinsically attached to the individual, are unable to change and adapt as circumstances alter, and believe the social order is eternal and immutable rather than temporary and manmade. Such individuals cannot help becoming the victims of confidence men because the latter's more labile sense of self and society gives them a flexibility in creating opportuni-

ties for action and an adaptability to changing circumstances that ensure victory.

The confidence man's major traits—his deep moral ambiguity and his
recognition of the historical contingency and transformability of the
social order—reflect important aspects of the historical development of
Italy and Europe in the age of the Renaissance. The Renaissance fascination with confidence men might be correlated, for example, with
the perception of an increased number of rogues and vagabonds, charlatans and mountebanks, of the poor in general, which humanists and
social reformers linked to the land enclosures precipitated by a developing capitalism, to the population shifts related to the spread of the
plague and other diseases, and to the furious wars that raged in the
period.[27] As we noted earlier, some Renaissance confidence men are indeed marginal characters who live at the threshold of poverty, wander
incessantly, and have no stable social position. The parasitical Falstaff
and Ligurio, the itinerant actor and juggler Martellino of *Decameron*
II, 1, homeless rogues such as Shakespeare's Autolycus and Jonson's
Subtle and Dol, the immense legions of the picaros—all may be seen as
reflections of Renaissance people's awareness that a very large class of
the poor and the dispossessed existed in their world. Renaissance writers also imagined a second, though related, group of confidence men,
characters who, like some of Boccaccio's gentlemen and ladies, Machiavelli's princes, Shakespeare's Prince Hal, and Molière's Don Juan, enjoyed established positions within the social order. The Renaissance
interest in confidence men, then, involves more than a superficial,
though real, perception of poverty and social dislocation; writers from
Boccaccio to Molière used the figure as a device to articulate and shape,
brood on and evaluate some of the central concerns of their age.

One of those concerns, which appears in all representations of confidence men, is the ideology of self-fashioning, the notion that human

---

[27]Javier Herrero points out that historians of the Renaissance have not determined
whether the numbers of the poor and the socially dislocated actually increased during
the period, but there was at least a perception among reformers, of whom More, Erasmus, and Vives are the most famous, that poverty was on the rise and that methods
needed to be adopted to deal with it; see his "Renaissance Poverty and Lazarillo's Family:
The Birth of the Picaresque Genre," *PMLA* 94 (1979): 876–79. The increased conscious
awareness of vagabonds, rogues, and petty confidence men in the period is reflected in
such works as Teseo Pini's *Speculum cerretanorum* (Mirror of charlatans, c. 1485), which
Giacinto De Nobili reworked and published as *Il vagabondo* in the seventeenth century,
and in all the "coney-catching" pamphlets produced in the last decades of the sixteenth
century in England.

beings are, in Erasmus's words, not born but made.[28] Humanists and humanist-trained artists—indeed, writers of practically every philosophical and theological persuasion in the period—paid homage to the Renaissance's distinctive conception of identity formation: they recognized human beings as unshaped, morally neutral, malleable creatures at birth who were capable of being educated and trained, open to development in many directions, able to play an incredible array of roles.[29] Fundamentally free from any a priori definition of the self and utterly detached from the traditions, crafts, and places by means of which medieval people normally acquired their identities, Renaissance individuals were conceived as creating themselves; they were the sons of their works more than the sons of their fathers.[30] Writers in the period thus spun out for themselves a myth of man as Proteus or as Faustus, freed from old allegiances, rising and changing solely through the efforts of his will, intelligence, and art. Human beings made themselves through their education, or they made and remade themselves continually as they played role upon role on the great stage of the world. In the most optimistic versions of this Renaissance myth, the versions of the Italian Neoplatonist Pico della Mirandola, the Spanish humanist Juan-Luis Vives, Erasmus, and Rabelais, men were even imagined as having the power to ascend to the heavens and become one with the gods.[31] Machiavelli's Castruccio Castracani expresses perfectly this ideological conviction: he starts out in life as a foundling, attracts the attention of a powerful ruler through his obvious talents, and eventually becomes the ruler of his state and a threat to the entire region in which he lives. Machiavelli heightens the mythical quality of his brief biography by modeling Castracani's early life on that of Moses and by comparing him

[28]"Homines . . . non nascuntur, sed finguntur," in Desiderius Erasmus, *Declamatio de pueris statim ac liberaliter instituendis*, ed. Jean-Claude Margolin (Geneva: Droz, 1966), p. 389. On the concept of self-fashioning and the idea of the flexible self, see Stephen Greenblatt, *Renaissance Self-Fashioning: From More to Shakespeare* (Chicago: University of Chicago Press, 1980), pp. 201-13 and passim; Thomas M. Greene, "The Flexibility of the Self in Renaissance Literature," and A. Bartlett Giamatti, "Proteus Unbound: Some Versions of the Sea God in the Renaissance," both in *The Disciplines of Criticism*, ed. Peter Demetz, Thomas M. Greene, and Lowry Nelson, Jr. (New Haven: Yale University Press, 1968); Jonas Barish, *The Antitheatrical Prejudice* (Berkeley: University of California Press, 1981), pp. 99-111; and Peter Burke, *Popular Culture in Early Modern Europe* (New York: Harper & Row, 1978), pp. 167-77.
[29]See especially Eugenio Garin, *L'educazione in Europa: 1400-1600* (Bari: Laterza, 1957), pp. 92-93 and passim.
[30]See Margolin, Introduction to Erasmus, *De pueris*, p. 46.
[31]See the opening pages of Giovanni Pico della Mirandola's "Oration on the Dignity of Man" and Juan-Luis Vives' "A Fable about Man," both in *The Renaissance Philosophy of Man*, ed. Ernst Cassirer, Paul Oskar Kristeller, and John H. Randall, Jr. (Chicago: University of Chicago Press, 1948). For Erasmus, see *De pueris*, p. 391. For Rabelais, see the chapters dealing with Pantagruelion at the end of the *Tiers Livre*.

with Alexander and Scipio. Like so many others in the Renaissance, Machiavelli clearly reveals in this work his deep personal investment in the ideology of self-fashioning.

Not all in the Renaissance shared such an optimistic assessment of human freedom, potency, and metaphysical as well as social and political mobility. Such a radical detachment from traditional values, though exhilarating raised the specters of fraud and exploitation, fears that one could assault the heights only by deceiving and then stepping on the backs of one's fellows. Lacking any theory to justify unrestrained individualism, such as the laissez-faire capitalism of Adam Smith in the eighteenth century, many Renaissance individuals denounced as greed and usury the accumulation of wealth that enabled individuals to rise socially. Satirists attacked the performing of self as role as an act of fraud, and one of its chief exponents, Baldassare Castiglione, voiced his concern over the fraudulence of role-playing at least once in his masterpiece, *Il libro del Cortegiano*.[32] Finally, the very writers who celebrated human beings' ability to ascend to the heavens qualified their visions with an awareness that many individuals were not capable of the journey, that it was possible only if one drastically modified notions of original sin, and that freedom of metaphysical and moral movement permitted one to descend to the level of the beasts as easily as to rise to that of the angels.[33]

Self-fashioning was greeted with fear and hostility for yet another reason: it was equated with the destruction of any stable identity. If identity is acquired and not innate, if it is based on the role one plays, and roles are by definition extrinsic, temporary, and changeable, then identity becomes a slippery matter, and the solidity and reality of the self beneath the roles could become questionable. Thus Renaissance satirists repeatedly mock *arrivistes* and slaves of fashion as people without inner selves, whose identities go no deeper than the clothes they wear.[34] For most individuals in the period, identity still depended on an

---

[32]Baldesar Castiglione, *Il libro del Cortegiano*, ed. Bruno Maier, 2d ed. (Turin: Unione Tipografico-Editrice Torinese, 1964), bk. ii, chap. xl, p. 252.

[33]Erasmus stressed that some men were incapable of being educated and that original sin was an obstacle to their rising; see his *De pueris*, pp. 397, 419. Pico emphasized that men could turn as easily into beasts as into angels.

[34]In the *sotties* or fool-plays produced in France from about the middle of the fifteenth century to the end of the sixteenth, one of the most frequent targets of satire is the *gens nouveaux* (also called *gorriers* or simply *sots*), whose identities change as they change costumes. In one play, *La Farce nouvelle nommée la Folie des Gorriers*, dating from about 1465, the *gorriers* actually lose their sense of identity when they don new garments and wonder out loud who they are. See the edition of the play in Société des anciens textes français, *Recueil général des Sotties*, ed. Emile Picot (Paris: Firmin Didot, 1902), 1: 165–75. For comment on this aspect of the *sotties*, see Heather Arden, *Fools' Plays:*

inextricable bond between self and role, and it should therefore not be surprising that two of Shakespeare's greatest heroes, Richard II and King Lear, once stripped of their roles as kings, should experience a disorienting, maddening loss of identity. Nor should it be surprising that the title character of the fifth-century *novella* "Il Grasso legnaiuolo" should, when a trickster has entered his shop and claims he is Grasso, experience a comical, bewildering loss of identity and feel that "quasi per certo gli parve essere un altro" ("it seemed to him as if for certain that he was another").[35] Thus it is understandable that in the Renaissance the ideology of self-fashioning should have aroused as much fear as enthusiasm.

Obviously, Renaissance writers were obsessed by the confidence man because through him they could crystallize their culture's profound ambivalence about the issue of self-fashioning. The confidence man is, after all, the self-fashioner par excellence. A protean figure who enjoys a genuine detachment from the traditional social order and its values, he triumphs over others precisely because he is a superb role-player, able, like Mosca in Jonson's *Volpone*, to "change a visor [i.e., mask] swifter than a thought"; to disguise himself literally, as Callimaco does, or metaphorically, as when Prince Hal "plays" the role of ideal king in *Henry IV, Part 2*, and *Henry V*.[36] If no confidence man ever quite makes it into the circle of gods, marginal figures with obscure social origins (Machiavelli's Castruccio Castracani, Marlowe's Dr. Faustus) do manage to acquire tremendous wealth, bed beautiful women, and achieve great social status and political power. And confidence men already established within the social order, including many of Machiavelli's princes and Shakespeare's Richard III and Henry IV, treat their roles self-consciously as roles, using them to manipulate their subjects as so many dupes and thus to acquire and maintain political power. At the same time, however, the confidence man's triumphs are by their nature acts of exploitation; indeed, in no other figure of Renaissance literature are the heady freedom, individualism, and mobility involved in self-fashioning so inextricably bound together with a sadistic preying on and deceiving of others. Frate Cipolla succeeds at the expense of the hapless Certaldans, Callimaco's union with Lucrezia makes a mockery of her

---

A Study of Satire in the "Sottie" (Cambridge: Cambridge University Press, 1980), pp. 116–36. Jonson frequently satirizes those who slavishly follow fashion; for a splendid commentary on the issue of absent or empty selves, see Thomas M. Greene, "Ben Jonson and the Centered Self," *Studies in English Literature, 1500–1900* 10 (1970): 325–48.

[35]Gioachino Chiarini, ed., *Novelle italiane: Il Quattrocento* (Milan: Garzanti, 1982), p. 250.

[36]Ben Jonson, *Volpone*, ed. Alvin B. Kernan (New Haven: Yale University Press, 1962), III, i, 29.

marriage to Nicia, and Prince Hal's manipulation of kingship depends in part on his willingness to use others and heartlessly to make Falstaff his dupe. Moreover, if confidence men create their identities through role-playing, they thereby render identity a problem, for their reduction of social life to role-playing suggests the absence of any solid self behind the masks they wear. They are all, as frate Cipolla's name implies, "onions," that is, layers and layers of masks with no center beneath them.[37] Like Shakespeare's Henry IV and Falstaff, like Machiavelli's Ligurio and his ideal princes, they are men whose motives are so obscure, so hidden in irony, or so at variance with their actions that their centers are total mysteries, frightening abysses beneath all the faces they put on for the world. Thus the contradictory and ambiguous nature of the confidence man offered Renaissance writers and ideal means to articulate both their hopes and their fears about the self-fashioning, individualism, and personal mobility that were fundamental issues in their culture.

Renaissance writers also used the confidence man as a means to brood on the deeper implications of the economic, social, political, and religious transformations their society was undergoing. The gradual development of capitalism in the period, for instance, brought to the fore the issue of credit, of *credito* or trust, which was essential in banking, in the expansion of international trade, and in the use of letters of credit, the forerunners of the modern checking system.[38] Capitalism also freed people from the land, permitted the rapid accumulation and loss of fortunes, and thereby abetted the increase in social mobility which characterized the Renaissance as a whole and distinguished it from the more stable and static traditional culture of the Middle Ages. That mobility was also made possible by the expansion of educational opportunities through the founding of colleges and universities; the centralizing of states all over Europe, which necessitated the creation of large bureaucracies filled by men of talent drawn from many strata in society; the constant wars, which changed ruling classes everywhere; and the spread of printing, which disseminated information about a vast reper-

---

[37]On the significance of frate Cipolla's name, see Millicent Marcus, *An Allegory of Form: Literary Self-Consciousness in the "Decameron,"* Stanford French and Italian Studies, 18 (Saratoga, Calif.: Amna Libri, 1979), pp. 75-77.

[38]On the development of capitalism and the use of letters of credit in the Renaissance, see Wallace K. Ferguson, *Europe in Transition, 1300–1520* (Boston: Houghton Mifflin, 1962), pp. 96–132, esp. pp. 104-6. The Italian word for letter of credit or bill of exchange was *lettera di cambio.*

tory of lifestyles and through the publication of self-help books allowed generations of autodidacts to improve their situations.[39] Although the possibilities for social advancement may not have been very great by modern standards, and indeed more people probably sank below the level of their parents than rose above it, large numbers of peasants did improve their condition by fleeing to the developing towns; numerous baseborn *condottieri* did become princes; lawyers such as Thomas More did rise to positions of power; and merchants and bankers, the Medici foremost among them, bought themselves and their families noble titles.[40] Thus social mobility was both a possibility and a fact, and it correlated perfectly with Renaissance people's ideology of self-fashioning, their myths of Faustus and Proteus. Like the development of capitalism, it betokened a dynamic world freed from rigid hierarchies and ascribed statuses and open to all manner of new possibilities.

Politics and religion, too, become more fluid. The traditional order of feudal society was no longer adequate for the centralizing states of western Europe, which needed new governmental forms and theories to buttress them.[41] A flurry of treatises appeared, arguing for a variety of governmental forms: Giovanni Conversino da Ravenna's *Dragmalogia de eligibili vite genere* of 1404–5 was followed by the works of More, Machiavelli, and Jean Bodin in the sixteenth century and by those of Thomas Hobbes and John Locke at the end of the period.[42] Changes in the forms and theories of government undermined the authority of political arrangements in general as well as the particular political order. At the same time, the authority of the church was being called into question; by its subservience to the French king in Avignon during the Babylonian Captivity from 1305 to 1377 and during the Great Schism,

---

[39]On social mobility, see Lawrence Stone, "Social Mobility in England, 1500–1700," *Past and Present* 33 (1966): 7–25; and Fernand Braudel, *Civilisation matérielle, économie, et capitalisme, XVe–XVIIIe siècle* (Paris: Armand Colin, 1979), vol. 2, *Les Jeux de l'échange*, p. 425. On education and social mobility, see Jack H. Hexter, "The Education of the Aristocracy in the Renaissance," in *Reappraisals in History* (1961; rpt. New York: Harper & Row, 1963), pp. 45–70. On social mobility and the printing press, see Elizabeth L. Eisenstein, *The Printing Press as an Agent of Change* (Cambridge: Cambridge University Press, 1979), pp. 243–48, 284–87.

[40]For a detailed description of how medieval Italian businessmen gradually increased their power and purchased hereditary titles, see Ferguson, *Europe in Transition*, pp. 148–50. On the epidemic of title-purchasing in seventeenth-century Europe, see D. H. Pennington, *Seventeenth Century Europe* (London: Longman, 1970), pp. 90–93.

[41]For this thesis see J. G. A. Pocock, *The Machiavellian Moment: Florentine Political Thought and the Atlantic Republican Tradition* (Princeton: Princeton University Press, 1975).

[42]On the debate over the best form of government, see Paul Archambault, "The Analogy of the 'Body' in Renaissance Political Literature," *Bibliothèque d'Humanisme et Renaissance* 29 (1967): 32–53.

when two popes ruled, one in Avignon and one in Rome, from 1377 to
1417; by the persistence of millenarian movements challenging the authority of the Holy See from the High Middle Ages onward; by the
emergence of the humanists as an educated class to break the clerical
monopoly on learning and the authority it conferred; and finally by the
Protestant Reformation, which denied papal authority absolutely and
then split itself into warring sects. These developments in the political
and religious spheres fed on one another, for separation of church and
state was inconceivable in the period. When they were combined with
the discovery of exotic human cultures in the remote reaches of Africa
and America, and with the growth of historicism, with Renaissance individuals' recognition of their distance and difference from the classical
past, the result was an inescapable sense of the historical contingency,
the relativism, of the contemporary social order.[43]

Such a realization could be—and was—liberating, for if society was
perceived as the creation of human hands, then it was open to transformation and improvement. That realization led directly to, and found
its loftiest social expression in, the utopian fantasies of the period. It
generated the dreams of the schoolteacher Vittorino da Feltre of creating a perfect educational environment and influenced Erasmus to
imagine the ideal settings for his dialogues. Most strikingly, it led individuals to envision perfect societies: More's Utopia, Rabelais's Thélème,
Tommaso Campanella's Città del sole, Francis Bacon's Atlantis. Finally,
it combined with the religious fervor of the age to spur people on to create ideal communities in fact, not merely in theory, from John Calvin's
theocratic Geneva to the Puritan cities on the hill of North America and
the Jesuit state of Paraguay. In short, complementing Renaissance individuals' exalted vision of the Proteuses rising up to become like the
gods is their utopian vision of human beings using their reason and will
to transform an imperfect society into heaven on earth.

As Renaissance self-fashioning had its dark side, however, so does its
sense of the contingency, relativism, and transformability of the social
order. If this perception allowed for personal mobility and encouraged
people to dream of grandiose social transformations, it could also seem
like a return to chaos to the vast majority of individuals who inherited
from the Middle Ages a model of the social order which was corporate,

---

[43]On the relationship between a perception of the contingency of the social order and
Renaissance historical self-consciousness, see Greenblatt, *Renaissance Self-Fashioning*,
p. 219; and Thomas M. Greene, *The Light in Troy: Imitation and Discovery in
Renaissance Poetry* (New Haven: Yale University Press, 1982), pp. 90, 148–54. See also
the seminal work of Eugenio Garin, *L'umanesimo italiano* (Bari: Laterza, 1965),
pp. 13–22.

organic, hierarchical, and static. Hence throughout the period the fear of chaos provoked repeated denunciations of *novi homines,* "new men," by scions of the traditional order who guarded their own privileges and stoutly resisted the rise of members of the lower classes.[44] Ironically, even in such books as Castiglione's *Libro del Cortegiano* and Stefano Guazzo's *Civil Conversazione,* which described the behavior of the upper class and thus made it accessible to those below, we find an insistence on the inimitability of that behavior which must be read as an attempt to deny the very social mobility the books make possible.[45] In addition, Thomas Wyatt satirized the corruptions of recently transformed political and religious authorities; Marlowe's and George Chapman's tragedies often focused on the instability caused by political revolutions; popular chapbooks expressed horror at contemporary social disorder through world-upside-down motifs featuring women ruling men and servants their masters; and Thomas Nashe attacked as innovators those who sought changes in the religious or political order.[46] Many individuals feared that if the traditional order were challenged, set aside, or merely perceived fleetingly as ungrounded, the result would be chaos and an unleashing of ruthless competition leading to a state of endless, ultimately self-destructive war. Always sensitive to the deepest concerns of his age, Shakespeare articulated this fear in Ulysses' famous speech on "degree" (that is, hierarchical position and order) in *Troilus and Cressida:*

> O, when degree is shaked,
> Which is the ladder of all high designs,
> The enterprise is sick. How could communities,
> Degrees in schools, and brotherhoods in cities,
> Peaceful commerce from dividable shores,
> The primogenity and due of birth,
> Prerogative of age, crowns, sceptres, laurels,
> But by degree, stand in authentic place?

[44]For attacks on "new men" in England, see Fritz Caspari, *Humanism and the Social Order in Tudor England* (New York: Teachers College Press, 1954), pp. 3-5. For France, see n. 35 above.

[45]On the paradoxical character of courtesy books, which both enabled and resisted social mobility, see Frank Whigham, *Ambition and Privilege: The Social Tropes of Elizabethan Courtesy Theory* (Berkeley: University of California Press, 1984).

[46]On Wyatt's satires, see Greene, *Light in Troy,* pp. 256-59. On the world-upside-down motif in popular chapbooks and broadsheets, see Natalie Z. Davis, *Society and Culture in Early Modern France* (Stanford: Stanford University Press, 1975), pp. 124-51; and David Kunzle, "World Upside Down: The Iconography of a European Broadsheet Type," in *Reversible World,* ed. Babcock, pp. 39-94. Both Davis and Kunzle rightly stress the ambiguity of the motif, which could be read by conservatives as an attack on popular disorder and by the people as an attack on entrenched privilege and an expression of rebellion. Either way, the motif points to a sense of social disturbance.

> Take but degree away, untune that string,
> And hark what discord follows. Each thing meets
> In mere oppugnancy. . . .
> Strength should be lord of imbecility,
> And the rude son should strike his father dead;
> Force should be right. . . .
> Then everything include itself in power,
> And power into will, will into appetite.
> And appetite, an universal wolf,
> So doubly seconded with will and power,
> Must make perforce an universal prey
> And last eat up himself.[47]

Shakespeare's vision here of a world in which the absence of an un-impeachable social and political authority is equated with apocalyptic strife is the nightmare inversion of the Renaissance's bright dream of human advancement and utopian harmony.

The world inhabited by Renaissance confidence men is presented as historically contingent, its institutions and rules arbitrary. It is funda-mentally a play, its members actors whether they realize it or not, and its script the work of human hands. In such a vision, where roles are extrinsic to the individuals who perform them and social mobility is a given, no more than a costume change is needed to make a gentleman into a doctor or a rogue into an alchemist. Moreover, to conceive society as a play is to see it implicitly as a relative phenomenon, a human-created set of institutions and rules for behavior which may be changed or replaced by others as human will and ingenuity dictate. To be sure, in most Renaissance works about confidence men, these figures do not aim at social transformation. They accept the status quo, using social institutions and roles as means to satisfy their personal desires for wealth, sexual conquest, and power. Still, their very act of treating social roles merely as roles and their general distance and detachment from society and its rules point to a firm sense of the arbitrariness of the en-tire social order.

Even though confidence men generally do not fashion radical plans to transform society, there is a bit of the utopian dreamer about at least a few of them. Consider Bruno and Buffalmacco's ability to conjure up Cloudcuckoolands for Calandrino and maestro Simone, and Subtle's encouragement of the millenarian fantasies of the Puritans he dupes. Indeed, Dr. Faustus, who becomes a confidence man in the third and

---

[47]I.iii.101–11, 114–16, 119–24, in William Shakespeare, *The Complete Works*, ed. Alfred Harbage (New York: Viking Press, 1969).

fourth acts of Marlowe's play, and Jonson's Volpone both at times enter-
tain fantasies of radical social change, to be brought about in the first
case by diabolic magic and in the second by gold. Even more striking,
works focused on confidence men frequently depict large-scale social
transformations, suggesting some subtle and indirect but necessary connection between the appearance of confidence men and dramatic, mo-
mentous social change. One need only recall that Boccaccio's
Decameron, that treasure trove of confidence artists, opens with a Florence all but destroyed by the plague and moves toward a reconstituted,
ideal city of wit and sophistication projected through the stories of the
sixth day. Similarly, in his second tetralogy of history plays, from
Richard II to *Henry V*, Shakespeare appears to correlate the transformation of England from a feudal system to a centralized Renaissance
monarchy with an outpouring of confidence men at every level, from
dissolute knights to the king himself. In a more sinister way, Jonson suggests a similar correlation for the Roman world in his *Sejanus*. Finally,
Machiavelli envisions confidence men–princes generally as social innovators and renovators, and in *Il principe* he calls for a redeemer to
transform a social world marked by decadence and despair. In short,
Renaissance writers fully grasp the historicity and relativity of their culture and so dare to dream, albeit fleetingly, of sometimes radical social
alternatives in which their confidence men play significant roles.

But in Renaissance works about confidence men writers also articulate their deep disturbance at the unsettled condition of their society.
In stories and plays they could express their realization that if social
structures and institutions were ungrounded, society's principal players
were necessarily frauds whose authority was illegitimate and inauthen-
tic, even though it was accepted by those they exploited and dominated
and whose birth and abilities placed them at the bottom of the heap. In
other words, Renaissance works about confidence men can be seen from
one perspective as exercises in social and political demystification. For
if those in charge during the period invoked religious sanctions, national
myths, and humanist rewritings of classical fables to fashion a legitimacy for themselves, works about confidence men are clearly satires of
such efforts, revelations of the naked truth about the emperor's clothes.
Such works offered a heavy threat to the political order and must have
been disturbing to most people, including their authors, since the specter that the chief authorities of the social order are predatory and bogus
was surely unsettling to individuals who could not imagine an ordered
society without such authorities.

Renaissance writers consequently shied away from dwelling on the
more politically disquieting implications of the confidence man's role-

playing and vision of society. Indeed, they often adopted strategies overtly designed to qualify the challenge he posed either in his utopian fantasizing or in his revelation of the ungrounded, exploitive nature of those in power. One such strategy was to identify the confidence man as a lower-class rogue, thereby suggesting that even if he did imitate the behavior of his superiors, this was a parody, which primarily demeaned him and linked his acts of fraud and exploitation to his class status rather than to those whose roles he played. This was the strategy used by Jonson in *The Alchemist* with Subtle, Face, and Dol, by Shakespeare in *The Winter's Tale* with Autolycus, and by the writers of the picaresque. Another strategy may be perceived in connection with Boccaccio's frate Alberto, Shakespeare's Toby Belch, Jonson's Volpone, and Tirso's and Molière's Don Juan: the confidence man eventually is punished for his transgressions, usually at the hands of a social superior. This second strategy purges the social order of its disturbing element and confirms the goodness and legitimacy of its traditional authorities. Both strategies, however, seem illegitimate insofar as they imply a wish to deny the essential moral ambiguity of the confidence man and to push him in the direction of melodramatic evil. Both strategies fail resoundingly, for at least three reasons: first, no matter what the outcome, in many works the confidence man's role-playing and social vision do undermine the established order by suggesting that those in power may be both fraudulent and predatory; second, even when in one work an author presents the confidence man as simply a rogue, in another he inevitably imagines him as a gentleman or lady, courtier or prince, thus forestalling the complete identification of the figure with the lower orders of society; and third—and most important—the authors of a large number of texts make their confidence men so engaging that audiences and readers are disturbed when punishment comes to them. In general, then, despite efforts to minimize their impact, Renaissance works about confidence men do present a serious and disturbing challenge to any notion of the legitimacy and benevolence of the established order. If they assume a radical freedom of social arrangements that allows for personal mobility and utopian fantasies, they simultaneously undermine any faith people could place in the normal institutions, hierarchies, and behavioral rules of their social world.

Because the confidence man is deeply ambiguous, it is not surprising that he proved irresistible to Renaissance writers who felt equally ambivalent about a social order that was undergoing signficant changes, if not crisis. Paradoxically, they interpreted the confidence man both as a symptom, if not a cause, of the ills of their age and, at least in the case of Machiavelli's prince and Shakespeare's confidence men-kings, as the best hope for a cure. If the Renaissance could be described as a liminal or threshold period, situated between the feudal, corporate social order of the Middle Ages to which it still paid homage and the emergent capitalist, contractual order of the eighteenth century, which it could not yet articulate, its fascination with the confidence man makes perfect sense.[48] For he is, after all, a liminal figure, a character betwixt and between, whose extreme individualism, ingenuity, and energy are presented as both destructive of the static, traditional social order and creative of new, as yet imperfectly realized social possibilities.

In all his writings about his personal experience and about politics as well as in his artistic creations, Machiavelli clearly shared the general Renaissance fascination with the confidence man. Deeply influenced by Boccaccio and conversant with the *novella* tradition after the *Decameron*, he followed the lead of writers before him and used the figure of the confidence man to help give shape to his thought and to reflect on the basic issues of his age. But Machiavelli differed from his predecessors in two very important respects. First, his vision of life as a confidence game was far more extensive than those of Boccaccio and such writers of *novelle* as Sacchetti, Gentile Sermini, and Masuccio Salernitano in the fourteenth and fifteenth centuries. The latter saw the confidence man primarily as a denizen of the lower orders of society, peasants, students, artisans, itinerant friars (Boccaccio's frate Cipolla), buffoons (Sacchetti's messer Dolcibene). On the few occasions when they allowed him to occupy a higher position, they identified him at most as a member of the gentry, as in the case of Boccaccio's Ricciardo Minutolo, famous for his "nobiltà di sangue" (*Decameron*, III, 6, p. 228: "nobility of blood") or Madonna Isabella, "la qual fu moglie d'un cavaliere" (VII, 6, p. 501: "who was the wife of a knight").[49] Earlier works about confidence men virtually ignored the upper reaches of the secular and ecclesiastical hierarchies; although they sometimes implied in subtle and indirect ways that those who actually held the reins of power were, or potentially could be, confidence men, as Boccaccio's story of Ciappelletto suggests about the king and pope who employed the protagonist, nevertheless those at the top of the social pyramid were not normally explicitly identified as swindlers. Machiavelli, by contrast, thrust the confidence man directly into the corridors of power, identifying emperors, princes, condottieri, cardinals, and popes with the figure. In other

---

[48]For a convenient definition of *liminal*, see Victor Turner, "Comments and Conclusions," in *Reversible World*, ed. Babcock, pp. 276-96. For the notion of the Renaissance as a liminal period, see p. 288.

[49]Giovanni Boccaccio, *Il Decameron*, ed. Carlo Salinari, 2 vols. (Bari: Laterza, 1966).

words, Machiavelli extended the figure of the confidence man from déclassé rogues (Ligurio) and peasants (Gianmatteo) through artisans (the
anonymous, extraordinarily Machiavellian spokesman in the Ciompi revolt; see *Ist*, III, xiii, 236–39) to princes (Castruccio Castracani and Cesare Borgia) and popes (Alexander VI).

Machiavelli's vision of life as a confidence game was also more extensive than that of his predecessors in another way: like his good friend
Francesco Vettori, he tended to see all of life almost exclusively in terms
of the game. One need only think of the *Decameron* by way of comparison: although many of its most memorable stories feature confidence
men, and although trickery and swindling figure in about half of them,
the other half focus on alternative modes of social relationship. By contrast, although Machiavelli's *Clizia* is not quite a confidence-man comedy and occasional characters in his works are unrelated to the type,
nevertheless his basic vision throughout his works is of a world in which
confidence men and dupes act the principal parts. In other words,
Machiavelli saw the world as a *beffa* or confidence game, although that
game had many forms involving a wide variety of stakes. Thus if
Machiavelli dubs Florence the "calamita di tutti i ciurmatori del mondo"
(*Let*, #141, 308: "lodestone of all the confidence men in the world"), it
was so only because in his imagination all the world was already teem-
ing with such men.

Machiavelli not only departed from his predecessors by extending the
social range of the confidence man and by seeing virtually all of life as
a confidence game; he also increased the figure's historical significance
and personal stature. The tricksters of Boccaccio and other *novella*
writers largely operate in relatively limited segments of the public arena:
they deceive local peasants or townspeople, seduce the wives of neighbors, swindle the occasional merchant they encounter in a strange city,
or at most pull the wool over the eyes of limited groups of people, as
frate Cipolla does at Certaldo and Martellino at Treviso. By contrast,
although some of Machiavelli's heroes, such as Callimaco and Gianmatteo, have a similarly restricted scope of action, when he extends the
figure into the realm of history, he has them carry out their stratagems
at the level of cities and states. Machiavelli's political confidence men
are empire-builders, and the enormous scope of their activities gives
them a weightiness and stature that earlier confidence men never had.
Moreover, their stature increases insofar as Machiavelli assigns great importance to the historical moment in which they live. Because they are
placed on the stage of an Italy in crisis, threatened by "barbarian" invasions and political collapse, their stature is enhanced both by their
historical context and by the mission of national salvation assigned them

by Machiavelli. Of course, the *Decameron* also reflected a social crisis—the plague—but its cause was presented as a natural phenomenon
that was restricted essentially to Florence. Moreover, Boccaccio did not
reflect self-consciously about that crisis or speak of a need for political
redemption in his book. Finally, even if his confidence men possessed
skills essential to the maintenance of civilization, they were never presented as potential redeemers. Machiavelli's confidence men, by contrast, are indeed presented in that way, and their courage, energy, and
political imagination are dignified if only by the elevated goals they
pursue. In short, thanks to their enlarged sphere of action and the critical state of Italy, which requires desperate measures from them, Machiavelli's political confidence men achieve enormous stature. It should
not be surprising that, as we will see, he should conceive them as heroes.

Their elevated mission and stature also make them candidates for
something close to tragedy. Before Machiavelli, confidence men were
inevitably the heroes of comic tales and seldom had to face either mo-
mentous social issues or dramatic personal crises. Two seeming exceptions to this rule in Boccaccio's *Decameron* are Ciappelletto (I, 1) and
frate Alberto (IV, 2). Ciappelletto faces death, but without fear or desire
to triumph over it. His parodic confession makes death neither a victory
nor a defeat for him; it merely becomes the pretext for a performance,
for his last, most brilliantly comic scene as a confidence man. Frate Alberto comes closer to being an exception to the rule, as his tale comes
on the fourth day of the *Decameron*, which is explicitly dedicated to
tragedy. Nevertheless, although frate Alberto does suffer and die, most
of the tale is a comic celebration of his exploits, and his final incarcer-
ation and death are relegated to a few clauses at the very end. By contrast, the enormously elevated goals Machiavelli's political confidence
men pursue bring them into direct, conscious conflict with time, death,
and human finitude, as they seek to found empires that will survive the
vicissitudes of fortune and the ineluctable movement of history's cycles.
Since they are thus caught in the web of mutability in a way their predecessors never were, death becomes a heroic challenge for them, a real
opponent, the frustration of their aspirations, the confirmation of their
tragic, human limits, the ultimate, unavoidable defeat that reality imposes on their attempts to shape and order it.[50] Perhaps it might be more
appropriate to speak of irony than tragedy here, for Machiavelli responds to his heroes' losses less with pathos and glorification than with

---

[50]According to Giorgio Barberi-Squarotti, the prince's inability to impose an ideal
form on a shifting and disorganized reality constitutes his tragedy; see *La forma tragica
del "Principe" e altri saggi sul Machiavelli* (Florence: Olschki, 1966), pp. 6-15, 25-26,
and passim.

bitter mockery and irritated laughter. No matter how one labels them, however, Machiavelli's confidence men clearly emerge as far more substantial, more serious, more troubled and troubling figures than the slighter comic characters who may, at some remove, have been their chief inspiration.

By extending the social and political range of the confidence man, increasing the magnitude of his undertakings, and granting him a lofty, almost tragic statue, Machiavelli transformed that figure into a new character who would have a most significant effect on the writers who came after him, a figure one might dub, following the Elizabethans, the "Machiavel." To be sure, many writers continued to fashion comic confidence men in the manner of Boccaccio during the next century and a half; one need only think of the Italian *commedia erudita*, with its continual mining of the *Decameron*, or of much of the *novella* tradition, which harks back to the same source. But these comic confidence men were joined by another group of more serious figures who appeared in the drama and fiction of Europe, such characters as Shakespeare's Richard III, Jonson's Volpone, Molière's Dom Juan, and Milton's Satan. Although only Richard was identified as a Machiavel during the Renaissance, in a gesture that explicitly acknowledged his ancestry, all four could easily be given that title, because of either the significant scope of their activities, their great stature, or the seriousness of their personalities and undertakings. Machiavelli's reshaping of the confidence man in his intense political visions made it possible for such sinister and tragic, indeed often mythic, figures to enter European literature.

The five chapters that follow are concerned with the many ways Machiavelli used the figure of the confidence man to conceive, shape, reflect on, and evaluate his experiences, whether personal, imaginative and literary, or political and historical. Machiavelli's confidence men do change from work to work, appearing more comic and carnivalesque in his letters and literary writing, more heroic and serious in his political and historical works. Nevertheless, they are all related figures, all reflections of the generic type he inherited from his predecessors. By beginning with *La mandragola*, we can specify the traits of that type in their purest, most literary form, and then use that analysis to illuminate the traits of less obviously literary characters in Machiavelli's other writings. All five chapters will reveal in different ways just how fully Machiavelli thought life through the genre of the *beffa* or confidence game, how he gave that game an intense seriousness in some of his works, how he recognized the risk of loss it entailed, and how he dealt with inevitable defeat, particularly in his personal experience. It is striking that throughout his works his protagonists' triumphs are never unqualified successes, and that if they continue to play their game despite the inevitability of defeat, they do so only because, for Machiavelli, it was the only game in town. All of his works, as a result, are in various degrees haunted by a sense of incompleteness and imperfection; all are characterized by bitter dissonances rarely resolved into harmonies.

Chapter 2 focuses on *La mandragola*, the most conventional and purely literary of Machiavelli's works dealing with confidence men, one that continues in basic ways the generic pattern established by Boccaccio and the *novella* writers of the fourteenth and fifteenth centuries. Machiavelli, however, goes significantly beyond his predecessors by dividing the entire cast of his play into just two types—confidence men and dupes—and thus establishing the rigorous division of the human race that characterizes the basic nature of the universe he imagines in virtually all his works. He also anticipates the shape of that universe by elaborating the confidence man's perception of life as theater and his recognition of the power inherent in language. *La mandragola* appears to be the rare work in Machiavelli's corpus in which his confidence men's manipulation of others leads to a final state of social equilibrium, happiness, and enduring harmony, and in that way it stands as the most fully Boccaccian of his creations, recalling in mood and theme, if not in every plot detail, the happily resolved stories of the third day of the *Decameron*. Machiavelli can create this impression of harmony at the end of his play because its world is purely fictional; it is a world in which confidence games can be played without risk of failure because the writer controls all the odds. In a subtle way, however, Machiavelli undermines this impression of apparent harmony and fulfillment by establishing a clear disparity between the power of Callimaco, which is based largely on social position and wealth, and that of Ligurio, which is based on wit, linguistic and rhetorical skill, and histrionic flexibility. This disparity leaves the audience at the end of the play with the sense that the equilibrium achieved in the last act is fragile and illusory, a sweet dream that the pressures of reality and desire will eventually, inevitably shatter.

Chapters 3 and 4 turn to Machiavelli's political and historical writings and focus on his radical extension of the figure of the confidence man into a realm that earlier writers generally did not let him enter, that of politics and history. Chapter 3 shows that Machiavelli's political and historical works, too, essentially divide the world into sharpers and gulls. It also shows that Machiavelli conceived politics and history basically as theater and that his ideal prince owes his ability to manipulate and dominate those about him to his grasp of this conception as well as to his command of language. Like Callimaco and Ligurio, the ideal prince is a clever showman who creates compelling spectacles for his people. But he is unlike the heroes of *La mandragola* and the protagonists of countless comic *novelle* in that he does not simply create a fictional image of himself to establish his authority and gain the trust and confidence of those he manipulates. Living in the world of history, which Machiavelli imagines as an arena of competition dominated by force, the prince must respond accordingly and embrace violence as an instrument, using it to fashion terrifying spectacles that ensure his subjects' allegiance. Thus, if the confidence men in *La mandragola* could triumph merely by being clever foxes, in the world of Machiavelli's political and historical works they must change their game and their nature and often behave as lions as well. As they do so, however, they are less interested in merely terrifying their subjects than in constituting themselves as objects of faith for them. They make themselves high priests or even gods in a religion of terror, thus resuscitating what Machiavelli saw as the defining features of Roman religion and redeeming Italy not by playing the part of Christian Messiah but by offering in their own persons a substitute for the defective Christianity that he blamed for the decadence of his contemporary world.

Chapter 4 continues the analysis by showing that Machiavelli's political and historical writings transform the confidence man by amalgamating him with the figure of the hero derived from ancient and contemporary epic, thus revealing yet again the profound influence of literary genres on his thought. The confidence man as hero loses many of the associations with carnivalesque pleasure and the sensuous body that he had in the *novella* tradition as well as in Machiavelli's own literary works. Though he is still a deceiver and manipulator, he is also a warrior and heroic leader, relentless in his pursuit of power and glory. In keeping with this transformation, the confidence man's defining feature becomes *virtù*, a concept that, though it may identify a wide variety of intellectual and physical qualities, has at its root the meaning of "manliness" and hence bespeaks heroic male activity for Machiavelli. *Virtù* he then repeatedly juxtaposes to *ozio*, or idleness, a suggestive term that not only defines the primary danger the prince must avoid by living a life of struggle and ceaseless questing but directly invokes the pastoral genre, which was felt to be the contrary of epic in both antiquity and the Renaissance. Machiavelli's rejection of *ozio* thus links him to the writers of heroic poems, as does his fear of women and Fortuna, whom he characterizes as temptresses, just as the writers of epic from Homer to Ludovico Ariosto did. Finally, when all the traits of the heroic prince are considered together — his cunning and violence, his heroic

questing, his constant struggle with male enemies and female temptresses—it becomes apparent that Machiavelli had in mind a particular
ancient hero, rather than ancient heroes generally, when he reshaped
his confidence man–prince in that direction.

Chapters 5 and 6 are, each in its own way, concerned with Machiavelli's further transformation of the figure of the confidence man as he
uses it to shape his own life and his relationships with others. Both
chapters document the powerful attraction the character held for him
and analyze the uses to which he put it in his life in an effort to regain
a measure of the power and status he lost after he was thrust from office
when the Medici were restored to power in 1512. Chapter 5 completes
the investigation of Machiavelli's political and historical works by examining the relationship he establishes in them between his readers and
the particular persona or mask he fashions for himself. Ironically, it
shows that in many of those works, although he explicitly identifies
himself as an adviser or counselor to men of superior social and political positions, upon closer inspection he turns out to function as a teacher
and guide who coerces them by his style into conceiving the world in his
terms. In effect, then, Machiavelli plays the role of confidence man in
these works and uses it to structure his relationship with his readers. Although he appears to play the servant and to defer to them, he is really
manipulating them, becoming nothing less than his masters' master and
reveling in the vicarious power that position grants him. Machiavelli's
strategy here allows him at best only a potential or hypothetical victory,
however, for no matter how cleverly his works manipulate his readers,
they cannot compel assent, guarantee understanding, or even ensure a
complete reading. Indeed, as their reception has revealed, this strategy
paradoxically both succeeded and failed for Machiavelli: *Il principe* and
the *Discorsi* have certainly changed the way people think, but they did
not secure much real political power, let alone a great following, for
their author during his lifetime, and since then they have produced in
readers at least as much misunderstanding and hostility as enthusiastic
acceptance. Thus Machiavelli's strategy relegates him to the uncom-
fortable, paradoxical position his confidence men have always been in:
it has made possible a partial victory but only at the risk of a defeat,
which occurs with fearsome inevitability. Seeing the world through the
confidence man–dupe dialectic, Machiavelli plays his confidence game
to avoid experiencing defeat and degradation, just as his heroes do, but
ironically, he always winds up, like them, the impotent dupe.

The sixth and final chapter focuses on a diplomatic mission Machiavelli made to Carpi in 1521, examining the letters he exchanged from
there with his friend and kindred spirit Francesco Guicciardini. The

letters record how in this episode, he turned his life into a confidence game, deceiving the Carpigiani to enhance his sense of personal dignity and power. The letters also show him embracing the carnivalesque side of the confidence man, a side involving pleasure, idleness, and an affirmation of the body, all of which were obscured and suppressed in his heroic version of the figure. Finally, the letters record how Machiavelli's trick was exposed, how he failed as a confidence man at Carpi and experienced the seemingly inevitable, intensely degrading defeat that was built into the game in which he, like all his heroes, was engaged. This defeat is a repetition *in nuce* of experiences which the socially inferior Machiavelli had to endure throughout his life and which became especially intense after the end of the Florentine Republic in 1512 and his exile to Sant' Andrea. As other letters show, he employed a variety of psychological strategies to deal with his sense that he was a worthless, degraded dupe, but they also show that all of those strategies were to some degree unsatisfactory. By contrast, the letters from Carpi reveal that in this episode, at least, Machiavelli learned to live with the degradation and humiliation of being a dupe. At Carpi he adopted the strategy, both psychological and artistic, of ironically distancing himself from his experience, thereby accommodating failure by recourse, one final time, to literature. Significantly, he did not attempt a futile escape from the confidence man–dupe dialectic; rather, he turned his experiences at Carpi into brilliant, ironic farce, scripting for himself the role of self-conscious carnival clown. Thus he found a means to tolerate degradation, to preserve his sense of personal integrity and his self-possession: he laughs at his own behavior and thereby prevents anyone else from ever having the last laugh. Never able to be the princely lion and a failure as a crafty fox, Machiavelli plays the ironist, defending himself from the lions of his world who gladly would have eaten him alive as well as from the foxes who would have gloated and smirked over his humiliation.

Language and Power
in *La Mandragola*

La *mandragola* is a highly original comedy, but it is also indebted to a number of important literary texts and traditions. Machiavelli draws on the literature of courtly love, for instance, as he fashions a lovesick Callimaco who complains of his frustration and suffering. A more important source is the Roman comedy of Plautus and Terence, from which Machiavelli took the notion of pairing his hero with a tricky servant who masterminds the plot of the play. And from Boccaccio's *Decameron*, certainly the most significant influence on the comedy, he derived the basic shape of his plot as an extended *beffa* and borrowed specific episodes, such as the one in which Nicia is given aloes to eat.[1] In significant ways, however, Machiavelli differs from these two principal sources. Discussion of his differences from Plautus and Terence will be reserved until the end of the chapter, but two important differences between Machiavelli and Boccaccio require treatment now to clarify the particular character of Machiavelli's work. First, unlike his predecessor, Machiavelli rigorously divides the world in his play into two species, confidence men and dupes or fools, two distinctive *cervelli*, minds or psychologies. Thus Callimaco, Ligurio, and Frate Timoteo all fall into the first category; they are amoral swindlers who delight in pulling the wool over Nicia's eyes. Sostrata is also something of a dupe, and though Lucrezia may begin as a paragon of virtue — and hence appears to escape Machiavelli's fundamental division of the world into tricksters and dupes — she has become a perfect confidence woman by the end of the play. Even the anonymous Florentine lady, who appears in only a

[1] For the influence of Boccaccio and other *novella* writers on Machiavelli, see Luigi Vanossi, "Situazione e sviluppo del teatro machiavelliano," in *Lingua e strutture del teatro italiano del Rinascimento: Machiavelli, Ruzzante, Aretino, Guarini, Commedia dell'arte*, ed. G. Folena (Padua: Liviana, 1970), pp. 8-11, 35-38.

single, brief scene, may be understood in terms of this dichotomy, for she appears a superstitious fool who has been used by her husband and is now being used by Timoteo and the church, although in both cases she is, like many a dupe in the *Decameron*, satisfied to be so used. By contrast, although many of Boccaccio's most famous stories center on confidence men and dupes, his work contains many characters who escape those categories: devoted lovers such as Federigo degli Alberighi (v, 9), witty philosophers such as Guido Cavalcanti (vi, 9), magnanimous monarchs such as King Carlo (x, 6). Even in stories that do focus on confidence men or fools, Boccaccio often provides auxiliary characters who are neither, such bystanders and witnesses as the Florentine usurers in the tale of Ciappelletto (i, 1) and the Florentine who laughingly exposes Martellino's trick (ii, 1). In short, the *Decameron* offers a wide range of characters, perhaps as a reflection of the wide range of generic forms it includes, whereas Machiavelli's play reveals an obsession with the two figures who stand at the center of his imagination.

The second major difference between Boccaccio and Machiavelli involves the question of morality. In Machiavelli's play we find no morally neutral characters and certainly no innocent ones. Some are innocent in the sense of being naïve and inexperienced, but at the same time they are morally compromised. Thus Nicia may be extremely naïve, but he is also greedy, status-seeking, and willing to sacrifice a human life for the sake of gaining an heir. Similarly, Sostrata is ready to compromise her daughter for the same end, as well as to ensure her own future security. And Lucrezia, who begins the play as the only character genuinely concerned about traditional morality, has become an adulteress by the end. Again, the *Decameron* is very different. Although many of its dupes are morally compromised by their lust or violence, we find as well some genuine innocents, in both senses of the word: such characters as the old friar who confesses Ciappelletto and many of the lovers in Days IV and V. Indeed, Boccaccio celebrates the morality of many of his protagonists, and nowhere more strikingly than in the legion of the magnanimous in the tenth day. By contrast, there are no ethical paragons in *La mandragola*, so that from this perspective the work clearly appears to share the dour estimate of humanity one finds in Machiavelli's political and historical writings, the notion that all men are by nature wicked and egotistical.[2]

[2]Giulio Ferroni, *"Mutazione" e "riscontro" nel teatro di Machiavelli, e altri saggi sulla commedia del Cinquecento* (Rome: Bulzoni, 1972), p. 39. On the general relationship between *La mandragola* and Machiavelli's political writings, see Martin Fleisher, "Trust and Deceit in Machiavelli's Comedies," *Journal of the History of Ideas* 27 (1966): 368; Luigi Russo, *Machiavelli*, 3d ed. (Bari: Laterza, 1949), p. 97; Giorgio Cavallini,

Machiavelli's presentation of his confidence men and dupes in *La mandragola* is based on an anthropology of desire. All the characters are consumed by the pursuit of personal gratification, some seeking money, some sexual pleasure, some family security, some vicarious immortality. Hence society becomes for them a war of all against all in which the love of wife for husband, servant for master, or priest for parishioner cannot stem the tide of desire; as Machiavelli says in *Il principe*, love is a weak "vinculo di obbligo," scarcely able to unite men and women together in anything resembling a community (xvii, 70). For Machiavelli people are distinguished less by the presence or absence of desire than by their relative abilities to satisfy it, to control it with reason, to reflect on it self-consciously, and to maintain a degree of distance from it so that it does not overwhelm their judgment.[3] Thus *La mandragola* can be read as a kind of anatomy of the modes of responding to desire, and it establishes a clear hierarchy among its characters in respect to those responses.

At the bottom of that hierarchy stand the anonymous Florentine lady and Nicia, both overpowered by poorly understood urges never reflected upon or made the basis of self-criticism. The lady, for instance, is filled not only with superstitious fears but also with sexual fantasies in which foreign invasions and ideas of "impaling" are linked to obscure recollections of strange and unnatural sexual practices her dead husband forced upon her.[4] She consciously broods on the threat of a Turkish invasion but is completely unaware of its connection with her sexual fantasies — or even that she has sexual fantasies. Desire of a different sort dominates the life of Nicia, but here it is the desire to have a child. The precondition for the success of Callimaco's plot (see 1.i.62-63), this desire is a "pazzia" (1.iii.66) that masters Nicia's responses and drastically reduces his ability to respond to the world with reason and detachment. He is especially concerned that the child be male (iii.viii.86), a small replica of himself, a little Nicia to ensure his own worldly immortality. So strong is this desire that he actually cries at the thought of his baby boy, and his imagination is so powerfully stimulated that he can fantasize, while Callimaco and Lucrezia are passing the night together: "Me lo pare tuttavia avere in braccio, el naccherino!" (v.ii.107-8: "It seems to me I actually have the little toddler in my arms!"). Moreover, Nicia

---

[3] See K. R. Minogue, "Theatricality and Politics: Machiavelli's Concept of *Fantasia*," in *The Morality of Politics*, ed. Bhikha Parekh and R. N. Becki (New York: Crane & Russek, 1972), pp. 152-56.

[4] Russo has noted that her scene is full of subterranean sexuality; see his *Machiavelli*, p. 121.

is mercenary, a trait underscored three times in the play: he is maneuvered twice, first by Ligurio and then by Lucrezia, into unwillingly giving large sums of money to Frate Timoteo (iii.iv.82; v.vi.112), and
Callimaco appeals to his greed by offering him 2,000 ducats if the magic
potion should fail (ii.vi.75). Finally, Nicia utterly lacks self-
consciousness about his feelings; he cannot detach himself from them
and shape them. In his soliloquies—unique opportunities for self-
reflection—he characteristically engages in dialogues with imaginary
opponents rather than in reflections about himself. Obsessed by his desires, Nicia lives in a world created in large measure by imaginative projection, by the egocentric fantasies spun out by his will.

Nicia is not the only character in the play obsessed by a desire for
progeny. Sostrata fears that a woman without a child—or that woman's
mother—will be homeless (iii.xi.89), and her desire for security leads
her to agree essentially to the prostitution of her daughter. Unlike Nicia,
though, Sostrata keeps her imagination under some measure of control
as she argues rationally and coolly with her daughter. Sostrata clearly
knows the price of security and is willing to pay it, no matter what the
moral cost.

Frate Timoteo evinces a similar detachment from at least some of his
desires. Like Nicia and Sostrata, he also has an obsession—money. He
likes donations, feels that money will protect him from scandal
(iv.vi.99), and equates his holy function with "mercanzia" (v.iii.109).
Unwittingly perhaps, he reveals his desire publicly when he argues the
acceptability of adultery to Lucrezia on the grounds that it will result in
another tithe-paying soul for his superior, "messer Domenedio"
(iii.xi.89). Nevertheless, his soliloquies reveal his awareness of at least
some of the tricks Callimaco and Ligurio are playing on him as well as
a dispassionate ability to calculate his own interests, even if, at the same
time, they show that he, like Sostrata, is unable to face fully the serious
moral issues involved in his actions. Moreover, just to add a bit of spice
to the character of this rascally friar, Machiavelli gives him a prurient
interest in Callimaco's and Lucrezia's lovemaking. His powerful imagination, which equals Nicia's in some respects, leads him to envision the
pair together, keeps him from sleeping all night, and has him focus on
the couple's tarrying over "the last few drops": "Ben si sono indugiati
alla sgocciolatura" (v.i.105). Frate Timoteo is no more aware of the significance of such an interest than is the anonymous Florentine lady of
what "impaling" really means to her. The frate's failure to recognize his
erotic interest and the ease with which Ligurio manipulates him through
his greed diminish his status as a confidence man despite his amorality,
his shamelessness, and his unbending pursuit of personal advantage.

Like all the other characters in the play, Callimaco is obsessed—indeed, besotted—by desire, but he displays an awareness of it and a control over it which elevate him above the others and identify him unmistakably as a confidence man. The potency of Callimaco's desire is underscored throughout the play by images identifying it with physical appetite. As he conjures up seduction plots in his imagination, for instance, he tells Ligurio that he feeds himself with hopes to mitigate his suffering (I.iii.67). Later, Ligurio compares the state of total disequilibrium which Callimaco's desire and desperate hopes have produced in him to the condition of drunkenness: "Tu mi pari cotto" (II.vi.77). And near the end Callimaco claims to have lost ten pounds through fear and anxiety (IV.iv.97), thus suggesting that although he may feed on his fantasies, desire needs more substantial food. In an exaggeratedly comic fashion, Callimaco repeatedly reports that he is ready to die because of the pressure produced by desire (e.g., I.iii.67, II.vi.77, IV.i.92-93), and that pressure is reflected in his syntax, as in the repetitions of the following passage:

> Meglio è morire che vivere cosí. Se io potessi dormire la notte, se io potessi mangiare, se io potessi conversare, se io potessi pigliare piacere di cosa veruna, io sarei piú paziente ad aspettare el tempo; ma qui non ci è rimedio. [I.iii.67]

> It's better to die than live thus. If I could sleep at night, if I could eat, if I could engage in conversation, if I could take pleasure from anything, I would be more patient in biding my time, but there's no remedy here.

In essence, desire has deprived Callimaco of his freedom, and, as Giulio Ferroni has claimed, has made him a ridiculous, comic figure who arouses the scornful laughter of the audience.[5]

But Ferroni goes too far in devaluing Callimaco, for if the man is moved by desire, so are all the other characters, down to the least of the servants, whose behavior is dominated by a need for money. By contrast with Nicia, and with Frate Timoteo to a lesser degree, Callimaco can make his passion, at least partially, an object of contemplation.[6] Unlike Nicia's, his soliloquies are full of self-reflection and a fitful, comic detachment from his sufferings. A high point is reached in Act IV, scene i, when he consciously confronts his madness ("furor") and the "womanish" nature of his passion while wittily embracing the prospect of divine punishment in hell because of his planned seduction of Lucrezia

[5] Ferroni, *"Mutazione,"* p. 49.
[6] Vanossi, "Situazione e sviluppo," p. 17.

(92–93). Moreover, whereas Nicia's passions burst forth uncontrollably, Callimaco consciously recognizes his need for release ("sfogarsi"), and he deliberately seeks out others to whom he can safely pour forth his feelings (1.i.62; IV.i.93). He releases his feelings only in front of servants he can trust, nor does he allow his desires and fantasies to interfere with the roles he has to play in the public arena. Furthermore, Callimaco's strong desire never blinds him to the nature of men and the world; he never naïvely trusts others to look out for his interests willingly. In reply to Siro's warnings that Ligurio may deceive him, for instance, Callimaco claims that the parasite may be trusted because his services have been purchased with a generous sum of money (1.i.63). In fact, although the broken syntax in some of Callimaco's speeches reveals the pressure of desire, he is also capable of speaking rationally and dispassionately, as in the following speech, which uses such logical connectives as "nondimanco" ("nevertheless") and "perché" ("because") and enumerates carefully all the advantages Ligurio would lose by an act of betrayal:

> *Ligurio.* Tu hai ragione, e io son per farlo.
> *Callimaco.* Io lo credo, ancora che io sappia ch'e pari tuoi vivino d'uccellare li uomini. Nondimanco, io non credo essere in quel numero, perché quando tu el facessi ed io me ne avvedessi, cercherei di valermene, e perderesti ora l'uso della casa mia e la speranza d'avere quello che per lo avvenire t'ho promesso. [1.iii.67]

> *Ligurio.* You're right. I'm the man to do it.
> *Callimaco.* I believe it, although I know that men like you live by gulling others. Nevertheless, I don't feel I'm in that number, because if you did it and I were aware of it, I would seek to avenge myself, and you'd lose the use of my house and the hope of having what I've promised you for the future.

Callimaco is equally cautious about Siro and reveals his rational skepticism about human nature when he admits that he does trust the man, but only after ten years of faithful service (IV.iii.97). Moreover, Callimaco does not simply depend on that loyalty but mixes appeals to it with others to his servant's self-interest: "la roba, l'onore, la vita mia e il ben tuo" (IV.v.98: "goods, glory, my life and your welfare"). Clearly, then, if desire makes Callimaco at times something of a clown, a farcical figure eloquently symbolized by his disguise as the "garzonaccio" (IV.ix.102), he is by no means simply that. In fact, he appears most of the time disguised as a doctor, a role involving a fair amount of dignity and respect within the world of the play and for the audience, and one he will continue to play indefinitely after the last act ends. And with his desire for Lucrezia satisfied, one may well imagine that the self-conscious, skeptical, prudent side of his character will become dominant, no longer qualified by ridiculous episodes of helpless suffering. Above Callimaco in the hierarchy of the play's characters stand Ligurio and perhaps Lucrezia. Lucrezia is surely "accorta" ("clever"), as the Prologue labels her (57) and her later suspiciousness suggests (III.xi.88–89). Although she starts out as a moral and devoutly religious person who spends hours at her prayers (II.vi.75) and who, alone in the play, worries seriously about the death of the "garzonaccio" (III.x.88), she is transformed by the end into a confidence woman who cooperates fully with Callimaco and Ligurio in deceiving her husband. Like all the characters in the world of Machiavelli's play, she turns out to be a creature of desire, who must certainly be attracted to Callimaco sexually, as he himself argues, but is able to play the moral and devoted wife in public at the same time.[7] Nevertheless, to make Lucrezia the heroine of the play, as Giulio Ferroni has done, may be going too far, for although her transformation is self-willed, what she wills to do is to subject herself to Callimaco and to carry on the play that Ligurio has scripted for them all.[8] Moreover, although at the end she does appear to Nicia to be a commanding figure, originating the plan to make "Doctor" Callimaco their "compare" and getting her husband to give Frate Timoteo a large sum of money, it is doubtful whether she could ever play the power behind the throne with the more self-conscious Callimaco or Ligurio.[9]

Of all the confidence men and women in the play, only Ligurio seems to have achieved an ideal control over his desires. Accordingly, he scorns Nicia as a fool, mocks Callimaco's indulgence in erotic passion (IV.ii.94), and instructs his employer to rein in his desperate spirits and control himself (I.iii.67). A figure of perfect composure who hardly ever exposes his desires to others, Ligurio also has no soliloquies that explore his motives and feelings. In fact, one may well wonder if he is moved by desire at all, for although Callimaco describes him as a parasite sponging off Nicia and stresses the financial reward he offers (I.i.63; I.iii.67), Ligurio himself never dwells on such motives. In this regard, as Ezio Raimondi has noted, he is quite distant from his model, the parasite in

---

[7]She has "gustato che differenzia è dalla iacitura mia a quella di Nicia, e da e baci d'uno amante giovane a quelli d'uno marito vecchio" (V.iv.109: "tasted the difference between my sleeping with her and Nicia's, and between the kisses of a young lover and those of an old husband").

[8]*"Mutazione,"* pp. 30–31, 46, 80–84.

[9]It is difficult to generalize about Lucrezia's motives and her relationship to other characters in the play because she appears in only a few scenes and says relatively little.

Roman comedy, who was obsessed with filling his belly.[10] Ligurio comes close to stating a motive for his actions only when he defends his trustworthiness to Callimaco:

> Non dubitare della fede mia, ché quando e' non ci fussi l'utile che io sento e che io spero, ci è che 'l tuo sangue si affà col mio, e desidero che tu adempia questo tuo desiderio presso a quanto tu. [1.iii.67]

> Don't doubt my faith, for if there weren't the utility I already know of and hope for, there's your temperament [blood] which resembles my own, and I desire that you accomplish your desire almost as much as you do.

This speech seems to suggest that although Ligurio acknowledges a mercenary motive, he is really moved by a capacity for empathy, an ability to enjoy vicariously the desires that others are satisfying.[11] This empathetic identification is not, as I shall argue later, so innocent as it may seem here, and it may be inferred that Ligurio satisfies a more substantial and interested desire through the action of the play. In any case, he clearly stands at the apex of all the characters as the one most fully in control of his desires and imagination and hence as its ideal confidence man.[12]

If dupes and confidence men in *La mandragola* form a hierarchy because of their ability to control their desires, this ability is a matter less of self-discipline and restraint than of their relative detachment from themselves and their distance from place, customs, and conventional morality. Nicia, from this perspective, is hopelessly parochial. A stay-at-home, though he claims to have wandered about (been "randagio") in his youth, he has gone only as far as Prato, Pisa, and Livorno (1.ii.65), nor does he readily leave his home nowadays (1.ii.64: "io mi spicco mal volentieri da bomba"). By contrast, the well-educated gentleman Callimaco has lived abroad, and the unattached, if not *déraciné*,[13] Ligurio shows a large experience of the world as he voices a sophisticated cynicism, especially about friars (III.ii.80), and details the problems one may encounter at the baths (1.iii.66). The naïve Nicia does not share such cynical knowledge and is amazed ("Io strabilio") when Frate Timoteo

[10]Ezio Raimondi, *Politica e commedia: Dal Beroaldo al Machiavelli* (Bologna: Mulino, 1972), pp. 210-11.

[11]This is an ability that Frate Timoteo also possesses, as his comments about Callimaco's and Lucrezia's night in bed together suggest.

[12]Raimondi, *Politica e commedia*, p. 161; Vanossi, "Situazione," p. 23; and Franco Fido, "Machiavelli, 1469-1969: Politica e teatro nel badalucco di Messer Nicia," *Italica* 46 (1969): 364.

[13]Raimondi, *Politica e commedia*, p. 211.

agrees to arrange an abortion (III.v.84). This reaction suggests that Nicia lacks not merely a wide-ranging experience, but freedom from custom and conventional morality. To be sure, he does not seem worried about the immorality involved in sending an innocent young man to his death (although he *is* worried about being caught), and he hardly seems religious when he criticizes his wife for praying too much (II.vi.75), rejects her religious scruples about the mandrake plot (IV.viii.100), and admits that he has not been to confession in ten years (III.ii.80). But if he largely ignores morality and religion in his headlong pursuit of desire, he is terribly worried about appearances, social conventions, and reputation.[14] Thus Callimaco overcomes Nicia's hesitations about the mandrake potion by reporting that the king and queen of France used it (II.vi.75), and Nicia is concerned that Siro should call "Doctor" Callimaco by the correct title, "maestro" (II.i.70). Just as Nicia is unself-reflective about the desires that dominate his life, so he is mechanical in responding to social conventions, qualities reflected in his decision to go to church at the end of the play to have his wife ritually purified and to thank Frate Timoteo. Ironically, this man who is so worried about social conventions is the only person in the play directly critical of his fellow Florentines (see II.iii.72–73), but that criticism relates only to what he considers his mistreatment at the hands of those in power and does not extend to a conscious rejection of the moral codes, social structures, or institutions of his society.

Frate Timoteo and Callimaco, by contrast, are both aware, in different degrees, that their courses of action are evil, although both consciously set morality aside so they can satisfy their desires (IV.i.92; IV.vi.99). In fact, Callimaco repeats traditional, even Augustinian arguments against the pursuit of desire, which gives him no rest anywhere.[15] He tells himself:

Che fai tu? se' tu impazzato? quando tu l'ottenga, che fia? Conoscerai el tuo errore, pentira'ti delle fatiche e de' pensieri che hai avuti. Non sai tu quanto poco bene si truova nelle cose che l'uomo desidera, rispetto a quelle che l'uomo ha presupposte trovarvi? [IV.i.92]

What are you doing? Are you mad? When you obtain her, what would happen? You will recognize your error, and you will repent of the difficulties and the thoughts you have had. Don't you know how little good

[14] Ibid., p. 207.
[15] For Machiavelli's relationship to Augustine, see Joseph A. Mazzeo, *Renaissance and Revolution: Backgrounds to Seventeenth-Century English Literature* (New York: Random House, 1965, 1967), pp. 77–85.

can be found in the things which man desires, in respect of those things which he presupposed to find there?

But Callimaco then goes on to dismiss any fear of hell and ultimately to accept his submission to desire. To achieve satisfaction, as he tells Ligurio earlier, he is ready to do anything, however "bestiale, crudo, nefando" (i.iii.67: "bestial, coarse, wicked"), and Ligurio, equally detached from conventional morality, later suggests to Callimaco that he can rule Lucrezia by indirectly threatening to ruin her reputation: "dicale el bene le vuoi; e come sanza sua infamia la può essere tua amica, e con sua grande infamia tua nimica" (iv.ii.96: "tell her the good you wish her, and how without infamy she can be your mistress, and with great infamy your enemy"). Basically, Ligurio is suggesting something close to rape: Callimaco, like Machiavelli's prince, should cast aside moral scruples and use force to have his way with Lucrezia. Callimaco, however, whose relative inability to control his desires has already made him something less than the hero of the play, also shows himself less than an ideal prince, for once in bed with Lucrezia, he attempts to persuade her to accept his love not merely by his display of superior, masculine potency but also by offering to marry her when Nicia dies (v.iv.109). Ligurio is, as his suggested treatment of Lucrezia indicates, freer than Callimaco from such moral and social restraints, as Lucrezia herself may be, since she does not respond to the offer of marriage, seemingly content to enjoy a *ménage à trois* with someone she speaks of as her "signore, padrone, guida, . . . padre, . . . defensore" (v.iv.109: "lord, leader, guide, . . . father, . . . defender"), but never as her husband, her "marito" or "sposo."]

The difference between confidence men and dupes in *La mandragola* is also that between those who, fully realizing that life is theater, act on the basis of that awareness, and those who can at most play the parts others have scripted for them. We have already noted the power of Nicia's and Callimaco's imaginations, which lead them to fantasize about a happy future based on projections of their present desires. In different degrees, however, both characters are locked inside their fantasies and hence unable to shape the world by carrying them out. By contrast, Ligurio is, as Ezio Raimondi has observed, a superb director and actor, who composes the play that all of them act out.[16] With Nicia as mute onlooker, for instance, he puts on a one-act play for Frate Timoteo, concocting the tale of the woman in need of an abortion to test the ras-

---

[16]Raimondi, *Politica e commedia*, p. 212.

cally priest's corruptibility (III.iv.83-84). With his shrewd ability to size up people and anticipate situations, Ligurio dismisses the defective scenario that Callimaco thought to use involving the baths (I.iii.67-68), and he not only writes the play of the mandrake but also shows great ability to improvise solutions to unanticipated problems, as when Callimaco discovers he is supposed to play the "doctor" and the "garzonaccio" at the same time (IV.ii.94-95).

Ligurio's play of the mandrake focuses attention on the various levels of "theatrical" understanding possessed by all the characters. If Callimaco and, later on, Lucrezia are not responsible for scripting or directing it, they nevertheless share a full awareness with Ligurio that they are in a play, and they perform the roles assigned them with skill, recognizing explicitly that they *are* roles.[17] Timoteo knows quite a bit as well, although just how much Ligurio has told him is hard to determine. By contrast, Nicia, Sostrata, and Lucrezia (up to her "conversion") are all unwitting participants in the play of the mandrake. Ligurio, Timoteo, Callimaco, and the "converted" Lucrezia have a sense that the world is theater and that appearances, even of religious images (v.i.105), are what count, but Nicia has no such sense; he can at best play a part in a masquerade that someone else has dreamed up for him and that is explicitly identified as a play. Moreover, in that masquerade, when all the other participants are aware that they are playing double roles, only Nicia does not know what everyone else does—that Timoteo has replaced "Doctor" Callimaco and that Callimaco is playing the "garzonaccio." In addition, Nicia gets terribly confused by the little playlet Ligurio devises to tempt Frate Timoteo (III.vii.86). It is thus fitting that he, the character with the least theatrical awareness, should dress the part of clown for the masquerade without realizing it (IV.vii.100) and should be made the ridiculous object of the play's one great visual joke when he is placed between the two "horns" formed by Ligurio and Timoteo. He simply does not see the dramatic image of his cuckolding which is right before his eyes.

With all his script-writing and acting, Ligurio certainly displays the most potent imagination of any character in the play. This imagination does not, however, trap him in a private fantasy world, but rather enables him to enter into and shape the public one, although, unlike Timoteo's, it does not rely on the images of a no longer potent religion to do so. Ligurio's imagination is as fully theatrical as those of Boccaccio's great confidence men, Ciappelletto, Frate Alberto, and Frate Ci-

---

[17]If Callimaco's role as doctor is, as Giulio Ferroni argues, a simple one to play, then so is Lucrezia's role of honest wife at the end of the play. In this way she hardly appears Callimaco's superior as an actress. For Ferroni's argument, see *"Mutazione,"* p. 50.

polla: it constructs a new and utopian reality out of the greedy desires and fantasies of men and then relies on those desires and fantasies to compel the prey to accept that new reality in place of the old. Instructively, at one point Nicia, who has been terribly confused by Ligurio's playlet with Frate Timoteo, breathes a sigh of relief when all seems clear again and remarks to Ligurio, "Tu mi *ricrei* tutto quanto" (III.viii.86, my emphasis: "You have entirely *brought* me *back to life again* [*recreated* me]"). Although Nicia means simply that his spirits have been restored, the theater metaphors suggest another significance for his notion of being "recreated." For indeed, as Ligurio improvises his script of the mandrake, he does just that—he *recreates* the people who participate in the play, assigning them parts and determining their identities in a way that they, immersed in their desires and fantasies, could hardly have done for themselves. What is more, Ligurio gives a deep sense of satisfaction to those he manipulates and preys on, for in using his skills as a playwright-actor-director, he brings a sense of order, albeit one based on illusion, into the otherwise chaotic, frustrated lives of the others.

Why does Ligurio take this role? Certainly his expenditure of effort and ingenuity exceed the financial reward he will receive, a reward he hardly mentions.[18] Nevertheless, an examination of his actions suggests that he does have another, more substantial motive: the desire to acquire and maintain power.[19] By scripting the play of the mandrake to satisfy everyone else, Ligurio is able simultaneously not merely to benefit himself monetarily but in a deeper way to satisfy himself that the world is shaped according to *his* designs, that *he* controls it. He reveals this desire in the way he fabricates his comedy and tells his actors how to play their parts. Almost from the start he withholds pieces of his plot from Callimaco in order to force his ostensible master to follow his lead (I.iii.68: "seguitando el mio parlare e accomodandoti a quello"), using the excuse that time is pressing. He similarly goes out of his way to keep Nicia in the dark about the tale to be told Timoteo, and he has Nicia play deaf and respond only to direct cues (III.ii.81). Later, when Ligurio reports to Callimaco that Nicia promised three hundred ducats to the friar but gave only twenty-five, and Callimaco wants an explanation for this discrepancy, Ligurio commands his employer not to inquire further (IV.ii.94: "Bastiti che gli ha sborsati"). By keeping back bits of information from other characters, including his master, Ligurio recalls the tricky slave of Roman comedy, but whereas the slave refused to

[18]Fido, "Machiavelli, 1469-1969," 368.
[19]Ligurio is also doubtless moved by the sheer pleasure of calculation, as Raimondi suggests in *Politica e commedia*, p. 211, but I think his motive is a more interested one than such an analysis indicates.

reveal his plot only occasionally and always in response to the pressures of the action, Ligurio does so repeatedly and, at times, gratuitously, thus indicating the motive of personal gratification underlying his behavior. Moreover, Ligurio also engages in two acts of gratuitous sadism directed at Nicia, which can best be explained as attempts to enhance his feeling of power. First, he commits the stingy dupe to give Frate Timoteo a generous sum of money for his help (iii.iv.82) and later, under the pretext of helping Nicia disguise his voice, Ligurio gives him aloes to put in his mouth, causing the hapless gull to spit and sputter ridiculously. Thus manipulating the others by means of the play he composes, controlling their performances by keeping them in the dark as much as possible, and occasionally having them make spectacles of themselves for his sadistic pleasure, Ligurio satisfies his hidden but real desire for power over his world, a power his status as an outsider with no social position otherwise denies him.

Ligurio is not alone, of course, in wanting power, for the desires of all the other characters may be seen as equivalents to or displacements of such a desire. Masculine sexuality is linked directly to power in several ways during the play. For instance, the curious little scene between Frate Timoteo and the anonymous lady identifies sexuality with the wild, exotic, and powerful Turks who threaten to invade Italy and fill the lady with fear of "impaling" (iii.iii.82). Moreover, when Nicia praises "Doctor" Callimaco as "valente," a term meaning "clever" but also "powerful," Siro jokes in a way that extends its meaning to include Callimaco's sexual prowess (ii.iii.72). More important, Callimaco credits his success with Lucrezia at least in part to his potent "lying" ("iacitura") with her, and she reportedly identifies her lover with a series of masculine roles, the last one of which makes him her "defensore" (v.iv.109: "defender"). She may have been thinking of Callimaco as a knight in armor here, reflecting the courtly language he is prone to use, but her image also identifies her lover as a masculine figure of power.[20] Finally, Ligurio's suggestion, to which Callimaco does not object, that Lucrezia be subdued by a threat to her reputation evokes the possibility that the key act toward which the play has been moving is rape, a sexual expression of masculine violence and lust for power. When Lucrezia is "reborn" at the end of the play and impresses Nicia with her commanding presence, he remarks: "La pare un gallo!" (v.v.110: "She seems to be a cock!"). To be a figure of power in the world of this play is to be a "cock" indeed.

[20] On Callimaco's courtly language, see Ferroni, *"Mutazione,"* p. 44.

Whereas Ligurio, Callimaco, Timoteo, and Lucrezia all satisfy their need for power by manipulating others, Nicia attempts to do so to compensate for a genuine powerlessness, both social and familial, of which he is fitfully and uncomfortably aware. Although a man of property and a doctor of laws, he confesses how hard it was for him to learn the necessary Latin (II.iii.72: "ho cacato le curatelle per imparare due hac"), and in his desire to show off his meager store of learning to Callimaco, he merely reinforces his sense of his own deficiency. Moreover, as a lawyer, he is a self-proclaimed failure; he offers as an excuse his unjust treatment by the government of the city, but he nevertheless feels keenly his lack of dignity and status. As he says, he and those like him are good only to work funerals and weddings, "o a starci tutto dí in sulla panca del Proconsolo a donzellarci" (II.iii.73: "or to sit around all day on the Proconsul's bench and waste time"). "Donzellarci" suggests the depth of Nicia's feeling that he has lost his adult manhood, for it means to act the part of an immature adolescent, a *donzello*. It must be remembered that the mark of mature manhood throughout the Renaissance was the siring of a family, and Nicia has been sadly deficient on this score. But Nicia's "donzellarci" may also suggest a slightly different meaning, for the word derives from *donzella*, meaning *young girl* or *damsel*, and may thus imply a feeling of emasculation in that sense as well. That Nicia feels emasculated is clear from his complaints about his wife, for they reveal that if she does not exactly dominate him like a shrew, he nevertheless has great difficulty managing her. In one of his soliloquies, he addresses her in her absence: "Io ho fatto d'ogni cosa a tuo modo: di questo vo' io che tu facci a mio. S'io credevo non avere figliuoli, io arei preso piú tosto per moglie una contadina" (II.v.74: "I've done everything your way, but in this matter I want you to do things my way. If I thought I would not have children, I would have sooner taken a peasant as my wife"). A peasant woman would have been easier to dominate. Lucrezia's resistance to Nicia's wishes only confirms his powerlessness. In addition, the fact that he addresses his rebuke not to Lucrezia but only to her image in his mind suggests his inability to confront her directly with his desires and underscores his lack of power in yet another way.[21] Finally, the unpleasant probability of his sexual impotence once again connects masculinity and power in the play.

Nicia attempts to compensate for his deficiency in several ways. The first is to attack everyone about him who cannot fight back, a tactic that

[21]Nicia must use intermediaries (Sostrata, Frate Timoteo) to persuade Lucrezia to sleep with the *garzonaccio*, and he does not appear together with her on stage until the very end of the play. It is almost as though he could not command her presence until then.

is limited and ineffectual with his wife and thus leaves him only the representatives of the inferior social classes, Ligurio and Siro, to bully (see, for example, I.ii.65 and IV.ix.102). His aggression is complemented by a fertile imagination, which allows him to assert that he has qualities he actually lacks. In response to Callimaco's suggestion of impotence, for instance, he claims to be "el piú ferrigno e il piú rubizzo uomo in Firenze" (II.ii.71: "the strongest and liveliest man in Florence"). And later, when he disguises himself to help catch the "garzonaccio," his imagination runs riot: "Chi mi conoscerebbe? Io paio maggiore, piú giovane, piú scarzo; e non sarebbe donna che mi togliessi danari di letto" (IV.viii.101: "Who would recognize me? I seem taller, younger, thinner, and no woman would ask money of me to go to bed with her"). Nicia is the tired old man of the stock May-December marriage, but his marriage also reflects Florentine social reality: men generally married much later in life than women, and young unmarried men spent a great amount of time and energy trying to seduce other men's wives.[22] Nicia's fantasy permits him to cling to the image of himself as a man of learning: he is sure that by his "scienzia" he can discover whether Callimaco is an impostor (II.i.69), and later he offers his services as a lawyer in exchange for Callimaco's as a doctor (II.ii.70). He adopts a superior air when he mocks the Florentines as "cacastecchi" (II.iii.72: "constipated asses") and claims he needs no one but himself, although clearly his self-image is dependent on the support of others. Nicia especially compensates for his lack of power and status by trying to adopt the role of the confidence man, playing the skeptic with Ligurio lest the parasite leave him in the lurch (II.i.69: "io non vorrei che mi mettessi in qualche lecceto e poi mi lasciassi in sulle secche"), and he even sticks his hand into the bed in which Callimaco and Lucrezia lie to make sure all goes well. He prides himself that he is not used to taking "lucciole per lanterne" (V.ii.107: "fireflies for lanterns"), enjoys being in on the plot Ligurio has cooked up, and adds to it the touch of coming out early in the morning to deceive his neighbors about how he and his family have spent the night (V.ii.106).

To heighten the irony of Nicia's vision of himself as a confidence man, when he splits the world into two groups, tricksters and dupes, the sane and the mad, adult men and foolish women or children, he does not realize that his behavior identifies him with the group he despises. Thus, playing the cynic and realist, he condemns his wife's moral qualms as stupidity and madness on several occasions (II.v.74; IV.viii.100), but he,

[22]See David Herlihy, "Some Psychological and Social Roots of Violence in Tuscan Cities," in *Violence and Civil Disorder in Italian Cities, 1200–1500*, ed. Lauro Martines (Berkeley: University of California Press, 1972), pp. 145-47.

not she, is the *sciocco*, the "fool" of the piece. More tellingly, he ridicules Ligurio at one point for supposed naïveté, telling him that he is a
baby, literally that his mouth is full of milk (i.ii.65: "Tu hai la bocca
piena di latte"). For Nicia—as for Machiavelli—to be a dupe is essentially to be a child, to be infantilized in a world in which to be an adult
is equivalent to being a sharper. Ironically, Nicia himself plays the child
throughout *La mandragola*. In a general way he behaves like a child by
failing to control his desires and imagination and displaying little self-
restraint. He even talks like a child at moments, especially when he is
first introduced, referring to his home as a "bomba" (i.ii.64), a "base"
in a child's game, and noting, with a child's wonderment, that the sea
is larger than the Arno "per quattro volte, per piú di sei, per piú di sette
mi farai dire" (i.ii.65: "more than four times, no, more than six, than
seven times, you'll have me say"). Most significantly, when Nicia, totally
confused by the playlet with which Ligurio has tempted Frate Timoteo,
is left alone onstage, he comments: "Ora m'hanno qui posto come un
zugo a piuolo" (iii.vii.86: "Now they've left me hanging here like a little
peg of a prick").[23] His imagery here equates his feeling of humiliation
with a sense of phallic exposure and inadequacy and thus suggests the
feeling of infantilization which is Nicia's lot in life and for which his
identification with the role of the confidence man is a desperate attempt to compensate. Ironically, although Nicia mocks others as children, *La mandragola* reveals that he is truly a babe in the woods.

Power, *La mandragola* shows, is directly related to, indeed dependent
on, one's mastery of language. The play underscores the importance of
language from the start, when the Prologue uses a gratuitous periph-
rasis equating Italy with its language (it is the part of the world where
"sí" sounds [58]). Moreover, in Callimaco's successful playing of the doctor's role, although learning and physical appearance are important, his
ability to speak Latin and talk in a dignified and learned manner are
crucial. Similarly, Lucrezia agrees to go along with the mandrake plot
in part because she is persuaded to do so by the frate, who produces an
eloquent *speech* for her and adduces the special authority inherent in

[23]In the edition of the play by Roberto Ridolfi, this line is punctuated slightly differ-
ently: "Ora mi hanno qui posto, come un zugo, a piolo" (*La mandragola* [Florence:
Olschki, 1965], iii.vi.124). With this punctuation, the line should be rendered: "Now
they've left me hanging here like a prick." The general sense is the same in both cases,
but the edition of Franco Gaeta, which lacks the two strategically placed commas of
Ridolfi's edition, emphasizes Nicia's infantilization by underscoring the small size of his
genitalia.

written words, in books, to support his arguments (iii.xi.88-89). *La mandragola* unmistakably shows that language is the instrument by means of which one puts on the play of life and that either it will be used self-consciously or it will remain merely a mechanical reflex that leaves one exposed to manipulation by the more rhetorically skillful.

Machiavelli's confidence men—Ligurio, Callimaco, and Frate Timoteo—all show themselves to be masters of language. The first two, for instance, demonstrate an ability to flatter their victim, Callimaco praising Nicia as being among the best men (ii.ii.70) and Ligurio flattering his supposed cosmopolitanism and the "prudenzia" with which he carried out the last stages of the mandrake plot (v.ii.107). Timoteo is adept at sophistical argument and the skillful manipulation of religious formulas, and the learned Callimaco not only speaks Latin but also is a master of the language of courtly compliment.[24] To some degree, however, Callimaco is trapped within his courtly language and in the role of elevated suffering it entails; although he can assume the artificial role and language of "learned doctor," he is ultimately unfree insofar as his courtly language controls him. Frate Timoteo seems less victimized by language as he plays his role of religious merchandiser, and he is somewhat less ridiculous a figure than Callimaco as a result. But the character who appears most in control of language is, of course, Ligurio. He reveals this control not only in his ability to flatter others and to concoct stories but in the skill with which he controls Nicia by using Nicia's language of proverbs and aping his misogynistic style.[25] A linguistic chameleon, he imitates Timoteo's argumentative style in persuading the friar to become an advocate for abortion (iii.iv.83-84). At the same time, he evinces a clear hostility to Callimaco's artificial language of elevated sentiment (iv.ii.94) and expresses impatience when Callimaco and Timoteo indulge in a flowery exchange of obviously insincere compliments. Ligurio cuts off the exchange with dry sarcasm: "Lasciamo stare le cerimonie" (iv.v.99: "Let's let the ceremonies go"). Possessing what critics and historians have identified as the characteristically "modern" mentality, a totally demystified and rationalistic world view, Ligurio disdainfully rejects a use of language characteristic of the "traditional" mentality, one still fully bound up in a ceremonious and ritu-

---

[24]Cavallini, *Interpretazione*, p. 51.
[25]Ligurio says he marvels at Nicia, "avendo voi pisciato in tante neve" (i.ii.65: "since you've pissed in so many snowfalls"); he says Callimaco is "uno uomo da metterli il capo in grembo" (ii.i.69: "a man who will make you bow your head"); and he apes Nicia's misogynism: "Io credo che sia perché tutte le donne son sospettose" (iii.ii.79: "I believe it's because all women are suspicious").

alistic world view.[26] Ligurio is not uniformly irritated by such a use of language and the mentality it implies, for he is content to manipulate it without complaint in dealing with Nicia, but he is irritated by his cronies' behavior because they supposedly share his own "modern," demystified mentality.

If Ligurio is the master of the language he speaks and the roles it defines, then Nicia is its victim.[27] His language is irregular, angular, and abrupt, and as he curses his wife, brusquely orders underlings about, and complains violently of his treatment at the hands of the Florentines, his speeches seem to erupt uncontrollably out of his psyche as an automatic reflex, an unstoppable welling forth of feeling and desire. In a sense, words are alien presences for Nicia; they control him far more than he controls them.[28] Moreover, these presences seem to have a genuine reality, an identity with the objects, activities, and persons they signify. As a result, he seeks through language to dominate the world, not by weaving fictions to manipulate others as Callimaco, Timoteo, and especially Ligurio do, but by the mere naming of things.[29] His cursing makes Nicia what Robert Elliott would call a primitive or magical satirist, one who believes that an execration pronounced against an enemy actually has the power to do him harm.[30] In essence, then, when Nicia dubs doctors "uccellacci" (I.ii.64) and Florentines "cacastecchi" (II.iii.72), it is as though by calling them such names he had the power to control them, to deprive them of the social position and status which they have and which constantly unman him.

In his violent diatribes, denunciation, and cursing, Nicia manifests an anal fixation, repeatedly referring to excrement and his *derrière*. Basically he wants to defecate on the world, for to excrete—to be able to excrete on others—is to manifest power. Appropriately, Nicia identifies those whom he would like to see as powerless, the Florentines for instance, as so many "cacastecchi" (II.iii.72: "constipated asses"), the

[26]For the distinction between "modern" and "traditional" mentalities, see Peter Burke, *Popular Culture in Early Modern Europe* (New York: Harper & Row, 1978), pp. 176-77; and Stephen Greenblatt, *Renaissance Self-Fashioning: From More to Shakespeare* (Chicago: University of Chicago Press, 1980), pp. 224-27. Both writers are indebted to Daniel Lerner, *The Passing of Traditional Society: Modernizing the Middle East*, rev. ed. (New York: Free Press, 1964).
[27]See Vanossi, "Situazione e sviluppo," p. 38: Nicia seems the image "di una coscienza imprigionata in uno spesso strato di 'parole'" ("of a consciousness imprisoned in a thick layer of 'words'").
[28]Raimondi, *Politica e commedia*, p. 209.
[29]According to Giorgio Barberi-Squarotti, language for Machiavelli is a mode of appropriating the world; see *La forma tragica del "Principe" e altri saggi sul Machiavelli* (Florence: Olschki, 1966), p. 81.
[30]Robert C. Elliott, *The Power of Satire: Magic, Ritual, Art* (Princeton: Princeton University Press, 1960), esp. pp. 49-99.

inability to excrete being equivalent in his mind to impotence. Moreover, if Nicia feels he gains power through logorrhea, through curses
and oaths such as "cacasangue" (III.iv.82), he also has a logical, con-
comitant desire to preserve his own body inviolate. Thus, when he indicates that he likes to avoid trouble, he uses a revealing and
characteristic image: he says he wants to keep from getting "qualche
porro di drieto" (II.iii.73: "warts on my behind"). Similarly, he sees
death, which he also wishes to avoid, as "cotesta suzzacchera" (II.vi.76:
"that filth"). After Lucrezia's experience with the "garzonaccio," Nicia
characteristically hurries her off to be purified in the church, an act that
suggests his closeness to the "traditional," ritualistic mentality. In
essence, then, what Nicia wants is to manifest power by verbally defe-
cating on the world while remaining clean, free of the excrement that
he, like Swift's Yahoos, has been hurling at others.

Ironically, of course, Nicia's cursing is doomed to fall short of its
mark; it cannot change the world and thus reminds him continually of
the power he truly lacks. Nicia is like those weak men whom Machiavelli
scorns in the *Discorsi* because, too fearful and lacking in energy to
engage in conspiracies against rivals or oppressors, they content themselves with impotent, fruitless cursing.[31] Nicia's inability to control his
language and the utter ineffectuality of his cursing are both beautifully
symbolized in Ligurio's joke with the aloes. This episode is, of course,
derived from Boccaccio's tale (*Decameron*, VIII, 6) in which Bruno and
Buffalmacco contrive to have Calandrino implicate himself in the theft
of his own pig when he is unable to eat a supposed truth-revealing pill
that is really a mixture of dog excrement and aloes. Like Ligurio's, this
trick is a sadistic practical joke played at the expense of a hapless gull.
In Calandrino's case it is particularly fitting because his obsession with
eating has been revealed not only in this story, in his refusal to share his
pig with his friends, but also in the earlier heliotrope story (VIII, 3), when
he was caught up in fantasies about mountains of pasta and fountains
running wine. Ligurio's trick has a very different sort of appropriate-
ness both to its victim and to the theme of language in the play. For here
the character with the best command of words punishes the character
who has virtually no command over words, and he does so in an appropriate way, befouling Nicia's already very foul mouth. The result is that

[31]"Pertanto gli uomini (perché dove ne va la vita e la roba non sono al tutto insani),
quando e' si veggono deboli, se ne guardano; e quando egli hanno a noia uno principe,
attendono a bestemmiarlo, ed aspettono che quelli che hanno maggiore qualità di loro
gli vendichino" (*Discorsi*, III, vi, 394: "For men [because where life and goods are concerned, they are not entirely crazy], when they see themselves weak, are careful, and
when they are tired of a prince, they turn to cursing him and wait for those of greater
power to avenge them").

Nicia is reduced to sputtering out a series of monosyllables, which evoke the words *caca* and *cucu* (iv.ix.101-2). These words erupt out of Nicia's mouth as pure linguistic reflex. The first of them is, of course, the infant's word for excrement which has been featured in so many of Nicia's curses; it fits perfectly both his anal fixation and his infantilized character. The second, the French word for cuckold, ironically identifies Nicia's impending condition. The episode suggests that although Nicia tries to control reality through his words, his words have a life of their own and control him instead.

Nicia's belief in the power inherent in words is reflected also in his constant use of proverbs. Ironically, these proverbs, as well as the many colloquial expressions he uses, make his language reflect the very Florence he denounces so bitterly.[32] Instinctively he turns to proverbs because they are repositories of traditional wisdom; they seem trustworthy and stable, giving him the illusion that the world is a place of solid realities and that it and the word are somehow in harmony.[33] But his proverbs do even more, for they preach a particularly worldly wisdom, a guile and cynicism that fit the morality of a would-be confidence man.[34] Hence they help him identify himself in that role and thereby contribute to his illusory sense of power.

Nicia's belief in the power of words is further manifested in his response to Callimaco's ability to speak Latin. Whereas Nicia reports that he expended an enormous effort to acquire his "due hac," the learned Callimaco can rattle off medical diagnoses in Latin that Nicia probably does not understand, because he responds not to the content of Callimaco's words but merely to their form, to the fact that they are Latin and fluently spoken. Callimaco's ability overwhelms Nicia. Just before meeting the "doctor," Nicia adopts the role of skeptic, criticizing doctors in general (i.ii.64) and insisting that he will not be deceived (ii.i.69). But once he actually hears Callimaco speak Latin, he becomes a true believer in three quick exchanges: first, thanks to a "Good day" in Latin, Callimaco becomes worthy of praise to him (ii.ii.70); then, after Callimaco has delivered an extended speech, Nicia declares he is "el piú degno omo che si possa trovare!" (ii.ii.71: "the worthiest man who can be found!"); and finally, with a second Latin outpouring a few scenes later, Callimaco cements his hold on his prey, who now says he is ready

---

[32] Raimondi, *Politica e commedia*, p. 210-11.

[33] Vanossi, "Situazione e sviluppo," p. 38.

[34] David Kunzle, "World Upside Down: The Iconography of a European Broadsheet Type," in *The Reversible World: Symbolic Inversion in Art and Society*, ed. Barbara A. Babcock (Ithaca: Cornell University Press, 1978), p. 74.

to "credervi piú che al mio confessoro" (II.vi.75: "believe you more than my confessor").

As this last quotation suggests, the basic issue in this situation, as in every work concerned with confidence men in the Renaissance, is faith or trust, although in the case of this particular trick, something much more significant is involved—religious belief. Callimaco explicitly asks Nicia whether "voi avete fede in me o no" (II.vi.75: "you have faith in me or not"); he is asking Nicia to accept him as a religious leader, to believe in him. And Nicia does. Filled with awe for a being who has seemingly mastered the prestigious, mysterious language of science, medicine, law, theology, and the arts, Nicia tells Callimaco: "Voi mi avete fatto maravigliare" (II.ii.71: "You've made me marvel"). Nicia looks up to "Doctor" Callimaco as a worshiper would to God, full of a "marvel" that was identified in the Renaissance as the appropriate response to the mysterious, the lofty, and the paradoxical, and hence a fit response to the deity.[35]

Nicia could also be said to look up to Callimaco as child to father, and it is appropriate, therefore, that he should give this "doctor," who saved him from a sterile future and has given his life new direction, the keys to his house. It is equally appropriate that Nicia should look upon Callimaco as the "bastone" (v.vi.111) for his old age, a "stick," which is, of course, a crutch for an impotent old man as well as an unconscious phallic joke. But with an irony Nicia can scarcely appreciate, that "bastone" is also the rod with which fathers and teachers beat delinquent children, unruly wives, and disobedient servants—social inferiors in general—during the Renaissance. Nicia's faith and awe are due simply to Callimaco's possession of and ability to control those magical forces, words. Interestingly, the anonymous lady who meets with Frate Timoteo also believes in the magic of words: she is convinced that prayer will keep the Turks away from Italy for a year (III.iii.81–82). She and Nicia share the same traditional mentality, with its view of language as a magical substance that can control the operations of reality.

The difference between Nicia's implicit conception of language and that of those who deceive him can be seen in their contrary responses to the capacity of language to engender multiple meanings. For Nicia, as I have said, words are realities or are linked to realities by powerful

[35]For the conceptions of the "marvelous" in the Renaissance, see James V. Mirollo, *The Poet of the Marvelous: Giambattista Marino* (New York: Columbia University Press, 1963), pp. 117–78; Rosalie L. Colie, *Paradoxia Epidemica* (Princeton: Princeton University Press, 1966), pp. 3–8; and Wayne A. Rebhorn, *Courtly Performances: Masking and Festivity in Castiglione's "Book of the Courtier"* (Detroit: Wayne State University Press, 1978), pp. 47–51.

npathies; anything but ambiguous, they mean just what they say. Hence he remains oblivious of the double entendres and puns of other characters, such as Siro's play on *valente* cited earlier, Ligurio's mockery of Nicia's inexperience in the guise of praise for his learning (III.ii.80), and Callimaco's joke that Lucrezia is "poorly covered" at night (II.vi.75). Nicia is also capable of creating unconscious double entendres himself, as when he claims to see in Callimaco the "bastone" of his old age or says he trusts the "doctor" more than Hungarians their swords (II.ii.72). By contrast, the confidence men of the play are all ironists and masters of the double entendre, people for whom words are not realities but instruments of deception precisely because they have multiple levels of meaning, because they do not always mean what they say. Beyond all others, Ligurio holds this view of language, and he turns his irony on the other confidence men though they never turn theirs on him. Thus he can mock the idea of Callimaco's praying to God in thanks for Frate Timoteo (IV.ii.94), and he can ironically tell Timoteo, after the frate has agreed to help perform an abortion, that now he seems to be "quello religioso che io credevo che voi fussi" (III.iv.84: "that religious I thought you were"). Essentially, the dupes and the confidence men in Machiavelli's play reside in different dramatic universes. Nicia lives in a world of farce in which the meanings of words are obvious, direct, and unambiguous, the humor physical and crude, and aggression everywhere triumphant. By contrast, Callimaco, Siro, Lucrezia, and especially Ligurio see life as a sophisticated comedy of manners which distinguishes people according to their ability to be ironic and witty, to communicate through indirection, to be fully the masters of the language they speak.

For Machiavelli as well as for his confidence men, although language is divorced from reality, capable of double meanings, slippery and illusory, it is still—perhaps for those very reasons—capable of potent effects. Ironically, as *La mandragola* shows, Nicia is right: language does have extraordinary power, but its power does not derive from some magical connection between words and things. Rather, words have power because human beings, living in a largely verbal universe, are creatures of desire and imagination, and language can shape their reactions through its ability to generate compelling illusions based on and appealing to that desire and imagination and thereby capable of eliciting faith.[36] The final *ménage à trois* demonstrates the way words, despite their separation from things, can engender coherent and compelling fictions for men to live by, for that situation, the product of

[36]See the article cited in n. 3.

what Ligurio and Callimaco say about their identities and intentions, is convincingly real and orderly for the deceived Nicia and Sostrata even though it is a total fraud. Their conviction of its reality and orderliness testifies to the supreme power of language to bring coherence into the world through the fictions it creates, to generate an illusory but satisfying society out of human beings' desires and illusions, and to compel their absolute belief in it. As it turns out, rhetoric, though ungrounded — indeed, precisely because it is ungrounded — is the true queen of the sciences.

Machiavelli underscores the power of language to create something out of nothing by his choice of his play's title. Ezio Raimondi has suggested that the beaker of wine that is passed off as a magical potion made of mandrake root, the *mandragola* of the play's title, is a verbal correlative for all the deceptions and machinations of the plot.[37] But it is more than that, for *mandragola* is a word without substance, although one that, paradoxically, has tremendous power. Solely by virtue of that word, that name, the beaker of wine becomes a magical drink, thus forcefully illustrating the fact that power resides in language, not things, as long as people can be manipulated rhetorically to believe in the reality of what they hear. Machiavelli's confidence men understand this truth, whereas his dupes do not. Their failure to grasp it is all the more ironic in this case because the mandrake root had well-known associations with quacks and charlatans in Renaissance Italy.[38] Simply because of its label, then, Nicia sees a glass of wine as a magical elixir whose name alone makes it real and potent, capable of conferring both death and new life. Although Machiavelli and his friends referred to his play familiarly as "Messer Nicia," he certainly knew what he was doing when he titled it *La mandragola* in his Prologue.[39] For the mandrake root, which never appears on stage, is the most forceful presence in the play, testifying to the power of language, a power lying at the very heart of dramatic fictions, to manipulate the desires and shape the fantasies of the credulous, to elicit the most reverent of responses, and thereby, at least for those who can be brought to believe, to bring into being an orderly, satisfying world.

The comic resolution of *La mandragola* seems to reflect the endings of many of Boccaccio's tales, and especially those of the first six days of the

---

[37]Raimondi, *Politica e commedia*, p. 255.
[38]Ibid., p. 256.
[39]On the title of the play, see Giovanni Aquilecchia, "La favola *Mandragola* si chiama," in *Collected Essays on Italian Language and Literature Presented to Kathleen Speight*, ed. Giovanni Aquilecchia, Stephen N. Cristea, and Sheila Ralphs (Manchester: Manchester University Press, 1971), pp. 74–77.

Decameron, in which witty confidence men successfully pursue their personal interests by using language to manipulate linguistically deficient dupes. If the latter lose something in the exchange, however— usually their wives' fidelity—they also gain something, for not only are they inevitably ignorant of their loss, but the fictions the confidence men spin out for them both compel their belief and satisfy some of their most profound needs. Those fictions enhance the dupes' sense of security as, for instance, Frate Cipolla's tale about his sacred coal's power to prevent harm does for the peasants of Certaldo (VI, 10). Or the fictions grant the dupes new positions of importance in the community, as his supposed stay in "purgatory" does for Ferondo, whom an unnamed abbot kept deceived in a cell for months on end while he enjoyed Ferondo's wife (III, 8). Or the fictions bring financial and spiritual reward to the dupes, as does the sainting of Ser Ciappelletto to the people of Burgundy (I, 1). The harmonies at the close of many of Boccaccio's tales throughout the first six days of the *Decameron*, then, are due to the fact that all the characters, confidence men and dupes alike, satisfy their desires, their satisfaction made possible by the fictions the confidence men have created with their words and within which they all live. Such a situation is, of course, exactly what Machiavelli appears to have provided at the end of his play.

That conclusion also resembles those of Boccaccio's tales in another respect, for it is thoroughly carnivalesque, a festive celebration of pleasure, sexuality, and renewed life. As in many of Boccaccio's stories, the climax of *La mandragola* is the sexual union of the lovers, and Machiavelli goes out of his way, as Boccaccio often does, to stress the pleasure of the experience, how Callimaco lingered in bed, how difficult he was to wake, and so on (v.i.105; v.ii.108; v.iv.110). This is healthy sexuality both literally and metaphorically: Nicia's "physical" shows Callimaco free from diseases and defects (v.ii.107); and it restores human beings to their animal nature, as Frate Timoteo's image of the couple's being in a lair together intimates (IV.x.103: "intanati"). The explosion of pleasure at the end of the play affects every character; all are satisfied as they are included in this happy society, whereas before they were anxious and frustrated. The play's affirmation of sexuality and pleasure is essentially an affirmation of life. Callimaco goes through the play declaring himself ready to die if his desire is not satisfied (e.g., II.vi.77, IV.i.92), and Lucrezia says she expects her experience to kill her (III.xi.90). But neither dies, and the play underscores the rebirth that comes to them and to all the other characters at the end.[40] It rejects the sterility of Nicia's household as well as the total denial of life involved in Lucrezia's insistence that she would not submit to "Doctor" Callimaco's cure even if she were the last woman on earth and the resurrection of the human race depended on it (iii.x.88). The play also casts aside all fear of hell and damnation as Callimaco, in Shavian manner, jokes that there are "tanti uomini da bene" (iv.i.92: "so many proper men") in Inferno that it ironically appears a desirable place in which to pass eternity. Finally, the play emphasizes its festive mood, from the opening chorus of shepherds who have elected to live "in festa e in gioia" (Canzone, 55: "in festivity and joy"), through the association with holiday pleasures of the baths to which Nicia and Lucrezia contemplate going, to the masquerading, literal and figurative, of the last acts, which strongly emphasize the carnivalesque mood of the work and its celebration of human transformation, satisfied desire, and earthy fecundity.[41]

The carnivalesque character of *La mandragola*, like that of Boccaccio's tales, also involves a complex setting aside of conventional morality. In the first place, its action and Lucrezia's successful "conversion" appear to constitute a rejection of conventional pieties in favor of an alternative morality based on life, pleasure, and the naturalness of desire, much like that to be found in such tales in the *Decameron* as those of Filippo Balducci (iv, Introduction), the pirate Monaco da Paganino (ii, 10), and messer Lizio di Valbona and the "nightingale" (v, 4). Machiavelli's characters, in their different ways, disregard conventional ethics, sometimes voicing their hesitations as Lucrezia and, to a lesser extent, Callimaco and Timoteo do, but in general acting as though standard morality were truly irrelevant from the viewpoint of desire and the renewal of life. Moreover, the deception of Nicia is presented as constituting a form of justice, just as the deception of the dupe so often is in the works of Boccaccio and other writers of the *novella* tradition. For Nicia is so egregiously stupid, self-centered, and unself-conscious that he deserves to be tricked, and his verbal violence, bullying, and lack of courtliness and civility prevent his eliciting much sympathy from the audience. Thus *La mandragola* seems to rewrite morality and justice, to substitute an ethics based on life and pleasure for one based on the narrow conventions and prejudices of a jejune society.

---

[40]Nicia is "recreated" by the friar's promise of help (iii.viii.86); Callimaco is restored by Nicia (v.ii.108); Lucrezia is "ardita," whereas before she appeared half-dead (v.v.110); and even Sostrata appears reborn (v.vi.112).

[41]Raimondi, *Politica e commedia*, p. 215.

This interpretation is too simplistic, however, for carnivalesque festivity is usually morally ambiguous and produces a morally ambivalent response in the audience.[42] Here it is not a matter of Machiavelli's inviting the spectators simultaneously to rejoice in Callimaco's and Lucrezia's affair while feeling some traditional moral reservation about it. For such a response is, indeed, almost completely subverted by the alternative morality established through the play's celebration of life and pleasure just as moral condemnations are undermined in Boccaccio's *Decameron.* Machiavelli shapes his play as an uncompromising satire on the decadence and corruption of his native city whereas Boccaccio holds a considerably milder view, offering a paean to an ideal Florence in Day VI which balances his vision of its externally caused collapse at the start of the first day.

Throughout *La mandragola* Machiavelli is consistently hostile to Florence. In his Prologue he attacks the anticipated smirking of the Florentine spectators as a sign of the degeneration of their ancient "virtú" (58). Later, in the play itself, he has Nicia condemn both his fellow citizens generally for being unable to appreciate "virtú" and the ruling powers of the city in particular for having unfairly monopolized all legal business (II.iii.72–73). Finally, most of the characters in the play are far more concerned with their own desires and with reputation and social proprieties than with the possibility that their behavior might be immoral or criminal or might involve them in murder or rape.

The play's harshest criticism of social corruption, however, is focused on religion, which was the central issue involved in Callimaco's deception of Nicia. The play also incidentally satirizes friars who pester pretty women in church (III.ii.80) as well as wicked confessors (II.vi.77), and it shows the church as a place where people plot seductions, meet and gossip with neighbors, and seek to make money rather than worship. Prurient, amoral, materialistic, and thoroughly corrupt, Frate Timoteo incarnates all these defects. For him religion has become a mechanical matter of performing rituals for a fee, and that is why he is obsessed with the need to keep the images in the church clean and attractive (V.i.105). Reformers such as Erasmus were railing throughout Europe at this time against just such a reduction of religion to empty rituals, a situation that, as Frate Timoteo reports, led to a decline in the faith of his flock (V.i.105). Ironically, the actions of Frate Timoteo's parishioners fit his mechanical, externalized conception of religion perfectly: Nicia is so distant from it that he has not been to confession in ten years; and the

---

[42]On the ambivalence of the carnivalesque, see Mikhail Bakhtin, *Rabelais and His World,* trans. Hélène Iswolsky (Cambridge, Mass.: MIT Press, 1968), pp. 11–12.

anonymous lady equates confession with psychological release (iii.iii.81), sees prayers as a comfortable magic, and thinks her conversations with her confessor no more important than the obtaining of a piece of linen owed her by a friend. Machiavelli is no Erasmus, of course, filled with Christian zeal for reformation, but he does genuinely regret, for his own reasons (which will be explored in Chapter 3), that religion has lost its importance or become a mere convenience. In a play full of ironies, Frate Timoteo's name ("God-fearing") betrays one of the most far-reaching, for it points to the absence of any real "fear of God" in any of the characters. Frate Timoteo thus serves as a symptom and a symbol of the corruption Machiavelli saw all about him in his contemporary world.

Machiavelli's satirical indictment of Florence has suggested to a number of critics that he intended his play as a bitter and savage attack.[43] This view, however, is too extreme and one-sided, for it ignores the genuine ambivalence of the play and especially the tremendous emphasis in the last acts on rebirth, fecundity, and festive joy. The action moves through a twenty-four-hour period and ends with a symbolically significant dawn. Never forgetting the decadence of his society, Machiavelli accepts the fact of human beings' immorality and egocentricity and builds his hope for a better world not on some futile, utopian belief that they could be transformed into moral exemplars but on a realistic perception of the nature of desire, imagination, and the power of language to shape their beliefs and order their social reality for them.[44] If, at the end, that ordering is, from the viewpoint of conventional morality, still corrupt, it is at the same time happy, healthy, well regulated, and sanguine about a future that is incarnated in the child Lucrezia will surely bear.

The basic ambiguity of the play is reflected in the religious imagery with which it is saturated. Most of its characters experience some sort of rebirth by the end; Callimaco is explicitly presented as God's gift to fulfill Nicia's desire (ii.i.69); the church figures as an important setting for the plot and the place for the final "consecration" of Callimaco's and Lucrezia's union; and Frate Timoteo tells Lucrezia she will — and she does — thank God for what her husband wishes her to do. Moreover, Lucrezia's transformation is conceived imagistically as a parody of the soul's journey to God (or Christ). When she is being tempted by Frate Timoteo, she uses the image of a journey as she asks him, "A che mi conducete voi, Padre?" (iii.xi.89: "Where are you leading me, Father?").

[43]Roberto Ridolfi, *The Life of Niccolò Machiavelli*, trans. Cecil Grayson (Chicago: University of Chicago press, 1963), pp. 170-71; and Raimondi, *Politica e commedia*, p. 263.
[44]See Cavallini, *Interpretazione*, p. 9.

Later, Timoteo prays that the angel Raphael will accompany her, an angel frequently discussed and depicted as a guide in the Renaissance, especially because of his connection with Tobias.[45] Appropriately, the Canzone following Act III celebrates deception ("inganno") as showing "il dritto calle all'alme erranti" (91: "the right path to erring souls"). Finally, when Lucrezia accepts Callimaco as her lover, she uses terms frequently applied to the deity and suggestive of a journey as well: "Io ti prendo per signore, padrone, *guida*" (v.iv.109, my emphasis: "I take you as my lord, leader, *guide*"). The illicit union of Callimaco and Lucrezia may thus be interpreted as a blasphemous parody of the marriage of Christ and the human soul, which was one of the meanings, according to standard allegorical readings, of the Song of Songs.[46]

All this religious imagery is completely ambiguous. Not just parody, it also functions to underscore the enormous value of sexual love and procreation. There is something sacred, in a metaphorical sense, about the couple's union, just as there is something sacred about the profane love John Donne celebrates in many of his lyrics. From the desperately "sick" Callimaco's viewpoint, his night with Lucrezia really does save his life, make him more blessed than the saints (v.iv.110), and guarantee that the two of them will live in a state of worldly salvation because of the "grazia" that Nicia has unintentionally bestowed on them (v.v.110). Indeed, the Canzone after Act IV identifies the hours of the night as "sante," as the sole source that makes "l'alme beate" (104: "souls blessed"). The "Via dello Amore, / dove chi casca non si rizza mai" (Prologo, 56: "Street of Love, / where he who falls does not rise again") may be only a side street painted on the backdrop of the stage, but it is clearly the street down which Callimaco and Lucrezia walk. And if the fact that the people who fall there never rise again may suggest moral degradation and even the Fall, that street is also the way to worldly bliss, to a sexual rising and falling, a goal that, in the spirit of carnival, the play simultaneously affirms.

If the basic ambiguity of *La mandragola* is reflected in its religious imagery, it is also reflected in the imagery of health. For the Florence of the play is sick, sick in a moral sense, but also sick in its lack of energy, vitality, and a healthy claim on the future. Thus Nicia and Lucrezia cannot have a child, and Callimaco languishes in frustrated desire, feel-

---

[45]See Elizabeth McCutcheon, "Thomas More, Raphael Hythlodaeus, and the Angel Raphael," *Studies in English Literature, 1500–1900* 9 (1969): 27–28.

[46]For the standard treatment of the commentary tradition on the Song of Songs, see Friedrich Ohly, *Hohelied-Studien: Grundzüge einer Geschichte der Hoheliedauslegung des Abendlandes bis zum 1200*, Schriften der Wissenschaftlichen Gesellschaft an der Johann Wolfgang Goethe-Universität, Geisteswissenschaftliche Reihe, 1 (Frankfurt am Main, 1958).

ing he will die if he does not obtain a "rimedio" (i.iii.67). The central action of the play is the curing of these illnesses, as Callimaco, with telling symbolic effect, takes on the role of doctor and administers his life-giving potion to Lucrezia, thereby curing himself as well. When Nicia worries about the life of the "garzonaccio" for a fleeting instant, Ligurio tells him, "Lasciatene la cura a lui" (v.ii.108: "Leave the care [or the cure] of that to him [that is, to Callimaco]"), and Callimaco does just that. In the Canzone placed after Act iii, his confidence trick on Nicia is identified explicitly as a cure, a "rimedio alto e raro" (91), and Callimaco's body, as Nicia discovers, is healthy, the source of health and vitality for a society whose rebirth at the end of the play is also a return to health. The cure, as Callimaco makes clear, depends on Nicia's faith (ii.vi.75), and it is ultimately due less to Callimaco's sexual potency than to his and Ligurio's cleverness with language. But in either case, it allows Frate Timoteo to bid the spectators, the real Florentines (and Italians) watching the Florentines on stage, "Valète" (v.vi.112), a word meaning "farewell" but also "be strong" or "be healthy," notions that identify the positive values the play has been asserting all along.[47] Of course, the restoration of health in *La mandragola* is by no means a restoration of moral or spiritual health in a conventional sense, as the play never lets its audience forget, even if the emphasis of the final scenes falls on the renewed vitality and happiness of the characters. For even as Callimaco establishes his life-giving liaison with Lucrezia, his offer to marry her when Nicia dies reminds the audience of the moral order that has been sacrificed for the sake of a happy ending.]

Although *La mandragola* seems to be very close to Boccaccio's *Decameron*, it departs from its model in a most significant, and troubling, way by undermining its own happy ending, suggesting that the social harmony achieved there is a matter of appearances, fundamentally unstable and precarious, and thus leaving the audience unsettled and disconcerted. Like virtually all carnivalesque works, *La mandragola* turns the established social order topsy-turvy. To be sure, for the most part Machiavelli does follow in Boccaccio's footsteps, parodying marriage, religion, and social proprieties as well as titles and hierarchies, and, more important, inverting social relationships, such as that between husband and wife. Thus, by virtue of her miraculous "conversion" from prude to confidence woman, Lucrezia becomes the power behind the throne in Nicia's home. As she performs her part in the play

---

[47]Frate Timoteo bids the anonymous lady farewell with the similar words "Andate sana" (iii.iii.82).

that Ligurio has scripted, she emerges as the real master of her lord and
master, a "gallo" who rules through trickery rather than force and who
is, as Ligurio says of her early in the play, "atta a governare un regno"
(I.iii.66: "fit to govern a kingdom").[48] This inversion, however, like the
basic moral situation in the play, is ambiguous: from the perspective of
the established order, it is subversive, a sign of decadence and disorder;
from the perspective of the play's celebration of life, energy, and fecundity, it is a laudable triumph of talent, the justified defeat of hoary
privilege. Like much contemporary art using the topos of the world upside down, *La mandragola* allows for both perspectives, albeit Machiavelli seems to lean a bit more toward the vitalistic than the
establishmentarian view.[49] But even as it turns the world topsy-turvy, the
play also does something Boccaccio does only rarely: it inverts and de-
stabilizes the normal relationship among masters and servants, suggesting a possibility of future rivalry that undermines the impression of
social harmony created by the close of the play.

The central action of *La mandragola*, Callimaco's "curing" of Nicia's
family, underscores the fundamental ambiguity and instability of the
master-servant relationship as Machiavelli conceived it. In that action,
which constitutes a play-within-the-play, Callimaco as "doctor" presents himself as Nicia's servant, someone engaged for money to render
services and hence by definition an inferior. As he speaks to Nicia, he
confirms his own inferiority and the latter's superiority through his
flattery:

> A me non fia mai discaro fare piacere a voi ed a tutti li uomini virtuosi e
> da bene come voi: e non mi son a Parigi affaticato tanti anni per impa-
> rare, per altro se non per potere servire a' pari vostri. [II.ii.70]

> To me it would never be displeasing to satisfy you and all the respectable,
> virtuous men like you, nor did I labor so many years in Paris to learn
> things for any other reason than to be able to serve the likes of you.

It is clear not merely that Callimaco is serving his own interests and
tricking Nicia into helping him do so but that he and not Nicia enjoys

---

[48]Sofronia in *Clizia* similarly controls her household and manipulates her husband,
but unlike Lucrezia, she does so on behalf of the social order and to bring him back to
his senses and restore his authority. Sofronia is no confidence woman but a clever and
wise (hence her name) defender of the proprieties, and thus one cannot really speak of
her actions as turning the world upside down. In fact, she is aiming to bring it right
side up.

[49]See David Kunzle's interpretation of the reception of world-upside-down broadsheet
illustrations in his "World Upside Down," pp. 82–84.

the real position of authority and power here. His assumed knowledge of medicine and his superior command of Latin enable him to control his nominal employer, to become the real master in the relationship, the "*domine magister*" (II.ii.70: "*learned master*"), as Nicia calls him at their first meeting. To say the least, the play reveals that in this particular instance the servant-master relationship is fundamentally ambiguous and unstable.

The ambiguous and unstable nature of Callimaco's and Nicia's relationship as "doctor" and client is mirrored in the peculiar—and deliberately unsettling—master-servant relationship of Callimaco and Ligurio. The character who most nearly controls the destinies of all the others because he possesses the deepest understanding of society and the power of language as well as the greatest imaginative range and linguistic virtuosity is not Callimaco but Ligurio—a parasite, social outsider, and servant for hire. Because of Callimaco's inferior abilities, the nominal master is forced to depend on his servant's skills and trustworthiness for the success of his endeavors. To be sure, as a confidence man in his own right, Callimaco displays a noteworthy caution, reasoning out loud to himself, for instance, about his servant Siro's loyalty: "Costui è stato dieci anni meco, e sempre mi ha servito fedelmente. Io credo trovare anche in questo caso fede in lui" (IV.iii.97: "This man has been with me ten years and has always served me faithfully. I believe I'll also find him trustworthy in this case"). Callimaco's assessment here seems sensible enough and hardly equates him with the overcredulous Nicia, despite the emphasis on "fede" in this speech, but his brooding on the matter indicates his—and Machiavelli's—recognition of an ever-present potential for betrayal. Thus, despite his skepticism, Callimaco's basic need to trust in and depend on others renders him potentially vulnerable to deception and exploitation by them.

Siro may be dependable, but Ligurio is another matter. Ligurio swears that Callimaco can trust him (I.iii.67), but his delight in power, in being the master of his masters, tends to undermine his credibility. So detached and so delighting in the manipulation of others is he that one can easily imagine him deceiving Callimaco along with everyone else. Indeed, the play subtly intimates such a possibility, suggesting that Ligurio is potentially primed to displace his master in Lucrezia's bed. As he explains his motives for helping Callimaco:

Non dubitare della fede mia, ché quando e' non ci fussi l'utile che io sento e che io spero, ci è che 'l tuo sangue si affà col mio, e desidero che tu adempia questo tuo desiderio presso a quanto tu. [I.iii.67]

> Don't doubt my faith, for if there weren't the utility I already know of and
> hope for, there's your temperament [blood] which resembles my own, and
> I desire that you accomplish your desires almost as much as you do.

Ligurio seems to be saying here that he empathizes with Callimaco, and
that his empathy, quite aside from reasons of utility, makes him identify
his own interests with his master's and hence guarantees his faithful service. But empathy, which involves the ability to share, to enter into and
grasp the mental operations and emotional state of others, is not a neutral matter for Renaissance confidence men in general or for Ligurio
here, for there is no guarantee that such an ability will be used benev-
olently or in the interests of the person to whom it is directed. Empathy
can be a means to achieve power over and exploit others, and as Stephen Greenblatt has argued, it was often used in precisely that way during the Renaissance.[50] Indeed, close scrutiny of Ligurio's speech might
tempt one to read it not only as a statement of empathy but also as an
indirect acknowledgment that he is capable of the same feelings as Callimaco; in other words, that when he identifies with Callimaco, he too
can have a sexual interest in Lucrezia. Ligurio is not the only confidence man in the play capable of such an interested form of empathetic
identification. Frate Timoteo tells the spectators at the end of Act IV
about his own aroused feelings for Lucrezia, and he is sure that they too
can empathize in such an interested fashion (x.103). Finally, although
Ligurio has frequently obtained money from Nicia, he has apparently
not managed to get into Nicia's house before Callimaco's arrival (I.i.63),
so that only now, thanks to his master's success, will he finally have the
opportunity to realize a desire he may come to feel and which his control over others will potentially allow him to satisfy.

Machiavelli drops yet another hint of the detached Ligurio's potential
for betraying his master, even if he is not yet actively planning to do so.
In the course of the kidnapping of the "garzonaccio" in Act IV, Ligurio
places the soon-to-be-cuckolded Nicia between two "horns," one of
which, appropriately, is "Callimaco" (IV.ix.102). This "Callimaco," of
course, is really the disguised Timoteo, whose slightly perverse sexual
interest in Lucrezia the play makes explicit a little later. And no less a
person than Ligurio serves as the other "horn." Thus through Ligurio's
speech and this visual signal in Act IV, Machiavelli subtly suggests that
Callimaco's servant is interested and able, if not yet ready, to replace
him in Lucrezia's bed. Since the play has shown that the person who

---

[50]On empathy, manipulation, and the will to power, see Greenblatt, *Renaissance Self-
Fashioning*, pp. 227–35.

controls language and uses it to manufacture the fictions by which others play out their desires and fantasies is the truly powerful one, it leaves open the possibility that if Callimaco can be made to play a role of Ligurio's devising at one time, he may certainly be maneuvered into playing such a role again, perhaps this time to suit Ligurio's pleasure and not his own. *La mandragola* makes it painfully clear that Ligurio is *il servo padrone*, the master of his master, and potentially the master of his master's mistress as well.

This division between Callimaco, the socially superior master, and Ligurio, the intellectually superior servant, creates a final imbalance at the end of Machiavelli's play, a suggestion of future rivalry and tension which undermines the seeming harmony of its ending. We do not find this device in the tales of the *Decameron*; in that work servants remain distinctly inferior to their masters and are generally kept firmly in their place. Frate Cipolla, for instance, has a grotesque servant who is also a trickster but who is merely an inferior version of his master and by no means a potential rival (VI, 10). Chichibio, the Venetian cook of Currado Gianfigliazzi, manipulates his master with his wit, but he does so by playing the clown, and Currado laughs at his antics, thus maintaining control firmly in his own hands (VI, 4). Finally, one of King Agilulf's servants sleeps with the queen and outwits the king, who attempts to discover him, but the king ends the episode by publicly, though indirectly, putting the servant in his place and thus eliminating any threat of future cuckolding (III, 2). In short, although servants may be clever in Boccaccio's tales, they are seldom cleverer than their masters, so that there can be no serious, harmony-threatening rivalry between them. Moreover, when confidence men work in tandem in the *Decameron*, as Bruno and Buffalmacco do with great success, there is no hint of any possible struggle or potential tension between them. As a result, when Boccaccio's confidence men create a happy society for themselves and their dupes as well, that happiness may be morally suspect, but it is tactically secure.

Servants tend to be equally benign in the *novelle* of the fourteenth and fifteenth centuries. Typical is a tale about Andreoccio da Perugia in the Sienese Gentile Sermini's *Novelle*, a collection dating from the first half of the fifteenth century. The Andreoccio here is very different from his namesake in *Decameron* II, 5; he is an old fool whose young wife takes a lover, pretends to die while her husband is away, escapes with her lover from Perugia to Milan, and returns claiming to be someone else and posing as her lover's wife. Almost a pastiche of Boccaccio's motifs, the story focuses on the issue of trust: trust between the two lovers, trust between them and the woman's mother, who agrees to aid

them, and — most important — trust between the lovers and two servants
for hire who agree to help them during the initial stages of their relationship. At the very start, the hero asks an old woman who sells clothes
to help him, telling her that he has decided to "fidarmi di voi" ("trust
myself to you") because of what he sees as her "affezione e amore"
("affection and love") for him and his family.[51] Here we see none of the
nervousness and hesitation of Callimaco in *La mandragola*; the old
woman immediately promises her aid, concocts a plot for her master,
and only then is given two ducats, a reward for her good offices rather
than a bribe to ensure her allegiance. The idea that servants work only
for their own advantage and would willingly betray those who hire them
clearly has not occurred to Gentile Sermini. Nor did it to Sacchetti, or
to Masuccio Salernitano, who published a collection of fifty stories in
his *Novellino* around the middle of the quattrocento.

Machiavelli breaks with the pattern established by Boccaccio and
other *novella* writers in part because he bases his work not merely on
the tales of his Italian predecessors but on Roman comedy as well. The
Roman comedic hero is characteristically coupled with a servant, a
social inferior who is either a clever slave or occasionally a parasite, an
individual on whom the hero is completely dependent for the fulfillment of his wishes and who is largely responsible for working out the
intrigue of the play. Nevertheless, although the tricky slaves of Plautus
and Terence must be accounted Ligurio's ancestors, a brief examination of their defining features quickly reveals that Machiavelli's character is worlds apart from them.

Plautus's *Miles Gloriosus*, for instance, seems very close to *La mandragola* in many respects. Like Machiavelli's work, it pits a large cast of
characters against a single, egregiously stupid dupe, the braggart warrior of the title, and it presents the tricky slave Palaestrio as the ingen-
ious architect and scriptwriter of the plot; all except the dupe knowingly
play roles he assigns. The fiction Palaestrio concocts in the course of the
play rivals Ligurio's in complexity, but Plautus does not maintain the
fictional vision in its totality beyond the last act. Indeed, whereas all is
harmony based on pure illusion at the end of *La mandragola*, with Nicia content and Ligurio's betrayal still hidden, the braggart warrior
Pyrgopolynices is deprived of the woman he pursued and publicly
mocked as a would-be adulterer, and Palaestrio's role in his deception
and subsequent undoing is made perfectly clear to him. Palaestrio is a
very different character from Ligurio, despite the irreverent intelli-

---

[51] Gentile Sermini, *Novelle*, I, in *Novelle italiane: Il Quattrocento*, ed. Gioachino
Chiarini (Milan: Garzanti, 1982), p. 91.

gence and theatrical sense the two of them share. Like all the slaves in plays by both Plautus and Terence, and unlike Machiavelli's hero, Palaestrio is completely loyal to his young master: he willingly sets off in pursuit of his absent master's beloved after she has been sold to Purgopolynices, and even after having been captured by pirates and sold to that same braggart warrior, he never falters in his devotion to his master.[52] Although clever slaves in Plautus and Terence may deceive the fathers of their young masters as well as pimps and braggart soldiers, they faithfully align themselves with their masters' interests. As a result, their trustworthiness, unlike Ligurio's, can never be doubted.

Erich Segal has analyzed the activities of the Plautine slave in terms of the Saturnalian or festive pattern C. L. Barber used for Shakespearean comedy.[53] In that analysis, such comedies as the *Miles Gloriosus* are seen as depicting a holiday world in which the normal social hierarchy is temporarily inverted: slaves dominate those who usually rule over them with an iron fist, and young men successfully pursue sexual pleasure rather than strive to exemplify *pietas* in serving the family, the state, and the gods. The plays create a new hierarchy based on intelligence and theatrical skill rather than money or social position: the lowest of the low are on top, sometimes literally, as when the tricky slaves of Plautus's *Asinaria* mount and ride their masters. To be sure, the Plautine pattern does not hold exactly for Terence; his slaves are a little less clever than those of Plautus, his fathers a bit more savvy, and his plots depend more on fortuitous discoveries of hidden identity than on human ingenuity. Nevertheless, in both cases the principal engineer of the action tends to be the clever slave whose impudence and ability to manipulate his nominal master testify to his freedom and to the topsyturviness of the world of the play he inhabits.

What separates this slave from Ligurio — and the world of ancient comedy from that of *La mandragola* — is that his freedom and dominance are overt and temporary rather than covert and potentially permanent. Not only is the Plautine or Terentian slave impudent with his betters, but his plots are always discovered so that he must be forgiven by his owner, the father of his young master, for the play to end happily. Moreover, he conceives of his activities as temporary, a holiday lark, whose end is the enjoyment of status reversal as well as food and drink

---

[52] On the loyalty of the slave in Roman comedy, see George E. Duckworth, *The Nature of Roman Comedy: A Study in Popular Entertainment* (Princeton: Princeton University Press, 1952), p. 251.

[53] The material in this paragraph is derived from Erich Segal, *Roman Laughter: The Comedy of Plautus* (Cambridge: Harvard University Press, 1968), esp. pp. 99-110, 114-16, 144-61, and 164-66.

on occasion. He does not seek a permanent change in his status from slave to freeman; freedom, for instance, is offered in passing as a gift of the title figure of Plautus's *Epidicus* rather than presented as something he has earnestly sought, and the issue of freedom is practically unique to this play. By contrast, although Ligurio occasionally expresses his exasperation with Callimaco, he generally remains respectful toward his employer and never allows Nicia to be disabused about his situation. Thus Ligurio conceals his role as the master manipulator of the plot and his dominance of his employer. Further, Ligurio is a free man, not a slave; that is, unlike his Roman predecessor, he is not confined legally to a structurally inferior social position from which there can only be a temporary, holiday release. Ligurio enjoys a relative ease of movement in his society which a slave could not duplicate, and because that society is ultimately shaped by his wit and theatrical insight, he remains potentially capable of controlling it insofar as he controls the illusions on which all the others base their lives. In the world of Roman comedy, the tricky slave offers an amusing release for the audience that contemplates him; in *La mandragola*, Ligurio offers a disturbance and a threat.

It might be objected that Ligurio resembles the parasites of Roman comedy more than the tricky slaves. In the Prologue to the play (57), Machiavelli calls him "parassito," and his name most likely derives from the Latin verb meaning "to lick" or "to desire ardently or greedily," a verb Plautus uses in connection with the parasite in the *Captivi* and Terence employs in the *Eunuchus*. Ligurio, however, does not behave like the typical parasite of ancient comedy, who is usually both a greedy sponger and a flatterer as well as a clown or buffoon who makes himself ridiculous to gain free meals from his patron.[54] Fittingly, Plautus names his parasite in the *Stichus* Gelasimus, from the Greek word for jester or buffoon, and although parasites in Roman comedy frequently mock in asides to the audience the foolish patrons who feed them, they remain fundamentally ridiculous figures. Audiences were doubtless expected to laugh, for instance, when parasites complained about comically exaggerated hunger pangs, to share the disdain frequently directed at parasites by other characters, including slaves, and to enjoy the occasional discomfiture of a parasite, as when everyone refuses to treat Gelasimus to a dinner at the end of the *Stichus*.

There are two parasites, however, who to some extent stand as exceptions to the rule: Gnatho in Terence's *Eunuchus* and the title character of Terence's *Phormio*. Nevertheless, although in each case the parasite is a clever plotter who helps the young protagonist in his amorous in-

---

[54]On the parasite as buffoon, see Duckworth, *Roman Comedy*, pp. 265–66.

trigue, Gnatho has a very secondary role to the tricky slave Parmeno and joins in the intrigue only at the very end, whereas Phormio plays a witty, impudent middleman carrying on an intrigue fashioned by the slave Geta. Moreover, although Gnatho sees himself as breaking with the tradition of the parasite as buffoon because he is clever and is making fun of his patron even as he flatters him, other characters still mock him as a parasite and thus remind the audience of his traditionally inferior status. And despite his impudence and intelligence, Phormio shares the typical parasite's focus on food and even makes himself somewhat ridiculous by joking about his appetite. Finally, the young men whom they serve never have any doubt about the loyalty of either parasite. Thus these two exceptions to the rule governing ancient comic parasites are very different indeed from Ligurio. Ligurio is supremely intelligent, never exposed to the mockery of other characters or the audience, and fundamentally untrustworthy. The ancient parasite's limited intellectual abilities and ridiculous hunger allow Plautus and Terence to fix him in a position of permanent social inferiority so that, like the slaves who also people their works, he is anything but a threat to the social order. Just the opposite, of course, is true of Machiavelli's Renaissance *parassito*.

The most important question has been left for last: Why did Machiavelli deviate from both Boccaccio and the ancient comic drama by making Ligurio not only responsible for the comic intrigue but also a person of questionable loyalty whose potential future actions undermine the illusion of harmony at the end of the play? One answer — probably the best one — is that in this regard the play responds to the social reality of Renaissance Italy just as it does when Machiavelli has Callimaco pursue a married woman rather than a courtesan, as a character in a Roman comedy would have done. In other words, Machiavelli's characterization of Ligurio and the place he occupies in the play can be related to both the ideology and the fact of class mobility in Italian Renaissance culture, and in particular to a perceived tension in the relationship between masters and servants which was related to that mobility. Philippe Ariès has claimed that an existential bond existed between masters and servants during the ancien régime so that service was not entirely equated with money, as it was to be later on; cash was offered as a reward rather than a payment for service.[55] Nevertheless, Renaissance servants did expect to be paid, and tensions and problems arose when they were not, as a quick glance through, say, Castiglione's

[55] Philippe Ariès, *Centuries of Childhood: A Social History of Family Life*, trans. Robert Baldick (New York: Random House, 1962), p. 396.

letters requesting funds from his various masters and complaining about not being paid will reveal. Indeed, for every devoted family servant, such as the Buto celebrated in Leon Battista Alberti's *Libri della famiglia*, there were doubtless many members of the Florentine *popolo minuto* for whom devotion was purely a matter of the cash nexus.

As early as the start of the fifteenth century the writings of the humanists display an ideology of movement that cut against the grain of a more static conception of the social order in which inferiors automatically and instinctively owed service to their betters. Consequently, moralists and satirists, according to J. R. Hale, attacked pretension in dress and manners less because it was symptomatic of large-scale movement within society than because it was identified specifically with a breakdown of this idea of service.[56] At the same time, social mobility was a fact, not a theory, in Machiavelli's world. If poor farmers' sons could not hope to grow up to become dukes, nevertheless individuals with modest material resources but large endowments of intelligence and energy could make fortunes for themselves and their families, learn aristocratic modes of deportment from such books as *Il cortegiano*, and eventually acquire noble titles, as the Medici did. Or they could, like Machiavelli himself, rise by means of their wits and skills from a relatively humble, impoverished, though by no means totally obscure family to become the head of the Second Chancery of the Florentine state. Cunning parasites such as Ligurio thus represented a hope to those near the bottom, a danger to those on top. In either case, Machiavelli's focus on his clever parasite in *La mandragola* clarifies the problematic character of service in his world and the ambiguous nature of the socially mobile.

Although Machiavelli does not brood directly on the issue of lower-class servants and parasites in his other writings, he does focus repeatedly on two different but closely related versions of the servant. First, in an important passage in *Il principe*, he instructs princes how to manage their counselors and warns them that counselors, especially talented ones, will inevitably betray them if they can (xxiii, 96). Second, Machiavelli repeatedly focuses his attention on another servant figure similar to the counselor, one who occupied center stage in the tragic drama of Renaissance Italy and whose loyalty—or lack of it—was the main issue associated with him. That figure is the mercenary, in particular the mercenary leader. Again and again Machiavelli argues that mercenaries are undependable because they are motivated only by their

[56] J. R. Hale, *Renaissance Europe: Individual and Society, 1480–1520* (Berkeley: University of California Press, 1971), pp. 178–79.

own monetary interests and are unwilling to die for their masters, and he scornfully denounces the Florentines and other Italians for foolishly trusting their fortunes to such men rather than training citizen armies on the Roman model (*Pr*, XII, 54; *Disc*, I, xliii, 231).[57] Yet, while expressing contempt for the general cowardice of mercenary armies, he recognizes the ambition that drives the best of them (*Pr*, XII, 54–55; *Disc*, II, xx, 339), and he genuinely admires such mercenary captains as Philip of Macedonia, employed by the Thebans to lead their army, and Francesco Sforza, similarly employed by the Milanese, because both had the energy and intelligence to realize their enormous ambitions and to achieve control over a state, even if they had to step on the dead bodies of their masters to do so (*Pr*, XII, 55; XIV, 62). It is, of course, most likely that Machiavelli, who did not come from the ruling classes of Florence but who nevertheless achieved several important political offices through his intellect and skill, saw himself reflected in such figures, just as he must have seen himself in the Lucchese condottiere Castruccio Castracani, whose rise from orphan to ruler of the state he served Machiavelli celebrated in his *Vita* of the man.

Strikingly, in *La mandragola* Ligurio plays a combination of counselor and condottiere. Just as mercenaries offered to conduct military campaigns in exchange for financial reward, so he offers to manage Callimaco's affairs in exchange for a promise of money. In one notable passage, when he goes with Nicia, Timoteo, and Siro in quest of the "garzonaccio," the parasite speaks in military metaphors as he arranges his "troops": "Io voglio essere el capitano, e ordinare l'esercito per la giornata" (IV.ix.102: "I want to be the captain and to arrange the army for the battle"). He then disposes the frate on one flank, himself on the other, and Nicia in between, leaving Siro as the rear guard. Machiavelli's language here may be intended to recall the language of conquest that Roman poets used in connection with love, but it may also be read as constituting an allusion to the practices of contemporary mercenaries. Like them, Ligurio leads his troops into a fraudulent battle, appearing to serve but really aiming to betray his deluded master, whose name, in this context, acquires an ironic resonance. For Nicia is doubtless named after the famous ancient admiral who, according to Machiavelli, spoke against but finally helped lead the ill-fated Athenian expedition against Syracuse, and whom Machiavelli praises in the *Discorsi* as a "uomo gravissimo e prudentissimo" (I, liii, 251: "most grave and prudent man"). The Nicia of *La mandragola* is anything but grave

---

[57]Machiavelli's distrust of mercenaries reflects a sentiment widespread in his culture. On this point, see ibid., pp. 192–93.

and prudent, and he is defeated openly not by a declared enemy but by his own paid servant. The same sort of defeat may well be in store for Ligurio's other "master," Callimaco, and it is no wonder that the latter, unlike any protagonist in a Roman comedy or a tale by Boccaccio, felt an almost instinctive compulsion to worry about Ligurio's—as well as Siro's—loyalty early in the play and had to reassure himself about them with elaborate arguments and guarantees. Those arguments and guarantees may have persuaded Callimaco, but they bespeak a fundamental blindness that may eventually turn him into Ligurio's dupe. For the play demonstrates in many ways that if Ligurio possesses the superior energy and intelligence of a Francesco Sforza, he also shares Sforza's ambition, his fundamental loyalty only to himself, and his deep potential to betray his Visconti masters. Like countless mercenaries and counselors in the world of Renaissance Italy, Ligurio is a parasite, but in the modern, biological sense of the word: he dines not *with* his host but *on* him. Thus he poses a genuine threat to all those he serves, just as his continuing presence in the play destroys forever the illusory harmony seemingly achieved by its end.

The central characters of Machiavelli's play, Callimaco and Ligurio, are worlds apart from the young heroes and the comic slaves and parasites of Roman comedy on whom they are modeled. They are much closer to the clever confidence men in the *novelle* of Boccaccio, Sacchetti, and other fourteenth- and fifteenth-century Italian writers. Like their predecessors, they are free from allegiance to the traditional social order, and they manipulate their prey by their masterly use of language and rhetoric. Perceiving life as theater, they create a compelling illusion for their dupes as they put on the play of the mandrake root, an illusion that satisfies everyone concerned. For the audience watching the play, however, the social harmony seemingly achieved is more disturbing than the ending of any Roman comedy or Italian *novella*, for the audience knows that it is an illusion, that it papers over the most fundamental social tensions and rivalries. If the audience can rejoice in the triumph of intelligence, energy, and creativity, it has also witnessed a play that evokes near-paranoia at times in regard to basic social relationships. It stimulates one of the most frequent worries produced by the Renaissance ideology of self-fashioning—the worry that the best-educated and most sophisticated members of society, such men as Callimaco, will not rise up to become like the gods but will descend and become fundamentally untrustworthy beasts. The play also calls forth an even deeper fear in a society that still defined social relationships in terms of service just as medieval society did—the fear that those who serve, from courtly counselors through mercenaries down to the humblest menials, were undependable. To return to Francesco Vettori's phrase, *La mandragola* does indeed illustrate the notion that all the world is a confidence game, but not in the largely positive sense Vettori intended. It leaves its audience with the frightening specter that the world is an endless succession of tricks and betrayals, that social harmony is only an illusion, and that service, so essential to life in society, has been reduced to a fatal, destructive form of parasitic predation.

3

Spectacles of Violence
and the Memory of Fear

In the seventh chapter of *Il principe*, Machiavelli describes a famous incident that reveals both the similarities and the awesome distance between the comic world of *La mandragola* and the grimmer one of his political and historical writings. That incident occurred just after Cesare Borgia had secured control of the Romagna. To stamp out the lawlessness that the impotence of the region's former rulers had allowed to reign, he sent his henchman Remirro de Orco there, a "uomo crudele et espedito, al quale dette pienissima potestà" (*Pr*, VII, 37: "man cruel and quick, to whom he gave the most complete power"). Remirro quickly pacified the region "con grandissima reputazione" (ibid.), and Borgia, judging that such excessive authority was not necessary and might render him hateful to the populace, decided to replace his lieutenant with a civil tribunal. Borgia's next action, in another context, may deserve to live in infamy.

> E, perché conosceva le rigorosità passate averli generato qualche odio, per purgare li animi di quelli populi e guadagnarseli in tutto, volle monstrare che, se crudeltà alcuna era seguíta, non era nata da lui, ma dalla acerba natura del ministro. E, presa sopr'a questo occasione, lo fece mettere una mattina a Cesena in dua pezzi in sulla piazza, con uno pezzo di legno et uno coltello sanguinoso a canto. La ferocità del quale spettaculo fece quelli populi in uno tempo rimanere satisfatti e stupidi. [*Pr*, VII, 37]

And because he recognized that the former harsh procedures had generated some hatred for him, in order to purge the spirits of those people and to gain them entirely for himself, he wanted to demonstrate that, if any cruelty had occurred, it was due not to him but to the bitter nature of his minister. And, seizing this opportunity, he had him put one morning in two pieces in the piazza at Cesena with a piece of wood and a bloody knife beside him. The ferocity of this spectacle made those people feel at once satisfied and awed.

Despite their savagery, Cesare Borgia's actions here are not censored or satirized; rather, they make him what Machiavelli considered an ideal prince. They also make him as much a confidence man as Callimaco and Ligurio, just as the response of the people of Cesena recalls the reactions of the dupe Nicia. Let us briefly review just what is involved here.

First, Cesare Borgia's management of this brutal spectacle reveals that he shares the amoral egotism apparent in the confidence men of Machiavelli's play. Neither biblical injunctions against murder, common considerations of fairness, feelings of loyalty to a subordinate, nor feudal obligations to a faithful servant are given a second's thought. Remirro's death is simply a matter of political expediency, a means for Borgia to maintain his power and reputation in the Romagna. Strikingly, the narrative shape of the text reduces the execution to the level of a purely physical operation in which Remirro is no longer a human being who has been killed but an object—actually, two objects ("pezzi")—like the piece ("pezzo") of wood and the knife. Ironically, Remirro was sent to the Romagna as Cesare's instrument of justice, and in his death he has become just that—an instrument.

If Machiavelli minimizes the condemnation of Borgia's deed, he also omits any justification of it. Contemporary scholars have debated Remirro's execution, some claiming he deserved death because of his cruelty and misdeeds.[1] But in the passage cited, although Machiavelli tells us Remirro was a cruel man, we find no indication that his actions in the Romagna were particularly wicked; the passage emphasizes that Remirro enjoyed an "eccessiva autorità" in Borgia's eyes and that his "rigorosità" generated hatred in the people. He hardly seems a monster of iniquity worthy of betrayal and murder. Machiavelli places Borgia's act in a zone beyond any simple moral judgment, whether good or bad, making him a figure as fundamentally amoral as the confidence men in *La mandragola* or as any of the *beffatori* in the *novella* tradition that lies behind that play. Moreover, the people of Cesena who witness the spectacle Borgia has created recall in their reactions the archdupe of Machiavelli's comedy. Just as Nicia was awed by Callimaco's ability to speak Latin and by the dignity of his costume and bearing, so the

[1]See, for example, Allan H. Gilbert, *Machiavelli's "Prince" and Its Forerunners: "The Prince" as a Typical Book "de Regimine Principum"* (Durham, N.C.: Duke University Press, 1938), p. 157; and J. H. Whitfield, *Machiavelli* (1947; rpt. New York: Russell & Russell, 1965), p. 81.

townspeople are awed by Borgia's actions. And just as Nicia emerged at the end of the play completely content with events, so the citizens of Cesena are rendered "satisfatti" by the dead body they see before them. Finally, the fundamental relationship between confidence man and dupe in the episode in *Il principe* resembles the one in *La mandragola*: in both cases the swindlers create fraudulent, theatrical spectacles to bilk their prey.

The differences between those spectacles, however, are immense. Most noticeable is the fact that Borgia's centers on the dead body of Remirro de Orco, whereas no one dies in *La mandragola*. To be sure, force was present in Machiavelli's play, in the shadowy form of Callimaco's threat of rape, but in the "ideal" world of the comedy, there was no need for such a threat ever to be carried out. In the "real" world of history in *Il principe*, people are murdered as well as deceived, states ruined as well as tricked by their conquerors. Of course, the people of Cesena do not suffer violence, but Remirro, every bit as much Borgia's dupe as they are, certainly does. Borgia's spectacle shows that fraud and force are not separate commodities in the world of history as Machiavelli imagines it, for that spectacle includes within it, indeed is based on, an act of carefully calculated violence totally extraneous to the world of his comedy. It is thus a spectacle of power in a double sense: first, its centerpiece is an awe-inspiring display of physical power; and second, as a result of that display, it is able to ensure the political power Borgia exercises over the people he rules. In the world of history, unlike the world of comedy, it takes power to breed power.

The other major difference between Borgia's confidence trick and the one Callimaco and Ligurio engineer is seen in the utter silence of the scene in the piazza at Cesena. Although the two confidence artists in Machiavelli's play do manipulate their prey through such mute means as dress and physical objects, their primary tool is language. By contrast, words have vanished from Borgia's spectacle, replaced by the absolute stillness of Remirro de Orco's dead body. As we shall see later, words will be an indispensable weapon in the arsenals of the confidence men, including Cesare Borgia, in Machiavelli's political and historical works. Moreover, the body, the piece of wood, and the knife in the piazza all "speak" in their own way to the citizens of the town. Nevertheless, words are singularly absent from Borgia's exemplary spectacle, and their absence suggests that in the world of history, unlike the "ideal" world of comedy, language, though profoundly important, is sometimes not enough. It must be supplemented and at moments replaced by thoughtfully contrived acts of brutality if the spectacles the confidence man creates in his pursuit of power are to have real, persuasive force. A rhetoric of words must, in short, be joined by or even yield to a rhetoric of carefully calculated violent spectacle.

As the following pages will show, the confidence men–princes and victims who appear throughout Machiavelli's political and historical works resemble the tricksters and dupes of La mandragola in basic ways. Indeed, the very world of history which Machiavelli imagines for those characters often reflects in its structure and operations nothing less than a classic beffa. As the episode of Remirro's murder has suggested, however, the confidence man and his dupe undergo significant metamorphoses when they step out on the stage of history. The reckless pursuit of power, violence, pain, and fear all now enter into their relationships, and the confidence games they play acquire a new seriousness. As Remirro and the people of Cesena discovered, those games become matters of life and death.

Although Machiavelli's imagined world of history contains characters other than confidence men and dupes, that pair repeatedly occupies center stage. Thus in Il principe, Machiavelli focuses on such figures as Ferdinand of Aragon, who manipulates the Spanish nobility and people into a holy crusade as a cover for his own pursuit of power; in the Discorsi, he presents Appius Claudius beguiling the Roman Senate and people, and Roman leaders and generals staging religious spectacles to inspire and intimidate their soldiers; Castruccio Castracani, in the Vita Machiavelli wrote of him, is paired with the rebellious Poggio family, whom he persuades to agree to a truce by a promise of good treatment and then has brutally murdered; and the Istorie fiorentine teems with confidence men who victimize Florence, from the infamous Duke of Athens down to Cosimo and Lorenzo de' Medici. In the twenty-second chapter of Il principe, which is concerned with the prince's selection of advisers and ministers, Machiavelli generalizes at the most abstract level about this pair of characters. Here he follows Livy in distinguishing three kinds of cervelli, that is, minds or mentalities: "l'uno intende da sé, l'altro discerne quello che altri intende, el terzo non intende né sé né altri" (Pr, xxii, 94: "one understands things by itself, another discerns what others understand, the third understands neither [by] itself nor [through] others"). Machiavelli judges the first two cervelli excellent and the third useless, and as he ponders whether the wise and clever Pandolfo Petrucci, prince of Siena, belongs in the first or second category, it becomes clear that his threefold distinction is actually a twofold one:

men are either excellent because they understand or worthless because they do not.[2] They are, in other words, either excellent confidence men or worthless dupes.

So profound is this distinction in Machiavelli's thought that it even governs the way he depicts the state of Rome and its relationship with neighboring states. Inspired perhaps by the traditional image of the state as a person, Machiavelli creates what Mark Hulliung has called a myth of Rome as a trickster, identifying it as a prince and describing its use of "inganno" (*Disc*, II, iv, 289: "deception") so that its allies gradually subject themselves to its power without realizing it.[3] Rome is a mistress of fraud and her allies are perfect gulls. Although even states can behave as confidence men and dupes, I shall refer to this pair by the terms to which Machiavelli returns again and again in his works, the *principe* or prince and the *popolo* or people, even though some of his "princes" are dukes and consuls and popes, and the "people" may include various groups from time to time.

Although Machiavelli is basically concerned with two different mentalities or psychologies in his works, he does have recourse to terms that were employed, as Felix Gilbert has shown, to distinguish social classes in Renaissance Italy. Florentine diarists and political writers, according to Gilbert, apparently either divided their city's inhabitants into three classes — the poor, the middle class (*mezzani*), and the wealthy — or they ignored the masses outside the Great Council, dismissing them as the *plebe*, the *infima plebe*, or the *vulgo*, and divided the city into two classes: on one side the *populari, mercatanti, populo*, or *populo minuto*, and on the other, the *nobili, grandi, ricchi, principali*, or *uomini savi*.[4] Machiavelli uses such terms loosely, employing *populari* and *populo* interchangeably with words designating the excluded lowest segment of the Florentine citizenry, the *plebe* or the *vulgo*.[5] More important, although he sometimes actually does identify different social classes by means of this inherited vocabulary (see, for example, *Pr*, IX,

---

[2]In a letter to a Lucchese chancellor, Machiavelli divides the world into those who believe things readily and easily and those who are cautious and prudent and follow the diplomat's way. See *Let*, #11, 48-49.

[3]For other references to Rome as a person and a trickster, see *Disc*, II, i, 277-79; xiii, 312-13; III, xxxi, 470. On this point, see Martin Fleisher, "A Passion for Politics: The Vital Core of the World of Machiavelli," in *Machiavelli and the Nature of Political Thought*, ed. Martin Fleisher (New York: Atheneum, 1972), p. 137; and Mark Hulliung, *Citizen Machiavelli* (Princeton: Princeton University Press, 1983), pp. 43, 51-54, 160-62. Hulliung identifies Machiavelli's view of Rome as a "myth."

[4]Felix Gilbert, *Machiavelli and Guicciardini: Politics and History in Sixteenth-Century Florence* (Princeton: Princeton University Press, 1965), pp. 23-25.

[5]Alfredo Bonadeo, "The Role of the People in the Works and Times of Machiavelli," *Bibliothèque d'Humanisme et Renaissance* 32 (1970): 351-77.

45, and *Ist*, ii, xii, 155), he is more concerned with different mentalities than with socioeconomic groups. In one famous passage in *Il principe*, for instance, he sets up a clear distinction between the prince (and the few like him) and the vast mass of humanity not by class but by mental capacity: "Li uomini in universali iudicano piú alli occhi che alle mani; perché tocca a vedere a ognuno, a sentire a pochi" (*Pr*, xviii, 74: "Men in general judge more by their eyes than by their hands, because all can see but few can feel"). Here, inverting the traditional hierarchy of the senses, in which sight was privileged over touch, just as he inverts the beast-man hierarchy in praising his prince as a lion and a fox, Machiavelli distinguishes between those who see things in a superficial way and those who grasp them in depth. In a later passage he again condemns the vast mass of men ("li uomini in universali"), this time appropriating one of the traditional words used to identify those Florentines outside the Consiglio Grande: "El vulgo ne va preso con quello che pare . . . e nel mondo non è se non vulgo" (*Pr*, xviii, 74: "The vulgar are taken with what appears . . . and in the world there is nothing but the vulgar"). *Vulgo* here is clearly not a class term but the label for a particular *cervello*.[6] Finally, in a chapter of the *Discorsi*, Machiavelli equates the Roman *plebe* with the *moltitudine*, a term normally used to designate the lowest stratum of the Florentine population still represented in the Consiglio Grande, not because the two classes are social equivalents but because both terms, once again, indicate the same mentality (i, xliv, 232).[7]

If Machiavelli frequently expresses contempt for the *popolo*, whether he uses the term primarily to designate a social class, a mentality, or both, it is not always an "animale bruto" (*Disc*, I, xvi, 173) in his thought, just as *prince* is often less than a term of praise. In the *Discorsi* especially he stresses the virtues of a well-trained populace, insisting, for instance, that if they may be deceived by generalities, they are much better than princes at judging particulars (i, xlvii, 237-40), mainly because the biases of many individuals in a group tend to correct one another whereas those of an autocrat can mislead his judgment. Moreover, even in *Il principe*, a work never accused of republicanism, Machiavelli deliberately rejects the trite proverb that *"chi fonda in sul populo, fonda in sul fango"* (ix, 47: "who builds on the people, builds

⁶Although Machiavelli seems to reverse this judgment of the *popolo* in the *Discorsi* when he praises its ability to judge particulars (i, xlvii, 237-40), in the same chapter he stresses its self-deception about generalities and contrasts its inability with the greater understanding of the magistrate Pacuvius Calavius Campanus. Thus, though he does not deny the *popolo* all intellectual ability, he continues to make a firm distinction between it and a select few on this score.

⁷Gilbert, *Machiavelli and Guicciardini*, p. 24.

on mud"). But he defends the constancy of the people in this passage
because he is talking about a people whom the prince has shaped and
disciplined, just as in the *Discorsi* he is talking about a trained Roman
people operating under the restraints of the Roman constitutional system. In either case, the people remain largely passive, objects of manipulation and direction by others, and particularly by figures whose
behavior identifies them as confidence men. And when the two are juxtaposed by Machiavelli, he inevitably sneers at the first, as he does when
he describes the Roman people rejoicing when the Senate, playing the
role of confidence man, convinced them that the pay they received for
military service was a present from the Senate when it was in fact taken
from the public treasury (*Disc*, I, li, 246). By contrast, Machiavelli reveals his admiration for the perception and cunning of his confidence
men even though they may have aimed to destroy Rome's republican
liberty, as did Appius Claudius, or been responsible for destroying the
freedom of Florence, as did the Medici.

   If *popolo* (or *moltitudine* or *plebe* or *vulgo*) designates a mentality as
much as a social class for Machiavelli, his works also make it clear that
prince by no means simply indicates someone who comes from the upper
classes or nobility. Although many of his princes are indeed aristocrats
or at least gentlemen, some also come from the lowest strata of society.
Thus Machiavelli stresses the humble birth of Moses and Cyrus, Romulus and Theseus (*Pr*, VI, 30), revises historical fact to make Castruccio
Castracani a foundling (*CC*, 10), and has a Venetian opponent of Francesco Sforza insult him as a baseborn bastard, prompting Sforza to a
reply that rings with Renaissance self-confidence: if he could not account for his parents' deeds, he would certainly vouch for his own (*Ist*,
VI, xviii, 414). Even more significant is the passage in the *Istorie* in
which Machiavelli, with consummate irony, puts an exposition of his
own political philosophy into the mouth of a plebeian participant in the
Ciompi Revolt. All men, this rebel claims, have the same ancestor, so
all are equal and traditional social hierarchies do not matter. He then
says, even more radically, that everything the ruling class has acquired
has been gained "o con inganno o con violenza" (III, xiii, 238: "through
deception or violence"), although it has covered its ugly gains with false
titles. Hence he concludes that since the social order is a fraud and people's fortunes are in their own hands, he and his fellow rebels should
cast aside all moral scruples and seize the main chance, "perché coloro
che vincono, in qualunque modo vincono, mai non ne riportono ver-
gogna" (ibid.: "because those who conquer, in whatever way they conquer, are never shamed by it"). Machiavelli's princely confidence men
belong, like Boccaccio's *beffatori* and the deceivers in Machiavelli's

Mandragola, to an aristocracy of intellect; it is because of their intellect that they achieve political power and become genuine social aristocrats as well.[8] Thus they constitute a parody of the traditional social order, turning it topsy-turvy in the very effort to preserve that order so that they may rise to the top of it and rule over those beneath.

In Machiavelli's political and historical works, just as in *La man-dragola*, he both presents the relationship between the prince and the *popolo* as a *beffa* or confidence trick and arranges his princely confidence men in a hierarchy. Usually, if Machiavelli employs any term to identify the relationship between the prince and the people, that term is *inganno* or *frode*, that is, deceit or fraud. On a pair of occasions in the *Istorie fiorentine*, however, he uses derivatives of *beffa* to describe that relationship, stressing the scorn and mockery the word signified. In the first instance, he recounts how Niccolò Piccinino tricked the pope into thinking him an ally and then, after having conquered many of the pope's possessions in northern Italy, added insult to injury by mocking him (v, xvii, 354: "lo volle . . . sbeffare"). Thus Machiavelli suggests that Piccinino's deception amounted to a *beffa* even if that word was never used. In the second instance, Cosimo de' Medici, pretending to advocate republican government, manipulated the Florentines so that his supporters were elected to the Great Council, making him the virtual ruler of the city. As a result, the powerful men who opposed him felt themselves "beffati e derisi" (vii, ii, 454: "tricked/mocked and ridiculed"), in other words, the ridiculous victims of a *beffa*. Indeed, Cosimo arranged to have his supporters on the Council mock ("sbeffare") one of their opponents so badly that he was literally driven insane (vii, iii, 455). In these cases, the various derivatives of *beffa* are employed in contexts in which a confidence game, albeit a serious political one, has been played. The presence of those terms evokes the *beffa* cultivated by Boccaccio and others, and it thus suggests that Machiavelli saw—and shaped—the world of history in good measure through that literary genre: his princes play particularly brutal confidence tricks on the people they manipulate and deceive. Although Borgia's bloody spectacle in Cesena is never labeled an *inganno*, let alone a *beffa*, can there be any doubt that that is just what it is?

Borgia's activities allow readers to rank Machiavelli's confidence men in a hierarchy, for Borgia is not only manipulating a population of passive dupes but also deceiving his lieutenant, a person whose intelligence and energy, one must suppose, might make him a confidence man as

[8]For Machiavelli's conscious awareness of this movement, see *Disc*, ii, xiii, 311-12. The title of this chapter is "Che si viene di bassa a gran fortuna piú con la fraude che con la forza" ("That one goes from low to great fortune more by fraud than by force").

well. In general, Machiavelli's princes are juxtaposed both to the hapless, unperceptive populace and to other confidence men whom they have to outfox, to beat at their own game. This is what Niccolò Piccinino does with the pope in the episode referred to above and what Filippo Visconti, Piccinino's ostensible employer, does to him in turn. Visconti keeps his condottiere dangling with promises of territory and an advantageous marriage until he finally betrays him into coming to Milan and leaving his army to be defeated by that of his archrival Francesco Sforza. Machiavelli sees Piccinino as a man of intelligence and *virtù* but also as something of a fool in going to Milan, abandoning "per uno incerto bene una certa vittoria" (*Ist*, VI, viii, 399: "for an uncertain good a certain victory") over Sforza. Moreover, at the end of this section of the *Istorie* Piccinino ruefully realizes that he has been deceived and then literally dies of shame because of it (VI, viii, 399-400). This episode reveals the profound dualism that characterizes Machiavelli's thought: the world is essentially divided between confidence men and dupes, so that when two confidence men collide and one is defeated, the loser is presented as a dupe. Thus Oliverotto da Fermo appears in one section of *Il principe* as a confidence man, albeit an especially wicked one (VIII, 42-43), but when Machiavelli describes how he was outfoxed and murdered by Cesare Borgia at Senigaglia, we find only a withering contempt for Oliverotto's "simplicità" (VII, 36). In Machiavelli's thought there is no middle ground: although a few characters may escape this dualism, in a world of constant trickery and competition almost all are either confidence men-princes or, by nature, misfortune, or miscalculation, their dupes.

Like the confidence men and dupes in *La mandragola*, the princes and the people in the political and historical works share a number of basic characteristics, for they participate in the same anthropology of desire, just as all the characters in *La mandragola* do. For Machiavelli, human beings are by nature acquisitive creatures who seek to satisfy their appetites primarily by getting possession of things: material goods, wealth, lands, even, Machiavelli suggests satirically, women.[9] Hence a prince can avoid men's hatred if he simply resists touching their things ("roba") and their women—and especially *their* things—"perché li uomini sdimenticano piú presto la morte del padre che la perdita del patrimonio" (*Pr*, XVII, 70: "for men forget more rapidly the death of their father than the loss of their patrimony"). No idealism or desire for spiritual goods is involved: if people desire freedom after they have lost

[9]*Pr*, III, 23: "E cosa veramente molto naturale et ordinaria desiderare di acquisitare" ("It is truly a very natural and normal thing to wish to acquire [goods]").

it to a tyrant (see *Disc*, I, xvi, 175-76), on close examination that freedom appears less an exalted ideal than the mere absence of interference by the powerful in their pursuit and enjoyment of goods.

Perhaps humans' most universal desire is their appetite for political power, their "appitito del regnare" (*Disc*, III, iv, 388), which Machiavelli labels "ambizione." At times he seems to suggest that ambition is restricted to members of the ruling class, the nobility or *grandi*, declaring that the people wish merely not to be oppressed, whereas the nobility wishes to oppress others (*Pr*, IX, 45-46). If a wise man does most of a prince's ruling for him, however, Machiavelli warns that that wise man will inevitably desire to rule himself (*Pr*, XXIII, 96), and Machiavelli dramatizes this generalization in the *Istorie fiorentine* when he recounts how the dying Cosimo de' Medici asked Dietisalvi Neroni, a seemingly fervent Medici supporter in whom Cosimo had the greatest confidence, to aid Piero de' Medici in managing the state after Cosimo's death. Neroni pledges his entire *fede* to Cosimo, but the temptation is too great, and as soon as Cosimo is dead, Neroni's *ambizione* induces him to begin scheming to seize the state (VII, x, 468ff). Similarly, in the *Discorsi* Machiavelli describes how the Roman populace went from merely desiring liberty to desiring political power and how that desire eventually led to the destruction of the republic. The title of the forty-sixth chapter in Book I of that work is most revealing: "Gli uomini salgono da un'ambizione a un'altra; e prima si cerca non essere offeso, dipoi si offende altrui" (235: "Men rise from one ambition to another; and first they seek not to be offended, and then to offend others"). Machiavelli explains that in defending their own liberty, people are inevitably impelled to take away that of others. Thus, whether their primary motive is political ambition or not, the behavior of the populace, like that of princes and *grandi*, confirms Machiavelli's generalization: "La natura degli uomini è ambiziosa" (*Disc*, I, xxix, 198: "Men's nature is ambitious"). If the spirit (*animo*) of the nobility is directly labeled *ambizioso*, while that of the populace is merely *inquieto*, one is forced to agree with Martin Fleisher that the former is merely a more intense version of the latter.[10] Just as Nicia flattered himself with the notion that he was a confidence man, so, given the right circumstances, even the humblest person in the world of history is for Machiavelli a would-be prince.

Desire rules the lives of all who live in the world of history. Humans cannot control their lust for land, goods, and power, so that even a

[10]See Fleisher, "Passion for Politics," p. 126; see also Bonadeo, "Role of the People," p. 375.

model prince such as Castruccio Castracani laments at the end of his life that he did not have the good judgment to stop his headlong pursuit of land and glory long enough to leave his successor a stable realm (CC, 33).[11] In fact, humans' desire is so irrepressible that they must always find release for it, and consequently, the verb sfogare (or sfogarsi) appears throughout Machiavelli's writings.[12] As the verb suggests, men burn with the fire (fuoco) of desire and must vent or release it lest it consume them.

For all human beings, desire is not only all-powerful but restless and ever changing. People, says Machiavelli, afflict themselves in bad times and get bored in good ones, fighting out of necessity or ambition, which never leaves them. He explains this situation in Augustinian terms:[13]

> La cagione è, perché la natura ha creato gli uomini in modo che possono desiderare ogni cosa e non possono conseguire ogni cosa: talché essendo sempre maggiore il desiderio che la potenza dello acquistare, ne risulta la mala contentezza di quello che si possiede, e la poca sodisfazione d'esso. [Disc, I, xxxvii, 215]

> The reason is that nature has made men so that they can desire everything but cannot attain everything, so that, desire always being greater than the power of acquiring, they lack contentment with what they possess and take very little satisfaction in it.

Unlike Saint Augustine, for whom an infinite object, God, could finally satisfy humans' infinite desires, Machiavelli remains totally within the

[11] Machiavelli knew the imperiousness of desire intimately, and he speaks in several of his letters of the tremendous power love exercised over him so that all else, including his favored political speculation, became secondary (see #145, 322, and #154, 347). In one letter to Francesco Vettori, he admits his inability to keep from speaking of politics, which was also a passion (see #124, 239).

[12] See, for example, Let, #140, 303: "Cosí rinvolto entra questi pidocchi traggo el cervello di muffa, et sfogo questa malignità di questa mia sorta" ("Thus caught among these lice, I wipe the mold from my brain and vent my feeling of being ill treated by fate"). Callimaco, desperate to bed Lucrezia, soliloquizes in La mandragola about his plight and wishes Ligurio were there so that he would have some means of release: "Pure, se io trovassi Ligurio io arei con chi sfogarmi" (IV.i.93: "If only I could find Ligurio, I'd have someone with whom to get it off my chest"). The Florentine people, full of rage ("rabbioso furore") at the Duke of Athens, release their anger on his subordinates: "Sfogata la moltitudine sopra il sangue di costoro" (Ist, II, xxxvii, 203: "The multitude, having vented its anger with their blood"). And in the Discorsi, conspirators are described as releasing their passion ("sfogare l'animo suo") in the act of killing their enemies (III, vi, 393).

[13] For Machiavelli's partial affinity with Saint Augustine, see Joseph A. Mazzeo, Renaissance and Revolution: Backgrounds to Seventeenth-Century English Literature (New York: Random House, 1965, 1967), pp. 77-85.

orbit of this world and stresses the fundamental dissatisfaction that springs from the disparity between desire and the world's inadequate means to satisfy it. This dissatisfaction fuels human beings' restless search for novelty and makes it impossible for them to be moderate or temperate.[14] Thus the world is always in motion, always unstable, always topsy-turvy.[15]

Men in Machiavelli's world are totally egocentric, and their desires for goods, women, and power are continually conjoined to desires for vengeance, refusals to keep faith when it does not satisfy their personal needs, and a sadistic, uncharitable delight in the pain and destruction of others. Old injuries, he says, are not forgotten, no matter how much time has passed since they were committed and how many benefits have been conferred in the meantime (*Disc*, III, iv, 387-88). Thus, Machiavelli counsels, it is dangerous to let men live on if one has taken their goods or injured their women, for they always have a knife left to use (*Disc*, III, vi, 391), and once they have recovered their own, they inevitably wish revenge (*Ist*, III, xi, 232-33). And since people are in general ingrates and deceivers, they will support a prince or benefactor only so long as he does them good and danger is far off, and will abandon him as soon as the wind changes (*Pr*, XVII, 69-70).

Although at times Machiavelli may seem to speak in relatively neutral tones about people's egocentric desires, he insistently characterizes them as wicked (*tristi*), both when they are pursuing material goods and when they are treacherously stabbing an enemy. In a famous passage of *Il principe*, he generalizes: "Li uomini sempre ti riusciranno tristi, se da una necessità non sono fatti buoni" (XXIII, 96: "Men will all turn out to be wicked toward you unless they are forced by necessity to be good"). Similarly, with a resigned shrug Machiavelli tells the founder of a state that he should presuppose "tutti gli uomini rei" ("all men evil"), that they will use their wickedness ("malignità") when granted an opportunity, and that if it is hidden now, it will eventually come to light (*Disc*, I, iii, 135). Thus it should not be surprising that he encourages the prince to be wicked toward others and never to feel any obligation to keep his word to them: "Se li uomini fussino tutti buoni, questo pre-

---

[14]See *Disc*, II, *Proemio*, 274; and III, xxi, 446. In the *Asino d'oro*, Machiavelli says that men are less happy than the animals, who know how to be contented (*SL*, 301-2, VIII, 94-117). And in the *Istorie fiorentine* he claims that men are less eager to seize what they can have than to desire what they cannot (II, xxxi, 184).

[15]*Disc*, I, vi, 145: "Ma sendo tutte le cose degli uomini in moto, e non potendo stare salde, conviene che le salghino o che le scendino, e a molte cose che la ragione non t'induce, t'induce la necessità" ("But since all human affairs are in motion and never remain fixed, they must either rise or fall, and many things that reason does not impel you to do, necessity does").

cetto non sarebbe buono; ma, perché sono tristi e non la osservareb-
bano a te, tu etiam non l'hai ad osservare a loro" (*Pr*, XVIII, 73: "If all
men were good, this precept would not be good; but since they are
wicked and will not keep it [faith] with you, you likewise do not have to
keep it with them"). Although this quotation inverts the Golden Rule
and demonstrates Machiavelli's distance from Christianity's notions of
love, humility, and forgiveness, his emphasis on humans' wickedness
reveals his profound acceptance of at least one part of the Judaeo-
Christian world view.[16] For he clearly embraces the myth of the Fall, although in his interpretation of it, Adam's prideful sin in the Garden is
overshadowed by the competition between his sons and Cain's betrayal
and violent murder of Abel. Most revealingly, in his poem "Dell'ambizione" he claims that ambition and avarice entered the world together
when humans were created, and that without them we would still enjoy
our original, happy state (*SL*, 319, ll. 13-15). Although it does mention
Adam's rebellion briefly (319, ll. 20-21), the poem rushes forward to
focus on Cain and Abel, who lived in peace until the envious stars sent
ambition and avarice to bring war and destroy concord (319-20, ll. 22-45).
Even in a time when the general level of poverty made those desires
ridiculous, Cain was nevertheless moved by them to commit the first
murder (320-21, ll. 46-60). Since then, the seed he planted has grown
until now it causes the rise and fall of realms and the pathetic variations
of our mortal condition (321, ll. 61-66). At the start of history, then,
Machiavelli situates a deed of violence prompted by ambition and avarice, and the result is that since that time, as the wise Romans knew, life
is war (*Pr*, III, 21).[17]

Machiavelli's myth of the Fall identifies a most important characteristic of human beings: their stunning capacity for violence and destruction. Such a capacity may have been hinted at in *La mandragola*,
appearing in such different forms as Nicia's bullying of his social inferiors and Callimaco's contemplation of raping Lucrezia. but in the political and historical works it emerges full-blown in all its glory. Thus *Il
principe* and the *Discorsi* offer countless examples of bloody assassinations, brutal murders, and devastating wars in which human beings
seem all too often to rejoice, just as the people of Cesena take grim sat-

---

[16]See n. 13 above.
[17]Fleisher summarizes all of this in "A Passion for Politics," p. 129: "The human condition, then, is one of: 1) discontent; 2) desire for the means to satisfy desires; 3) domination of animo by these powerful desires and not by reason; 4) competition or conflict
with others for these means; 5) scarcity and not abundance by virtue of the nature of
human desire."

isfaction at the sight of the mutilated body of Remirro de Orco lying in their town square (see also *Ist*, II, xxxiv, 191).

Human beings' capacity for mindless, savage, unpredictable violence is a major preoccupation of the *Istorie fiorentine*. As Machiavelli records instance after instance of violence perpetrated primarily, though not exclusively, by his fellow Florentines and Tuscans, he focuses repeatedly on the tearing and mutilation of the human body until that action becomes a symbol of the explosive potential for destruction lying dormant in everyone. Thus he describes how the Bianchi-Neri conflict began in Pistoia when the father of a young man who was wounded slightly in a scuffle seizes the assailant, who has come to apologize, and has the young man's hand cut off in retaliation (II, xvi, 160-61). Later Machiavelli dramatically documents the cannibalistic savagery of the Florentines, who, in throwing off the despotic rule of the Duke of Athens, literalize the metaphor used by Machiavelli's plebeian spokesman during the Ciompi Revolt when he said that in this world, "gli uomini mangiono l'uno l'altro" (III, xiii, 238: "men eat one another"). Thus when the Florentines revolt against the duke, the murder of two of his henchmen becomes a horrific feeding frenzy: "Quelli che non poterono ferirgli vivi gli ferirono morti, né saziati di straziarli col ferro, con le mani e con i denti gli laceravono" (II, xxxvii, 203: "Those who could not wound them alive wounded them dead, and not satiated with using swords to cut them apart, ripped them with their hands and their teeth"). Still later in the *Istorie*, Machiavelli tells that during the Ciompi Revolt a certain ser Nuto, who had been designated *bargello* or sheriff by the nobles, was dragged by a mob to the gallows, hanged there by one leg, and violently torn apart until nothing remained of him "altro che il piede" (III, xvi, 245: "other than the foot"). Such fearsome violence was not confined to Florence and Tuscany; in a later episode Machiavelli describes how the people of Genoa, rebelling against the rule of Milan, caught the old Milanese governor, killed him, cut him up, and dragged the pieces of his body about the city (V, vii, 336-37).

The violence and mutilation mount in a crescendo during the course of the *Istorie*, reaching an almost apocalyptic climax near the work's end with the defeat of the Pazzi conspiracy against Giuliano and Lorenzo de' Medici. Although the men who attacked and killed Giuliano escaped temporarily, the two assassins who attacked Lorenzo and failed were almost immediately caught, killed, and then dragged about the city (VIII, v, 519). Later, when the people, who were largely partisans of the Medici, had defeated the entire party of the conspirators, they cut them up, "e le membra de' morti, o sopra le punte delle armi fitte o per la città strascinate si vedevano" (VIII, ix, 522: "and the pieces of the bodies of the dead were seen either stuck on the points of weapons or being dragged about the city"). Finally, after Jacopo Pazzi, the head of the family, had been executed, the mob took his body from his ancestral tomb and buried it in unconsecrated ground near the walls of the city, then dug it up, dragged it naked to the Arno, and heaved it into the swollen waters (523). The Pazzi conspiracy, with its combination of deceit and murder and its bloody aftermath, thus demonstrates Machiavelli's unblinking recognition of the savagery in human beings. It constitutes a final indication that for him the world of history is a chaos of force and fraud, of treachery, murder, and war, all symbolized by the barbarous mutilation of the human body. It is noteworthy that in the *Istorie fiorentine*, Machiavelli never presents human beings as engaging in ordinary occupations or enjoying leisure time or play, and that holidays and festivities are mentioned not because they had sacred associations or were moments of celebration but because they were opportune occasions for political assassination and rebellion. The *Istorie fiorentine* vividly documents Machiavelli's conviction that man is a creature who desires — and who kills.

Both princes and people in Machiavelli's political and historical works share one final but crucial trait — imagination. In general, Machiavelli insists on the primary role of imagination in human action and on the uniqueness of the imagination of each individual. In a famous letter to Piero Soderini, explaining how a single tactic can have diametrically opposed results while different ones can achieve a single end, he begins by stressing the diversity of men and, in particular, of their imaginations:

> Credo che come la natura ha fatto all'huomo diverso volto, cosí gli habbia fatto diverso ingegno et diversa fantasia. Da questo nasce che ciascuno secondo lo ingegno et fantasia sua si governa. [#119, 230]

> I believe that as nature has fashioned different faces for men, so it has given them different minds and imaginations. From this arises that each one governs himself according to his mind and imagination.

Hence, because times and circumstances vary continually but each man has a particular, determined *ingegno* and *fantasia* that generate his distinctive "modo del procedere," sometimes he will succeed and sometimes fail.[18] In *Il principe* Machiavelli explains the successes and failures

[18]He also identifies men's interior dispositions with the terms *la natura* and *la disposizione*; see K. R. Minogue, "Theatricality and Politics: Machiavelli's Concept of Fantasia," in *The Morality of Politics*, ed. Bhikha Parekh and R. N. Backi (London: George Allen & Unwin, 1972), p. 152.

of princes largely in terms of this principle: "Credo, ancora, che sia felice quello che riscontra el modo del procedere suo con le qualità de' tempi; e similmente sia infelice quello che con il procedere suo si discordano e' tempi" (xxv, 99: "I believe also that he is successful who fits his mode of proceeding to the qualities of the times; and similarly, he is unsuccessful when the times do not fit his mode"). Machiavelli goes on to analyze the career of Julius II, whose violent and impetuous nature suited the times, but who would have failed if they had been different, for he, like most men, would never have "deviato da quelli modi a' quali la natura lo inclinava (*Pr*, xxv, 101: "deviated from those modes to which nature inclined him"). Machiavelli concludes that even the most flexible and adaptable prince will inevitably fail at one moment or another to suit his "modo del procedere" to the times and so will eventually go down to defeat. Imagination is thus clearly as powerful in human beings as are desire and the urge to violence, and like them, it constitutes an ultimate limit to human freedom.

Although Machiavelli's prince and people share the basic characteristics of desire, violence, and imagination, their mentalities are nevertheless as distinct as those of the confidence men and dupes in *La mandragola*. At the simplest level, they have different abilities to see, as was implied in the passage from the *Discorsi* cited earlier in which the people were praised for their ability to see particulars, princes for theirs to see farther and wider (I, xlvii, 237-40). Usually, however, Machiavelli emphasizes the *popolo*'s inability to spot its own true interests and the ease with which it is deceived by false appearances (*Disc*, I, liii, 249-52). By contrast, the prince is a clever fox who sees the traps laid for him (*Pr*, xviii, 72). In general, Machiavelli says that the prince sees more deeply into things than the *popolo* does, and so is not taken in by "quello che pare" (*Pr*, xviii, 74: "that which seems").

The distinction between the prince's and the *popolo*'s vision is based on a fundamental assumption that runs through all of Machiavelli's works: the world is a place of appearances and illusions that obscure and displace realities. In this connection, Machiavelli's language in the following quotation is suggestive:

> Colui che desidera o che vuole riformare uno stato d'una città, a volere che sia accetto e poterlo con satisfazione di ciascuno mantenere, è necessitato a ritenere *l'ombra* almanco de' modi antichi, acciò che a popoli non paia avere mutato ordine, ancorché in fatto gli ordini nuovi fussero al tutto alieni dai passati; perché lo universale degli uomini *si pascono* cosí di quel che pare come di quello che è: anzi molte volte si muovono piú per le cose che paiono che per quelle che sono. [*Disc*, I, xxv, 192; my emphasis]

> He who desires or wants to reform a government of a city and wants it to
> be accepted and maintained to the satisfaction of all must necessarily
> retain at least *the shadow* of ancient modes so that to the people it does
> not seem to have changed its basic institutions, although in fact its new
> institutions were entirely different from the old. For the general run of
> men *feed themselves* on that which seems as much as on that which is; in
> fact, frequently they are moved more by things that seem than by those
> that are.

Here Machiavelli sees people living in a world of illusions which nourishes them so that they ultimately become dependent on those illusions
for their lives, more taken with them than with realities. Moreover, the
world of illusions is imagined as a shadow world, a place of darkness
which recalls Plato's cave, an image that clearly harmonizes with that
of blindness and sight found throughout Machiavelli's texts. This realm
of darkness and opacity constitutes a large limit for human beings, and
it is to this notion, or something like it, that Machiavelli refers when he
speaks at times of fortune as the ultimate power in the world of history.
Unable to see through the darkness, the vast majority of people in
Machiavelli's works are easily taken in by appearances, from the Orsini,
who are deceived by Cesare Borgia's gifts and assurances (*Pr*, vii, 36;
SP, 43-44), through the Poggio family in Lucca, who rebelled against
Castruccio Castracani and then were foolishly persuaded to place themselves in his hands (*CC*, 20-21), to the people of Florence, who were
gulled by the Medici's strategy of respecting the traditional forms of republican government while really ruling as autocrats (*Ist*, vii, v, 459; viii,
x, 527). In the world of shadows, it is easy to be misled by appearances,
to be attracted to what seems good and useful without realizing it will
ultimately be destructive (*Disc*, i, liii, 250). Hence all the more praise
must be given to those Machiavellian princes who see at least some light
through the illusions about them.

Although the darkness of the world obstructs human beings' vision,
Machiavelli insists that the blindness that afflicts most of them comes
from within, not without. Just as writers of *novelle* from Boccaccio on
gave the dupe's inordinate appetites almost as much responsibility for
the tricks played on him as the confidence man's guile, so Machiavelli
repeatedly points out that the strong force of desire within human beings
blinds them to the illusions of the world and the treachery of their fellows. Thus the Roman people, he says in the *Discorsi*, foolishly subjected themselves to Appius Claudius because because their "eccessiva
voglia . . . gli acceco in modo che concorsono in tale disordine" (i, xl,
229: "excessive desire . . . blinded them so that they rushed into that

disorder"). Similarly, later in the same work he remarks that military leaders are often taken in by apparent mistakes made by their enemy because their desire to win blinds ("acceca") them (III, xlviii, 503). Although he never uses *cieco* ("blind") when discussing the hapless Niccolò Piccinino's ultimate betrayal at the hands of Filippo Visconti, the way he described it places the blame largely on Piccinino's desire, which impedes his understanding: when Visconti calls him out of the field to discuss "cose importantissime," Piccinino should have known better, but, "cupido di intenderle, abbandonò per uno incerto bene una certa vittoria" (*Ist*, VI, viii, 399: "eager to hear them, he abandoned for an uncertain good a certain victory"). In all of these examples—and more could be added (see *Disc*, I, liii, 250; II, xxi, 341; III, xxviii, 464)— Machiavelli clearly places the blame for people's undoing on their own shoulders, even in situations in which one might be tempted to exonerate them. For instance, he suggests, perhaps somewhat unfairly, that people who open their gates to a new prince because they are eager to better their lot deceive themselves and will find themselves bitterly disappointed in the end (*Pr*, III, 17). As Machiavelli sees it, their inability to control their desires and passions makes humans pathetic and ridiculous, as it does Francesco de' Pazzi, whose killing of Giuliano de' Medici constitutes a brutal, but also grimly comic, example of the force of passion in the *Istorie*. For after having cleverly engaged Giuliano in small talk all the way to the church where he was to be slain, Francesco not only threw himself down on the already fatally wounded body of his enemy, stabbing it repeadedly, but, "obcecato da quel furore che lo portava, se medesimo in una gamba gravemente offese" (VIII, v, 518-19: "blinded by the fury that possessed him, seriously wounded himself in the leg").

If most human beings, blinded by their overwhelming desires, wound themselves in the leg, Machiavelli's princes are distinguished by their ability to master the passions seething within them. The following quotation from the *Discorsi*, which is attributed to Ferdinand II of Naples, illuminates the differences between the prince and the *popolo* on this score.

Gli uomini . . . spesso fanno come certi minori uccelli di rapina, ne' quali è tanto desiderio di conseguire la loro preda, a che la natura gl'incita, che non sentono uno altro maggiore uccello che sia loro sopra per ammazzarli. [*Disc*, I, xl, 229]

Men often act . . . like certain small birds of prey, in which the desire to attain their prey is so strong, to which nature incites them, that they do not sense another larger bird that is over them in order to slay them.

This quotation suggests that although all human beings are urged on by the same predatory nature, the prince has a clearer, larger vision than the mass of men, a grandeur or stature that raises him above them. Moreover, if Machiavelli never directly states that the prince enjoys a relative freedom from and control over his desires, he does at least suggest it indirectly when he presents examples of princes who fail, as most seem to do sooner or later. Thus he describes how the Duke of Athens defeats himself through his lust for women (*Ist*, II, xxxvi, 197), how Castruccio Castracani's ambition leads him to overextend his realm, and how the hapless Niccolò Piccinino, an extremely cunning condottiere, finally fails to resist the lure that Filippo Visconti holds out to him.

If the prince is superior to the *popolo* by virtue of his relative control of desire, he is also superior because he enjoys a complex freedom the *popolo* cannot match. Related to the latter's subjection to desire is its almost total immersion in the present: "Li uomini sono molto piú presi dalle cose presenti che dalle passate, e quando nelle presenti truovono il bene, vi si godono e non cercano altro" (*Pr*, XXIV, 97: "Men are much more taken by present things than by those of the past, and when they find the good in present things, they enjoy it then and do not search elsewhere"). Like little birds of prey, they enjoy the food before them, taking every day for itself, never believing the unexpected can occur (*Let*, #135, 280).[19] Their memory is short, so that they forget the causes of innovations in time as they readjust to a new present. Because of their immersion in the present and their lack of a wide acquaintance with human affairs through either travel or reading, they are always being deceived by accidental happenings (*Disc*, II, xxii, 343), always exposed to manipulation by others: "Sono tanto semplici li uomini, e tanto obediscano alle necessità presenti, che colui che inganna troverrà sempre chi si lascerà ingannare" (*Pr*, XVIII, 73: "Men are so simple and so obedient to present necessities that he who deceives will always find someone who will let himself be deceived"). Most human beings are thus like Nicia, who knows little but the present world in which he lives.

Machiavelli's insistence on humans' immersion in the present may seem to contradict his equal insistence that they dwell on past injuries and hold grudges. Even Nicia's memory burns when he recollects how his fellow Florentines have humiliated him. Nevertheless, this contradiction may be only apparent, for Machiavelli seems to be pointing to a general incapacity in most people to make their remembered dissatisfactions the basis for rational plans. Although they are capable of sporadic outbreaks of violence in pursuit of vengeance, they are generally

---

[19] Ibid., p. 158.

absorbed in the affairs of the present, reluctant to engage in conspiracies that require long-range planning. By contrast, Machiavelli's prince enjoys a decided detachment from the present and an ability to plan out the future. Like Callimaco and Ligurio, he has traveled widely both in fact and through the study of geography, and he has studied history and can analyze events in a discriminating fashion (*Pr*, XIV, 64). He has thus precisely the necessary distance from the present not simply to recall the past with rational clarity but to project a future on the basis of that past. He is, in Machiavelli's conception, truly prudent and can manipulate the rest of humanity who are not.[20]

If most human beings are driven by almost uncontrollable desires, they are equally tyrannized by custom, by the usages, traditions, and conventions of their social world. They resemble Nicia, who does not want to change his routines by going to the baths and who totally accepts the social system of Florence even though he suffers from its inequities and prejudices. For Machiavelli, most human beings *are* their habits; they cannot think of changing them, just as the French, for instance, accustomed to winning with Swiss mercenaries, assume they cannot do so without them (*Pr*, XIII, 60). Consequently, people fiercely resist innovative changes in the social order (*Disc*, I, Proemio, 123), believe in innovations only when they are no longer new (*Disc*, I, ii, 130; II, xix, 333-34), and cling to the customary even when it is to their disadvantage to do so, as when Florentines through habit remained faithful to the Medici after Cosimo's death (*Ist*, VII, xxiv, 489). Because dramatic changes in customs and traditions are so traumatic for most people, Machiavelli concludes that it is easier for a hereditary monarch to keep his throne than for a new ruler to do so (*Pr*, II, 16), and he repeatedly advises his prince to maintain the customs, laws, and taxes of a newly conquered realm, eliminating only the old rulers, and doing that quickly (*Pr*, III, 18; VIII, 44). As he says in the passage of the *Discorsi* cited earlier, when a prince reforms a state, he should keep at least a shadow ("ombra") of ancient modes, "acciò che a' popoli non paia avere mutato ordine" (*Disc*, I, xxv, 192: "so that it does not appear to the people to have changed its basic order"). So powerful is the hold of custom on human beings that they will adapt to almost any social order once it has existed for a while (*Pr*, V, 28-29).[21]

[20] Ibid., p. 154.
[21] Although Machiavelli may be right in principle, Florence did in fact accept the Medici as absolute rulers despite a long tradition of republican freedom. Machiavelli's warning to the Medici that they could not impose absolute rule on Florence in his "Ai Palleschi" (1512) was, from the Medici point of view, wisely ignored.

Of course, Machiavelli does recognize that people sometimes want change. The very pressure of desire renders them always at least slightly dissatisfied with things as they are, always ready to improve their situation, always filled with hopes for a golden future (*Pr*, III, 17). What they really want, however, is not fundamental changes in institutions and social structures but quantitative improvements (i.e., more and better "roba"), changes that bring the world more perfectly into conformity with their desires. Hoping for such changes, Machiavelli sardonically concludes, they are usually disappointed (ibid.).

Machiavelli stresses that the people's subjection to custom is one of the most important reasons that clever confidence men can manipulate them so easily. To dominate the inhabitants of a conquered country, he says, it is merely necessary for a ruler not to appear to rule and to allow the people to keep their own laws and traditions; like so many hapless children, they will then be ready to throw themselves in his lap (*Disc*, II, xxi, 341). The people, he says with bitter humor in the *Discorsi*, is a brute animal, and if it has been kept in a cage for a long while and is then suddenly freed, it will not know how to adapt to its new circumstances and will become "preda del primo che cerca rincatenarlo" (I, xvi, 173: "prey to the first person who seeks to put it back in its cage"). Nevertheless, although Machiavelli insists that human beings are slaves to custom, he also insists with equal vehemence that they are animated by powerful egocentric drives, so that although they are capable of adapting to practically any conceivable social order, the prince cannot count on their doing so. To gain and hold a state, he has a strong ally in custom, but he must also blunt the egocentric drives of his subjects, and for that, as we shall see, he must have recourse to force.

Free not only from the pressure of custom and tradition, the prince enjoys a more profound and disturbing freedom, a freedom from allegiance to the conventional moral system of his society. This does not mean, as critics have argued since the Renaissance, that Machiavelli is advocating evil *tout court*,[22] but rather that he sees the different spheres of life, the private and the public, the ethical and the political, as estranged and discontinuous.[23] What is politically good and necessary, such as the ruthless murder of all holdovers from a preceding regime, is

[22]The most forceful advocate of this position is Leo Strauss. See his *Thoughts on Machiavelli* (Glencoe, Ill.: Free Press, 1958).
[23]Sheldon S. Wolin, "The Economy of Violence," in Niccolò Machiavelli, *The Prince*, ed. and trans. Robert M. Adams (New York: Norton, 1977), p. 193; Neal Wood, "Machiavelli's Humanism of Action," in *The Political Calculus: Essays on Machiavelli's Philosophy*, ed. Anthony Parel (Toronto: University of Toronto Press, 1972), p. 47; Brayton Polka, "Commentary," in *Machiavelli and the Nature of Political Thought*, ed. Fleisher, p. 181; and Mazzeo, *Renaissance and Revolution*, p. 72.

by traditional morality wicked and pernicious. Whether one interprets Machiavelli as saying that politics requires the perpetration of evil or constitutes a separate "moral" system, in either case he is stressing the prince's ability to switch systems freely.[24] This ability allows the prince to plan the future, to concoct elaborate schemes of political conquest without being sidetracked by moral considerations, and to use violence as an instrument of policy whenever he feels it is necessary to do so. Needless to say, the *popolo* can do nothing of the sort.

The prince resembles folk tricksters and the *beffatori* of Boccaccio and other *novella* writers in that he dwells in an amoral no-man's-land without ethical imperatives. He exists in the free space between or among systems, always on the threshold between politics and morality, able to move in any direction. Thus he is free to use cruelty or piety toward his subjects as circumstances dictate (*Pr*, xvii, 68–69); adjusting quickly to every variation of fortune, he cleaves to the good if he can but enters into evil when he must (*Pr*, xviii, 73–74). The prince actually differs somewhat from many folk tricksters and literary *beffatori* in that his amorality is less a condition of his being than a conscious intellectual position. In other words, whereas tricksters and *beffatori* normally act in an amoral manner without thinking about the moral consequences, the prince always consciously chooses to abandon traditional morality whenever necessary in the political arena. In this regard, he resembles Callimaco in *La mandragola*, who consciously brooded about hell and the absurdity of his desires. Of course Callimaco's meditation was exaggerated, comic, and partly tongue-in-cheek, whereas the prince's is always in deadly earnest.

The prince's consciousness of moral choice also separates him from the people, for they carry out the dictates of their morality just as mechanically as they adhere to the rules of custom and tradition. Although Machiavelli does not dwell at length on most humans' blind subservience to conventional morality, he implies it when he remarks that an ideal prince, if he is to survive in a world of wicked individuals, has to distinguish himself from the people by *unlearning* that morality: "E necessario a uno principe, volendosi mantenere, imparare a potere essere non buono, et usarlo e non usare secondo la necessità" (*Pr*, xv, 65: "It is necessary for a prince who wants to maintain his position to learn not to be good, and to use and not use that ability according to neces-

[24]Isaiah Berlin, "The Originality of Machiavelli," in *Studies on Machiavelli*, ed. Myron P. Gilmore (Florence: Sansoni, 1972), pp. 147–206. Machiavelli never claims a higher goodness for those who serve the state by doing immoral deeds; he merely claims for them a political goodness. On this point, see also John Plamenatz, "In Search of Machiavellian *Virtù*," in *Political Calculus*, ed. Parel, p. 170.

sity"). Machiavelli also indicates the power of traditional morality over most people's minds when he complains that those who wish to be tyrants usually do not have the courage of their convictions – or of their desires: halfheartedly wicked, they inevitably wind up losing their realms (*Disc*, I, xxvi–xxvii, 193–95). On this score he attacks Piero Soderini because, to maintain Florence as a republic, he was not willing to flout conventional morality and kill the "sons of Brutus," that is, those Florentine aristocrats opposed to republican rule (*Disc*, III, iii, 386–87). By contrast, he admires the coolness of Francesco and Bernardo de' Pazzi, who entertained Giuliano de' Medici with idle chatter on his way to the church where they would kill him, whereas most men would have been paralyzed by moral scruples in such a situation (*Ist*, VIII, v, 518).

Since Machiavelli insists on human beings' innate wickedness and violence, his simultaneous insistence on their adherence to conventional morality may seem contradictory. But in both cases he is talking about automatic behavior: the morality people adhere to is habit, reflex action, not conscious choice, just as their explosions of evil are instinctual rather than rational and calculated. In this regard, they resemble Messer Nicia, for whom murder and a pious regard for social titles were equally compelling and equally mechanical. In the prince, by contrast, Machiavelli presents a carefully calculated, fully conscious setting aside of morality and an indulgence in violence, betrayal, and murder whenever they are necessary to satisfy his political ends.

Thanks to his freedom from custom and morality, the prince alone is capable of being a true innovator, that is, of founding a state or of reordering one by taking it back to its origins once it has grown corrupt.[25] The *popolo*, insists Machiavelli, cannot form itself into a state or reorder a corrupt one, for to do so requires the use of "grandissimi straordinari, i quali pochi sanno o vogliono usare" (*Disc*, I, xvii, 179: "extraordinary means, which few know how or want to use").[26] As J. H. Whitfield has shown, Machiavelli puns here: most men live totally within the framework created by the constitution or ordinary arrangement ("modi ordinarii") of their state; while only the prince has the detachment needed to do the extraordinary ("lo straordinario") (*Disc*, I,

---

[25]See J. G. A. Pocock, "Custom and Grace, Form and Matter: An Approach to Machiavelli's Concept of Innovation," in *Machiavelli and the Nature of Political Thought*, ed. Fleisher, p. 172.

[26]See Gennaro Sasso, *Niccolò Machiavelli: Storia del suo pensiero politico* (Naples: Istituto italiano per gli studi storici, 1958), pp. 349, 418. In the *Istorie fiorentine*, Machiavelli stresses that it is easier to preserve a good order than to find one out and then impose it on the state (III, xi, 233).

xviii, 182).[27] When he discusses conspiracies, Machiavelli comments that most human beings make many errors of judgment in such actions, which are by their natures extraordinary, and he similarly notes how difficult it is for conspirators to adapt to unforeseen events as they carry their plots forward (*Disc*, III, vi, 399, 402). By contrast, in creating a new political order, the prince reveals himself as a master of the extraordinary, prepared to change absolutely everything—laws and rulers, class structures, even the locations of cities (*Disc*, I, xxvi, 193–94). Moreover, since the *popolo* can normally be expected to resist such basic innovations, the institution of "lo straordinario" usually necessitates violence if the people are to be brought to accept it (see *Disc*, I, xviii, 182; xxxiv, 210–11). Machiavelli argues that the renewal of the state is not inevitably bloody, however, for the prince can sometimes be a leader to imitate rather than a savage reformer (*Disc*, III, i, 382), and he also insists that the people's conservative adherence to custom and the tendency of their many voices to balance each other will maintain the form of a state far better than a prince will, because he cannot control his passions and desires absolutely at all times (see *Disc*, I, lviii, 264; lix, 268; III, ix, 417; xvii, 439; xxxiv, 478). Nevertheless, Machiavelli concludes that though the vast majority of human beings may be better than the prince at preserving the status quo—and hence that a republican form of government is to be preferred to a principality—the people cannot match the prince as a social innovator (*Disc*, I, xxxix, 223).

In his ability to create new social and political institutions, the prince resembles trickster figures in general, from mythic heroes to sophisticated swindlers in Italian Renaissance *novelle*, who are associated not just with fraud but with social recreation, albeit sometimes indirectly.[28] In their self-serving deception of others, they may subvert and parody the social order, but their moral freedom simultaneously allows them to offer glimpses of alternative systems of social norms and behaviors or at least to allow for the possibility of imagining them. Folk tricksters are often the sources of basic social institutions and even biological practices, and a *beffatore* such as Boccaccio's Ciappelletto, who hoodwinks the faithful, also creates a new saint for them even while he is indirectly giving those who see through his fraud a new vision of the very institution of sainthood, thereby allowing for the possibility of its transfor-

---

[27]J. H. Whitfield, *Discourses on Machiavelli* (Cambridge: W. Heffer, 1969), pp. 146–48.
[28]In *Fortune Is a Woman: Gender and Politics in the Thought of Niccolò Machiavelli* (Berkeley: University of California Press, 1984), pp. 25–79, Hanna F. Pitkin has argued that the prince's behavior makes him at least two distinct figures, the deceiving trickster and the founder of states, but as I argued in Chapter 1, folk tricksters and Renaissance confidence men typically embrace both behaviors.

mation. In this tradition, then, the foxlike trickery and the capacity for founding states which Machiavelli assigns to his prince are not unconnected behaviors; they are simply different expressions of his fundamental freedom. Like the trickster, he is a walking paradox: at once satirist and creator, exploiter and benefactor, demon and deity.

If the prince and the *popolo* differ in their relationship to desire, custom, and morality, they also differ profoundly in their basic perception of social life, the prince grasping fully what the *popolo* does not: the world is a place of illusion, a theater. This metaphor has less prominence in Machiavelli's political and historical works than in *La mandragola*. In fact, Machiavelli never directly employs the world-as-theater commonplace in those works, and although he refers to Cesare Borgia's treatment of Remirro de Orco as creating a ferocious "spettaculo" for the people of Cesena, he uses that word only a few times. His spokesman in the *Arte della guerra* praises military exercises as creating a "bello spettacolo" for youth (1, 354), and in the *Istorie fiorentine* he tells us that the severed head of the Florentine commander Baldaccio d'Anghiari, murdered by the thugs of the gonfaloniere Bartolomeo Orlandini, was left in the piazza as a "spettaculo" for the people to gaze on (VI, vii, 397). Finally, in the *Discorsi*, Machiavelli describes how the Samnites instilled courage in their soldiers by means of a terrifying "spettacolo" (1, xv, 172): those who refused to swear allegiance were publicly slaughtered before the assembled army. These four occurrences of the word *spettacolo* suggest that Machiavelli uses it to refer to specially staged incidents, not to define the bulk of reality as theater.

Nevertheless, we find many indirect indications in the political and historical works that Machiavelli does generally conceive of social life in such terms. He repeatedly emphasizes the way that princes manipulate the people through pomp and splendor, describing how such performances can stop a conspiracy dead in its tracks (*Disc*, III, vi, 403) and how the mere appearance of gravity and dignity can cow a mob (*Disc*, I, xiii, 168; liii, 249; liv, 252). Moreover, Machiavelli directly and indirectly presents his princes as actors. In *Il principe* he stresses the need for the prince to appear to have such virtues as liberality and religiosity, and he insists in a famous passage that the prince must know how to use "la persona della golpe e del lione" (xIx, 80: "the persona [or role, or mask] of the fox and the lion"), thereby implying that since all of his activity must involve either foxlike fraud or lionlike force, social life for the prince must be a continuous masquerade. In the *Discorsi* he cites a passage from Livy referring to Appius Claudius's ability to wear a mask (1, xl, 226), and he later says that humanity is a "parte" people desire to see in their leaders (III, xx, 445). Even when Machiavelli does not directly label his princes actors, he praises them for their histrionic ability, as when Ferdinand of Aragon is celebrated for using religion as a "mantello" or cloak for his political aims (*Pr*, xxi, 89-90). And he describes how Castruccio Castracani engaged in a wonderfuly egocentric bit of theater. When he was made a Roman senator out of gratitude for his quelling of an uprising in the city, he took his office "con grandissima pompa," dressing up in a brocaded toga "con lettere dinanzi che dicevano: *Egli è quel che Dio vuole*; e di dietro dicevano *E' sarà quel che Dio vorrà*" (*CC*, 24: "with letters on the front which said, 'He is the one God wants,' and others behind which said, 'He will be the one God will want'").

In all these examples, Machiavelli's princes are the active agents, the people their largely passive audience. For the latter, as for Nicia in *La mandragola*, social life is accepted as fact, or as having only limited spheres in which fairly obvious forms of deception may operate. By contrast, Machiavelli's princes recognize that social life is theater, a set of manipulable fictions through which they can control others and ensure their own power. They are even urged at periodic intervals to stage spectacles, to "tenere occupati e' populi con le feste e spettaculi" (*Pr*, xxi, 93: "keep the people occupied with festivities and spectacles"), and in the *Istorie fiorentine* Machiavelli notes that Florentine leaders, and especially the Medici, used spectacles and festivities to divert the people and keep them from thoughts of rebellion (vii, xii, 470-71; xxi, 485-86; viii, xxxvi, 575). Realizing that life is spectacle and acting on that insight, Machiavelli's princes clearly resemble Ligurio and Callimaco; it should hardly be surprising that they would enjoy the same enormous advantage over the *popolo* that that pair of characters did over Nicia in Machiavelli's comedy.

An actor and director staging spectacles in the great theater of the world, the prince is likewise a superb rhetorician; in fact, to say he is the first is really to say he is the second as well. Rhetoric, regarded with suspicion as a highly ambiguous art since Plato, does not aim at reaching transcendent truth, but contentedly operates in the realm of opinion, assuming always that the world is a place of illusions and that words and things are necessarily disjunctive. These are precisely the assumptions Machiavelli makes. Not only does he recognize the illusory quality of experience, but he stresses repeatedly the gap between language and the world. Thus he claims that Caesar would have been a dictator even if the word did not exist (*Disc*, i, xxxiv, 209), and he has his plebeian spokesman in the Ciompi Revolt spout Machiavellian philosophy by saying that all rulers have used force and fraud to gain their positions and then sanctified them with a "falso titolo" (*Ist*, iii, xiii, 238: "false title").

In both cases, Machiavelli suggests the insubstantial character of language, its inferior reality in comparison with things. He reiterates this judgment elsewhere in the *Discorsi* when he says that a weak and disorderly army, put to flight by mere words, has been moved by "vento" (III, xiv, 431: "wind"). Yet wind, as Machiavelli well knows, can have enormous force, and insubstantial words and phrases have in fact routed entire armies. As *La mandragola* reveals, words, no matter how ungrounded in reality they may be, do contain the power to move human beings.

Machiavelli stresses not only the power of language but also the ambiguity of that power. He notes with praise at one point that eloquent language can play a positive role in making the truth accessible even to the *popolo*.[29] Using characteristically vivid images, he crystallizes this insight into their responsiveness to words by contrasting it with the tyrant's imperviousness:

> A un popolo licenzioso e tumultuario gli può da un uomo buono essere parlato, e facilmente può essere ridotto nella via buona; a un principe cattivo non è alcuno che possa parlare né vi è altro rimedio che il ferro. [*Disc*, I, lviii, 265–66]

> A licentious and tumultuous people can be spoken to by a good man and can easily be led back to the good way; to a wicked prince there is no one who can speak, nor is there any remedy but the sword.

More typically, however, Machiavelli insists on the power of language to deceive. Thus elsewhere he recounts at some length that the Roman leaders, having removed their kings but needing someone to perform an animal sacrifice that the kings used to do, created a "Re Sacrificulo," thus deceiving the people into thinking that their customary life had not changed merely because the names of things remained more or less the same. Machiavelli generalizes about such practices: anyone who wants to innovate, to change an old, established mode of existence in a city ("un antico vivere in una città"), should make his alterations retain as much of the old modes as possible. In particular, he should keep the old

[29]Machiavelli, however, qualifies his assertion that the people can understand the truth in the following passage: "E quando queste opinioni fossero false e' vi è il rimedio delle concioni, che surga qualche uomo da bene che orando dimostri loro come ei s'ingannano; e li popoli, come dice Tullio, benché siano ignoranti sono capaci della verità, e facilmente cedano quando da uomo degno di fede è detto loro il vero" (*Disc*, I, iv, 138: "And although these opinions were false, there is a remedy in public discussions in which some good man rising up and speaking may show them how they are deceived, and the people, as Cicero says, although ignorant, are capable of the truth and easily yield when a man worthy of faith tells it to them").

name, so that "se i magistrati variano e di numero e d'autorità e di tempo, degli antichi . . . almeno ritenghino il nome" (*Disc*, I, xxv, 193: "if the magistrates vary in number and authority and length of service . . . at least they should retain the names of the old ones"). The heads of the various parties in Florence (the *sette*), Machiavelli observes, have learned this lesson about the ability of language to create a smokescreen to hide their ambitions: they aim at tyranny, he says, but "la intenzione e fine loro con un piatoso vocabolo adonestono" (*Ist*, III, v, 220: "they make their intention and end seem honest with a pious word"). Consequently, openness to manipulation by words indicates a praiseworthy accessibility to language which a tyrant does not share but also a large capacity to be duped by it, to be led to serve the interests of those who can use it for their own ends.

It is thus easy to see why rhetoric, the art of manipulating human beings by the use of words, should be indispensable to Machiavelli's princely confidence man, and why Machiavelli should insist in a variety of ways that the prince must be an orator.[30] In the *Discorsi* he says that a military leader—and the prince must be such a leader—should possess the ability to use words to instill courage and determination in his troops (III, xxxiii, 475), a point he returns to in the *Arte dell guerra* (IV, 440-42). He ends the biography of Castruccio Castracani with a list of sayings to illustrate the man's mastery of language (*CC*, 36-40), and he does something similar, though more briefly, when he praises Cosimo de' Medici in the *Istorie fiorentine* (VII, vii, 461-62). Still later in that work, he recounts a speech Lorenzo de' Medici delivered to rouse the Florentines to defend themselves against the pope and the king of Naples, and he says that Lorenzo'a eloquence reduced his audience to tears (*Ist*, VIII, x, 525-28). Finally, Machiavelli's prince, enjoying a thorough mastery of language, must himself always remain beyond the magical power of words, as all the advice on counselors and flatterers in *Il principe* makes clear (XXII-XXIII, 93-96).

Machiavelli also identifies the prince as a rhetorician by using the important word *colore* and its verb form *colorire* over and over again to describe the prince's behavior. Thus he says that the prince must know how to "colorire" his ambitious nature by making it seem virtuous (*Pr*, XVIII, 73); he praises Septimus Severus as a sly fox who managed to persuade his troops to go to Rome under the "colore" of avenging the death of the emperor Pertinax (*Pr*, XIX, 81); he counsels that one should invent a "colore" to attack the ally of a third party with whom one wishes

[30]It should be remembered that Machiavelli himself was an *oratore*, that is, a diplomatic representative and negotiator whose task was to manipulate words and appearances to gain the confidence of others and use them for his own and his city's ends.

to go to war but does not wish to attack directly (*Disc*, II, ix, 301); he recounts how Castruccio Castracani invented "colori" to kill all his rivals who aspired to rule in Lucca (*CC*, 22); and he praises Francesco Sforza for knowing how to "colorire" his designs on Milan (*Ist*, VI, xvii, 411).[31] The word *colore* means in all these examples color, pretext, covering, or even deception, but it also has the common meaning in Renaissance Italian of rhetorical ornament.[32] Therefore, to say that the prince is a master of disguising his motives and acts by means of some "colore" or other is to identify him as a master rhetorician.

The prince's rhetorical ability extends to more than his command of words, however, for Machiavelli sees his entire being and activities as a rhetorical performance, a calculated display in which dress and actions are joined to speech.[33] If the wise prince uses a verbal "colore" to disguise his true purposes, he will, more profoundly, learn to "colorire" his very "natura" to do so (*Pr*, XVIII, 73).[34] This coloring of his nature is another way of saying, of course, that the prince is an actor-director-scriptwriter in the play of life, and he shapes his identity with care because he wishes to create an image for others. Machiavelli wants his prince to appear to have such traditional virtues as generosity, humanity, and religion, and especially "dignità" and "maestà." Throughout the *Discorsi* he stresses the powerful effect of the appearance of gravity, dignity, and grandeur: a certain Publius Ruberius, a "cittadino grave e di autorità" (I, xiii, 168: "citizen grave and possessing authority") was capable of reducing a disorderly *plebs* to obedience; the Roman Senate saved itself from a raging mob by shielding itself behind certain "vecchi ed estimati cittadini" (I, liii, 249: "old and esteemed citizens"); and he has an entire chapter on the subject of "quanta autorità abbi uno uomo grave a frenare una moltitudine concitata" (I, liv, 252: "how much authority a grave man has to stop an excited multitude"). A wise prince will thus work to maintain and enhance this image of gravity and maj-

[31]For additional examples of the words *colore* and *colorire*, see *Pr*, XVIII, 73; *Disc*, II, xxxii, 375; III, vi, 399; xii, 427; and *Let*, #3, 33.
[32]According to the *Grande dizionario della lingua italiana*, ed. Salvatore Battaglia (Turin: Unione Tipografico-Editrice Torinese, n.d.), this meaning goes back to Dante, Bandello, and Firenzuola.
[33]In one passage of the *Discorsi*, Machiavelli describes how Francesco Soderini, then bishop of Volterra, stopped a mob about to sack his family's home in Florence by means of the splendid presence he was able to create through dress and words. As soon as he heard the noise and saw the crowd, says Machiavelli, "messosi i piú onorevoli panni indosso, e di sopra il roccetto episcopale, si fece incontro a quegli armati e con la presenzia e con le parole gli fermò (I, liv, 253: "having put on his most honorable clothes and his bishop's chasuble over them, he approached the armed men and stopped them with his presence and his words").
[34]See Michael McCanles, "Machiavelli's *Principe* and the Textualization of History," *MLN* 97 (1982): 4.

esty. Felix Gilbert has noted that humanist treatises on the prince reflect Renaissance political reality in emphasizing the importance of displaying signs of power (*majestas, magnificentia*), so that in this case Machiavelli appears to adhere to humanist precedent.[35] Nevertheless, he is more clearly aware than the humanists that the display of majesty and magnificence is just that—a display, an image rhetorically manufactured to carry out an elaborate strategy of power.

More important than dignity and majesty, however, is an image of strength, controlled violence, and military success. In the twenty-first chapter of *Il principe*, devoted to the kind of esteem a prince ought to cultivate, Machiavelli opens by speaking in general terms of "grande imprese e . . . rari esempli" (89: "great undertakings and . . . rare examples"), but when he gets down to particulars, he focuses exclusively on the "reputazione" (90) that accrued to Ferdinand of Aragon from his military exploits. The power of a reputation for military valor and success is so great, Machiavelli observes in the *Discorsi*, that a victorious army, even though weakened by losses, will demoralize and thus easily defeat a stronger opponent (II, xxii, 344), and he notes in *Il principe* that as soon as Louis XII of France gained a reputation for military skill by taking Lombardy, a host of Italian city-states threw themselves at his feet (*Pr*, III, 22). Consequently, he stresses his princes' conscious recognition of the need for such a reputation and their energetic pursuit of it. Cesare Borgia, he notes, gained a useful reputation by defeating his enemies the Orsini and recognized how much greater his reputation was when he relied on his own troops than when he used mercenaries (*Pr*, VII, 36; XIII, 59), and Castruccio Castracani was acutely aware of the need to establish his reputation as a successful warrior (*CC*, 18). By contrast, Machiavelli observes that those princes who are not famed as men of force and military skill earn the scorn of their subjects and especially of their soldiers, and thus inevitably lose their realms (*Pr*, XIV, 62). A reputation for other virtues may aid a ruler, but a reputation for the successful use of force is absolutely essential.

As a military figure, Machiavelli's prince must be less a brilliant strategist than a warrior and a stern leader not averse to the use of violence when necessary—and violence not directed solely at the enemy. Recall the four examples cited earlier in which Machiavelli used the word *spettacolo*: from Cesare Borgia's treatment of Remirro de Orco through the murder of the Florentine commander Baldaccio d'Anghiari to the Samnites' slaying of soldiers who refused to swear alle-

[35]Felix Gilbert, "The Humanist Concept of the Prince and *The Prince* of Machiavelli," in Machiavelli, *The Prince*, ed. and trans. Adams, p. 158. (This article was originally published in *Journal of Modern History* 11 [1939]: 449–83.)

giance, they all involved princely leaders who slaughtered their own followers in bloody events staged to enhance their reputations with their own people or at least to intimidate their followers into obedience. Further, Machiavelli tells the prince not to fear the name of "crudele" ("cruel"); in fact, he ought to seek it out, provided he avoids real hatred, because without it an army could not be kept in order and a state would be difficult to manage (*Pr*, xv–xvii, 64–71). Machiavelli is sufficiently bothered by the question of whether cruelty or kindness works best for a leader that he discusses it in both *Il principe* and the *Discorsi*. Although he opts for cruelty in the first work, in general he does not resolve the dispute in the second. Nevertheless, since he praises Hannibal's cruelty without qualification in that work while noting that Scipio's kindness at one point led his troops in Spain to rebel (*Disc*, iii, xxi, 447), his preference for cruelty may be detected, even if the great prestige Scipio enjoyed among Machiavelli's humanist predecessors may have limited his criticism of the Roman general.[36] In short, then, Machiavelli wants his prince to be not just an astute commander and well-trained fighter but a compelling figure of force, creating spectacles of terror to discipline his followers.

Words may have a place in the creation of such spectacle, but words are not enough. Near the end of the *Discorsi* Machiavelli comments that family and associates may give a person a reputation, but that such a reputation is fragile; one based on deeds is far preferable (iii, xxxiv, 478–79). The deeds he praises here include giving laws to one's country and bringing accusations against malefactors. In general, however, the deeds he emphasizes throughout his political and historical works are those of consciously calculated violence rather than lawgiving. They are deeds in which words and verbal persuasion are supplemented — and at times even displaced — by spectacles of power in which the mute display of force persuades the audience to do the prince's will. They are evidence of Machiavelli's conviction that in the world of history, unlike the "ideal" world of comedy, fraud must include force and a rhetoric of words must sometimes yield to a rhetoric of violence.

To say that the prince is a rhetorician of violence is not to explain why he must be one. Machiavelli's political and historical works do, of course, suggest an answer to this question, which at first appears simple: violence persuades through intimidation and thus compels obedience. This answer emerges whenever Machiavelli considers the prince's alternative to violence — dependence on the love and devotion of his

[36] For a fine discussion of this issue, see Pitkin, *Fortune Is a Woman*, pp. 73–79.

subjects. Since Machiavelli sees the world as a place of continual combat, he concludes that it is best to operate on the assumption that all
human beings are one's enemies (*SP*, 58) and to rely as little as possible
on their faith or love.[37] Although their self-interest makes it easy to defeat them, for they do not trust one another and can thus be picked off
one by one (*Disc*, I, lvii, 260), to depend on their love is the height of
folly: "L'amore è tenuto da uno vinculo di obbligo, il quale, per essere
li uomini tristi, da ogni occasione di propria utilità è rotto" (*Pr*, XVII,
70: "Love is held by a chain of obligation, which, because men are
wicked, is broken on every occasion of their own self-interest"). But if
human beings cannot be trusted to love, they can be compelled to be
faithful (*Pr*, XXIV, 97), and the most effective and dependable way to
compel fidelity is through fear-inspiring spectacles of violence. Whereas
love is a weak chain, "il timore è tenuto da una paura di pena che non
ti abbandona mai" (*Pr*, XVII, 70: "fear is held by a dread of punishment
which never abandons you"). Cesare Borgia's decision to create a terrifying spectacle in the piazza at Cesena thus makes perfect sense as rhetoric; it is based on the simple proposition that as a means to gain and
maintain human beings' loyalty, nothing surpasses fear.

Yet the particular way in which Machiavelli has shaped this passage
reveals his conviction that more than a simple visceral reaction of fear,
no matter how powerful, is involved. Indeed, the very language that describes the killing of Remirro de Orco indicates that Machiavelli wants
his readers to see that the act does more than merely intimidate the people of Cesena, although it certainly does that. Strikingly, he never says
that Cesare Borgia sought to frighten the people of Cesena, but rather
"purgare li animi di quelli populi e guadagnarseli in tutto" (*Pr*, VII, 37:
"to purge their spirits and win them over wholly to himself"). Nor does
Machiavelli say that Borgia's spectacle terrified the citizens; rather he
claims that it rendered them at once both "satisfied and awed" ("satisfatti e stupidi"). These important details suggest that, as Machiavelli has
shaped this episode, Borgia's spectacle, albeit viscerally frightening,
aims to have — and does have — an effect on the citizens of Cesena which
looks more like ritual purification and religious conversion than sheer
terror. Further consideration of this brief but complex episode reveals
that purification and conversion are precisely the reactions involved.

The killing of Remirro de Orco, as Machiavelli imagines it, subverts
the normal processes of public executions in Renaissance Italy. Executions were almost always elaborate spectacles, political rituals designed

---

[37] See Dante Germino, "Machiavelli's Thoughts on the Psyche and Society," in *Political Calculus*, ed. Parel, pp. 62–63.

to impress the populace with the power of the authorities as they punished malefactors, heretics, and political opponents.[38] Although investigations and trials were carried out behind closed doors, executions were usually open to the people and the bodies of the executed were almost always publicly displayed. The condemned, especially if he were not noble, was often tortured before the people's eyes, drawn in a cart through the city, and finally dispatched in an impressively brutal ceremony. Werner Gundersheimer reports that more serious crimes in Ferrara were punished by decapitation, less serious ones by hanging, and to judge by Luca Landucci's *Diary*, the same system seems to have been generally followed in Florence during this period.[39] The form of punishment was often made into a theatrical representation appropriate to the crime, as when a blasphemer's tongue was cut out or the execution was performed at the scene of the crime. The people played audience to these spectacles, doubtless terrorized by them but also curious as to how the condemned would bear up to the ultimate ordeal. Landucci reports that the Florentines expected great words from Savonarola at his execution, and when they got none, they threw stones at the dying man and many of them lost their faith as a result (143). There were, of course, many private executions in Italy generally and in Florence in particular, although the body of the dead man or woman was usually hung out of a window or the head displayed on a pole so that all could see it.[40] The people's presence was essential at all these executions, for as an audience it bore witness to the power and justice of the authorities, as the Florentines did when they rejoiced at seeing the severed head of the supposedly traitorous Paolo Vitelli in 1499 (Landucci, 162). There was also, however, a potential for Saturnalian protest in those public executions, for the solemn official rituals could be counterbalanced by a release of antiauthoritarian feeling as the people identified with the condemned, who frequently cursed their judges. Even the displaying of a severed head after a private execution might provoke the wrong reaction.

In some ways the killing of Remirro de Orco is true to the pattern of such executions: it is a public spectacle demonstrating the power of the

[38]On executions during the *ancien régime* generally, see Michel Foucault, *Discipline and Punish: The Birth of the Prison*, trans. Alan Sheridan (New York: Random House, 1977), pp. 25–63.

[39]Werner L. Gundersheimer, "Crime and Punishment in Ferrara, 1440–1500," in *Violence and Disorder in Italian Cities, 1200–1500*, ed. Lauro Martines (Berkeley: University of California Press, 1972), pp. 115–16; Luca Landucci, *A Florentine Diary from 1450 to 1516*, trans. Alice de Rosen Jervis (London: J. M. Dent, 1927), pp. 4, 27, 75, 146, 176, 213.

[40]The conspirators against Lorenzo were hanged from the windows of the Bargello in 1481, and Paolo Vitelli's head was shown at its windows in 1499. See Landucci, *Florentine Diary*, pp. 32, 162.

authorities, in this case, of Cesare Borgia; it fits Remirro's "crimes," a swift and brutal end to a man who obviously had been carrying out a swift and brutal form of justice; and it involves the people as an audience, affirming through feelings of satisfaction and awe the union of power and justice revealed in the spectacle. But this execution varies from the norm in significant ways. First, there is its terrible suddenness. In the letters of his *Legazione* to Cesare Borgia in 1502–03, Machiavelli says that Remirro was seized by his master and placed in a tower, where he remained for several days.[41] A later letter then recounts the discovery in the piazza:

> Messer Remirro questa mattina è stato trovato in dua pezi in su la piaza dove è anchora; et tucto questo populo lo ha possuto vedere; non si sa bene la cagione della sua sorte, se non che li è piaciuto così al Principe, el quale mostra di sapere fare et disfare li huomini ad sua posta, secondo e' meriti loro.[42]

> Messer Remirro was found this morning in two pieces in the piazza where he still is, and all the people have been able to see him. The cause of his death is not known, unless it is that it was thus pleasing to the Prince, who shows he knows how to make and unmake men at his will, according to their merits.

A reader of these letters would have perceived Cesare Borgia's disposal of Remirro as a process, perhaps one involving an investigation and judgment, which lasted several days, whereas in *Il principe* the execution seems no sooner thought of than done. Although the letters stress that Borgia's behavior did enhance his power in the eyes of the people of Cesena, the suddenness of the execution in *Il principe* enhances that power even more, making Borgia seem almost omnipotent as he dispenses with such preparatory stages as investigations, arrests, and trials and executes a brutal justice with terrifying speed.

The slaying of Remirro also differs from the typical execution by dramatically transforming the rituals involved. The people of Cesena witness, in fact, not an execution but the results of one. Of course, sometimes that is exactly what happened in Renaissance Italy, especially in the power struggles that marked Florentine history. Nevertheless, in this case Cesare Borgia's reduction of the execution to a kind of dumb show is a strategy that reveals real political acumen, for if he de-

---

[41]See the *Legazione* of 23 December 1502, in Niccolò Machiavelli, *Legazioni, Commissarie, Scritti di governo*, ed. Fredi Chiappelli (Rome: Laterza, 1973), 2: 363.
[42]The *Legazione* of 26 December 1502, in ibid., p. 365.

prived the citizens of Cesena of a great portion of the typical ritual, he also avoided the possibility that in the hour of his death Remirro could have attacked and undermined Borgia's authority and connected him directly with the brutal repression visited on the people of the Romagna. By showing the citizens of Cesena only a dead body, Borgia has minimized and carefully channeled their ability to identify with Remirro: they can see themselves, like Remirro, as potential victims of Borgia's wrath if they misbehave or rebel, but they cannot identify with him as a spokesman for rebellion against Borgia's authority.

Although Machiavelli has Borgia change the pattern of more orthodox Renaissance executions to eliminate the possibility of Saturnalian protest, that does not mean the people of Cesena are deprived of participating in ritual. On the contrary, the passage stresses that Borgia acted as he did to purge the spirits of the townspeople. What he is purging them of is, to be sure, their hatred of an oppressive judge, but he is also allowing them to release vicariously their more diffuse, sadistic impulses, that instinct for violence which Machiavelli documented so vividly in the *Istorie*. Borgia thus transforms Remirro into a scapegoat whose death takes with it the violent impulses of his audience, purging them of that violence and rendering them more tractable subjects as a result. Borgia can thus be seen indeed as providing a carefully controlled, ritualized experience, a solemn funeral in which the viewing of the corpse takes place not in a church but in the politically more appropriate public space of the town square. Borgia's act, of course, also enhances his power in the eyes of the citizens of Cesena, for it shows that he can both do away with traditional rituals and replace them with powerfully compelling ones of his own devising.

Machiavelli also shapes the Remirro de Orco episode to stress its symbolism, a symbolism that is simultaneously transparent and opaque. The citizens of Cesena come upon the dead body at the highly symbolic moment of dawn, for example; by this device they enter into a ritual space, a threshold between an old epoch that has come to an end and a new one that has just begun.[43] This bit of ritual symbolism also elevates Borgia, for it makes it seem as though his power were so great that it could, in one night, alter the entire order of the world.

The spectacle of Remirro de Orco is more remarkable for its explicit symbolism: the pieces of the body are not just dumped in the square, as bodies frequently were in Renaissance Florence, but laid next to a bloody knife and a piece of wood, which force the audience—and the

---

[43] McCanles has argued that the killing of Cesare Borgia was an act of communication demanding to be decoded; see his "Machiavelli's *Principe* and the Textualization of History," 7. Here I attempt just such a decoding.

reader—to construct a symbolic reading. Renaissance people were, of course, used to reading allegorical meanings in public spectacles, and those who staged them usually took pains to invite symbolic interpretations. In the *Istorie fiorentine*, Machiavelli recounts a comparable incident in which a treacherous Florentine *podestà*, who not only gives up his castle to the forces of the Visconti of Milan but encourages them to attack Tuscany, is imprisoned by his captors and given only papers painted with serpents ("biscie") to eat until he dies (IV, xii, 286). The allegory of the serpents is clearly intended as a comment on the man's treachery, although it has an additional ironic meaning because the *biscia* was the emblem of the Visconti. Again, in another part of the *Istorie*, Machiavelli says that Piero degli Albizzi, who came from a powerful Florentine family and conspired with certain Florentine exiles to attack the city, was discovered, and someone sent him as a gift a silver bowl full of sweetmeats among which a nail was hidden. Although the motives of the sender remained obscure—was the gift meant to prepare Piero for his fall or mock him because of it?—the allegory was clear to everyone: it was read as an invitation to Piero to stop Fortune's wheel when he was at the high point, before it turned around and brought him to destruction, as of course it did (III, xix, 251). Both of these incidents dramatize the allegorical frame of mind of Renaissance Italians and also indicate that the symbolic message involved in such a gesture was usually fairly transparent and unambiguous.

As Machiavelli presents it, Borgia's allegorical show, though simple, is very different. For although capable of being interpreted in a clear manner, it is open to more than one reading and becomes ambiguous as a result. From one perspective, the knife and wood can be read as referring to the executioner's sword and block, so that the scene becomes a direct representation of public justice. From yet another perspective, they may refer to the equipment of a butcher and be interpreted either as recalling Remirro's treatment of the Romagna or as pointing to a fundamental savagery in Remirro's nature. From still a third perspective, the piece of wood—a bludgeon—may refer to Remirro's crude justice, and the knife—a rapier—to Borgia's subtle finesse. Machiavelli's text enhances the spectacle's ambiguity for his readers because he offers no explanation of the symbolism involved. Indeed, he never even explains just what two pieces Remirro's body was divided into. Since the man's "crimes" were serious, one might suppose that the "dua pezzi" were the head and trunk, but the passage remains resolutely silent on this matter, just as the event itself is bathed in silence. More than a dumb show, it seems like the dramatic version of a hieroglyph from a Renaissance emblem book. Borgia has created a mysterious picture that is transparent in that it may be read by its audience but opaque in that its meanings are ambiguous and contradictory. Like a Renaissance emblem, it is mysterious as it allegorically points to hidden knowledge; indeed, it is all the more mysterious because, unlike an emblem, it lacks any explanatory text.[44] The mysterious, symbolic character of Borgia's hieroglyph not only enhances the ritualistic nature of the spectacle but also profoundly affects his image in the minds of the audience. For the silent mystery forces his audience, already predisposed to read human affairs allegorically, to supply in their minds the absent explanatory text, thereby increasing its hold on them because their imaginations are so deeply engaged in it. The silence and mystery of the scene especially bring the people of Cesena to envision Cesare Borgia, the only possible author of this dramatic hieroglyph, as a being larger than life, one whose wisdom transcends theirs as it creates spectacles that go beyond simple, clear explanations, just as his power transcends theirs as it overturns the order of the world in a single night. In effect, by stimulating people's incredibly powerful imaginations, Machiavelli shows Borgia bringing his audience to engage in nothing less than a supreme act of self-mystification.

The spectacle of Remirro de Orco is all the more mysterious and compelling because of Borgia's simultaneous presence in and absence from the scene. Normally the authorities were always present at Renaissance executions, either directing the spectacle or personified by the executioner, or at least symbolically indicated when the dead person's body or head was displayed in or near a building, such as the Palazzo della Signoria, associated with those authorities. In fact, when one compares the letters of Machiavelli's *Legazione* with the later passage in *Il principe*, one is struck by how much he has minimized Borgia's presence in the latter. In the letters Machiavelli reports that Remirro was incarcerated in a tower "da questo Signore," whereas in *Il principe* he says merely that Cesare Borgia wanted to show ("volle monstrare") he was not responsible for Remirro's cruelty and that he had the dead body placed ("lo fece mettere") in the piazza one morning.[45] Thus the later text indicates that Borgia was absent from the scene, working through others from a distance. Indeed, if one reads that text alone, one has no indication that he was even at Cesena, although the *Legazione* makes it perfectly clear that he was. What is more, Machiavelli ends the passage

[44] On emblems, see the classic studies of Rosemary Freeman, *English Emblem Books* (London: Chatto & Windus, 1948), and Mario Praz, *Studi sul concettismo* (Florence: Sansoni, 1934).
[45] See the *Legazione* of 23 December 1502, in Machiavelli, *Legazioni, Commissarie, Scritti di governo*, 2: 363.

in *Il principe* by indicating the effect of the spectacle on the people but
without attempting to reconstruct their thoughts, whereas in the letters
he explains that they clearly attributed the slaying to their "Principe."
Thus the passage in *Il principe* paradoxically says two things at once:
Borgia is responsible for the slaying and hence deeply involved in it; and
yet he stands apart, maintaining an enormous distance from it. This
paradox renders Borgia's power immensely mysterious and enhances its
image in the eyes of the citizens of Cesena, while allowing the less mys-
tified reader to admire the brilliance of Borgia's brutal genius in creating such a spectacle.

Machiavelli clearly wants his reader to think that far more than
intimidation and visceral fear are involved here. For although the
description of Remirro's murder certainly allows one to conclude that
the people of Cesena were terrified into submission, it also intimates
Machiavelli's conviction that they were, in a profound way, inspired as
well. As he has Borgia manipulate the traditional rituals of execution,
create a silent, mysterious, compelling emblem, and paradoxically appear both present and distant from the scene, he makes this ideal prince
into a figure of overwhelming power for the citizens of Cesena. Indeed,
Borgia becomes nearly godlike. No wonder Machiavelli insists that the
spectacle in the public square rendered its audience both satisfied and
awed, for he presents it as a manifestation of something verging on divine power. It should now also be apparent that the violence in that
spectacle is indispensable and is meant to do far more than intimidate.
It is not wanton or random but aims to reveal the awe-inspiring presence of a savage god.

The passage about the killing of Remirro de Orco points to an aspect
of Machiavelli's anthropology that was omitted earlier but is of the
utmost importance. Human beings are not merely aggressive individualists prone to violence; they also have a deep capacity for religious belief. Like Nicia, they all want someone or something to have faith in.
Such a religious instinct Machiavelli identifies in different ways
throughout his works as he sees it directed at different objects. For instance, in the *Discorsi*, when he deals with Roman religion, he documents extensively human beings' capacity to revere the state. This
matter comes up in *Il principe* as well, when Machiavelli reassures the
prince that although a few individuals may see through his disguises,
they will not be able to act against the will of the majority, who will be
totally awed by "la maestà dello stato" (xviii, 74: "the majesty of the
state [or, more accurately, the government]"). For the most part, however, Machiavelli focuses on people's capacity to revere individuals rather
than cities or states. Thus, in *Il principe*, he says that a successful prince

will gain and maintain what he calls the "credito" (IV, 27) of the people, a word that could be translated as "trust" or "credit" but can also be rendered as "belief" or "faith."[46] Similarly, in the *Discorsi* Machiavelli says that nothing can restrain an excited crowd as much as its "riverenzia" for a man who is grave and possesses authority (I, liv, 252–53), a "riverenzia" that is clearly already present in the instincts of the *popolo*. As the famous sixth chapter in the third book of the *Discorsi*, the chapter on conspiracies ("Delle congiure"), indicates, human beings may respond with religious awe even to a prince they do not like simply because he is a prince: "E tanta la maestà e la riverenza che si tira dietro la presenza d'uno principe, ch'egli è facil cosa o che mitighi o che gli sbigottisca uno esecutore" (403: "The majesty and reverence that the presence of a prince engenders are so great that they easily either soften or dismay a conspirator"). Finally, in the *Istorie fiorentine* he identifies a capacity for reverence in the people of Florence when he says that, divided into factions, they sent for a leader from elsewhere to unite them, seeking one "per adorarlo" (II, xxv, 175: "to worship him"). Machiavelli is looking down with scorn on the Florentines here, for the capacity for belief and sheer credulousness are never distinct in his thought. Nevertheless, he does recognize that such a capacity exists and is a powerful determinant of human behavior.

Granted human beings' profoundly reverent response to the individuals and states that control their lives, it should not be surprising that Cesare Borgia is not the only prince in Machiavelli's works to attempt to fill the people with something like religious awe. Ferdinand of Aragon is praised for having kept the spirits of his subjects suspended in amazement ("sospesi et ammirati") by his great deeds and military campaigns (*Pr*, xxi, 90), and, in language reminiscent of the passage on Remirro de Orco, the Roman emperor Septimus Severus is celebrated for his *virtù*, which kept his soldiers "attoniti e stupidi" (*Pr*, xix, 80: "astonished and awed") and his people "reverenti e satisfatti" ("reverent and satisfied"). The profound capacity Machiavelli sees in human beings to worship the prince who leads them is also eloquently demonstrated by what happened to Jacopo Pazzi after the failure of the Pazzi conspiracy. In Machiavelli's account, the partisans of the Medici feel such deep reverence for their leaders that they see the conspiracy as verging on sacrilege. This religious feeling leads them to remove Jacopo Pazzi's body from his family's crypt and to bury it near the walls of the city "come scomunicato" (*Ist*, VIII, ix, 523: "as though he had been excommuni-

---

[46]Such meanings were possible for the word as early as the fifteenth century; see *Grande dizionario della lingua italiana*.

cated"). Finally, they dig it up again and throw it into the Arno, almost as if they were ritually cleansing the city of a source of pollution. Significantly, Machiavelli makes no mention of the great storms that occurred in those days, which the people superstitiously interpreted as a sign of God's wrath over the Pazzi conspiracy. Since God does not enter into Machiavelli's account, he thus makes the people's religious horror seem purely a response to an assault on their "sacred" leaders.

Machiavelli's political and historical works generally reveal that the people revere their princes primarily because of the controlled violence the latter engage in themselves or cause others to perpetrate on their behalf. Whether he is speaking of Cesare Borgia betraying Remirro de Orco, Ferdinand of Aragon driving out the Moors from Spain, or Septimus Severus conquering all his rivals for the emperor's crown, Machiavelli is always concerned with princes engaged in acts of violence against enemies, subjects, or both. Violence is thus unmistakably the handmaiden of faith.

But why should faith require spectacles of violence? Perhaps the answer is simply that those spectacles intimate the existence of a power that provides human beings with a source of order and direction for their world. People, in Machiavelli's view, are buffeted by the winds of fortune and the changing pressures of their desires, and the prince's power thus rescues them from potential chaos, giving them a reference point by which to guide their lives. At the start of the world, says Machiavelli, when there were few people scattered over the face of the globe like wild beasts, they began to gather together for protection, and to defend themselves better they sought out one who was "piú robusto e di maggiore cuore" (*Disc*, I, ii, 131: "more robust and of greater heart") to be their leader. Since people's natures have not changed since that time, according to Machiavelli, one can conclude that they cleave to the powerful now as then for order and protection. One need not indulge in speculation on this point, however, for in one of his letters Machiavelli recalls that when Cesare Borgia first sent Remirro de Orco into the Romagna as his surrogate, the violent punishments Remirro meted out provided authority and order for the people there: "Fece quei popoli uniti, timorosi dell'autorità sua, affectionati alla sua potenza, confidenti di quella" (#163, 375: "He made those people united, fearful of his authority, affectionate toward his power, and confident in it"). There could be no clearer indication of Machiavelli's belief that a controlled display of violence will generate in people not just fear but dependence and confidence—a form of faith. No wonder he concluded that the people of Cesena, living in what was formerly a highly disorderly region (*Pr*, VII, 37: "quella provincia era tutta piena di latrocinii, di brighe e di ogni altra ragione di insolenzia") and feeling oppressed by Remirro's actions, found Cesare Borgia's superior display of violence not just intimidating but inspiring in a distinctly religious way as well.

To maintain their godlike authority over their subjects, Machiavelli's princes must project an image of dignity which raises them above the acts of violence they instigate, just as Machiavelli showed Cesare Borgia remaining detached from and above the brutality visited upon Remirro de Orco at Cesena. Thus, although a prince may actually lead his men into battle against an external enemy, he will let his subordinates do the ugly work of disciplining the populace, while he distributes benefits from his own hand. He will never do what the Roman emperor Commodus did, whom Machiavelli faults not only for being rapacious and allowing his troops to be licentious but also for a more significant failing:

> Non tenendo la sua dignità, discendendo spesso ne' teatri a combattere co' gladiatori, e facendo altre cose vilissime e poco degne della maestà imperiale, diventò contennendo nel conspetto de' soldati. [*Pr*, xix, 82]

> Not preserving his dignity, frequently descending into the theaters to combat with the gladiators, and doing other things most base and little worthy of the imperial majesty, he became contemptible in the sight of his soldiers.

Commodus failed as a leader because he made himself a spectacle in others' eyes, rather than organizing spectacles that manifested his power while maintaining his superiority. Machiavelli's passage has Commodus literally lowering himself ("discendendo") so that people could not help but look down on him and as a result scorn him, conspire against him, and kill him. A true prince never lowers himself thus, but always maintains the dignity and majesty of his person and his office.

The prince's use of violence to generate reverence and awe is circumscribed in yet another way: he cannot indulge in it continually. If the power he manifests must be lofty, it must also be firm and stable if it is to provide human beings with a sense of order and direction. Thus Machiavelli frequently stresses his prince's need for firmness, telling him, for instance, that his judgment ("sentenzia") in the public affairs of his subjects should be irrevocable (*Pr*, xix, 75). Similarly, the ruler of a newly acquired realm is instructed to put his shocking deeds of violence quickly behind him and then to distribute benefits gradually, living with his subjects in such a way that "veruno accidente o di male o di bene lo abbia a far variare" (*Pr*, viii, 44: "no accident, whether for good or ill, would have to make him change"). Indeed, Machiavelli warns his prince that it is dangerous to cause people to live in continual fear by perpetrating a prolonged series of randomly spaced violent deeds, for although people respond well to the spectacle of power, too frequent and erratic a display produces insecurity. Thus, concludes Machiavelli, it is best for the prince to do all his evil deeds at one stroke, "e dipoi rassicurare gli uomini e dare loro cagione di quietare e fermare l'animo" (*Disc*, I, xlv, 235: "and then to reassure men and to give them reason to calm and steady their spirits"). Living in a world of constant change and variability, people clearly yearn for security, and the wise prince will ensure his rule by using carefully calculated displays of violence to make himself appear a figure of fearsome, awe-inspiring, and especially stable power. He will become the firm center of the universe for his people, a god of mystery and power who satisfies human beings' deep need for faith and order.

Why should Machiavelli make the prince a god of mystery and power in a religion founded on the memory of fear? To this most important question there are two complementary answers, one negative and one positive. The negative answer is that the prince must become such a figure because of what Machiavelli sees as the general decadence of religion in the modern world. Most notably in the *Discorsi*, when he attempts to explain why modern Italy is in such dire straits, he points to the failure, really the double failure, of Christianity.[47] First, it does not command human beings' allegiance in the modern world. As Frate Timoteo observes in *La mandragola*, and as that play documents generally, religion has been reduced to empty formulas, and its rites and places of worship no longer command crowds of the faithful. Similarly, the *Istorie fiorentine* indicate that religious festivities are either used by political leaders as means to keep the masses occupied or serve as settings for political assassinations. Machiavelli's political and historical works generally illustrate the decline of religious authority in his world: popes and cardinals, having given so many examples of wicked behavior, have lost their spiritual power over the masses (see *Disc*, I, xii, 165); kings and other secular leaders feel free to wage war on and imprison ecclesiastics; and prophets fail, as Savonarola did, because their spirituality cannot command allegiance. This last example points to the problematic nature of *credito* or belief in the modern world. Savonarola's government fell because he was an unarmed prophet and lacked the troops and weapons necessary to enforce belief. Machiavelli concludes: "La molti-

[47]See Hulliung, *Citizen Machiavelli*, pp. 61-62.

tudine cominciò a non crederli; e lui non aveva modo a tenere fermi quelli che avevano creduto, né a far credere e discredenti" (*Pr*, VI, 32: "The multitude started not to believe in them [Savonarola's governmental arrangements], and he did not have the means to hold firm those who had believed or to make the disbelievers into believers"). The modern world is skeptical and rationalistic, as Machiavelli's own attitude in his work attests; religious faith withers under such conditions.

More profoundly, Christianity is also a failure for Machiavelli because it unrealistically relies on human beings' willingness to love rather than on their fear, and because, although it recognizes the egocentric drives animating every individual, it wants those drives denied: "Se la religione nostra richiede che tu abbi in te fortezza, vuole che tu sia atto a patire piú che a fare una cosa forte" (*Disc*, II, ii, 282: "If our religion asks that you have strength, it wants you to be apt to suffer more than to do a strong deed"). The result is that the modern world — and particularly Italy — is weak because so many people prefer to take a beating rather than avenge it, thus leaving the field to the wicked. Admittedly, Machiavelli does say that Christianity itself is not at fault because, interpreted correctly, it may be consistent with patriotism (283). But this disclaimer may merely be an attempt to anticipate censorship, since Machiavelli's attack on the Christian ideals of humility and contemplation is an attack not on some perversion of Christian doctrine but on its very essence. Thus Christianity is damned in his mind both because it has become decadent and ineffective in the modern world and because it is unrealistic, denying human beings' individualism and giving them no defense against their enemies.[48]

In his attack on Christianity, Machiavelli once again seems to be contradicting himself: how can he say that Christianity prevents people from seeking to avenge themselves while he simultaneously argues that they manifest their evil, egocentric natures by pursuing vengeance, an argument that he supports by countless examples? This contradiction may be unresolvable, and yet one answer does suggest itself. Machiavelli is really angry with Christianity not because it tries to blunt humans' aggressiveness but because it does not accept that aggressiveness and use it constructively. In effect, what Machiavelli is calling for in his works is anything but an acceptance of lawless vendettas and deadly party fac-

---

[48]To say that Machiavelli was hostile to Christianity on political grounds does not mean that he was antireligious in his personal life. Letters replete with pious phrases, a chapter from the *Discorsi* revealing a belief in portents (I, lvi, 258–59), and the *Esortazione alla penitenza* all indicate a general orthodoxy, if not a fervent faith. Moreover, before he died, his son Piero reported that he confessed his sins and had a friar stay with him to the end (see *Let*, #238, 509).

tionalism; he wants human aggression to be accepted, but he also wants it to be disciplined so that his fellow Italians can unite, regain the power and direction of their Roman forebears, and thrust out the "barbarians" from the north.

What Machiavelli wants becomes clearer if one examines what he says about Roman religion, for in his eyes that religion was everything Christianity is not. Operating on the supposedly correct assumption that human beings are egocentric individualists filled with enormous capacities for violence as well as awe, Roman religion depended not on the weak chain of love to keep people united and faithful but on fear. It could educate the people and make them a disciplined body, creating a civilizaton out of sheer barbarism, both because, accepting human aggression, it trained the people to be tough and to defend themselves and their state and because it imbued them with an absolute terror of divine retribution if they failed in their duty or refused to obey their leaders (*Disc*, I, xi, 160). Repeatedly in the *Discorsi*, Machiavelli shows how the Roman *plebs* was brought to agree to political changes when its leaders invoked that terror. At one point, for instance, he says that it accepted the selection of its own representatives, the tribunes, from the nobility because it was "sbigottita da questa religione" (I, xiii, 167: "dismayed by this religion"), and at another, that it believed a consul rather than the tribunes "per paura della religione" (I, xiii, 168: "for fear of religion"). In general, Machiavelli praises Roman antiquity because "per più secoli non fu mai tanto timore di Dio quanto in quella republica" (I, xi, 160: "for many centuries there was never so much fear of God as in that republic").

Machiavelli, to be sure, is working here with a myth of Roman religion. It is a myth in the same way that his presentation of the state of Rome as a confidence trickster outfoxing its enemies is one: Machiavelli reads into the Roman past only those traits he admires and ignores those that do not fit, just as he sets up a deformed and partial vision of Christianity as a kind of straw man. Thus his vision of Roman religion ignores that religion's positive stress on achieving the gods' favor and its basic concerns with ethics and justice, while his vision of Christianity slights that side of it which harps on the fear of God's wrath, its use of impressive spectacles to shore up belief, and the religious inquisitions that often led to intimidating shows of violence in Machiavelli's own time. Strikingly, when he praises Roman religion, he frequently speaks of "God" rather than "the gods," as he does when refers to the "timore di Dio" ("fear of God") in the passage quoted above. One might thus be tempted to conclude that the very Christianity he rejects ironically helps shape his vision of the Roman religion he admires.

Machiavelli makes Roman religion not only into a religion of terror but into a confidence game as well, for leaders who may or may not have been believers used it and its authority to manipulate the people into doing their bidding. Thus Numa is celebrated for having falsely claimed a divine sanction for his wishes: "Simulò di avere domestichezza con una Ninfa, la quale lo consigliava di quello ch'egli avesse a consigliare al popolo" (*Disc*, I, xi, 161: "He feigned to have been familiar with a nymph, who advised him what he had to say to the people"). Other Roman leaders, Machiavelli notes, were perfectly willing to manipulate auspices and portents, although he claims that they did so with discretion, so as not to discredit them, and that they then interpreted them according to political and military needs. They relied on the authority embodied in those auspices and portents to persuade the people, to fill them full of "confidenza," so that they would carry out the will of their leaders and faithfully serve the state (*Disc*, I, xiv, 169-71; see also *Arte*, IV, 441). Because those leaders sought not to satisfy their own ends but to serve the state and augment its glory, it may not be exactly right to classify them with such confidence men as Ligurio, Cesare Borgia, and Castruccio Castracani. And yet when we consider how often Machiavelli shows Roman leaders serving their own class interests by using religion to deceive and manipulate the people, the line that separates them from their more modern counterparts is very fine indeed.

Finally, in Machiavelli's conception, the ancients did not merely invoke the power of the gods through prayer but created terrifying religious spectacles, rituals of violence centered on blood sacrifices. In a striking passage in the *Discorsi*, Machiavelli compares unfavorably the humility and delicate pomp of Christian *sacrifizi* with the magnificence, ferocity, and bravery of Roman ones. He praises the latter:

Qui non mancava la pompa né la magnificenza delle cerimonie, ma vi si aggiugneva l'azione del sacrificio pieno di sangue e di ferocità, ammazzandovisi moltitudine d'animali: il quale aspetto, sendo terribile, rendeva gli uomini simili a lui. [II, ii, 282]

Here ceremonies lacked no pomp or magnificence but there was added the action of sacrifice full of blood and ferocity and the slaying of multitudes of animals. This spectacle, being terrible, made men similar to it.

Religion here is clearly a powerful educating force, which relies on human beings' capacity to imitate—in this case, the controlled violence they see in their rites—to turn them into a disciplined force of warriors. For Machiavelli, the display of violence in religious spectacles is a way to manifest the power of the gods and to implant the memory of fear in people so that their faith and loyalty will persist even after the spectacle is done.

In one episode of the *Discorsi* Machiavelli not only dramatizes the important role he saw violence playing in ancient religion but shows leaders' willingness to improvise acts of violence when normal rituals were insufficient. It also shows how violence supposedly generates faith. The episode involves the Samnites, the Romans' enemies and, for Machiavelli, their equivalents in religion. The Samnites had been defeated by the Romans in a series of engagements, and, desperately turning to religion to inspire their army for one final effort, they decided to repeat an ancient ceremony. The high priest, in the midst of the dead sacrificial animals and the burning altars, made all the leaders swear to carry on the fight and afterward called forth all the soldiers one by one.

> Ed intra quegli altari, nel mezzo di piú centurioni, con le spade nude in mano, gli facevano prima giurare che non ridirebbono cosa che vedessono o sentissono; dipoi con parole esecrabili e versi pieni de spavento gli facevano promettere agli Dei d'essere presti dove gl'imperadori gli mandassono, e di non si fuggire mai dalla zuffa. . . . Ed essendo sbigottiti alcuni di loro, non volendo giurare, subito da' loro centurioni erano morti: talché gli altri che succedono poi, impauriti dalla ferocità dello spettacolo, giurarono tutti. [I, xv, 172]

> And among those altars, in the midst of many centurions, with their swords naked in their hands, they made them first swear not to repeat anything they saw or heard; then, with curses and charms full of terror, they made them promise to the Gods to be ready to go where their leaders sent them and never to flee from the battle. . . . And some of them, dismayed and not wanting to swear, were immediately killed by their centurions, so that all the others who followed them then, frightened by the ferocity of the spectacle, swore.

Violence and the threat of violence are everywhere in this scene: in the altars streaming with sacrifice, in the curses and charms, in the upraised swords, in the invocation of the gods. Testifying that even such a spectacle could not always overcome people's egocentric — and perfectly understandable — desires for personal safety, the episode emphasizes that some of the soldiers refused to swear. But it then goes on to show how the Samnites dealt with such a problem in a truly Machiavellian fashion: they added physical violence to the more purely symbolic violence in the spectacle, transforming and enhancing the ritual involved, thereby ensuring the loyalty of the army. Ironically, however, Machiavelli reports that the Samnites lost, defeated by the superior "virtù" of the Romans, who possessed an equally effective religion (i, xv, 172–73). Of course, there is another possibility, which Machiavelli's myth of Roman religion does not allow him to acknowledge. The Samnites may have lost because the terror instilled in the soldiers did not last beyond the ritual itself and because their all too human fear returned and overwhelmed them when they faced the Romans in battle one last time. In other words, even in the ancient world the capacity for religious awe that Machiavelli sees in people may have been no match for the egocentric concern for self he also saw in them.

Machiavelli felt he lived in an age when a religion such as the one he imagined for the Romans no longer existed and when the one that did exist was corrupt and decadent, lacking in authority and unrealistic. He was also sure that only a religion like Rome's could truly regenerate the modern world. In a passage discussing that religion, he declares: "La osservanza del culto divino è cagione della grandezza delle republiche . . . [e] . . . dove manca il timore di Dio, conviene . . . che quel regno rovini" (*Disc*, i, xi, 162: "The observance of religion is the cause of the greatness of states . . . and . . . where the fear of God is lacking, . . . that state must go to ruin"). Finally, Machiavelli was convinced that such a religion could and should be recreated in the modern world. His belief is based not only on his myth of ancient religion but on the assumption that human nature has not changed: people are still violent, egocentric, and possessed of powerful imaginations; they still need to live in an orderly world, and no order is more effective than one based on fear; and they still have an enormous capacity for religious awe. The passage cited above goes on to say that if the fear of God is lacking, a state may be "sostenuto dal timore d'uno principe che sopperisca a' difetti della religione" ("upheld by the fear of a prince who may supply the defects of religion"). Thus Machiavelli believes that Italy can be saved by an able prince who is both a figure of force and, through his spectacular displays of violence and the awe they inspire, able to take the place of ancient religion. Interestingly, this conception of the prince solves one of the major problems in Machiavelli scholarship involving the gap between the last chapter of *Il principe*, in which the prince is a redeemer for Italy, and the first twenty-five chapters, in which he appears merely as a self-serving combination of fox and lion. For the prince is at his core a religious figure, a god, and hence always potentially a redeemer. But he is hardly a redeemer in a Christian sense, for the religion he incarnates and propagates is not a religion of love and mercy but one of power, violence, and fear.

Although Machiavelli ends *Il principe* on an optimistic note — his prince can redeem Italy and lead it back to the greatness of Rome — and in the *Discorsi* he makes it clear that the prince can accomplish this end by becoming himself a god in a substitute religion, Machiavelli concludes pessimistically, in the *Discorsi* if not in *Il principe*, that no prince can be truly successful in reaching such a goal. The reason he gives is simple: princes can behave like gods, but they are not divine, and when they die, their power dies with them. Moreover, Machiavelli's works reveal another, more profound reason why princes cannot reestablish something like Roman religion, for those works document eloquently the tenuous hold all princes have on their subjects. Although Machiavelli argues that human beings can be intimidated and even converted by spectacles of violence, he also shows that that intimidation and conversion are of very short duration and less powerful than people's egocentric drives for self-preservation or their urge to personal aggrandizement. Thus, if Machiavelli describes the brilliant spectacles his princes stage, he also recounts the endless conspiracies, assassination attempts, and betrayals with which they have to deal and which prove dramatically just how desperate all their attempts to become the focus of a substitute religion really are.

The Medici, according to Machiavelli, came up with a solution of sorts to the prince's problem in the period between 1434, when Cosimo came to power, and 1494, when the family went into exile. Every five years, he says, they "retook" the state in the sense of regaining political offices and punishing opponents. What they were really doing was trying to keep alive the memory of fear in the people by reawakening "quel terrore e quella paura negli uomini che vi avevano messo nel pigliarlo" (*Disc*, iii,i, 382: "that terror and fear in men which they had put there in taking it [i.e., the state]"). Although this technique did succeed in keeping the Medici in power, they lasted only sixty years, and it did not prevent successful and unsuccessful assassination attempts during that period as well as the family's final expulsion. By contrast, the Roman state endured in grandeur for centuries because, as Machiavelli saw it, its political and social order was grounded in a supernatural religion of terror which transcended the life of any single leader; that religion was part of the *ordini*, the basic arrangement, of their state. Hence what Machiavelli really wants for the modern world is a full-scale restoration of ancient religion. He never specifies, however, how such a restoration is to be accomplished — or even if it could be. At most he expresses the cautious and qualified hope that if the rough men of the earliest Roman times could be persuaded to accept the new religious order of their state by Numa and others, it is not impossible ("non è . . . impossibile") that the civilized men of the modern world could be persuaded to accept a return to Roman religion — and, through it, to Roman greatness. After all, he remarks, admittedly with a witty sneer, even the people of Florence, who are neither ignorant nor uncivilized, were persuaded that Savonarola talked with God (*Disc*, 1, xi, 163).

The sneering tone here reveals unintentionally the final reason why his hopes for a revival of his vision of Roman religion and Roman grandeur in the modern world are doomed. As Machiavelli himself saw only too well, the modern world is dislocated and skeptical, suspicious of its authorities, which have discredited themselves in many ways, and diffident of belief. Machiavelli recognizes that religious faith was potentially threatened by skepticism in the ancient world, but in his myth he stresses the discretion with which the Romans acted so that the skepticism of their leaders never infected the mass of the people. By contrast, Machiavelli's political and historical works document his conviction that such a situation does not obtain in the modern world. Moreover, those very works, filled with sneering remarks that mock the *credito* of the Florentines as childish credulity, actually contribute, as they spread abroad their skeptical attitude, to the impossibility of any full restoration of the ancient faith Machiavelli dreamed of. The most that his works allow one to glimpse is a world in which princes satisfy human beings' capacity for religious awe sporadically and temporarily. By creating spectacles of violence whose fearfulness generates faith, those princes do indeed command the *credito* of the people, but only for the little while that the memory of fear remains.

4

The Heroic Prince

At the end of his *Vita* of Castruccio Castracani, Machiavelli records a long list of clever sayings attributed to the Lucchese condottiere, almost all of which actually come from the ancient writer Diogenes Laertius' *Lives of the Philosophers*, and which Machiavelli includes in part to satisfy his audience's generic expectation that biography should contain such things and in part to further his glorification of Castracani.[1] Among those sayings are many that evoke for their supposed speaker a life of festivity and merriment, eating and drinking heavily and chasing after women (*CC*, 36-41), although such matters are virtually ignored in the biography itself, which precedes them. That biography focuses instead almost exclusively on Castracani's activities as a military leader and ruler, and it portrays him not merely as not philandering but as actually renouncing marriage in favor of his former patron's heir (*CC*, 34). One may, of course, read between the lines and presume that the man ate and drank and was involved with women (he was, in fact, married), but the picture Machiavelli paints of him makes him an utterly serious, grimly determined, puritanical figure obsessed with power politics and war. Consequently, since Machiavelli studiously avoids associating Castracani with either play or pleasure throughout the bulk of the biography, the references to such matters at its end come as a shock. They are unbelievable even for the reader who knows that Machiavelli pirated them all from antiquity.

The idea of indulgence in play or pleasure would be equally shocking were it mentioned in connection with any of Machiavelli's princes. To judge from his political and historical works, one could not imagine a

[1] For Machiavelli's borrowing from Diogenes Laertius and other ancient writers at the end of the *Vita di Castruccio Castracani*, see the introduction to that text, pp. 3-4.

Cesare Borgia, an Appius Claudius, or even a Lorenzo de' Medici, the author of one of the most famous *carpe diem* poems in the Renaissance, eating a good meal with gusto or participating with gay abandon in a popular celebration. Although all of Machiavelli's confidence men recognize the theatrical nature of social life and are adept at putting on spectacles for the *popolo*, they themselves never enter into spectacles or shows with complete abandon; they are never free of distance and reserve, self-conscious control. Participation in such spectacles is for them always a form of work, not play. Moreover, when Machiavelli does mention holidays or festivities in his political and historical works or speaks of individuals at banquets or pursuing women, such events are occasions when one must be doubly on one's guard, for they are almost inevitably associated with assassinations, political vendettas, and conspiracies. Ironically, the prince who entertains others can never enjoy an entertainment wholeheartedly; he who strives to bring peace and stability to his realm and people can never relax. When he is not engaged in protecting himself from attackers inside and outside his state, he is pursuing glory in the field and seeking to extend the reputation on which his security depends. At one point in *Il principe*, Machiavelli says that the ultimate goal of his princes is to be "potenti, securi, onorati, felici" (VI, 32: "powerful, secure, honored, happy"), but this last goal—happiness—has little to do with bodily pleasure or festive fun and everything to do with power and glory bought at the price of self-denial and unflagging labor.

Chief among the qualities that distinguish the prince from the confidence men of the literary tradition is his puritanical seriousness. Renaissance confidence men, like their folk cousins, are basically carnivalesque characters. Their activities celebrate the life of the body, its pleasures and creativity, and they are motivated by powerful drives for food and sex as well as wealth and power, drives shared by Ligurio and Callimaco. They are gay characters, at times almost practical jokers or clowns, like Boccaccio's Bruno and Buffalmacco or like Brunelleschi and the other Florentines who deceive the title character in the "Novella del Grasso legnaiuolo" ("The Story of Fatso the Carpenter"). Finally, as they turn the world topsy-turvy with their tricks and pranks, confidence men derive a real joy, not unrelated to aesthetic pleasure, from the trickery they engage in, trickery often conceived of as a game or as play.

By contrast, Machiavelli's princes could hardly be said to celebrate the soft, open, grotesque, procreative body Mikhail Bakhtin associates with carnival.[2] They favor rather the tough, hard physique of the soldier. Indeed, in reducing the literary confidence man's motives and goals to an obsession with political power, they treat the body not as a locus of pleasure but purely as an instrument, a tool of politics, and a means to conquest. More important, Machiavelli's princes are never depicted as enjoying either the quest for or the fruits of power, and there is nothing playful about their activities. Machiavelli's political confidence men are, on the whole, too tough, too consistently self-disciplined, and too relentlessly serious to be grouped with his more carnivalesque confidence men Callimaco and Gianmatteo or with the countless confidence men, picaros, and rogues who abound in Renaissance literature. Clever foxes like all the other confidence men and tricksters, his princes have also simultaneously turned into ferocious lions whose lives are spent in endless, unrelenting political activity.

How can one account for this striking deformation undergone by the confidence man in Machiavelli's political and historical works? It does not suffice to say that he has been changed simply by his shift from the realm of literature into history, for there is no reason why even the most princely lion could not be depicted as enjoying his kill or playing with his mate or his cubs. But we can explain the changes Machiavelli has made in his prince by noting that his characteristics—high seriousness, an overwhelmingly significant political goal in the world of history, and a rejection of relaxation and festivity, play and women—all link him directly to another character of great importance in Renaissance culture: the epic hero. Machiavelli's prince can thus be read as a conflation or amalgam of two figures, the tricky confidence man of medieval and Renaissance tradition and the heroic warrior and leader of men who was celebrated in ancient epics, was revived in transmogrified form by Dante in the *Divina commedia*, and preoccupied Renaissance poets from Matteo Boiardo and Ludovico Ariosto, through Torquato Tasso and Edmund Spenser, down to Giambattista Marino and John Milton. Through this conflation, Machiavelli significantly modifies the confidence man he inherited from tradition, deepening the ethos of that figure by giving him the lofty purpose and general earnestness of the hero. His prince is thus different from his confidence-man ancestors not just

[2]Mikhail Bakhtin, *Rabelais and His World*, trans. Hélène Iswolsky (Cambridge: M.I.T. Press, 1968), pp. 5–12.

because he has entered upon the stage of history but because his origins—the literary models preceding him—are different as well.[3]

Although Machiavelli's prince is an amalgamation, the historical figures who exemplify the ideal fail uniformly and consistently to manifest the traits of both confidence man and epic hero. Cesare Borgia, for instance, more often performs as a tricky deceiver than as a warrior, and Ferdinand of Aragon is more warrior than deceiver. Even more striking, in the *Discorsi*, Scipio Africanus, the conqueror of Carthage, is a model lion, almost never a fox; Fabius Maximus, who saved Rome through guile, is just the reverse. These failures suggest why Machiavelli ultimately prefers republican government to the rule of one individual: not because he believes in some lofty democratic ideal but because the many people involved in running a republic allow it to shift swiftly from role to role, from deceiving trickster to forceful warrior, as circumstances dictate, whereas single individuals could never match such flexibility. Nevertheless, although real princes in the world of history can neither achieve an absolutely perfect union of fox and lion in themselves nor move from one role to the other with ease, Machiavelli still imagines his ideal prince as coming close to a perfect amalgamation of confidence man and epic hero.

Machiavelli's knowledge of epic heroes is not in dispute. Although he did not know Greek and thus could not have read Homer in the original, he may have read him in translation, and he certainly knew Vergil and Dante extremely well.[4] He had, moreover, read deeply in the ancient Roman historians, especially Livy, who saw Roman history as an epic and singled out various figures from the past as heroes to be imitated. Machiavelli was also acquainted with contemporary epics. In a letter to him, Roberto Acciaiuoli, his fellow bureaucrat and Florentine diplomatic representative, cites a pair of lines from Luigi Pulci's late-fifteenth-century epic *Morgante maggiore*, obviously assuming that Machiavelli had read Pulci's work and would grasp the allusion (*Let*, #92, 186). Acciaiuoli was right, for in a later letter to Francesco Vettori, Machiavelli quotes from memory, albeit with slight inaccuracy, two

---

[3]Giorgio Barberi-Squarotti sees the prince as heroic and tragic because of his struggle to dominate the world of brute matter; see *La forma tragica del "Principe" e altri saggi sul Machiavelli* (Florence: Olschki, 1966), pp. 25–26. His concept is close to but not identical with mine, which is greatly influenced by the work of Ezio Raimondi, especially his *Politica e commedia: Dal Beroaldo al Machiavelli* (Bologna: Mulino, 1972), pp. 141–72, 265–86; and "Machiavelli and the Rhetoric of the Warrior," *MLN* 92 (1977): 1–16.

[4]On Machiavelli's knowledge of Greek, see John H. Geerken, "Homer's Image of the Hero in Machiavelli: A Comparison of Areté and Virtù," *Italian Quarterly* 14 (1970): 45–50.

lines from the same epic poem (*Let*, #163, 376). Finally, it is clear that Machiavelli knew a version of the *Orlando furioso*, for he complains in a letter of 1517 that Ariosto left him out of the catalogue of great poets in that work. But because Machiavelli did not read Ariosto's poem until late in 1517, it could not have had a serious impact on *Il principe*, which was completed before that date, and may not have had much effect on the *Discorsi*, which was most likely begun at the same time as *Il principe* in 1513 and may well have been completed by 1517.[5] Nevertheless, it should be clear that even if Machiavelli did not know Ariosto when he was composing his most important political works, he had many other sources from which to shape his idea of the epic hero.

Machiavelli's deep engagement with epics and their heroes emerges in various ways throughout his writings. He directly cites such figures as Achilles, Alexander, and Cyrus as models for his prince (*Pr*, XIV, 64), and the *Discorsi* are full of praise for the heroes of Roman history, particularly Scipio Africanus, the hero of the Punic Wars and the victor over Hannibal, and Fabius Maximus, on whose name Machiavelli's work literally ends. Machiavelli also directly cites or imitates passages from epics: in *Il principe* he quotes two lines from the *Aeneid* stressing the difficulty of the prince's founding a new realm (XVII, 69), and he opens the "Decennale primo," a work focused on that modern "hero" Cesare Borgia, in the manner of epic with a lofty statement of theme and an invocation to the muses (*SL*, 236). Moreover, Machiavelli frequently defines the typical action of his princes with a suggestive word, *impresa*, which could be translated in a fairly colorless way as "undertaking" but might better be rendered as "epic quest," since it had great currency in medieval romance, in which it meant something nearer to "quest," and was used by sixteenth-century writers of epic to identify the actions of their heroes.[6] Thus Machiavelli speaks of his Romans' heroic conquests as "le imprese loro" (*Disc*, II, i, 278); in the *Istorie fiorentine*, he praises the first crusade, which would later inspire Tasso and other writers of Renaissance epics, as a "generosa impresa" (I, xvii, 101), and he has his plebeian spokesman in the Ciompi Revolt urge his comrades on in their "imprese" (III, xiii, 239); and in *Il principe* he characterizes his princes' activities by the same term (XXVI, 103). He ends this last work by urging

[5]For the dating of *Il principe* and the *Discorsi*, see the introductions to those works in the volume used, pp. 3-10, 109-16.

[6]*Impresa* is defined as meaning *prodezza di cavaliere* in the fourteenth century, according to the *Dizionario etimologico italiano*, ed. Carlo Battisti and Giovanni Alessio (Florence: G. Barbera, 1952). The *Grande dizionario della lingua italiana*, ed. Salvatore Battaglia (Turin: Unione Tipografico-Editrice Torinese, n.d.), gives a similar definition and references from works by Giovanni Villani, Dante, Boccaccio, and Ariosto. The latter uses the word in the opening stanza of *Orlando furioso* (I, i, 2).

the redemption of Italy on Lorenzo de' Medici as an "impresa" that will render his house "illustre" (xxvi, 104) and by citing lines from Petrarch calling for a revival of "l'antico valore" in modern Italian hearts (xxvi, 105). Finally, the general goals Machiavelli repeatedly stresses—the conquering of enemies in battle, the securing, founding, or reviving of states, the acquisition of personal glory—all are the goals of epic heroes from Achilles and Aeneas down to Ariosto's Orlando and Ruggiero. In short, wherever one turns in Machiavelli's political and historical works, epics and their heroes are a major determinant of his conceptions.

An examination of the prince's qualities, and especially those that make him more a lion than a fox, confirms his deep affinity to the epic hero. The hero is a figure of energy and activity, a clever strategist and an eloquent leader of men, and above all, a warrior, whether one speaks of Odysseus wandering and fighting across the Mediterranean, Achilles slaying Hector at Troy, or Aeneas leading the Trojans into battle against the Latins. Machiavelli's prince is just such a character. He is tough, courageous, and energetic, and the most important component of his reputation, a component that must be based on his acts and not simply on others' opinions, is his military success as a warrior and leader of men. Machiavelli also emphasizes the prince's firmness and resolution, his ability to remain unchanged no matter what adversity he faces (see *Disc*, ii, xiv-xv, 314-15). Machiavelli took pride in a similar quality he saw in himself, his ability to withstand torture in prison (see *Let*, #122, 234), and he generally praised a stoic ability to remain firm in spirit in every situation (*Disc*, iii, xxxi, 469-73). Although from time to time he may suggest that one can accomplish more by the confidence man's guile than by the lion's force,[7] force certainly has a prominent place in the constitution of the prince.[8] Indeed, Machiavelli underscores the great importance of force by focusing on it in the first three chapters of *Il principe*, emphasizing its ability to drive rulers out of their states (ii, 16), to instill fear in the people on whom it is used (iii, 18-20), and to create

[7]In the "Descrizione del modo tenuto dal duca Valentino nello ammazzare Vitellozzo Vitelli, Oliverotto da Fermo, il signor Pagolo e il duca di Gravina Orsini," Machiavelli stresses Cesare Borgia's preference for fraud (*SP*, 44), and in the *Vita di Castruccio Castracani* he stresses that Castracani used it as well (*CC*, 36). The title to chap. xiii of Bk. ii of the *Discorsi* is "*Che si viene di bassa a gran fortuna più con la fraude che con la forza*" (311).
[8]Raimondi, *Politica e commedia*, pp. 156, 276-80, and "Machiavelli and the Rhetoric of the Warrior," 1-16. See also J. E. Siegel, "Violence and Order in Machiavelli," in *Violence and Aggression in the History of Ideas*, ed. Philip P. Wiener and John Fisher (New Brunswick: Rutgers University Press, 1974), pp. 58-59.

the all-important reputation of the prince (III, 17). And in the *Istorie fiorentine* he mocks those princes and military leaders of recent Italian history who have used "inganni" ("deceptions") and "astuzie" ("ruses") to win battles and gain an undeserved reputation as warriors because they lacked the real military skill such a reputation should indicate (v, i, 327).

Indeed, Machiavelli declares at one point in *Il principe* that the prince's only art should be the art of war and that he should never stop thinking of it even during peace:

> Debbe adunque uno principe non avere altro obietto né altro pensiero, né prendere cosa alcuna per sua arte, fuora della guerra et ordini e disciplina di essa; perché quella è sola arte che si espetta a chi comanda. [XIV, 62]

> A prince should thus have no other object or thought nor take anything as his art beyond war and its principles and discipline, because that is the only art expected in one who commands.

Of course, the art of war involves mental training and the intellectual skills of strategy, organization, and leadership, but Machiavelli particularly stresses the toughening and disciplining of the body, instructing the prince to avoid "delicatezze" (*Pr*, XIV, 62) so that he can eventually lead his own troops into battle (*Pr*, XII, 54; *Disc*, I, xxx, 201). In the *Arte della guerra*, Machiavelli has one of its characters, Cosimo Rucellai, speak on behalf of a truly Spartan—and Roman—existence for both the young man in training and the adult in action: washing in cold water, sleeping out of doors, going naked, despising wealth (I, 331-32). Castruccio Castracani provides a model both of what an ideal prince should do as a warrior-ruler and of how he should prepare himself for that life, for Machiavelli emphasizes not only Castracani's resoluteness and cunning as a warrior but the preparation for that role which essentially occupied his youth. Thus, although his foster father began to train Castracani intellectually for the priesthood at fourteen, says Machiavelli, the young prince-to-be distanced himself from his family, left his religious books, and turned to arms. He came to delight solely in handling arms and in competing with other youths in running, jumping, and wrestling, sports directly related to his future tasks as a warrior. Ironically, when Castracani did read from time to time, "altre lezioni non gli piacevano che quelle che di guerre o di cose fatte da grandissimi uomini ragionassino" (*CC*, 11: "no readings pleased him but those that treated of war or of deeds done by the greatest men"). This

model heroic prince, then, spends most of his time toughening his body
in preparation for a life to be spent in battle, and that physical training
is supplemented and reinforced, rather than complemented or counterbalanced, by intellectual training, which has a distinctly secondary role
in his formation.

Chief among the various kinds of training Machiavelli recommends
to prepare the prince as a warrior is hunting; the prince, he says, "debbe
stare sempre in su le caccie" (*Pr*, xiv, 63: "must constantly engage in
hunting"). Although Machiavelli justifies his preference on quasi-
intellectual grounds by explaining that such an activity can teach a great
deal about geography, the first and obviously most important benefit
credited to hunting is its ability to toughen and discipline the body as it
teaches the prince how to "assuefare el corpo a' disagi" (ibid.: "accus-
tom his body to hardships"). In a significant passage in the *Discorsi*,
Machiavelli makes an explicit connection between hunting as a preparation for war and the training of a hero. The subject comes up when
he discusses the military leader's need to know the lay of the land; nothing teaches him this skill better than hunting, Machiavelli says.

> Però gli antichi scrittori dicono che quegli eroi che governarono nel loro
> tempo il mondo, si nutrirono nelle selve e nelle cacce: perché la caccia,
> oltre a questa cognizione c'insegna infinite cose che sono nella guerra
> necessarie. [iii, xxxix, 491]

> Therefore, ancient writers say that those heroes who governed the world
> in their time were nourished in the forests and on hunting, because hunt-
> ing, beyond this knowledge [of geography], teaches us an infinite number
> of things that are necessary for war.

Machiavelli goes on to cite Xenophon's *Cyropaedia*, thus identifying the
"antichi scrittori" he had in mind. This is virtually the only place in his
political and historical works in which the word *hero* occurs, but since
he consistently praises hunting and the skills it fosters, it should be clear
that in thinking of his princes as hunters he is thinking of them as
heroes.

Machiavelli's conception of the education of his prince and particularly of the role hunting should play in it sharply distinguishes him from
his humanist predecessors and contemporaries. Without exception,
from Petrus Paulus Vergerius at the start of the fifteenth century
through Erasmus in the first decades of the sixteenth, humanists all included physical training in their educational programs, but also without exception they assigned that training a distinctly secondary role.

They sought primarily to train human beings' intellects and moral sen-
sibilities; the main functions of a sound body were to house a sound
mind, to prevent diseases, and to allow the important work of intellectual training and moral formation to go on.[9] The humanists were involved with the teaching of the European ruling classes, and their
preferences cut directly against the grain of late-medieval notions about
aristocratic training and behavior, according to which book-learning
was relegated to "clerks" (i.e., clerics) and noblemen were to spend their
time fighting, ruling—and hunting.[10] Nevertheless, possibly because the
humanists' pupils were rulers and noblemen, this aristocratic bias remains in their theorizing about education, with resultant ambivalence,
especially in regard to hunting. This ambivalence can be seen in Alberti's dialogue *I Libri della famiglia*. Alberti's first instinct is to reject
hunting altogether, whether for education or for life generally, and to
contrast it with more important matters, such as the management of the
household and the individual's personal perfection in virtue. Hunting,
says one of his speakers, makes human beings beasts themselves and
turns adults into children playing a game.[11] This speaker does not have
the last word, however; Alberti has others argue that hunting does serve
a purpose as exercise and as training in arms. Nevertheless, although
he makes this concession to aristocratic preference, he clearly feels un-
easy about the effect of hunting on human beings, who are defined in
terms of a hierarchy that gives preference to mind over body, a hierarchy that the practice of hunting might disturb. Consequently, he, like
the other humanists, can accept hunting, but only if it remains a sub-
sidiary activity that aids the training of the mind and leaves the basic
hierarchy of the human faculties unscathed.[12]

[9]On the need to strengthen the body for the sake of the mind, see Petrus Paulus
Vergerius, *De ingenuis moribus ac liberalibus studiis*, trans. in William H. Woodward,
Vittorino da Feltre and Other Humanist Educators (1897; rpt. New York: Teachers College, Columbia University, 1963), p. 116; Aeneas Silvius Piccolomini, *De liberorum
educatione*, ed. J. S. Nelson, Studies in Medieval and Renaissance Latin Language
and Literature, 12 (Washington, D.C.: Catholic University of America Press, 1940),
pp. 102–6; and Leon Battista Alberti, *I Libri della famiglia*, ed. Ruggiero Romano and
Alberto Tenenti (Turin: Einaudi, 1969), pp. 87–88. Erasmus writes in one of his treatises
that some exercise is useful for the sake of the mind but that excessive concern with the
body is regrettable: "Nec enim athletam fingimus, sed philosophum, sed Reipublicae
gubernatorem, cui satis est adesse prosperam valetudinem, etiamsi non adsit Milonis
robur" (*Declamatio de pueris statim ac liberaliter instituendis*, ed. Jean-Claude Margolin
[Geneva: Droz, 1966], p. 423: "For we are forming not an athlete but a philosopher, the
ruler of a state, for whom the presence of good health is sufficient, even if the strength
of Milo is missing").
[10]On this point, see Philippe Ariès, *Centuries of Childhood: A Social History of Family
Life*, trans. Robert Baldick (New York: Random House, 1962), pp. 138–45, 365–69.
[11]Alberti, *Libri della famiglia*, pp. 338–39.
[12]On hunting, see also Vergerius, *De ingenuis moribus*, p. 116.

When one contrasts Machiavelli's praise of hunting with the humanists' views on the subject, his radically different conception of education
and his even more radical subversion of the traditional mind-body hierarchy emerge with dramatic clarity. Machiavelli strives to create not an
intellectual giant or a moral paragon but an exemplar of toughness, a
general and leader who needs a physically well-trained, superior body
for the wars he will wage in a career of conflict and conquest. For such
a figure, hunting is not merely preparation for a vastly different end
than any contemplated by the humanists; it is also an initiation into and
a symbol of the life the prince will always lead. Hunting defines the very
mode of his existence as it never could for the idealized princes of the
humanists.

Machiavelli also considers hunting, like physical training, a means,
but the ends he assigns his princes—triumph in combat, the conquest
of nations, military glory—are vastly different from those of the
humanists. As a result, he effectively stands their traditional Christian
hierarchy of mind and body on its head, elevating the body at least to
the level of the mind (*Pr*, VII, 39; *Disc*, II, ii, 282). For Machiavelli, life
is war in a literal, not a figurative or spiritual, sense, as it was for the
humanist Erasmus in his *Enchiridion Militis Christiani* (*Handbook of
the Christian Soldier*), and hence he embraces just what Alberti most
feared, the possibility that in their aggressive actions humans could
come to resemble beasts. In a world constantly at war, affirms Machiavelli, the prince cannot fight only with laws, the mode proper to
humans, but must use force, the mode proper to beasts (*Pr*, XVIII, 72).
Insisting on the prince's bestial side, Machiavelli says he wants him to be
like the ancient hero Achilles, who was trained by and came to resemble
his mentor, Chiron the centaur. The prince must imitate Achilles and
strive to become, at least metaphorically, "uno mezzo bestia et mezzo
uomo" (ibid.: "a half beast and half man"), a grotesque amalgam at
the opposite extreme from what Bakhtin sees as the soft, procreative,
grotesque body of carnival.

Machiavelli's emphasis on the toughness of his prince and his celebration of hunting are completely consistent with what has been described
as his "primitivism."[13] To be more precise, Machiavelli falls into the
camp of what A. O. Lovejoy has called "hard primitivists," those who

---

[13]On Machiavelli's primitivism, see Alfredo Bonadeo, *Corruption, Conflict, and Power
in the Works and Times of Niccolò Machiavelli*, University of California Publications in
Modern Philology, 108 (Berkeley: University of California Press, 1973), pp. 9-10; and
Daniel Waley, "The Primitivist Element in Machiavelli's Thought," *Journal of the History
of Ideas* 31 (1971): 91-98. For Machiavelli's celebration of the primitive toughness of the
Germans, see "Rapporto delle cose della Magna," *SP*, 202; and *Disc*, II, xix, 334-36.

imagine the original state of human beings as being not marked by edenic bliss, harmony, and order, but rather by competition, strife, and destruction—in Hobbes's famous words, an existence "nasty, brutish, and short."[14] Machiavelli's acceptance of the myth of the Fall and his notion that at the start of the world humans banded together under the protection of the strongest and most robust among them (*Disc*, I, ii, 131) point to this hard primitivism and suggest ambivalence about it: the first idea implies a negative moral judgment of human beings' primitive aggressiveness and the second suggests a positive evaluation of it. A positive evaluation appears also in Machiavelli's praise of the Swiss in the *Arte della guerra* for being close to the ancients in military matters (II, 375), for in his mind the Swiss, whom he associated with the Germans, were generally supposed to be more primitive ("rozzi," or "rough and uncivilized") than his fellow Italians (see the "Rapporto delle cose della Magna," for instance, in *SP*, 201). That positive evaluation of primitive aggression also surfaces elsewhere in the *Arte*, when he says that the simple, rough people of the country make better soldiers than the soft ones of the city: they not only are used to hardships but actually welcome them, preferring to stay in the hot sun rather than relax in the shade (I, 345). In general, then, although Machiavelli sometimes characterizes human beings' primitive aggressiveness as "wicked" in Christian terms, he more consistently values it as a necessity in a world where war is the norm.

As a hero, the prince also shares with Achilles and Aeneas, Orlando and Ruggiero, one other, interrelated set of qualities defined by such words as *daring*, *boldness*, *resolution*, and *courage*. Willing to risk everything, including his life, to obtain his ends, he disdains petty, self-protecting measures and would readily go with Odysseus into the Cyclops' lair or square off with an Orc like Ruggiero. One recalls in this connection Machiavelli's admiration for the coolness of the Pazzi conspirators, who joked with Giuliano de' Medici as they walked him to the church where they planned to kill him (*Ist*, VIII, v, 518), and Castruccio Castracani's grand indifference to the disease-bearing wind that caused his death (*CC*, 33). In his daring and risk-taking, the prince is a gambler, and although Machiavelli never actually uses that metaphor in his works, he does refer to politics as a chess game in a letter to Francesco Vettori, stressing the element of risk-taking rather than the calculation involved in that game (#159, 366).[15] Gambling and running risks have

---

[14]On soft and hard primitivism, see A. O. Lovejoy and George Boas, *Contributions to the History of Primitivism: Primitivism and Related Ideas in Antiquity* (Baltimore; Johns Hopkins University Press, 1935).
[15]Francesco Vettori also sees politics as a game; see *Let*, #139, 297.

to be exercised with discretion, kept within bounds, of course, and Machiavelli consequently condemns those princes and states for the "temerità" of their decisions when they cast caution to the winds and behave in self-destructive ways, as the Venetians did by inviting Louis XII into Italy (*Pr*, III, 23) and the Roman emperor Antoninus did by murdering the brother of a centurion and then keeping the latter in his personal service (*Pr*, XIX, 82). Like the hero, the prince is bold, not foolhardy.

The prince's daring stands out in high relief when he is compared with the *popolo*, whom Machiavelli scorns for lack of resolution and courage. Thus he remarks with contempt that most people "sono sempre nimici delle imprese dove si vegga difficultà" (*Pr*, X, 49: "are always the enemies of [heroic] undertakings in which they see difficulties"), using the word *imprese* here to mark their distance from true heroism. Similarly, he mocks the people for their reluctance to attack adversaries and their hesitation to engage in conspiracies or to carry out plots (*Pr*, XIX, 76; see also *Disc*, III, vi, 411-12). Machiavelli had long experience of his fellow Florentines' hesitation to engage in perilous enterprises, and he frequently attacked the dubious wisdom of their policy of constantly temporizing, "usando il benefitio del tempo" (*Let*, #6, 39: "using [or taking] the benefit of time"), according to a popular Florentine proverb.[16] He feels that modern Italian princes have lost Italy to the barbarians not because they are not devious enough but because they lack the courage and daring required in that most difficult of all enterprises — war (*Disc*, II, xvi, 320). The ideal prince, then, is to be distinguished from such failures by his willingness to engage in battle, to risk all in the hope of gaining all.

One word sums up the heroic qualities of Machiavelli's prince and also identifies the intelligence, foresight, and cunning that make him a confidence man as well: *virtù*. Although he does not use it in a philosophically systematic fashion, most discussions of *virtù* link it to two interconnected sets of properties, including, on one side, the more physical or bodily traits of strength and military prowess, courage and daring, and, on the other, the more intellectual or spiritual traits of

---

[16] On the proverb, see Felix Gilbert, *Machiavelli and Guicciardini: Politics and History in Sixteenth-Century Florence* (Princeton: Princeton University Press, 1965), p. 33.

strength of will, skill, foresight, insight, and imagination.[17] Machiavelli himself points to the doubleness of *virtù* when he speaks of "virtú d'animo e di corpo" (*Pr*, VIII, 41: "*virtù* of spirit and body"), and the chief synonyms scholars have tracked down for this key term—*animo*, *gagliardia*, *fortezza*, *destrezza*, and *ingegno*—and such related concepts as *furore*, *prudenzia*, *industria*, *astuzia*, *inganno*, and *arte*, all point to the toughness of the warrior as well as the cunning of the confidence man. Most scholars agree that although a civic form of *virtù* is defined in the *Discorsi* and associated with devotion to the republic and the law, the term has the double set of meanings described above in *Il principe* and in Machiavelli's political and historical works generally, where it is also fairly consistently associated with the disciplined and self-conscious use of violence.[18] *Virtù* may even be, as John Geerken has argued, exactly analogous to *arête*, the quality defining the activity of Homeric heroes,[19] although one must remember that Machiavelli did not know Greek and that *virtù*, meaning force or energy, was a common term employed by many Renaissance Italian writers.[20] Still, as the word's synonyms and related concepts indicate, *virtù* for Machiavelli meant that conjunction of force and fraud, the lion and the fox, the warrior and the confidence man, that defines his prince as a transmogrified ancient hero.

Virtù may point to both the heroic and the trickster sides of the prince, but it does not do so evenhandedly. For Machiavelli has chosen as his key term a word derived from Latin, and he uses it in a way consistent with its root. *Virtù* is thus equivalent to *virtus*: at its base, it means manliness (according to Cicero, *virtus* is derived from *vir*, the

[17]See, for example, John Plamenatz, "In Search of Machiavellian *Virtù*," in *The Political Calculus: Essays on Machiavelli's Philosophy*, ed. Anthony Parel (Toronto: University of Toronto Press, 1972), pp. 158–64; Bernard Guillemain, *Machiavel: L'Anthropologie politique* (Geneva: Droz, 1977), p. 358; Joseph A. Mazzeo, *Renaissance and Revolution: Backgrounds to Seventeenth-Century English Literature* (New York: Random House, 1965, 1967), p. 93; Russell Price, "The Senses of *Virtù* in Machiavelli," *European Studies Review* 3 (1973): 337–38; and Hanna F. Pitkin, *Fortune Is a Woman: Gender and Politics in the Thought of Niccolò Machiavelli* (Berkeley: University of California Press, 1984), pp. 25–26. For a useful discussion of *virtù* as an improvisational quality, see Thomas M. Greene, "The End of Discourse in Machiavelli's 'Prince'" *Yale French Studies* 67 (1984): 57–71.

[18]Plamenatz, "In Search of Machiavellian *Virtù*," pp. 167–68; Price, "Senses of *Virtù*," 328; Neal Wood, "Machiavelli's Concept of *Virtù* Reconsidered," *Political Studies* 15 (1967): 162–65; Jack H. Hexter, "The Loom of Language and the Fabric of Imperatives: The Case of *Il Principe* and *Utopia*," *American Historical Review* 69 (1964): 956; and Siegel, "Violence and Order," p. 60. On the notion that *virtù* means prowess in the use of political violence, see Mark Hulliung, *Citizen Machiavelli* (Princeton: Princeton University Press, 1983), p. 203.

[19]Geerken, "Homer's Image of the Hero in Machiavelli," 62–75.

[20]Price, "Senses of *Virtù*," 320.

Roman word for *man*), and manliness, in turn, is the physical and military prowess, the energy, discipline, and furor of the warrior.[21] Although Machiavelli also uses *virtù* to define such intellectual qualities as cunning and foresight, these meanings may be perceived as extensions of its fundamental sense. As a result, when he defines the prince as a creature of *virtù*, Machiavelli may be pointing to both sides of that figure's character, to both the heroic lion and the cunning fox, but the word he has chosen also suggests that however important the cleverness and prudence of the confidence man may be, the toughness, resolution, and daring of the hero are more basic. Why such a hierarchy should exist, why one set of meanings should be given prominence over another, will emerge as we proceed.

Normally, students of Machiavelli stress his opposition of *virtù* to *fortuna*, but it is also opposed to a somewhat different but equally important term in Machiavelli's lexicon, *ozio*, a word that could be translated as "inactivity," "leisure," "idleness," or perhaps even "sloth."[22] If *virtù* defines the mode of existence of the hero, *ozio* defines the contrary condition, the absence of struggle, freedom from political and military competition, and peace. Although such a condition might be worth a hero's striving, Machiavelli almost uniformly condemns it. The only instance of a positive — or better, neutral — use of the term occurs in a passage early in the *Discorsi* when he says that the *ozio* the Venetians enjoyed because of their geographical position allowed them to achieve their present greatness (I, i, 126). This passage also makes it clear, however, that what counts for Machiavelli is the Venetians' rise to political greatness, and that the leisure they enjoyed is valuable not in itself but only as a means to that end. More typical of Machiavelli's attitude is his warning in *Il principe* that hereditary rulers, unlike "new" princes, could become "oziosi" because they can keep their realms through the force of custom and do not have to struggle to hold onto them, and that their idleness could consequently cost them their realms (*Pr*, IV, 27). Similarly, he shakes his head over the sons of Francesco Sforza, who, having fled discomforts ("disagi"), thereby ensured the loss of the state they inherited from their father (*Pr*, XIV, 62). In general, he faults contemporary rulers for trying to avoid difficulties and discomforts and especially for running away from conflict and war; their idleness, he insists, is the main reason that so many of them have lost their realms and

---

[21]See Hulliung, *Citizen Machiavelli*, pp. 28–29.
[22]Among the various antonyms to *virtù*, Price includes *ozio* as well as *viltà*, *ignavia*, and *debolezza*; see his "Sense of *Virtù*," p. 315.

that Italy is in such a sorry state (see *Ist*, ı, xxxix, 135-36; *Arte*, vıı, 518). In short, an indulgence in *ozio* means a basic refusal to engage in heroic activity and spells inevitable political disaster as a result. Hence Machiavelli repeatedly insists that his prince not stay idle at court but actively rule his realm and take charge of his army in the field (*Disc*, ı, xxx, 201). He may fault Alexander and Caesar for their ambition and tyranny, but he admires them because they were anything but idle (*Arte*, vıı, 517-18).

If *ozio* is a danger for individual princes, it is also one for states. In the *Discorsi* he observes that "l'ozio e la pace" (ıı, xxv, 357: "idleness and peace"), by allowing dissension and corruption to appear in republics, will lead to their ruin (see also *Disc*, ı, vi, 145). Machiavelli sees states going through inevitable cycles from a condition of "virtuous" struggle to one of peace and *ozio*, which lead in turn to disorder, ruin, and then to a cataclysmic reordering and a return to the *virtù* of their beginnings.[23] *Ozio* thus represents the bottom of the circle, the nadir in the life of the state. Machiavelli wants for the state what he wants for his prince: a life that is, paradoxically, both orderly and marked by constant toil and struggle both with other states and within itself, because orderly, circumscribed struggle is a sign of its vitality, whereas a giving in to *ozio* is a sign of decadence and death. Not surprisingly, then, Machiavelli is hostile to ideal republics and utopias, to visions such as Castiglione's Urbino, More's Utopia, and their classical models. In the famous fifteenth chapter of *Il principe*, he says such states betray his sense of human beings' fundamentally evil, unstable, restless, egocentric natures, but it is also clear that he dislikes them because they would fail politically. The *ozio* they would enjoy would render them flaccid and weak, the helpless prey of stronger, more aggressive states. By contrast, Machiavelli extols his mythic Rome, whose success, he claims, derived from an institutionalization of conflict that kept its citizens vigorous and engaged in public life (*Disc*, ı, iii, 135). To be sure, such conflict could degenerate into destructive party factionalism, as it had done in Florence (*Ist*, ıı, ii, 141). It also makes the state inherently unstable, as was the case with Rome: the internal struggles that were the source of the city's vitality and greatness eventually caused its demise. Nevertheless, Machiavelli praises those struggles, for Rome grew long and gloriously because of them (*Disc*, ı, xxxvii, 218).

The state for Machiavelli is a body politic, a metaphor he takes seriously. Like all bodies since the Fall, it is by its nature, according to

---

[23]For the fullest presentation of the cycle of history, see *Ist*, v, i, 325. See also *Disc*, ı, ii, 131-34; ıı, Proemio, 271-74; the *Asino d'oro*, *SL*, 287, v, 31ff.

Renaissance medicine, filled with humors in a permanent condition of disequilibrium and constantly at war with one another, so that it is the height of folly to attempt utopian projects of reformation. Instead, a good state provides outlets for its humors when they endanger its health (*Disc*, I, vii, 146-47); it allows for political parties to express class interests, and it creates wars to distract the general populace. Moreover, because of its humors, the state will always be in slightly bad health, always open to disease, always exposed to corruption and death, although its body, unlike the bodies of humans, can come back from the grave to live again. Clearly the best state is like Rome, which accommodated its nature and arranged its basic institutions to allow the longest and most glorious survival. Instructively, whereas the commonplace of the body politic was used from the twelfth century through the Renaissance usually to argue that the authority of princes derived from the peoples they ruled, Machiavelli uses the metaphor to underscore the paradoxical identity of disease and vitality, the life-begetting struggle that defined the nature of the state for him.[24]

Machiavelli's rejection of *ozio* as a goal for either the individual or the state is a radical move that places him at odds with a major tendency in Western thought. In *The Garlands of Repose*, Michael O'Loughlin has shown that leisure in various guises was the end sought by most important ancient thinkers and writers, by Christian philosophers and theologians in the Middle Ages, and by writers representing all facets of Renaissance culture.[25] He begins with the symposium, a time of leisure presented as ideal by Homer in *The Odyssey*, and then shows that both Plato and Aristotle embraced a comparable vision of civic leisure, a festive, collective celebration, as the goal that made all the work of society worthwhile. Later, when the advent of the Hellenistic period meant that the *polis*, or city-state, ceased to be the central means for human self-definition, and individualistic philosophical systems as divergent as Stoicism and Epicureanism appeared, leisure still remained the ideal, although now it was the leisure of the personal life of retirement. Although the Romans—the actual Romans, not those of Machiavelli's mythical republic—valued hard work and struggle, service and self-sacrifice for the public good, they too saw leisure as the goal to be achieved, imagining it, according to O'Loughlin, in Vergilian terms as the return of the Age of Gold under Augustus, or in Horatian terms as

[24]Paul Archambault, "The Analogy of the 'Body' in Renaissance Political Literature," *Bibliothèque d'Humanisme et Renaissance* 29 (1967): 48-53.

[25]This paragraph is based on Michael O'Loughlin, *The Garlands of Repose: The Literary Celebration of Civic and Retired Leisure* (Chicago: University of Chicago Press, 1978). The quotation from Saint Benedict occurs on p. 180.

a private escape into the country, or the country of the mind, where one could be free from the cares of business and the state. Christianity continued the same emphasis by assimilating the idea of civic leisure to the pastoral free time of the heavenly city. Through monasticism, Christians sought to turn a philosophical and poetic idea of leisure into an existential reality by creating communities that attempted to realize the ideal city on earth. Western monasticism especially placed what O'-Loughlin calls a georgic (after Vergil's *Georgics*) stress on work and action in history and distrusted quotidian idleness—Saint Benedict proclaimed that "otiositas inimica est animae" ("idleness is the enemy of the soul")—but the labor advocated was always justified by the ultimate leisure, the contemplative beatitude, it was intended to lead to. Finally, in the Renaissance if there was a revival of the Roman notion of the active life, that life was still sanctioned by the ultimate attainment of some golden existence to be achieved in this life and represented in such things as the earthly symposium of Erasmus's *Convivium religiosum* (The godly feast) and Rabelais's utopian Abbaye de Thélème. Moreover, those who, like Petrarch and Montaigne, opposed the concept of the active life in the Renaissance did so in the name of an ideal of private retirement which had little to do with Christian contemplation but was nevertheless an ideal of leisure. For this entire tradition, then, *negotium*—work, business, engagement in public affairs—was always perceived, as the construction of the word suggests, as a negation, an absence; it was a denial of *otium* (*neg-otium*), of that leisure or retirement which had primary value. Machiavelli has turned this tradition dramatically upside down.

In his rejection of leisure, Machiavelli appears to recall Cicero, who was also at odds with that tradition. Both men were intensely active in affairs of state, and both were forced into an unwilling retirement by political events, Machiavelli by the Medici takeover of Florence and Cicero by the Roman civil wars. Cicero characteristically praises Scipio for occupying his leisure thoughts with business ("in otio de negotio congitare") and insits that his own forced retirement does not find him idle.[26] Cicero, however, could accept the idea of Scipio's voluntary retirement, and his notion of involvement in civic affairs was a matter of carrying out a duty, a public responsibility. Although Machiavelli echoes Cicero's dislike of forced retirement as he insists that even in such a situation he is not idle (see the "Proemio" to the *Arte della guerra*, 325–27), he differs from his Roman alter ego in two significant ways.

[26]For the quotation from Cicero, see Marcus Tullius Cicero, *De Officiis*, ed. Walter Miller (Cambridge: Harvard University Press, 1961), p. 270.

First, he does not conceive the life of action as a moral duty but in more profound, existential terms: human beings are defined by heroic action; not to act is thus to be less than human, to enter into an existential void. That is why Machiavelli is willing even to serve the Medici he opposed so fervently during the years of the Soderini republic. In the famous letter in which he confesses this desire to Francesco Vettori, he never says that his motive is patriotism, despite his intense love for Florence, and although he admits he is pressed by financial needs, he goes on to say that he simply wishes to be used by the Medici, "se dovessino cominciare a farmi voltolare un sasso" (*Let*, #140, 305: "even if they should just begin to have me roll a stone about").[27] He will accept even the humblest position, for to act is clearly better than to lose one's identity through idleness. Machiavelli's second difference from Cicero is equally profound, for he sees both the individual and the state as existing in a condition of constant struggle and turmoil. The mind is not ideally the center of peace and harmony for him, as it was supposed to be for much of the Western tradition before him and especially for Platonists and Christian contemplatives, but rather the scene of dynamic desires and the constant conflict of will and reason.[28] And his version of the ideal state of Rome, as has been shown, involves a situation of perpetual internecine strife. Cicero could imagine an ideal republic at peace and could praise Scipio for embracing a voluntary retirement; such options for Machiavelli were clearly neither realistic in a psychological or political sense nor admissible in an existential one.

Though Machiavelli's notion of *ozio* was far from the Christian position, Christianity did shape his conception in important ways, just as it strongly influenced his vision of fallen human beings as prone to evil. For although Machiavelli dislikes *ozio* on existential and political grounds, he also condemns it as a vice for what it does to the character of those who embrace it. A person who is *ozioso* does not merely turn away from heroic action but embraces evil; that person is not merely idle but slothful. Like Saint Benedict, Machiavelli distrusts *otiositas* as the potential ruin of the spirit, as the workshop of evil, the "balia de' vizii."[29] Consequently, it is not by chance that *ozio* is constantly presented as either leading to evil and degeneracy or paired with them. At various points in his works, he links it to such clearly despised traits as "delica-

[27]For a splendid commentary on this phrase and on Machiavelli's desires for political activity, see Raimondi, *Politica e commedia*, pp. 166-72.

[28]Martin Fleisher, "A Passion for Politics: The Vital Core of the World of Machiavelli," in *Machiavelli and the Nature of Political Thought*, ed. Martin Fleisher (New York: Atheneum, 1972), pp. 118-23.

[29]Alberti cites the old Italian proverb "L'ozio si è balia de' vizii" in the *Libri della famiglia*, p. 92.

tezze," "sontuosità," and "lascivia" (*Pr*, xiv, 62; *Disc*, i, ii, 131) and condemns it for its potential to make a republic "effeminata" (*Disc*, i, vi, 145; see also *Disc*, iii, x, 420). In the following sentence, for example, Machiavelli mixes together the idle with those who are morally depraved and those who are cowardly, as if there were little difference among these categories in his mind: "Sono . . . infami e detestabili gli uomini distruttori delle religioni, dissipatori de' regni e delle republiche . . . , come sono gl'impii, i violenti, gl'ignoranti, i dappochi, gli oziosi, i vili" (*Disc*, i, x, 156: "Men who destroy religions and dissipate reigns and republics . . . are infamous and detestable . . . , as are the impious, the violent, the ignorant, the worthless, the idle, the cowardly"). To indulge in *ozio* is to degenerate morally, in essence to rot, as Machiavelli suggests when he speaks of certain Roman legions "marcendo nell'ozio" (*Disc*, ii, xx, 338: "rotting in idleness"), coming to love their sloth, and as a result losing their patriotism and their reverence for the Senate. In the *Istorie fiorentine*, Machiavelli tells us that the youth of Florence at one point responded to a time of peace by throwing money away on clothes, banquets, and "altre simili lascivie" ("other similar lascivious pursuits"), and, "essendo oziosi, in giuochi e in femmine il tempo e le sustanze consumavono" (vii, xxviii, 494: "being idle, wasted their time and substance on games and women"). Indeed, the evil inherent in the life of idle pleasure is felt to be so contagious that if one captures "una città o una provincia piena di delizie" (*Disc*, ii, xix, 337: "a city or a state filled with pleasures"), one's intercourse with it will surely lead to one's own corruption, as Machiavelli saw it did in the case of Rome. Nevertheless, although Machiavelli's conception is clearly influenced by Christianity here, his *ozio* is juxtaposed not to a life of Christian virtue and contemplation but to political and military activity; it is either arms or "delicatezze" for him (*Pr*, xiv, 62). And those who succumb to *ozio* are condemned not to suffer for eternity in hell but to endure more mundane fates: they are forced into political exile or slain by their more *virtuosi*—more heroic—opponents.

If the prince's *virtù* and his *imprese* imply epic, then the *ozio* to which he is opposed also evokes a literary genre, one felt to be precisely the contrary of epic in both antiquity and the Renaissance—namely, the pastoral. Typically, the pastoral involves a celebration of pleasure and idleness, turning its back on both the urban landscape and the heroic quest.[30] It takes place, as does Vergil's programmatic First Eclogue, "sub

[30]On the pastoral, see, among others, Renato Poggioli, "The Oaten Flute," *Harvard Library Bulletin* 11 (1957): 147-84; Mia I. Gerhardt, *La Pastorale* (Assen: Van Gorcum, 1950); Harold E. Toliver, *Pastoral Forms and Attitudes* (Berkeley: University of Califor-

tegmine fagi / . . . / in umbra" (ll. 1, 4: "under the cover of a beech /
. . . / in the shade"), rather than in the world of work and struggle, and
the precondition that allows it to exist is leisure.[31] As Vergil's idle shepherd Tityrus says to his friend Meliboeus in the same eclogue, "deus
nobis haec otia fecit" (1.5: "a god gave us this leisure"). Moreover,
although the mutability of the form of the pastoral allowed it to be
adapted to a wide variety of themes in the Renaissance, both in that
period and in antiquity it is specifically associated with love and sensual
pleasure, from the love complaints of the shepherds in Theocritus and
Vergil down to those of Jacopo Sannazaro, Maurice Scève, and Christopher Marlowe. Indeed, Machiavelli's friend Francesco Vettori makes
explicit the connections among *ozio*, love, and the pastoral when in two
letters he writes of his and Machiavelli's amatory experiences: first, he
links love to idleness in the manner of Ovid (*Let*, #161, 369: "Ovidio
dixe bene che l'amore procedeva da otio"), and then citing a verse from
Vergil's Second Eclogue (l. 69), he identifies himself as a pastoral lover:
"E' sono piú mesi che io intexi benissimo in che modo amavi, e fui per
dirvi: *Ah, Coridon, Coridon, quae te dementia cepit*" (*Let*, #162,
370-71: "For many months I have understood very well how I loved and
was ready to say to you: *Ah, Coridon, Coridon, what madness has taken
you*").[32] Finally, most pastoral works, if not explicitly antiheroic, at least
see themselves as standing at the opposite extreme from the epic.[33] Vergil, for instance, in the Sixth Eclogue defines this opposition when, in
the role of Tityrus the shepherd, he reports that Apollo plucked him by
the ear, rebuking him for thinking of kings and battles, the subjects for
an epic bard, not a pastoral swain, and instructed him instead to stick
to his sheep and to the "deductum . . . carmen" (l. 5: "slender . . .
poem") appropriate to such a singer. In a complementary fashion, many
Renaissance epics may include the pastoral in some way, as do those of
Sir Philip Sidney, Tasso, and Spenser, but they are usually concerned to
point out the limitations of that genre and the lifestyle it adumbrates in
part simply through its placement in the larger context of epic. Consequently, it should now appear perfectly natural—historicaly determined, really—that when Machiavelli celebrates heroic activity and epic

nia Press, 1971); and Thomas G. Rosenmeyer, *The Green Cabinet: Theocritus and the European Pastoral* (Berkeley: University of California Press, 1969).
   [31] P. Vergili Maronis, *Opera*, ed. Frederic A. Hirtzel (Oxford: Clarendon Press, 1900).
   [32] On the connection between the pastoral and courtly love in the Renaissance, see O'Loughlin, *Garlands of Repose*, pp. 192-96.
   [33] On the opposition between pastoral and epic, see Patrick Cullen, *Spenser, Marvell, and Renaissance Pastoral* (Cambridge: Harvard University Press, 1970), pp. 6-10. See Rosenmeyer, *Green Cabinet*, pp. 4-8.

achievement, he should simultaneously disparage pastoral leisure, love, and pleasure.

That Machiavelli was familiar with pastoral and its basic conventions can be easily proved, not merely by the fact that Vettori felt free to cite a line from Vergil's Second Eclogue in a letter to him but by reference to Machiavelli's own works. We find, for instance, the "Capitolo pastorale," a love poem, and the pastoral choruses opening *La mandragola* and *Clizia*. Those two choruses are sung by nymphs and shepherds, and the first especially celebrates a life of pleasure, of "festa" and "gioia" (55: "festivity" and "joy"), in the midst of a world of "pene," "inganni," and "noia" (ibid.: "suffering," "deceptions," and "trouble"). By affiliating the world of his comedy with that of pastoral, Machiavelli links the "ideal" quality of the one with that of the other and implicitly juxtaposes both to the "real" world of history and politics, a world that clearly shows up the limitations of the pastoral. In Machiavelli's opposition of pastoral *ozio* to the *virtù* of his heroic confidence man there may also be a touch of the traditional opposition between the country bumpkin and the city slicker, as when he notes that the Roman emperor Maximinus, who was a failure as a prince, started out his life as a shepherd in Thrace and was despised as a result (*Pr*, XIX, 83). Finally, there is a disparity between Machiavelli, who could write pastoral poems and plays with pastoral choruses while still giving primacy to politics, and his prince, for whom politics has elbowed everything else aside. Machiavelli, we shall see, could enjoy leisure and the pleasures of the body, taking them as at least salutary interludes in his committed public life; his prince knows only a life of discipline, struggle, and total seriousness.

Machiavelli's rejection of pastoral in favor of epic can also be related to — may indeed help shape — his distinctive, heroic conception of time. The pastoral depicts a timeless moment in which all is play and the will is utterly relaxed. The pastoral pleasance is free from the pressures of history, from any striving after the future, which is glimpsed at most in the haze hovering beyond its borders; if time moves there at all, it does so only according to leisurely, diurnal rhythms. In the shepherd's world there is always room for song and play, for love laments and contests, for indulgence in poetry. The epic, by contrast, is profoundly concerned with temporal movement, with the forward rush of history, with a past to be fulfilled and a future to be encountered, if not always joyously embraced. Not by chance do epics frequently dwell on prophecies and interrupt their plots to recount the genealogies of their heroes. Moreover, whereas pastoral is essentially static and stationary, those epic plots, from Vergil's through Boiardo's and Ariosto's down to Milton's,

are shaped as and by quests in which movement in time is complemented by movement in space. The epic is, in short, dynamic, teleolog-
ical, and concerned with origins; the pastoral celebrates immanence.

In keeping with his preference for *virtù* over *ozio*, for epic over pastoral, Machiavelli is obsessed by history, by a past from which to draw
lessons and a future in which to apply them. He is everywhere concerned with beginnings and endings, and especially with the new beginnings he imagines his ideal princes can bring about. It should
consequently be no surprise that he utterly rejects pastoral leisure,
heaping scorn upon the notion of living in and for the moment and
consistently attacking the folly of those princes who complacently think
they can rest secure in the present and stop worrying about future con-
tingencies (see *Let*, #135, 280). Human beings, he feels, live in a world
driven relentlessly by time: "el tempo si caccia innanzi ogni cosa, e può
condurre seco bene come male e male come bene" (*Pr*, III, 22: "time
chases everything forward and can produce good as well as evil, evil as
well as good"). Hence it is a catastrophic mistake to do what the supposed "savii" of the present urge and try to "godere el benefizio del
tempo" (*Pr*, III, 22: "enjoy the benefit of time"), for in a world where
time is ever-moving and, as Machiavelli says the Romans knew (*Pr*, III,
21), struggle and war are inevitable, whether one elects them or not, to
lie passive before time in pastoral idleness is not only to renounce any
chance for self-definition as a hero but to make oneself inevitably the
victim of others as well. Like so many writers of Renaissance epics,
Machiavelli thus condemns the happiness and security of pastoral *ozio*
as treacherous illusions, and just as those writers expose the fragility of
the pastoral world and the insubstantiality of the boundaries it erects
around itself for protection, so Machiavelli condemns self-indulgence in
the pleasures of idleness for exposing one to destruction, to submer-
gence beneath the ever-moving stream of history.

Machiavelli is also like countless writers of epic in associating the pastoral bower with moral decadence and dereliction of duty. From Homer
to Ariosto to Milton, the bower is a place of sensual indulgence and personal, psychological regression, a place where the hero abandons his
quest out of sheer physical weariness and spiritual collapse. Instead of
struggling onward through a world full of dangers and pain, he simply
stops and gives up, as Odysseus does when he lingers on Circe's isle for
a full year after he has tamed her magic and as Ariosto's Ruggiero does
when he succumbs to Alcina's fatal charms. Such episodes have a sexual
component, to be sure, but far more important is the fact that the
temptress offers food, shelter, and a life free from responsibility, offers
the hero essentially a chance to become a child again and avoid the work

and trouble of manhood. Appropriately, in poem after poem, he is depicted as lying at his ease in utter idleness, stripped of his armor, totally
absorbed in his emotional and sensual life rather than continuing his
journey and carrying on the good fight.

Since Machiavelli identifies *ozio* as the chief, most disastrous vice
afflicting such city-states as Florence, he has few opportunities to describe actual pastoral landscapes in his political and historical works.
Nevertheless, there are moments when such landscapes do appear, so
rich and fertile that they seem to require almost no work to be fruitful.
There a benevolent, pastoral nature appears, which potentially offers
humans an abundance of leisure. Consequently, it may seem strange
that Machiavelli, with his distrust of pastoral *ozio*, should sometimes
view those spots positively. In the *Istorie fiorentine*, for instance, he
praises the peace of the Roman Empire, which allowed the inhabitants
of Florence to descend out of the mountains and settle the fertile plain
near the Arno, a beneficial site that he lauds for having allowed the city
to grow and become prosperous (*Ist*, II, ii, 139). Likewise, he notes, this
time specifically using words that allude to the *locus amoenus*, the
pleasance characteristic of pastoral, that the barbarian invasions of Italy
forced the Venetians to leave "luoghi amenissimi e fertili" (*Ist*, I, xxix,
121: "most pleasant and fertile spots") and to flee to the sterile, com-
fortless islands of their lagoon, which they nevertheless managed to
make "non solo abitabili, ma dilettevoli" ("not only inhabitable, but delightful") in a short time. This last example reveals that what Machiavelli really values is not the benevolent nature of the pastoral bower but
human beings' ability to transform even a harsh, unpleasant landscape
into a splendid city by their art and labor. In general, he does not consider nature particularly benevolent, and he revealingly praises the
Romans at one point in the *Arte della guerra* for not depending on the
nature of the site when they set up their military encampments but using
their art to make the site fit the orderly arrangement they preferred (VI,
464). In all of these examples, the fertility or sterility of the landscape
may seem almost a neutral matter for Machiavelli, but in one extremely
important passage in the *Discorsi* he unmistakably indicates that nature
in the pastoral world poses a serious moral danger. This passage occurs
near the start of that work, when Machiavelli is discussing the founding
of cities. Initially he wants them built on a sterile site because the difficulties it imposes will act as a constant constraint on their inhabitants'
desires and imaginations; it will force them to be virtuous because they
will be "meno occupati dall'ozio" (I, i, 127: "less occupied by idleness").
Here *ozio* is a presented as a profound danger, which could possess the
very beings of those who were exposed to it. Then, however, Machiavelli

decides that republics really need rich sites, just as he said Florence did, so that they can grow in size and strength and avoid becoming the easy prey of other, larger states. Still, since the richness of such a site presents a moral danger to the citizens, he concludes by insisting that good laws and extraordinary military discipline must be used to counteract "quell'ozio che le arrecasse il sito" (ibid.: "that *ozio* which the site would entail for them"). He not only describes those dangerously rich sites in pastoral terms, speaking of "paesi amenissimi e fertilissimi" and of "l'amenità del paese," but declares that such pleasances are "atti a produrre uomini oziosi ed inabili a ogni virtuoso esercizio" (ibid.: "apt to produce men who are idle and incapable of every action involving *virtù*"). Clearly, then, for Machiavelli as for the writers of Renaissance epics, the pastoral bower is indeed a bower of bliss, a treacherous, morally disastrous place from which the epic hero must flee and over which Machiavelli's citizens can triumph only through the most stringent controls, the most extreme discipline.

Pastoral *ozio* and the lack of heroism and *virtù* are responsible, according to Machiavelli, for the political ruin he saw all around him in the Italy of the early *cinquecento* (see *Disc*, II, xxx, 371; "Capitolo dell'ambizione," *SL*, 322, ll.115-20; *Arte*, VII, 517-18). Specifically, he attacks two of the dominant institutions in his world, the church and humanist courtly culture, as being corrupted by *ozio* and responsible for the decadence of everything else. The church is faulted because, although it may once have rallied men for heroic crusades, in the present world the Christian worship of humility and aspiration to celestial heights have made men weak, effeminate, and inclined to dismiss as unimportant the maintenance of a strong state. Machiavelli does not attack Christianity directly, but rather attacks the "viltà degli uomini" (*Disc*, II, ii, 283: "baseness of men"), for he insists that Christianity theoretically permits the exaltation and defense of the *patria*. In this context, he directly connects people's baseness to *ozio* and opposes it to *virtù*: human beings' failure, he insists, is that they interpret Christianity "secondo l'ozio e non secondo la virtú" (ibid.: "according to *ozio* and not according to *virtù*"). By contrast, he praises the great enemies of Christendom, the Moslem Egyptians and Turks, for their *virtù*, and he specifically identifies them with their religion, celebrating them as "quella sètta Saracina che fece tante gran cose ed occupò tanto mondo" (*Disc*, II, Proemio, 273: "that Saracen sect which did such great things and occupied so much territory"). In Machiavelli's mind, then, religion can foster heroism just as surely as it can be corrupted by pastoral *ozio*.

If Machiavelli hedges his attack on Christianity, he feels no constraint in attacking the humanist and courtly culture of his own day.[34] In particular, he lashes out at contemporary gentlemen, defining them thus:

> Gentiluomini sono chiamati quelli che oziosi vivono delle rendite delle loro possessioni abbondantemente, sanza avere cura alcuna o di coltivazione o di altra necessaria fatica a vivere. Questi tali sono perniziosi in ogni republica ed in ogni provincia; ma più perniziosi sono quelli che oltre alle predette fortune comandano a castella, ed hanno sudditi che ubbidiscono a loro. . . . Tali generazioni di uomini sono al tutto inimici d'ogni civilità. [*Disc*, I, lv, 256]

> They are called gentlemen who live idly and in abundance on the returns from their possessions without any care about cultivation or any other trouble involved in living. Such men are pernicious in a republic and in every country; but more pernicious are those who in addition to the aforementioned advantages rule from a castle and have subjects who obey them. . . . Such generations of men are absolutely the enemies of all civilization.

Gentlemen are disparaged because they live in what Machiavelli characterizes as a pastoral situation: their lives are spent in *ozio*, and they are freed from any obligation to struggle in order to live. They were not always thus, according to Machiavelli, and in the *Istorie fiorentine* he laments the loss of modern gentlemen's ancestors, the old feudal nobility, who were devoted to war and whose degeneration into citified and courtly idlers has brought about the decline of Italy (III, i, 212–13). Machiavelli also indicts contemporary gentlemen because their possession of lands and retainers grants them the means to pursue their petty personal ambitions, with the result that the states they live in are doubly weak: weak because those who should stand in the first rank as warriors are idle and inconsequential, and weak because the internecine strife fomented by gentlemanly ambition undermines political unity. Finally, in *Il principe*, he notes that contemporary gentlemen, however prone to fractiousness, are sufficiently manipulable that they can easily be neutralized by money, and he praises Cesare Borgia for adopting just such a strategy with the rival Orsini and Colonna families in Rome and making all their adherents his own "gentili uomini" (VII, 36).

If Machiavelli condemned the idleness and decadence of gentlemen, in the course of his career he also finally came to condemn the aesthetic humanist culture by which gentlemen defined themselves. Thus, al-

[34]See Raimondi, "Machiavelli and the Rhetoric of the Warrior," p. 6.

though in the *Discorsi* he could still praise writers and warriors in the same breath (i, x, 156), by the time he composed the *Istorie fiorentine* he had changed his mind. Now he follows Cato the Elder and rejects letters and philosophy altogether because they are, he says, the products of *ozio*, albeit an "onesto ozio," and therefore will corrupt the citizens of the state (*Ist*, v, i, 325). Clearly, then, Machiavelli stands at the opposite pole from his contemporary Castiglione, who reflected the opinion of so many people in *cinquecento* Italy when he saw in the refined, aesthetic life of court society a vision of the highest civilization possible.[35]

Because Machiavelli condemns contemporary civilization as decadent, it is easy to read him as a primitivist. Unless qualified, however, such a reading would be a mistake, for if he praises "bestial" qualities such as violence and fierce cunning while attacking the refinements of such idle pastimes as literature, that does not mean he idealizes a condition of lawless violence. As the passage quoted earlier indicates, he rejects idle, effete gentlemen not in the name of savagery but because they are "inimici d'ogni civiltà" (*Disc*, i, lv, 256: "enemies of every civilization"). For Machiavelli, a true civilization will retain human beings' natural capacity for fierceness, their animal cunning and force; yet it will also be sure to discipline and shape those qualities, subjecting people to the restraints of law, education, and, as we have seen, religion. Human beings will be useful citizens, he insists, only if their egocentric tendencies are counterbalanced by the force of necessity and they are made to live under the constraints imposed by a relative scarcity, hunger, and poverty, as well as by the force of good laws (*Disc*, i, iii, 136; cf., iii, xii, 425). Thus Machiavelli notes that the Romans prevented their own decadence for a long period by creating censors to oversee public morality (*Disc*, I, xlix, 241), and that they gave their colonists very little land lest wealth lead them into trouble (*Disc*, ii, vii, 296). By contrast, he observes in the *Istorie fiorentine* that unhealthy "humors" increased

---

[35]Castiglione expressed reservations about the ideal civilization he celebrated in Urbino. At the start of Bk. iv of *Il libro del Cortegiano*, he has Ottaviano Fregoso object to the courtly pursuits of the ideal courtier on the grounds that they are "leggerezze e vanità" ("frivolities and vanity") and that they have done nothing less than "effeminar gli animi, corrumper la gioventù e ridurla a vita lascivissima; onde nascono poi questi effetti che 'l nome italiano è ridutto in obbrobrio, né si ritrovano se non pochi che osino non dirò morire, ma pur entrare in uno pericolo" (*Il libro del Cortegiano*, ed. Bruno Maier, 2d ed. [Turin: Unione Tipografico-Editrice Torinese, 1964], iv, iv, 450: "make spirits effeminate and corrupt youth, leading it into the most wicked life, from which the effect is that the Italian name is held in contempt, and only a few can be found who would dare, I will not say to die, but merely to enter into danger"). Ottaviano's terms here are similar to those used by Machiavelli throughout his writings. Obviously, both men were voicing not merely their personal beliefs but an attitude generally shared within their culture.

in Florence after its war with Lucca, for peace released the "freno" (*Ist*, IV, xxviii, 312: "rein") imposed by the necessities of war. Ironically, war is thus a blessing as well as an inevitability, granted the nature of the world, and a good state will not only keep its citizens poor but constantly engage them in wars, as Rome did (*Disc*, III, xvi, 437). Machiavelli seems to contradict his emphasis on keeping citizens in a relatively deprived condition when he says that a state must have a fertile site and must grow rich and prosper if it is to become great, but what he really wants is the creation of an artificial condition of want in which the public treasury of the state is full and all the inhabitants must work hard to sustain themselves. For the private accumulation of riches could lead to *ozio*, and *ozio* would mean decadence and the end of civilization.

To create his version of civilization, Machiavelli places his faith not in nature but in art, not in human beings' natural drives or some illusion about the benevolence of the world but in the shaping power of human intelligence and the force of human will. That is why he consistently gives the palms to law and religion, discipline and industry, praising their ability to tame both people and the world they live in. He insists, for instance, that no matter how defective the nature of a country is, no matter how weak and effeminate the people, a good prince can successfully train them to become excellent soldiers and citizens (*Disc*, I, xxi, 186–87). He even makes the initially puzzling claim that discipline and good order are a better source of the fury needed for war than human beings' aggressive nature, but he clarifies his meaning when he praises the discipline of the Romans because it rendered their fury in battle both dependable and consistent, whereas the lack of such discipline made the uncontrolled, natural fury of the French fitful and self-defeating (*Disc*, III, xxxvi, 484–85). Machiavelli also praises the ability of human industry to tame the natural world not only when he notes that the Romans could successfully adapt every site to the requirements of their military encampments but also when he lauds their practice of sending out colonies. Since nature, he says, cannot be depended on to fill a country evenly and to prevent certain parts of it from becoming deserts while others suffer from overcrowding, "è necessario supplisca la industria" (*Ist*, II, i, 138: "it is necessary that industry should supply [this deficiency]") through the establishment of colonies. In short, although Machiavelli recognizes and accepts human beings' "animal" nature in a way he feels Christianity does not, he also insists that if civilization is to emerge, their nature must be — and can be — trained and shaped. Ironically, his faith in that training and shaping directly recalls a similar faith shared by earlier and contemporary humanists, a faith epitomized in Erasmus's belief that "efficax res est natura, sed hanc vincit efficacior institutio" ("nature is efficacious, but a more efficacious training will conquer it")[36] and dramatized by the basic institutions of More's humanist Utopia. Nevertheless, Machiavelli's goals—the production of fiercely heroic individuals and the achievement of a republic marked by constant, vital internecine strife—are a world away from anything the humanists dreamed of.

Machiavelli clearly conceives of civilization as dynamic, evolving and developing through human direction. He speaks on two occasions, in most suggestive language, of a corrupt state returning to the "vera via" (*Disc*, III, xvi, 437: "true way") and of an uncorrupted one's going along the "diritta via . . . alla perfezione" (*Disc*, I, ii, 134: "right way . . . to perfection"). Machiavelli may be recalling the "diritta via" in the third line of Dante's *Inferno* and suggesting a contrast between Dante's conception of the "right way," which leads through faith, hope, and love to paradise, and his own conception of that way, which leads through discipline and training to a secular state whose constant internal strife might make it seem, to a Christian, like hell. Whatever Machiavelli may have intended by his language, he clearly conceives of civilization as something achieved through art and effort, as moving and changing over time, and the images he uses for it underscore its temporal dimension. In *Il principe*, for example, he frequently imagines it as a building whose foundations must be well laid and which, by implication, must be constantly maintained, can fall into disrepair, and may eventually become a ruin (see, for example, VI, 33; VII, 34, 39; XII, 53). Machiavelli also sees the state as a changing human body (an image already discussed) and as a growing plant. When he explains in the *Discorsi* that all the good of Rome came from its laws and disciplined mode of proceeding, he envisages it as a tree or plant so well cared for that its roots could plunge deep and thus could sustain its growth for a very long time (II, iii, 285-86). Similarly, in the *Istorie fiorentine* he says that because the secular states established by various popes lacked *virtù*, their roots could not hold them firm against the wind (I, xxiii, 113). But whether the state is imaged as a house, a body, or a plant, it is always vital and growing, constantly in need of care.

That care is provided for the state by its leader, by the heroic prince who establishes its constitution, manages its wars and internal struggles, and leads it back to its origins when it becomes flaccid and decadent. Appropriately, Machiavelli identifies that prince not as a willful beast or unrestrained savage but rather consistently as an artist or artisan, and the images used for him correspond directly to the various images used

[36]Erasmus, *Declamatio de pueris*, p. 385.

for the state. Thus, although sometimes the prince is imagined as a sculptor shaping the malleable mass of the populace, he is more frequently a builder or architect who puts down solid foundations for his state or channels the floodwaters of fortune by means of dikes (see *Pr*, VII, 33, 34, 39; XII, 53; XXV, 98–99).[37] As a builder, the prince complements the natural and historical world about him, which is constantly in motion and whose developments Machiavelli repeatedly describes by the verbs *nascere* and *partorire*, as though they were organic processes (see, for example, *Pr*, XVI, 68, and *Disc*, III, v, 389). More frequently the prince is presented, implicitly or explicitly, as a doctor for the body politic, whose health he must manage and whose disorderly condition he must return to its original robustness (*Pr*, III, 19, 21; *Disc*, III, i, 379; XLIX, 504). At the end of *Il principe*, the doctor is transformed into a redeemer: Italy is sick spiritually and needs a doctor to cure her, a savior to redeem her (XXVI, 102–3). Machiavelli uses a word to define such an action in the *Discorsi*, a word that identifies doctoring with religious redemption, when he speaks of the Roman tribunes acting to ensure the "salute" of the state (III, xxx, 467).

Perhaps the most striking and most truly characteristic image of the prince is that of a farmer tending the great plant of the state. This image can be traced to the fact that Machiavelli's admired Romans were, at their origin and for some time thereafter, a race of farmers, whose values of hard work and self-sacrifice the epics of Vergil and Livy attempted to define and preserve. Thus it is not surprising that Machiavelli should have given that image a prominent place in his works, stressing that the Romans wished to treat their state "ad uso del buono cultivatore" (*Disc*, II, iii, 285: "in the manner of a good farmer") and praising those modern republicans, the Venetians, for curing the unhealthfulness of their city's swampy site by means of "la cultura" (*Ist*, II, i, 138). Too, many of his beloved heroes of the Roman Republic were in fact farmers. Thus he singles out for praise in the *Arte della guerra* Regulus Attilius, who led the Roman army to glory against the Carthaginians but then willingly returned to his fields (I, 337–38). And in the *Discorsi* Machiavelli celebrates one of the most famous ancient Romans, Cincinnatus, who had only a "piccola villa" (III, xxv, 457: "small farm") but was chosen to lead the Roman army, refused to take booty for himself or allow his men to do so, and willingly returned to his plow at the end of his tenure as general. Machiavelli looks back with nostalgia at the period of Roman history in which these men lived, turning it into a mythical time in which heroes were grand in battle, fearlessly scorning the princes, kings,

[37]See Raimondi, *Politica e commedia*, p. 153.

and powerful states who were their enemies but showing an entirely different temper when they once again were private citizens; then "diventavano parchi, umili, curatori delle piccole facultà loro, ubbidienti a' magistrati, reverenti alli loro maggiori" (*Disc*, III, xxv, 458: "they became frugal, humble, devoted to their little properties, obedient to the magistrates, reverent to their elders"). Although Machiavelli may claim that their education, discipline, and religion made the ancient Romans thus, this passage practically pushes them beyond human nature, or at least beyond the human nature Machiavelli described as egocentric, aggressive, self-serving, and vindictive.

Machiavelli's image of the farmer-warrior allows him to bring together several of the most important strands of his thought in a single figure, for the farmer-warrior is by profession a *cultivator*, a reverent upholder of the *cult* of the state, and as someone who domesticates nature, the supreme representative of *culture* or civilization. Moreover, as a throwback to a simpler, earlier form of social organization, he escapes the decadence Machiavelli sees in contemporary Christian and courtly culture without at the same time becoming a primitive or a savage. The image of the prince-as-farmer may differ from that of the prince-as-hunter, for in the first image the emphasis falls on the discipline and hard labor involved, in the second on toughness and the controlled use of violence. Nevertheless, the two images have a great deal in common: both hark back to a simpler, earlier, if not exactly primitive condition; both strive to dominate a neutral or even hostile nature; both use intelligence or cunning as well as force and energy, though the proportions differ between them; and both lead lives of self-reliance and vigorous effort. Most important, both the prince-as-farmer and the prince-as-hunter deny the carefree leisure that characterizes pastoral in favor of a life of strenuous exertion and struggle—the life, in other words, of the hero.

Machiavelli presents most dramatically his preference for epic *virtù* over pastoral *ozio* as well as his image of the princely soldier as a rugged Roman farmer-warrior in the one prose work whose publication he carefully oversaw during his lifetime, the *Arte della guerra*.[38] This work is ostensibly a dialogue carried on between, on one hand, the old condottiere Fabrizio Colonna, and, on the other, the group of young men— Cosimo Rucellai, Zanobi Buondelmonti, Battista della Palla, and Luigi Alamanni—who formed a circle of disciples around Machiavelli from

[38]For a fine discussion of this work which parallels my own in many ways, see Pitkin, *Fortune Is a Woman*, pp. 63-73.

about 1516 to 1520 and encouraged him in his political writing. Colonna, however, almost totally usurps the conversation as Machiavelli's spokesman, effectively transforming the work into a monologue interrupted by occasional questions. Ironically, in this dialogue celebrating the art of war and describing such matters as tactics and military fortifications, the setting is not a battlefield but a pastoral garden planted by the grandfather of Cosimo Rucellai, the patrician Bernardo Rucellai. The old warrior Fabrizio Colonna himself directly evokes the pastoral nature of the garden when he initially praises it as "dilettevole" (1, 330). Even more evocatively, the group flees the heat of the day to place itself "sotto l'ombra d'altissimi arbori" (ibid.: "under the shade of the loftiest trees"), thus recalling the cool shade that is one of the most important symbols of the pastoral world. On being informed that the garden has been planted in imitation of the ancients, Colonna hesitates to offer to express his true opinion of it, but he goes on to say that he wishes people would imitate the ancients "nelle cose forti e aspre, non nelle delicate e molli, e in quelle che facevano sotto il sole, non sotto l'ombra" (1, 331: "in matters of strength and hardness, not delicacy and softness, and in those things that they did in the sun, not in the shade"). Colonna thus rejects the very setting in which he will present his ideas on the art of war, beginning what will become a wholesale rejection of the corruption of the modern world, a corruption symbolized by the *ozio* of pastoral and its delightful shade.

The *Arte* is so consistently hostile to the pastoral that as soon as Colonna has attacked Cosimo Rucellai's garden, the latter joins in the attack himself. He says his grandfather actually would have preferred to have imitated the ancients in things tough and difficult, would have preferred to go naked in summer and winter like them, sleep out of doors, and wash in cold water. But because a person who did so, "essendo nato in tanta corruttela di secolo, . . . sarebbe tenuto pazzo" (1, 331–32: "having been born in such a corrupt century, . . . would be considered crazy"), old Bernardo had had to content himself with imitating the ancients in their gardens. Colonna reminds the young man that one could imitate the Romans in less radical fashion, but when he describes what he likes about the Romans—their practice of honoring and rewarding *virtù*, their lack of contempt for poverty, their esteem for military discipline—it becomes clear that the difference between the two characters is merely one of degree.

Fabrizio Colonna, Cosimo Rucellai, and all the other speakers agree on their opposition to *ozio* and everything related to it. Thus Colonna prefers European republics in general to a large Asiatic despotism such as that of the ancient Persians, because, he says, such a state is "ozioso"

(II, 393) and few men of *virtù* can emerge from it. He also praises the discipline and good order of his model Roman army, which he opposes to modern ones that cannot abstain "da' giuochi, dalle lascivie, dalle bestemmie, dalle insolenze" (VII, 516: "from games, from lascivious pursuits, from cursing, from insolence"). Colonna's entire presentation builds up to a full-scale denunciation, replete with bitter irony, of the idle and corrupt princes who are responsible for the loss of Italy to the northern "barbarians":

> Credevano i nostri principi italiani, prima ch'egli assaggiassero i colpi delle oltramontane guerre, che a uno principe bastasse sapere negli scrittoi pensare una acuta risposta, scrivere una bella lettera, mostrare ne' detti e nelle parole arguzia e prontezza, sapere tessere una fraude, ornarsi di gemme e d'oro, dormire e mangiare con maggiore splendore che gli altri, tenere assai lascivie intorno, governarsi co' sudditi avaramente e superbamente, marcirsi nello ozio, dare i gradi della milizia per grazia, disprezzare se alcuno avesse loro dimostro alcuna lodevole via, volere che le parole loro fussero responsi di oraculi; né si accorgevano i meschini che si preparavano ad essere preda di qualunque gli assaltava. [VII, 518]

> Our Italian princes used to believe, before they had tasted the blows of the wars from beyond the Alps, that it was enough for a prince to know how to think up an acute response in his study, to write a beautiful letter, to demonstrate wit and alacrity in sayings and words, to know how to weave a deception, to adorn himself with gems and gold, to sleep and eat with greater splendor than others, to keep enough lascivious goings-on about him, to behave with his subjects in an avaricious and haughty manner, to rot in idleness, to give military appointments as favors, to be scornful if anyone showed him a praiseworthy way, to want his words to be taken for oracles; nor did the wretches realize that they were preparing themselves to be the prey of anyone who assaulted them.

This passage has been quoted at length because it touches practically all the characteristics that so far have been associated with *ozio*, from moral degeneracy, sensual indulgence, political ineptitude, and exposure to the predation of others, down to what someone like Castiglione would include among the arts of civilizaton—witty language and a beautiful style in words and dress. This rejection of the refined arts of civilization, which has already been noted in the *Istorie fiorentine*, shortly surfaces again when Colonna draws a parallel between contemporary Italy and Greece just before Philip of Macedonia conquered it, when that entire country, he says, with derision in his voice, "stava in ozio e attendeva a recitare commedie" (VII, 519: "was idle and occupied themselves with performing plays").

The *Arte della guerra* is also hostile to the body as a source of pleasure and to festivity. The body should be toughened, subjected to discipline and hardships, used to make war. Sex and any association with women are out of the question, and indeed, women are conspicuous by their absence from the dialogue. Nor can there be any indulgence in food and drink. As if in illustration of this preference, Machiavelli reports that the group ate their meal quickly in order to get to what they felt was really "important," the intellectual discussions with Colonna (I, 330). This minimizing of the importance of eating and drinking involves a larger rejection, that of "convivali piaceri . . . e . . . ogni ordine di festeggiare" (ibid.: "convivial pleasures . . . and . . . every kind of festivity"). The reason for this striking rejection of festivity becomes apparent later in the dialogue, when Colonna explains that he wants his model army to exercise on "giorni festivi" ("festival days"), because those are "giorni oziosi" ("idle days") and the people otherwise would stand about "vilmente . . . oziosi" ("basely . . . idle") (I, 354). As we noted earlier, Machiavelli's ideal prince is almost puritanical in his opposition to pleasure and the body, never for a minute ceasing to work, never engaging in games or play, so that his very being constitutes a rejection of festive celebrations in which pleasure and the body come into their own. In Fabrizio Colonna's imaginary army and state, such a prince would clearly have plenty of company.

The dialogue's attack on pastoral *ozio* and everything associated with it is counterbalanced by praise for the life of military action, a life marked by toughness, discipline, reverence, and restraint — the life of the heroic warrior. From the start of the work, Colonna places the emphasis on *industria*, on human art and effort: exercise and training can make good soldiers no matter where they come from, he says, for "dove manca la natura, sopperisce la 'ndustria, la quale in questo caso vale piú che la natura" (I, 344: "where nature is lacking, it is made up for by industry, which in this case is stronger than nature"). Consequently, Colonna stresses the importance of preparation and planning: "Gli uomini che vogliono fare una cosa, deono prima con ogni industria prepararsi, per essere, venendo l'occasione, apparecchiati a sodisfare a quello che si hanno presupposto di operare" (I, 333: "Men who wish to do something must first prepare themselves industriously so that when the time comes, they will turn out to accomplish what they have imagined they would"). For the soldiers of the model army preparation involves intensive physical exercise as well as firm discipline (II, 371). Colonna endorses very harsh punishments for soldiers who are derelict in their duty, although he also calls for rewards for those who excel (VI, 476-77). In keeping with Machiavelli's sense of the purpose of religion,

Colonna also expects that his model army would be trained to be reverent, essentially so that its discipline could be reinforced by the fear of God (vi, 478). Colonna's ultimate goal is to produce an army and a civilization with the disciplined aggression and energy of heroes, what he and Machiavelli both call *virtù* (ii, 393).

The central symbol that Machiavelli develops in the *Arte della guerra* for the heroic life of *virtù* is the sun, a symbol at the opposite extreme from the pastoral shade with which the work opens. The sun is associated throughout with heat and discomfort, with a virtuous, praiseworthy life spent out in the open, in struggle and military encounters. Thus when Cosimo Rucellai and the young men in the dialogue flee the heat of the day by going "nella piú segreta e ombrosa parte del suo giardino" (i, 330: "into the most secluded and shady part of his garden"), Colonna rebukes them by saying they should imitate the ancients in things hard and difficult, in things that were done "sotto il sole, non sotto l'ombra" (i, 331: "in the sun, not in the shade"). Later he proclaims that his model army should be filled with soldiers taken from the country, once again linking a praiseworthy toughness and willingness to endure hardships with a life spent in the sun and a rejection of the shade: all writers on military matters agree, he says, that men from the country are to be preferred because they are "avvezzi a' disagi, nutriti nelle fatiche, consueti stare al sole, fuggire l'ombra, sapere adoperare il ferro, cavare una fossa, portare un peso, ed essere sanza astuzia e sanza malizia" (i, 345: "used to discomforts, nourished on difficulties, accustomed to stay in the sun and to flee the shade, know how to use the sword, to dig a ditch, to carry a weight, and are without cunning and malice"). The sun thus functions as the appropriate symbol of the ideal farmer-warrior, and it is not by accident that Machiavelli celebrates in this work the Roman hero Regulus Attilius, who led the army against Hannibal but then willingly returned to his little farm (i, 338). The sun is also a symbol of truth: the ancients who worked and fought in the sun knew the truth about military and political matters, and that truth Colonna is now imparting to his young interlocutors. Appropriately, Colonna's task is to make them see, and Machiavelli allows him to do so almost literally when, in the middle of the work, he has the old condottiere describe in vivid detail how his ideal army engages in an imaginary battle and easily defeats its enemy (iii, 409-10). Colonna also reinforces the association of the sun with truth and with sight in other ways: the judgment that mercenaries are useless is "piú chiaro che il sole" (i, 338: "clearer than the sun"), he says, and he implies that the smoke from the artillery he condemns (the ancients, of course, relied on foot soldiers) blinds men on the battlefield because it blocks out the sun (III, 413).[39] The physical blindness produced here by the cannons is clearly meant to be an analogue for the spiritual blindness of the modern world, an inability to see, to which Colonna also alludes when he stresses the world's preference for living in the shade, and when he praises the Swiss for possessing at least "alcuna ombra" (II, 375: "a shadow") of ancient military practices.[40] Although the modern world lies in darkness, Colonna does have hope for it or he would not offer it the light he brings. After all, young Florentines do listen to him, and there are still simple, rough men living in the country who might yet be trained as farmer-warriors.

If the *Arte della guerra* is consistently hostile to *ozio*, in an important way that hostility is qualified, for the work attempts to accommodate pastoral leisure, to find a place for the beautiful Rucellai gardens. It does so much as Plato does with the spot beneath the plane tree in the *Phaedrus* and Cicero with the suburban villa in *De Oratore*, two works that clearly are models for Machiavelli. That is, it allows the pastoral world to serve as a setting for the education of the young; it is thus acceptable, not as the end of civilization but as a means, as a useful interlude that prepares those who partake of it for the active life of *virtù*. As a result of this ideological dispensation, although Colonna prefers a life in the sun, he does not get up from the garden and walk out from under its shady trees. Moreover, the young men who listen to him praise him as a tree whose shade makes them happier than that of the real trees about them (I, 333), shade in this context becoming acceptable because it is equivalent to the great man himself and the instruction he imparts. Finally, it must be remembered that the *Arte* opens with a eulogy for Cosimo Rucellai, who died after the dialogue Machiavelli describes supposedly took place, and whom it praises for what might seem a surprising activity: he wrote love poems during his brief youth. Machiavelli does not offer this praise ironically; he justifies the young man's writing as a means to sharpen his mind, as an exercise to prepare himself for life, not as a sign of the degeneration implied by actual sexual involvement. In those poems, he says, Cosimo, "come che innamorato non fusse, per non consumare il tempo invano, tanto che a più alti pensieri la fortuna lo avesse condotto, nella sua giovenile età si esercitava" (I, 328-29: "as

[39]Colonna is aware that the sun can be blinding on the battlefield if it shines in an army's eyes and that one must accommodate oneself to it (III, 413; IV, 426-27). It is not clear whether the sun can still be read as a symbol of truth in these instances (a truth too blinding to look at directly?), but the army still remains in its proper place—outdoors, under the sun.

[40]In the *Discorsi* Machiavelli says that when the Roman emperors became bad and started paying mercenaries to fight for them, they started loving "più l'ombra che il sole" (II, xxx, 370: "the shade more than the sun").

he was not in love and in order not to waste time, so drilled himself during his youth that fortune might have led him to loftier thoughts"). Cosimo is praiseworthy because even in the act of writing love poetry he was disciplining himself and because he was, like a would-be epic hero, avoiding any waste of time. Cosimo clearly functions as a model in the *Arte* just as Colonna does: both use leisure, whether that afforded by the pastoral Rucellai garden or that involved in the writing of poetry, as a period of preparation for what really counts, the life of *virtù* and heroic action. Machiavelli's work thus essentially aims to teach the reader how to take the *ozio* that is so much a part of modern society and use it to reform that society, to lead it away from its immersion in the dangerous, ultimately self-destructive pastoral bower and bring it back to the epic world of its glorious Roman past.

If Machiavelli seldom seems to describe pastoral bowers in his political and historical works, those few green spaces of refined leisure he does present or allude to also seem to lack a standard feature of such places in Renaissance epics: they lack a temptress. In a sense, however, this lack is only apparent, for Machiavelli's works continuously refer to women young and old, who, although scorned for their stupidity, fearfulness, and pusillanimity, are nevertheless inevitably a danger to the men who come into contact with them.[41] They are also both repeatedly linked with pastoral *ozio* and opposed to heroic *virtù*. One may recall, in this connection, the many times *ozio* is linked to moral degeneracy, which often is defined as an indulgence in *lascivie* or an involvement with *femmine*. Moreover, women also appear in Machiavelli's works as the cause of political disasters and wars, such as the conflict between the Guelphs and the Ghibellines (*Ist*, II, iii, 142-43), and Machiavelli even devotes a brief chapter in the *Discorsi* to this subject: "*Come per cagione di femine si rovina uno stato*" (III, xxvi, 459: "*How a state is ruined because of women*"). Castruccio Castracani is an ideal prince in part because of his refusal to marry, and Machiavelli agrees with the ancient opinion that accorded Scipio more praise for sending a chaste young wife back to her husband than for defeating Carthage (*Disc*, III, xx, 445). Women are similarly excluded from the discussions in Cosimo Rucellai's garden, and Machiavelli praises the discipline of the Roman army for being so great that the troops would not go awhoring ("si meritricava") without the order of their consul (III, xxxvi, 484).

Machiavelli's insistent focus on a single mythic female figure who embodies all the traits he imagines in individual women reveals his pro-

---

[41] On Machiavelli's sense of the danger women present to men, see Pitkin, *Fortune Is a Woman*, pp. 109-37.

found ambivalence in regard to them. That mythic female figure is, of course, Fortuna. *Fortuna* is admittedly as vexed a term in Machiavelli's lexicon as *virtù*, and one of the main problems scholars have encountered in defining it is its fundamental ambiguity.[42] Thus sometimes Fortuna appears within the prince's control or even as an aid in presenting him with occasions to display his prowess, and sometimes she is seen as his great opponent and especially as the opponent of *virtù*. Hanna Pitkin points out that, whatever the word may mean conceptually, Fortuna is always a woman for Machiavelli, and that his ambivalence about her is an extension of a basic ambivalence about women.[43]

Fortuna had been a woman, of course, throughout the Western tradition: the Romans imagined her as a fickle but ultimately benevolent female, a goddess who bestowed goods and possessions on humans; Christians in the Middle Ages saw her as a wicked stepmother, albeit one working under God's plan, and opposed her to the benevolent, maternal Virgin; and Renaissance writers, continuing these identifications, saw her as a fickle, even malevolent deity and stressed her female identity in visual representations that juxtaposed her to the male figure of Virtus. Therefore, when Machiavelli personifies Fortuna as a woman throughout his works, his response is consistent with the long tradition he inherited from his culture. In Machiavelli's thought, however, Fortuna is not an aloof Roman goddess or a medieval agent of the divine. She behaves like a fickle, cunning woman, though one vastly superior in power to actual women (and men) and she has a human hunger for power which she displays by being whimsically hostile to some men while favoring others. Fortuna rules the world, and Machiavelli sometimes urges that she be attacked, sometimes placated. She is essentially a mythic vision of woman less as a sexual being than as an all-powerful mother, and this notion supplies the key to her ambiguity and to Machiavelli's ambivalence about her. For as mother she is a threat to male autonomy, a reminder of infantile dependence, and an invitation to regression. But as mother she is also necessarily associated with generation, and in Machiavelli's thought she is related to and overlaps with nature, so that she is simultaneously threatening to and yet indispensable for men, the literal and symbolic source of their life, energy, and creativity. Machiavelli also identifies the movement of historical events that lie beyond human control with Fortuna; indeed, since that move-

---

[42] For the many different meanings of Fortuna, see Mazzeo, *Renaissance and Revolution*, pp. 72-78, 91-94; and Thomas Flanagan, "The Concept of *Fortuna* in Machiavelli," in *Political Calculus*, ed. Parel, pp. 128-56.

[43] My discussion in this and the following paragraphs is generally indebted to Pitkin's *Fortune Is a Woman*, pp. 139-69, although my emphases are quite different from hers.

ment is suggestively defined over and over again by the verbs *nascere* (to be born) and *partorire* (to give birth), the world of history, like that of nature, becomes a kind of mythic mother. In such a scheme, men play subordinate roles with only limited powers to intervene in processes that threaten always to overwhelm them but that they nevertheless help generate, partially direct, and even, in a sense, assist into being as doctors, or better, as male midwives. Thus as mythic mother, Fortuna is an ambiguous creature for Machiavelli, a threat to male identity and a source of vital energy and creativity, a power to be both feared and harnessed for projects determined by the male will.

Machiavelli gives far more emphasis to the threat of women's power than to their usefulness to men. He repeatedly characterizes women as shrews, such as the wife in "Belfagor," or stresses their role in men's degeneracy, so that he excludes them from his vision of a preferred society, such as that depicted in the conversations in Cosimo Rucellai's garden, except for carefully managed bouts of sexual release. A few positive images of women can be found in Machiavelli's works, but upon close inspection, even these admirable women turn out to pose a threat to men. One thinks in this connection of the astute Lucrezia in *La mandragola*; of Sofronia, the directing spirit of *Clizia*; and of Caterina Riario, the Countess of Forli, the one full-fledged, heroic confidence woman in Machiavelli's political writings. Thus, although the two heroines of his comedies assist men (Callimaco in *La mandragola* and, without his knowing or willing it, Nicomaco in *Clizia*), they are presented not only as duping and manipulating men but as humiliating and ridiculing them. And Caterina Riario is no different. Machiavelli tells us in the *Discorsi* that when she and her children were seized by conspirators who had just killed her husband, she promised, if she were released, to persuade those loyal troops in the citadel who were still holding out to surrender. Once she was safely inside the citadel, however, though she had been compelled to leave her children behind as hostages, she climbed atop its walls, menaced the conspirators with vengeance, and "per mostrare che de' suoi figliuoli non si curava, mostrò loro le membra genitali, dicendo che aveva ancora il modo a rifarne" (III, vi, 408: "to show that she did not care about her children, she showed her genitals, saying that she had the means to make more"). Realizing they had been tricked and faced with such an awesome display of women's unmatchable power as mothers and sources of generation, the conspirators lost heart, were defeated, and wound up in perpetual exile. Once again, a woman who is positively evaluated by Machiavelli winds up not only defeating but humiliating and ridiculing men.

When Machiavelli focuses on Fortuna rather than women and on the assistance she gives to men, once again a figure who could be seen as benevolent emerges from his imagination shrouded in menace. In this connection, it is important to remember that Machiavelli repeatedly insists on Fortuna's enormous power in the world, a power so great that it seems at times almost to undermine the very possibility of significant human action as well as Machiavelli's faith in human art and effort. For in his mind Fortuna defines that mysterious quality, that opaqueness, in events which puts them so often beyond the control of human reason and will.[44] He points to this opaqueness and to humans' limited powers when he emphasizes how difficult it is to foresee all eventualities (*Disc*, II, xxix, 365), how many unexpected accidents occur every day (*Disc*, III, xlix, 504), and says that the wise prince is the one who finds not the most secure but the least insecure mode of action (*Pr*, XXI, 92). In his letters he points to a different aspect of Fortuna's power when he says that human beings can act only if she is willing to let them (#119, 231; #160, 368), and in the *Discorsi* he dilates on this point, suggesting that even as Fortuna aids a person, she remains in charge, so that from one perspective humans may well seem like little more than pawns in her hands:

> Fa bene la fortuna questo, che la elegge uno uomo, quando la voglia condurre cose grandi, che sia di tanto spirito e di tanta virtú che ei conosca quelle occasioni che la gli porge. Cosí medesimamente, quando la voglia condurre grandi rovine, ella vi prepone uomini che aiutino quella rovina. E se alcuno fusse che vi potesse ostare, o la lo ammazza o la lo priva di tutte le facultà da potere operare alcuno bene. [II, xxix, 366–67]

> Fortune does this well, for when she wants to accomplish great things, she selects a man who has such spirit and *virtù* that he will recognize those occasions she offers him. Likewise, when she wants to accomplish great ruins, she proposes men who aid that ruin. And if there were anyone who could oppose her, she either slays him or deprives him of all means to effect any good.

In keeping with such a conception of Fortuna's power, Machiavelli even sees that exemplar of heroic action and princely *virtù*, Castruccio Castracani, as her creature in a certain way, declaring at the start of the *Vita* that Castracani's rise from a humble beginning is attributable to

---

[44]Flanagan, "Concept of *Fortuna*," p. 152; and Gennaro Sasso, *Niccolò Machiavelli: Storia del suo pensiero politico* (Naples: Istituto italiano per gli studi storici, 1958), pp. 272–73.

the fickle goddess who allows men their successes in order to show that she, and not their own prudence, is responsible for what they are (9).

Nevertheless, in *Il principe* Machiavelli declares his conviction that human beings can share equally with Fortuna in the control of their own affairs (xxv, 98–101), and he writes the *Discorsi* specifically to dispute Plutarch's and Livy's claim that Rome owed her greatness to that fickle goddess rather than to its own *virtù* (ii, i, 275–79). Indeed, all the images he conjures up for his prince — as architect, doctor, farmer, and hunter — imply a faith in art and a belief that humans can exercise some control over the worlds of nature and history. Consequently, although in the game of life Fortuna holds the cards and people can play only with the hand she gives them, Machiavelli does, admittedly illogically, insist that they can beat her on occasion. He never faces this problem squarely in his works, insisting to the end on Fortuna's omnipotence while still asserting that human beings have the resources to deal with her.

If Fortuna is a mythic female who menaces men with her enormous physical power, Machiavelli also sees her, and women generally, as possessing an equally threatening but far more insidious power over them. They have the power to enter men's inner worlds, to play to their passions, desires, and weaknesses, to seduce them to do their bidding. They are, in other words, temptresses like the sinister figures in Renaissance epics — and their classical ancestors — who waylay knights in the midst of their quests by luring them into their seductive bowers of bliss.[45]

In general, Machiavelli links men's degeneracy to their involvement with women, and at times he explicitly describes Fortuna as though she played Delilah to the prince's Samson. Thus he says that she first lulls men into complacency and inactivity, into *ozio*, by granting them limited and temporary portions of luck, a delusion of security, and then ruins them when they have lowered their guard and lie weak and exposed to her blows. Fortuna holds out hopes of benefits as well as prospects of fear, he writes in a letter to Francesco Vettori, psychological delusions that are human beings' "maggiori nimiche" (#160, 368: "greatest enemies"). He devotes an entire chapter of the *Discorsi* to the fickle goddess's practice of blinding people who trust in her so that they cannot perceive her designs and hence cannot oppose them (ii, xxix, 365–67), and in *Il principe* he says that some foolish princes trustingly and naively depend on her and wind up ruined (xxv, 99). Although Machiavelli is attacking Fortuna here, he also holds humans partly, per-

[45]Machiavelli's characterization of Fortuna as a temptress has roots in tradition; see Howard R. Patch, *The Goddess Fortuna in Medieval Literature* (1927; rpt. New York: Octagon Books, 1974), pp. 47–55, 82–83, 101.

haps largely, responsible for their own undoing, for as she deceives them, she is appealing to desires and fears deep inside them which they are too weak to resist. Thus he mocks Fortuna's victims for getting drunk ("inebriano") on their temporary good luck and thinking their own *virtù* has gained what she has given them, and then behaving in a base and cowardly manner when their luck changes (*Disc*, III, xxxi, 469-70). In effect, those individuals are the victims of themselves, of their own desires for security and power. Thus if Machiavelli's political and historical works never place women or Fortuna at the center of a pastoral pleasance, those works are as replete with temptresses as any Renaissance epic. What is more, women and Fortuna are so closely associated with *ozio* in Machiavelli's mind that no sooner does he mention that a man or a state may rot ("marcire") in leisure, like the immobilized hero of one of those epics, than a malevolent *femmina*, the equivalent of a bewitching temptress such as Alcina or Armida, enters the scene. It should not be surprising, then, that when Machiavelli describes Fortuna in his "Capitolo di fortuna," he should not only depict her as two-faced and duplicitous but dub her an "antica strega" (*SL*, 313, l. 55: "ancient witch"), who moves on wheels rolled by "Necessità" and "Ozio" (313-14, ll. 55-84).

Playing the temptress, women and Fortuna in Machiavelli's works do to men what such characters as Circe and Medea, Alcina, Armida, and Acrasia do to epic heroes: they unman them. Or rather, the heroes unman themselves, placing themselves under the control of their seducers, abandoning their endless quests and restless activities and giving in to their passions. They can be led to do so because the epic life is hard; it requires so much restraint and repression that however committed to it they may feel, they must also have deep and powerful yearnings to abandon it. Thus the temptress appeals less to their sexual adventurousness than to their existential and moral fatigue, their restiveness under the stern yoke of duty, their profound longings for the rest, relaxation, and freedom that her pastoral bower promises. As those heroes of Renaissance epics who have forsaken the quest languish in the arms of their seductive temptresses, their creators inevitably pronounce them, in one way or another, *effeminato*, a term that pinpoints their weakness and unmanliness as well as their subjection both to their own passions and to a woman.[46] Machiavelli also uses this term to condemn both men and states that have abandoned the life of heroic struggle and succumbed to pastoral leisure (for example, *Pr*, XIX, 80; *Disc*, I, xix,

[46]For the notion that excessive passion made a man "effeminate" in the Renaissance, see J. Leeds Barroll, "Antony and Pleasure," *JEGP* 57 (1958): 708-20; and "Enobarbus' Description of Cleopatra," *Texas Studies in English* 37 (1958): 61-78.

183, 184; III, xlvi, 501). Indeed, if *ozio* or *ozioso* appears in his texts, *effeminato* is never far behind (for example, *Disc*, II, ii, 283; III, x, 420). In essence, to give in to *ozio* is to become *effeminato*, to forsake the heroic quest, to become unmanly as a result, to abandon one's very identity as a man.

When the hero of an epic chooses to enter the temptress's pastoral oasis, he may be seeking sensual pleasure, but his immobility there, his dependence on the temptress for food and drink, his passive participation in play and games, all suggest that his "unmanning" is really a regression to childhood, to a period before the heroic quest became the defining mode of his existence. From this perspective, the temptress is a deceivingly benevolent mother who nourishes and cares for the hero only in order to entrap and infantilize him. Consider, for instance, Circe, who feeds and offers shelter to Odysseus; Dido, who provides a luxuriant resting place for the tired Aeneas; Alcina, Armida, and Acrasia, who hold their infantilized lovers in their laps. In the *Orlando furioso* Ariosto directly compares the enchanted Ruggiero to a "fanciullo" ("child").[47] Being a hero is hard work, so that the temptation to return to childhood even at the risk of losing one's identity is perfectly understandable. Homer consequently allows Odysseus to be sent into Circe's bed and has the hero's men protest their stay on her island only after a year has passed: though dangerous, a little rest and relaxation obviously do not hurt. In Rome of the first century B.C., when Vergil composed his *Aeneid*, however, the epic hero had come to live in a decidedly moral universe, and Mercury is sent not to urge Aeneas into Dido's bed but to reprimand him for tarrying with her instead of hastening on to Italy. Aeneas is guilty not of the sin of sensuality but rather of dereliction of duty, of replacing a lofty political goal with a less lofty, personal one. Finally, by the time Ariosto writes at the start of the Renaissance, the last step has been taken, and the hero's entry into the bower of bliss is presented not merely as abandonment of masculine identity and political failure but as moral decadence and degeneracy. Deviation from the heroic quest is now moral deviation as well; to become a child again is not to regain innocence but to lose it.

Like the writers of epics, Machiavelli organizes the world of his works in terms of an adult-child as well as a male-female dialectic. When his heroic princes succumb to the lure of *ozio*, they, like classical and Renaissance heroes, are basically regressing to a childlike condition marked by physical pleasure and freedom from care, a condition that

---

[47] Ludovico Ariosto, *Orlando furioso*, ed. Remo Ceserani (Turin: Unione Tipografico-Editrice Torinese, 1962), VII, lxxi, 1.

is consistently presented as decadent and degenerate, though more of a political failing than a true sin in any Christian sense. Thus Machiavelli generally faults men in the modern world for spending too much time in "giuochi" (*Arte*, VII, 516), and he numbers among Lorenzo de' Medici's "vizi" ("vices") not only his attraction to the pleasures of Venus but the fact that "si dilettasse di uomini faceti e mordaci, e di giuochi puerili piú che a tanto uomo non pareva si convenisse" (*Ist*, VIII, xxxvi, 576: "he delighted in witty, biting men and in children's games more than seemed fitting for such a great man"). Great men in Machiavelli's world do not play games. Moreover, Machiavelli uses a somewhat peculiar locution to describe the behavior of those men who fail the test of heroism because they lack the energy and wit to keep from being outmaneuvered: such men, he says, throw themselves into the laps of their enemies. The opponents of Rome, for instance, who gave up without a struggle, "se gli sono volontari rimessi in grembo" (*Disc*, II, xxxii, 376: "voluntarily threw themselves into her lap"). Even more strikingly, in a letter to Francesco Vettori, Machiavelli says that either the pope (Leo X) must fight the viceroy of Naples—and thus act the part of the heroic, adult male—or he will "mettere il capo in grembo a questo viceré, et lasciarsi per questa via governare alla fortuna" (#232, 501: "put his head in the lap of this viceroy and let himself in this way be ruled by fortune"). As these words indicate, to be weak and give up the heroic fight means to become a child again and place one's head in the lap of that treacherous, malevolent mother Fortuna—which is just what the heroes of Renaissance epics do when they succumb to the lure of the women or goddesses who tempt them. The brief interludes of personal regression that Homer could tolerate in his hero and that the subsequent epic tradition roundly condemned on political and moral grounds, Machiavelli views with the most intense scorn. Thus in one of his letters he mocks the current pope for being passive and letting himself be trapped in Rome by his enemies like "un binbo" (#226, 491: "a baby"), and his scorn finds its most savage, unpitying expression in the epigram he wrote about his former master Piero Soderini, who was driven out of the city by his enemies and thereby failed the test of heroism:

> La notte che morí Pier Soderini
> l'anima andò de l'inferno a la bocca:
> gridò Pluton: "Ch'inferno? anima sciocca,
> va su nel limbo fra gli altri bambini." [*SL*, 365]

> The night that Piero Soderini died,
> his soul went to the mouth of hell;

> Pluto shouted: "Come to hell? foolish spirit,
> go up to Limbo with the other children."

Clearly, "child" is virtually an imprecation in Machiavelli's lexicon.

If one reviews the two major characteristics of Fortuna in Machiavelli's thought—her immense power over events in the world and her tricky ability to seduce men from their heroic pursuits—then it should become apparent why she is the supreme opponent of the prince, for Fortuna is something like his alter ego, a figure of force and fraud just as he is, a serious opponent who can often best him in their encounters. She is, in other words, a confidence trickster of mythic proportions, and she turns men as well as women into her agents so she can defeat her opponents. Moreover, if she plays the confidence woman, her victims can be seen, in a complementary way, as sharing the characteristics Machiavelli assigns the dupe throughout his writings, from the infantile Nicia to the passion-driven murderer of Giuliano de' Medici who wounds himself with his own knife. All of Fortuna's victims are presented as stupid and incapable of calculation; all are weak, childish creatures who cannot control their passions; and, most important, all are made to appear largely responsible for their own undoing, for they are described as throwing themselves into their enemies' laps or willingly and stupidly playing the child.

In a sense, everyone in Machiavelli's works, even the most heroic confidence man, sooner or later becomes Fortuna's victim, if only because all human beings are mortal and will eventually succumb to her as she appears in the guise of nature and death. And since, in Machiavelli's starkly Manichean universe, everyone is either a confidence man or a victim, to go down to such a defeat, however "natural" and unavoidable, is to become a dupe. Two of Machiavelli's most successful and heroic confidence men, Cesare Borgia and Castruccio Castracani, are made to present themselves as ultimate failures—and hence as dupes—for neglecting to solve all their problems before they contracted fatal diseases; it is almost as though Machiavelli holds them responsible for not controlling the timing of their own deaths (*Pr*, vii, 39; *CC*, 33). In both cases, their defeats are simultaneously pronounced the victory of Fortuna: Machiavelli equates Borgia's failure through death with Fortuna's rejection of him as Italy's redeemer (*Pr*, xxvi, 102), and Castracani says of his miscalculations that he was not allowed sufficient intelligence by "la fortuna, che vuole essere arbitra di tutte le cose umane" (*CC*, 33: "fortune, who wants to be the judge of all things human"). In the great, grim confidence game that is life as Machiavelli sees it, Fortuna all too often enjoys the last, mocking laugh.

But although Fortuna's control over events in the world of history is very great, and although she will always ultimately defeat her opponents, if only through their deaths, Machiavelli refuses to accept his recognition of her omnipotence. To do so would be to deny his princes — and himself — the possibility of a meaningful identity as he conceived it. Consequently, he suggests that there are two ways for his princes to grapple successfully with Fortuna, the first of which can be summarized in a word: self-possession. Thus, he says in the *Discorsi*, the prince with true *virtù* is never shaken by little accidents, and he cites a passage from Livy contrasting the Romans' reliance on themselves and their own arms with the inferior reliance of their enemies on Fortuna (III, xxxiii, 476–77). Even more important, in the same work, he defines what he means by great men or heroes:

> Gli uomini grandi sono sempre in ogni fortuna quelli medesimi; e se la varia, ora con esaltarli ora con opprimerli, quegli non variano, ma tengono sempre lo animo fermo ed in tale modo congiunto con il modo del vivere loro che facilmente si conosce per ciascuno la fortuna non avere potenza sopra di loro. [III, xxxi, 469]

> Great men are always the same no matter what their fortune; and if it varies, now raising them up, now overwhelming them, they themselves do not vary, but always keep their spirit firm and so consistent with their manner of living that everyone else easily recognizes that fortune has no power over them.

Machiavelli may appear to contradict himself here, as he first has Fortuna raising and lowering great men and then insists that their actions show that she has no power over them. He believes, however, that human beings can fashion meaningful identities for themselves despite Fortuna's power, because those identities are based not on externals but on an inner self-possession and a consistency of attitude and behavior akin to Stoicism.[48] Furthermore, when he says in *Il principe* that such self-possession and consistency keep the prince from appearing to be driven to act in certain ways (VIII, 44), it is clear that he values those qualities because they bespeak the freedom that is the basis of personal autonomy. To preserve that freedom and that autonomy, Machiavelli essentially tells his princes to maintain a strict distance from Fortuna and the women who often serve in her stead. They must never allow themselves

---

[48]For Stoicism as a traditional response to Fortune, see Patch, *Goddess Fortuna*, p. 13; J. G. A. Pocock, "Custom and Grace, Form and Matter: An Approach to Machiavelli's Concept of Innovation," in *Machiavelli and the Nature of Political Thought*, ed. Fleisher, p. 158; and Flanagan, "Concept of *Fortuna*," p. 143.

to trust or depend on such creatures, never throw themselves into Fortuna's lap or become "drunk" on the good luck she gives them. They
must constantly avoid imitating their fellow heroes of epic who succumb
to the lure of pastoral *ozio* and sensual pleasure. For to behave like those
heroes is to cooperate in one's own undoing, to become the complete
dupe, so that one not merely is defeated by Fortuna on the stage of history but surrenders the fortress of the inner self, the very citadel of
identity, to her without firing a shot in self-defense.

As usual, Castruccio Castracani provides a splendid example of a
prince who made the right choice. First, the character Machiavelli fabricates in his biography never puts himself in the power of women. Thus
he renounces marriage, and among the witty sayings Machiavelli steals
from Diogenes Laertius and assigns to Castracani at the end of the *Vita*,
three suggest directly or indirectly his skeptical detachment from women
and his sexual self-possession. In one, he is credited with rebuking a
youth for having visited a bawdyhouse (36); in another, he ridicules the
practice of choosing a wife merely by sight rather than testing her as one
would a piece of pottery (39); and in the most striking of the three, when
he is reported to have been involved in an affair and is mocked by a
friend for having let himself be chosen by a woman, he replies that his
critic errs, for "io ho preso lei, non ella me" (37: "I took her, not she
me"). Castracani thus exemplifies Machiavelli's notion of the way a truly
heroic prince deals with members of the opposite sex: to maintain his
self-possession, he either avoids them, evaluates them as though they
were objects, or possesses them as such ("io ho preso lei") lest they possess him ("non ella me"). Machiavelli ends the biography by praising
Castracani as the equal of Philip of Macedonia and Scipio Africanus,
for, despite his final defeat through disease and death, he triumphantly
maintained his self-possession and personal integrity. Castracani, he
concludes, lived "quarantaquattro anni, e fu in ogni fortuna principe"
(40–41: "forty-four years, and in every fortune he was a prince").

Such stoic self-possession and inner freedom may allow the prince to
maintain an identity, but only a fairly minimal one. Like the epic hero,
he needs glory as well as integrity, and the way to glory lies through
conquest. He must, in other words, not merely insulate himself from
Fortuna and her minions but do battle with and defeat her, and despite
her enormous power, Machiavelli expresses his conviction on numerous
occasions that his prince can do just that. Thus if Machiavelli's prince is
encouraged in one way to keep his distance from Fortuna and women,
it is even more important that he actually engage them — and the worlds
of nature and history which they symbolize — but on his own terms, that
is, in combat. Thus he confronts the feminine and the world in the same

way, a way that conflates masculine sexuality with military conquest and imperialism. He seduces or "takes" women as Castracani did, and he treats states in the same way: his typical actions have him occupying territory, penetrating the walls of besieged cities, and seducing states by making them his "amica" ("friend" or "mistress") as Cesare Borgia did the Romagna (*Pr*, VII, 36) and Scipio Africanus did Spain (*Disc*, III, XX, 445). His acts of seduction are violent assaults, as one of the most famous passages in *Il principe* reveals with dramatic clarity, a passage in which Machiavelli is teaching his prince how to make an "amica" of the most resistant woman of them all, lady Fortuna:

> La fortuna è donna; et è necessario, volendola tenere sotto, batterla et urtarla. E si vede che la si lascia piú vincere da questi, che da quelli che freddamente procedono. E però sempre, come donna, è amica de' giovani, perché sono meno respettivi, piú feroci, e con piú audacia la comandano. [XXV, 101]

> Fortune is a woman, and it is necessary, if one wishes to master her, to beat and hit her. And it can be seen that she lets herself be conquered more by such a man than by those who proceed coldly. And therefore she is always, like a woman, the friend [mistress] of young men, because they are less restrained, fiercer, and command her with more daring.

In this vivid text, seduction stands revealed as rape. The prince will thus actually do what Callimaco in *La mandragola* only contemplated fleetingly: violently assault both women and the world in order to conquer and possess them, thereby forging an identity for himself as a hero.

As the prince brutally rapes Fortuna, he clearly plays the part of the violent lion much more than that of the cunning fox. Machiavelli thus suggests that force has precedence over fraud in the prince's character, a preference already implied in his decision to make *virtù* the prince's defining attribute. This preference is based not simply on Machiavelli's irrational, misogynistic fears or on an unthinking commitment to violence but on his epistemology and his sense of human beings' limits. Although he may evince at times an enormous faith in human reason and art, he is also well aware of just how ineffectual they can be. Because of the darkness and opacity of the world and the unpredictability of Fortuna, even the most cunning prince will frequently be in doubt, so that at such moments Machiavelli urges him to rely on his capacity for forceful action and boldly, impetuously to plunge ahead. Though he admits in the *Discorsi* that one may always be in Fortuna's power, rising and falling as she wills, able only to weave, not alter, her designs, he goes on to say that the obscurity and uncertainty that mark the human situation actually give people a paradoxical, if illusory, freedom to direct their own lives. It is imperative, he says, that they act and not abandon themselves, not give themselves up into Fortuna's possession: "hanno sempre a sperare e sperando non si abbandonare in qualunque fortuna ed in qualunque travaglio si truovino" (II, xxix, 367: "they always have to hope, and while hoping, they should never abandon themselves, no matter what fortune and what difficulty they find themselves in"). To temporize in unresolved doubt because of the inscrutability of the world is not to act, and not to act is to abandon the effort to wrest an identity for oneself through heroic conquest. Thus it should not be surprising that Machiavelli repeatedly praises his princes for boldness and resolution, or that he says states need to act resolutely and with dispatch (*Disc*, II, xiv-xv, 314-17). In the words of his plebeian spokesman in the *Istorie fiorentine*, men's fortunes are in their midst and are more open "alle rapine che alla industria" (III, xiii, 238: "to violent seizures than to industriousness").

Just before he recommends the rape of Fortuna, Machiavelli directly confronts the issue of impetuosity. Some princes succeed by diffidence and others by impetuosity, he notes, and a continuous use of one of these modes will sooner or later lead to defeat. Although Julius II always managed to find success through impetuosity, he would have failed if he had lived longer, for the times would have changed. Consequently, one expects Machiavelli to conclude that a truly clever, adaptable prince should be sometimes diffident and sometimes impetuous. Instead, he says that "sia meglio essere impetuoso che respettivo" (*Pr*, xxv, 101: "it is better to be impetuous than diffident"). The reason, as we have seen, is that Fortuna is a woman and has to be beaten. One can see that Machiavelli's conclusion is based not solely on his fear of women but also on his epistemology, on his sense that the waters of this world are so murky that reason and calculation sometimes cannot fathom them. In such situations, only violence and resolute action will truly allow his prince to triumph over Fortuna. Impetuosity here does not mean for Machiavelli a mindless reflex or a constant tossing of caution to the winds, which is what he denounced in Julius II, but rather a bold and decisive abandonment of reason at the point where reason reveals its insufficiency, as it does only too frequently. Impetuosity is thus a form of madness not totally unlike the madness of ancient heroes, the rage of Achilles and the furor of Ajax. In a letter to Francesco Vettori, Machiavelli makes his preference for madness explicit. He declares that in many situations reason remains so puzzled that one must act with madness ("alla impazzata"), for such "disperazione" — his word for impetuosity here — can find remedies that thoughtful choice cannot (#234, 505).

Thus Machiavelli concludes that to face Fortuna, his heroic prince must, at bottom, be a bit more the lion than the fox, for in the grim and often baffling game that is history, a game in which one's wits are no match for those of that inscrutable confidence woman Fortuna, the force, impetuosity, and heroic madness of the lion are the best weapons the prince has.

Although Machiavelli clearly conceives his prince to be a warrior-hero as well as a confidence man, it shoud now be possible to supply a specific epic model for the figure or at least to identify the epic character with whom he has the greatest affinity. That character cannot be Achilles, despite Machiavelli's mention of him in the eighteenth chapter of *Il principe* and despite Cicero's praise of him as both orator and warrior in his *De Oratore* (III, 57).[49] For if the heroic prince does share with Achilles both eloquence and the force of the lion, it must be stressed that he, unlike that ancient hero, is a fox, a tricky confidence man, as well. He is, moreover, an exemplar of the active life, a restless quester for whom relaxation is inconceivable, a vigilant opponent of idleness and pastoral leisure, and the creator and defender of a dynamic civilization. Finally, he struggles against fierce masculine opponents who strive to outwit or overpower him, and he fights his greatest battles— internal ones—against women and Fortuna, temptresses who would lure him from his journey into their deceptively pleasurable but ultimately treacherous bowers. Struggling against such figures in a terrifying universe marked not merely by death but by the violent rending of the human body, the heroic prince can sometimes outwit his enemies, can occasionally overpower Fortuna with masculine force, but, barring divine assistance, can never hope for permanent victory. It should now be apparent that the epic character to whom Machiavelli's heroic prince is most closely related is none other than that "man of many turns," Homer's polytropic Odysseus.[50] Odysseus is the one Greek hero who is both fierce warrior and eloquent confidence man, whose life is continual questing and struggle, who stands for an active vision of civilization, who must battle monsters that characteristically tear their victims apart

[49] Raimondi, "Machiavelli and the Rhetoric of the Warrior," 4.
[50] The resemblance between Machiavelli's prince and Odysseus has been noted; see Hulliung, *Citizen Machiavelli*, pp. 200-201; and Silvia Ruffo-Fiore, *Niccolò Machiavelli* (Boston: Twayne, 1982), pp. 34-35. It has also been discussed in J. G. A. Pocock, "Machiavelli in the Liberal Cosmos," *Political Theory* 13 (1985): 559-74. Pocock identifies Machiavelli's princes as being either warriors or tricky Odysseus-like figures. My argument is that Odysseus is both warrior and trickster and thus the perfect model for that generic amalgam which is the prince.

or threaten them with engulfment and a total loss of identity, and who must defeat alluring goddesses not by his wits but by masculine force.

It is unlikely, of course, that Machiavelli knew the figure of Odysseus directly from Homer's *Odyssey*, although he could have read that work in the Latin translation of Raffaello da Volterra, published in Rome in 1510.[51] But he did not need to have a firsthand acquaintance with Homer, for the identification of Odysseus as a figure of both force and fraud had been made by Vergil in the *Aeneid* and repeated by Dante in the *Inferno*, works with which Machiavelli was well acquainted. Dante also stressed the importance of the quest and a life of active striving for the ancient hero. Moreover, a passage in his incomplete satire, the *Asino d'oro*, makes it clear that Machiavelli was fully cognizant of the nature of Odysseus' chief female temptress, Circe, a figure who also appeared in Ovid's *Metamorphoses*, a work so central to Renaissance education that Machiavelli must surely have known it. In the *Asino*, Machiavelli describes his encounter with a woman he identifies as Circe's servant. He banquets with her and eventually sleeps with her, although his initial reluctance to approach her in bed makes him appear a ridiculous figure, hardly Odysseus' match (*SL*, 284, ll. 92–102). Machiavelli says he felt like a new bride timidly joining her husband in bed for the first time, and Circe's servant mocks him for his lack of *virtù*, thus underscoring not merely the masculine character of that quality but its explicitly sexual character as well (*SL*, 285, ll. 112, 129). Moreover, in the last completed *capitolo* of the *Asino*, Machiavelli engages in a dialogue with a pig, one of Circe's enchanted victims, who argues for the superiority of animal to human life. This episode is based on a dialogue by Plutarch between Circe, the pig Gryllus, and Ulysses, which constituted an attack on Ulysses' active, heroic vision of life and had been translated into Latin at least as early as 1508.[52] If Machiavelli temporarily shares Plutarch's viewpoint in the *Asino*, defending a life of *ozio* and pleasure, he hardly does so in his political writings, where he makes the heroic questing of Odysseus into an unchallenged ideal and totally rejects pastoral leisure. Finally, the affinity between Machiavelli's heroic prince and Odysseus may be explained by the prominence of Odysseus-like fig-

---

[51] This is the earliest translation of the *Odyssey* I have been able to find which was in print in Machiavelli's lifetime. There was also a translation by a G. Maxillus which was printed by Johan Scott in 1510 in northern Europe, but one may well doubt that Machiavelli had access to this volume. Both works are listed in the *Catalogue général des livres imprimés de la Bibliothèque Nationale, Auteurs* (Paris, Imprimerie nationale, 1920), vol. 73, col. 344.

[52] "Bruta animalia ratione uti, sive Gryllus." It was translated by Raffaello Regio and published in Venice in 1508 and in Paris in 1514, according to the *Catalogue général des livres imprimés de la Bibliothèque Nationale*, vol. 139, col. 321.

ures in the Renaissance epic, questers who battle masculine opponents and who must resist the blandishments of temptresses who wish to lure them into deadly inactivity in their pastoral bowers. Indeed, those temptresses often share the traits that Machiavelli's Fortuna inherits from tradition, as the Fata Morgana does in Boiardo's *Orlando innamorato*.[53] Thus Machiavelli did not have to know Homer's work in order to fashion his prince as a hero along the lines of Odysseus. Nevertheless, it is remarkable that his heroic prince should duplicate so many of the ancient Greek hero's traits, just as *virtù* captures so much of what Homer called *arêtê*, and that force and fraud should unite at the core of both figures. It is almost as though Machiavelli had seen around the screen erected between himself and Homeric culture by the works of the Romans and had grasped what was most essential to it.

Although Machiavelli deeply admired the Romans, he clearly did not share the negative judgment of Odysseus' deceptiveness and violence to be found in the *Aeneid* and in Dante. His positive evaluation of Odysseus' traits likewise puts him at odds with ancient philosphers and Renaissance humanists who also valued the Greek hero but turned him into an allegorical figure of wisdom and obscured or devalued his deviousness and violence.[54] Living in an Italy that he saw as decadent and degenerate, a world whose structures and institutions had become so fluid that appearances were unreliable, Machiavelli dramatically rejected all of his predecessors' assessments. He saw that an Odysseus-like ability to be both tricky fox and violent lion, to be both confidence man and heroic warrior, was necessary if that world were ever to be redeemed.

Nevertheless, Machiavelli's prince is not exactly an *Odysseus redivivus*. First, the two figures have strikingly different relationships to their cultures and communities. In Odysseus' world, deceit and violence were morally acceptable to his peers and even possessed divine sanction: Athena cozied up to the rugged old warrior precisely because she admired his trickiness, and his savage slaughtering of all the suitors at the end received divine sanction. There is, to be sure, a certain ambiguity about Odysseus' trickery, precisely because it was a trait he shared with merchants who were anything but aristocratic warriors, but on the whole it was admired and celebrated within the *Odyssey* by other bona

[53] Patch, *Goddess Fortuna*, p. 23.
[54] On Ulysses' reputation from antiquity to the Renaissance, see W. B. Stanford, *The Ulysses Theme: A Study in the Adaptability of a Traditional Hero*, 2d ed. (Ann Arbor: University of Michigan Press, 1963). On the positive evaluation of Odysseus as a figure of wisdom by the ancients and by Renaissance humanists, see Gérard Defaux, *Le Curieux, le glorieux et la sagesse du monde dans la première moitié du XVIe siècle: L'Exemple de Panurge (Ulysse, Démosthène, Empédocle)* (Lexington, Ky.: French Forum, 1982), pp. 36–38, 54–60.

fide heroes, as when they praised him for the stratagem that allowed them to take Troy. Thus Odysseus enjoyed an exemplary position within his culture, and if his wanderings were, by the end, solitary, he was valued as a companion, and he had a definite place within a family deeply devoted to him, a state many of whose inhabitants genuinely loved him, and an aristocratic community of heroes.

Machiavelli's heroic prince is a more troubled and troubling figure. Although always in the midst of a crowd of people, he is nevertheless utterly and completely alone. The nature of his world forces him to live a somewhat paranoid existence, making him keep his distance from women and regard even his seemingly most devoted servants, courtiers, and allies as potential traitors and assassins. There is also no recognizable public community of aristocratic heroes to which he could belong, mainly because his deceit and violence, unlike Odysseus', contradict the orthodox morality of his culture. Indeed, Machiavelli repeatedly emphasizes that his prince can succeed only if he is willing to violate the dearest values of Renaissance Christian society whenever necessary. Thus, while Homer's hero can operate fully within his culture, Machiavelli's must stand at a distance from his. This distance is salutary, of course, for without it he could not grasp the nature of his society, free himself from its limits, and then act to renew it. Ironically, however, at the same time it stands in the way of his full recognition as a hero within his community—almost no one but Machiavelli in Renaissance society would have dubbed Cesare Borgia a hero. As a result, Machiavelli's prince, in effect because of his very nature, denies himself the heroic glory for which he strives. By definition, then, he cannot be truly an Odysseus reborn; he can never enjoy the cultural centrality or the community of Odysseus, no matter how important his activities may be for his culture's survival.

There is yet another ironic difference between Machiavelli's prince and Homer's hero. Odysseus and his descendants in Renaissance epics all manage to escape from the temptresses they encounter. When their own human strength and willpower fail, they are aided by the gods or the gods' representatives. There is no such aid for Machiavelli's hero, no hope that he can forever elude Fortuna's clutches. This is yet another reason that Machiavelli's prince is so relentlessly serious, so desperately unable to relax and play, why he lives constantly in a state of siege. Machiavelli celebrates him for his self-reliance, but the truth is that this solitary figure must be so, for he has no one else on whom to rely. By contrast, Homer's Odysseus can earn his moments of security, pleasure, and idleness through his enormous heroic efforts; he can embrace leisure as a goal and truly enjoy eating, drinking, and the sensual life; and thanks to the gods, he can finally return home to the stability and tranquility of his bed in Ithaca, where his exploits can be told over in peace, a still center from which he can reestablish a dependable community around him. Unlike Odysseus — and unlike Machiavelli's mythical Romans, who could return to their farms, if not to idleness and leisure, after their battles were done — the restless, solitary modern prince lives in a world without gods, or at least without benevolent and caring ones, and he not only has no community, but he really has no home to return to after his labors. We find here none of the profound comedy of Homer's work, the glorying in reunion after hardship and separation; Machiavelli's works are filled with nostalgia for the past and bitterness and pathos about the present. His prince is an almost tragic figure, living in an inhospitable universe ruled by the inscrutable and malevolent Fortuna, doomed to quest endlessly for a home and community he will never reach.

5

Il Servo Padrone

In June 1508, upon his return from a diplomatic mission to Germany, Machiavelli wrote a report, the "Rapporto delle cose della Magna," concerning his activities for the Ten (Dieci di Libertà), and in 1509 he supplemented it with two more works concerning Germany: the "Discorso sopra le cose della Magna e sopra l'Imperadore," which was intended to aid Giovanvittorio Soderini and Piero Guicciardini, who were then being sent to the emperor; and the "Ritratto delle cose della Magna," a literary elaboration of the earlier "Rapporto." All of these works are addressed to men who were his political and social superiors, and even though Machiavelli headed the Second Chancery at this time, he still speaks of them with great deference. He identifies himself explicitly in the "Rapporto" as a good servant ("servitore"), offering his master ("signor suo") what he has understood (*SP*, 199), and in the "Discorso" he defines the task of an ambassador ("oratore") as the making of good conjectures so that his "superiore" will understand them (*SP*, 207-8). In both works Machiavelli puts in the foreground his socially inferior position, insisting on his role of humble adviser, the "servitore" to those in power. He generally adopted that role in all the dispatches and treatises he composed during the period of the Florentine Republic (1498-1512).

He played the deferential servant because he had to. Although Machiavelli had worked his way up to be head of the Second Chancery, which dealt to a large extent with foreign relations, and although he became the confidant and adviser to Piero Soderini, who headed the government as *gonfaloniere a vita* from 1502 on, he was the social and political inferior of the men who composed the ruling class of the city. Thus he had no say in legislative matters, and when sent on diplomatic missions, he was inevitably coupled with a person of higher social standing, at least in part because the states to which he went were reluctant to recognize someone from a minor branch of a nonnoble family.[1] But another reason for such treatment was the nature of the city he served. Although an urban and commercial Florence had freed itself from feudal status systems well before Machiavelli's birth, it was still an intensely hierarchical society, dividing itself by various formulas along a vertical axis into such classes as the *grandi*, the *popolani grassi*, the *popolo minuto*, and so on.[2] The Machiavelli clan in the fourteenth and fifteenth centuries was considered *popolani grassi* or "rich commoners," a status that would have severely limited Machiavelli's participation in government service even if his branch of the family had not fallen on hard times and was even suspected to be illegitimate.[3] Thus his lack of sufficiently elevated position in the social system of Florence doomed him to play the role of perpetual *servitore* to those who ruled the city.

Nevertheless, Machiavelli did enjoy a certain power. He was a successful bureaucrat who served as head of the Second Chancery for fifteen years, and his correspondence is filled with letters from inferior civil servants and others begging favors (see, for example, *Let*, #43, 105–6, and #91, 184–85). He was, in addition, so well ensconced as Soderini's friend and counselor that his enemies jealously labeled him the Gonfaloniere's *mannerino* ("little hand"), his lackey or tool, and thus he participated indirectly in the ruling of Florence (Ridolfi, 99). His career reached a high point in the spring of 1507, when, in addition to running the Second Chancery and serving informally as Soderini's chief adviser, he was appointed secretary to the Nine (Nove Ufficiali dell'Ordinanza e Militia Fiorentina) and to the Council of Ten (the Dieci) (Ridolfi, 96). Finally, he was frequently singled out for important diplomatic missions on which he was expected to understand, manipulate, flatter, and deceive the powerful men and women with whom he came into contact. He apparently did so with a fair amount of success (Ridolfi, 56, 97, 108, 230). In 1504, for instance, even though there was a ranking ambassador on the spot, he was sent to France on a special mission to make sure the French did not abandon their Florentine allies in Italy; according to Roberto Ridolfi, this decision was prompted by a lack of confidence in the ambassador's judgment and a great deal of confidence in Machiavelli's (77). He was also able to dom-

---

[1] J. R. Hale, *Machiavelli and Renaissance Italy* (New York: Collier, 1963), pp. 18–19.
[2] On the degrees and ranks of Florentine society, see Felix Gilbert, *Machiavelli and Guicciardini: Politics and History in Sixteenth-Century Florence* (Princeton: Princeton University Press, 1965), pp. 24–25.
[3] Roberto Ridolfi, *The Life of Niccolò Machiavelli*, trans. Cecil Grayson (Chicago: University of Chicago Press, 1963), pp. 1–2. Future citations to this work in this chapter will be incorporated in the text as "Ridolfi," followed by the appropriate page numbers.

inate the men under whom he nominally served on such missions (Ridolfi, 102). These examples and Machiavelli's career in general make it
clear that what power he enjoyed he owed to his intelligence, his ability
at political analysis, and his capacity for handling people. Consequently, Machiavelli must always have felt a degree of frustration: to be
so keen an observer and judge of people and situations and yet always
to have to work behind the scenes without sufficient money, political
authority, or public standing! As Hanna Pitkin puts it, he "was always
in but not of the world of power, an insider and yet an underling."[4] Machiavelli had the ability to be a master, but his social and political position always forced him into the role of servant.

If Machiavelli knew frustration during the years of the Soderini
Republic, he knew downright despair after its fall and the restoration
of Medici rule over the city. Tortured as a possible conspirator against
the new rulers of Florence and forced into exile at Sant' Andrea in Per-
cussina, Machiavelli became an outsider to the political world he once
knew so well. Whatever power he had enjoyed before was now gone, and
although he eventually gained the confidence of the Medici and advised
them occasionally on political and military matters, he never again
wielded the power he had enjoyed during the Soderini years.[5] In place
of his position as head of the Second Chancery, he had that of official
historiographer to the city; instead of being sent on diplomatic missions
to France, he went to Carpi to collect a preacher for Lent or acted as
go-between among the Medici and their agents; and rather than have
direct access to the rulers of the state, he usually had to offer his advice
humbly, through such intermediaries as Vettori and Guicciardini. The
best he could manage was to be elected secretary in 1526 to the newly
formed magistrature of the Curators of the Walls (Procuratori delle
Mura), which was charged to oversee the defenses of Florence against a
possible attack by the emperor's forces, and then to be sent into the field
in Lombardy to act under Guicciardini's command and thus to assist in
the war effort (Ridolfi, 227-32). These were assignments of limited importance, and when a truce brought the war to a halt, Machiavelli's
military career came to an abrupt end. From 1512 to the end of his life,
Machiavelli never enjoyed even the qualified power he had had earlier;

---

[4]Hanna F. Pitkin, *Fortune Is a Woman: Gender and Politics in the Thought of
Niccolò Machiavelli* (Berkeley: University of California Press, 1984), p. 26. In my analysis of Machiavelli's career I am indebted to Pitkin's book, although my emphasis differs
in significant ways from hers.

[5]On Machiavelli's powerlessness during the Medici years, see Ridolfi, pp. 180-81,
186-87, 237.

humiliated and used for menial tasks, he had become the *servitore* with a vengeance.

He still possessed his formidable intellect, however, which was responsible for the little advancement he gained while the Medici held the reins of the city. Both Vettori and Guicciardini valued him for that quality, as well as for his warm friendship, and Vettori wrote on more than one occasion asking Machiavelli to analyze political matters he felt were beyond his grasp (see, for example, *Let*, #127, 249 and #132, 270). Machiavelli was similarly valued by the young men who gathered around him in the Orti Oricellari, the gardens of Cosimo Rucellai, to listen to him discourse on political and military matters, who encouraged his writing of works such as the *Discorsi* and the *Arte della guerra*, and who may well have helped him settle some of his many debts (Ridolfi, 168–69). In his poverty and his humiliating position as lowly servant to the great, Machiavelli could count on his enormous intelligence and the esteem of his friends to salvage his self-respect; at least in the sphere of the intellect he could feel he was a true master, not a servant.

Since Machiavelli did not live in the sphere of the intellect, however, but in the real social and political world of Florence, his status as a master rather than a servant was always in jeopardy. During the republic, when he enjoyed a fair amount of power both in his public roles as chancellor and *oratore* and in his private dealings with Soderini, he could portray himself with equanimity as the *servitore* of those to whom he addressed his writings, perhaps simply because he knew that his voice carried some weight with them. Such equanimity was, however, impossible after 1512. Speaking in the person of Fabrizio Colonna in the *Arte della guerra*, he reveals his feelings of frustration and powerlessness when he has that character complain that nature has given him knowledge without power: "E io mi dolgo della natura, la quale o ella non mi dovea fare conoscitore di questo, o ella mi doveva dare facultà a poterlo eseguire" (VII, 519: "And I complain of nature, which either should not have given me knowledge of such [military and political] matters or should have given me the ability to put it into effect"). Colonna's situation is, of course, Machiavelli's. Consequently, practically all the works he produced during the rule of the Medici, literary as well as political and historical texts, can be seen as direct or indirect expressions of his frustration, and in a variety of ways they represent attempts to deal with it.

First, almost all of Machiavelli's works after 1512 were written with the practical end of helping him reacquire the status and power he had lost, from *Il principe* and the *Istorie fiorentine*, which he dedicated to members of the Medici family, down to *Clizia*, which was first pre-

sented as an entertainment for leading members of the Florentine ruling class, including one of the Medici.[6] Those works can also be read as
psychological release, a direct, purely intellectual unleashing of his
frustrated political energies, in which speculation substitutes for the
combination of action, observation, and analysis that marked his former life. As he says in a letter to Francesco Vettori in 1514, writing
served generally as a means of release for him during this period of his
life: "Io . . . vi scrivo questo, . . . solo per sfogarmene" (#152, 343: "I
. . . write you this . . . only to unburden myself of it"). The works
Machiavelli produced from 1512 on can even be seen as a vicarious participation in politics and diplomacy, for they allowed him to reenter, at
least through his intellect and imagination, the world of history from
which he had been so painfully excluded. As Giorgio Barberi-Squarotti
has argued, Machiavelli subjected the world to analysis in his works in
order to achieve a positive and superior relationship to it, to control
what he otherwise could not.[7] Machiavelli expected his works to have an
impact on others; as Fabrizio Colonna says, he shared his knowledge with
his listeners because, although he was now too old to put it into effect,
they were not (VII, 519). And in the Proemio to the Second Book of the
Discorsi, Machiavelli says directly that he writes because it is his duty to
show others how to do what he has been unable to because of the ma-
lignity of Fortuna and the times he lives in (274).

At the most fundamental level, however, Machiavelli's works are a direct expression of power, for they reveal that if he no longer had much
influence over the destiny of Florence, he could at least exercise power
over his audience through his rhetoric. And since he knew that some of
those who read his treatises and attended his plays would be members
of the Medici and other ruling families of Florence, he could achieve a
potential intellectual dominion over them as well. In short, by crafting
a rhetorical relationship with his audience, the lowly servo could turn
the tables on his superiors and become their padrone, his rhetoric of
power transforming him into the master of his masters.

Machiavelli adopts a specifically antirhetorical stance at times. He
evinces a general distrust of words in the Discorsi, (II, xv, 315), and he
directly attacks empty ornamentation in the dedication of Il principe, a
work he says is not "ornata né ripiena di clausule ample, o di parole
ampullose e magniche, o di qualunque altro lenocinio o ornamento

[6]On the original audience for Clizia, see Ridolfi, p. 210.
[7]Giorgio Barberi-Squarotti, La forma tragica del "Principe" e altri saggi sul Machiavelli (Florence: Olschki, 1966), pp. 18-24.

estrinseco" (13: "adorned or filled with fulsome clauses or bombastic or grandiloquent words, or with any other farfetched or extrinsic ornament"). And indeed Machiavelli's style is lean and sinewy, full of unexpected turns and twists, anything but Ciceronian.[8] His purpose, he declares in *Il principe*, is thoughtful, penetrating analysis, not flashy shows of verbiage; he does not appeal to the eye, which sees only surfaces, but to the sense of touch, which plumbs the depths, "perché tocca a vedere a ognuno, a sentire a pochi" (xviii, 74: "because everyone can see, few can feel"). This last statement indicates that although Machiavelli eschews an ornamental rhetoric solely in the service of self-display, he is still an intensely rhetorical writer, profoundly concerned to persuade his audience and aware of just how much power words can have, even if those words are, as we noted in Chapter 3, ungrounded, divorced from the situations they refer to. Indeed, an antirhetorical stance is a standard tool of the rhetorician, a means of gaining credibility with the audience, not an abandonment of any attempt to persuade or manipulate. Machiavelli's antirhetorical rhetoric is thus a trick intended to bring his audience under his control.

Machiavelli's insistence that he writes for those who feel, who penetrate the essence of things, rather than for those who see only surfaces, reveals one of his major rhetorical techniques. He divides the world into two groups, those who are and those who are not clever and deep enough to grasp his analyses. This division is, of course, identical with the one between princes and the *popolo* which he makes in his political and historical works, but now it is applied to the hypothetical members of his audience rather than to the inhabitants of ancient Rome or Renaissance Florence. It is, moreover, a rhetorical technique of some power, for it coerces the audience into identifying themselves with the first group rather than the second, thus maneuvering them into linking themselves directly to the author and embracing his teaching. Machiavelli's antirhetorical stance is thus not only a trick but an application of force, even a subtle bullying.

In carrying out his rhetorical program, Machiavelli first uses mockery, irony, and sarcasm to distance his audience from the vast majority of the people who are incapable of unprejudiced analysis. Such people are like the dupes he ridicules throughout his writing, for they passively rely on traditional authorities and proverbial wisdom. In *Il principe*, for instance, he remarks that "solevano li antiqui nostri, e quelli che erano stimati savi, dire come era necessario tenere Pistoia con le parte e Pisa

---

[8] J. R. Hale, "The Setting of *The Prince*: 1513–1514," in Niccolò Machiavelli, *The Prince*, trans. and ed. Robert M. Adams (New York: Norton, 1977), p. 148.

con le fortezze" (xx, 86: "our forefathers, and especially those who were deemed wise, used to say that Pistoia had to be held by factions and Pisa by fortresses"). The heavy sarcasm here is not evident at first, but it becomes clear as Machiavelli explains why the maintenance of factions in a city can never be beneficial. His sarcasm thus undermines the authority of the Florentine "forefathers" and the proverbial wisdom of those who were and still are reputed to be "savi," and it forces his audience to separate themselves from such wisdom lest they be numbered in the company of fools. Similarly, in the *Discorsi* he once again rejects proverbial wisdom, the "comune opinione" that money is the sinew of war (II, x, 303), and when he defends his praise of Roman antiquity, he distinguishes himself from those who blindly accept past things simply because of the authority inherent in tradition (II, Proemio, 272). Finally, Machiavelli takes pains to separate his audience from those who are, like the *popolo*, mired in the present and make misjudgments because they lack broad experience of the world (*Disc*, II, xxii, 343).

Machiavelli is particularly contemptuous of those individuals who like Nicia in *La mandragola*, believe in a world full of magic and marvel. With consummate irony in *Il principe*, for instance, he remarks that the use of mercenaries will bring a leader "miraculose perdite" (XII, 56: "miraculous losses")—miraculous, that is, because seemingly inexplicable and unpredictable to those who have failed to understand the clear arguments he has advanced against mercenaries. Similarly, some people will marvel that Alexander the Great took Asia so quickly and that it did not rebel against his successors after his death (it did do so, of course, historically); for the benefit of those who are capable of understanding, Machiavelli provides an explanation (IV, 25-26). Indeed, he says at the start of the *Discorsi* that his work is addressed to those who will not marvel ("non si maraviglieranno") that Rome, given its beginnings, its laws, and its political arrangements, lasted as long as it did (I, i, 125). For those who do marvel, who see the world as a mysterious place full of strange and magical events, Machiavelli clearly feels nothing but disdain.

Throughout his political and historical works, Machiavelli is consistently critical of people who prefer mercenaries, or want a prince to be truly virtuous, or think fortresses offer real protection. He hits at the shallowness of those supposedly learned individuals who criticize Rome's internal political disturbances: they hear only the noise, he says with subtle irony, and fail to see the good effects those tumults caused (*Disc*, I, iv, 137); and he openly mocks those who think so "superficialmente" (I, xxiv, 191), that they say a republic should not punish its heroes when they commit crimes. In general, Machiavelli is scathing in his criticism of what he dislikes, and since he usually provides compelling arguments for his position, no one in his right mind would be encouraged to hold a contrary opinion, for Machavelli could handily demolish it with withering sarcasm.

Not only is Machiavelli ironic and sarcastic in his works, but he frequently plays the bullying satirist as well, manipulating his audience by making them fear his biting wit. His satire is pervasive, though intermittent, in the bulk of his writing, and it dominates two of his creations, *La mandragola* and the *Istorie fiorentine*. As we have seen, *La mandragola* may be read as a denunciation of Florence's immorality, venality, and general decadence. Machiavelli sets the tone of his play in a prologue that explicitly divides his audience into two groups, just as his political works do. On the one hand are the potential detractors who will not understand or like the play and will greet it with smirks and jeers (Prologo, 58). Such individuals are denounced in a witty *argumentum ad hominem* as being responsible not only for the author's "tristo tempo" (57: "wretched situation"), because they deny rewards to merit, but also for the general decline of *virtù* in the century. Machiavelli's spokesman warns them that his first art was satire ("dir male") and that they had thus better be quiet (58). Opposed to this group are the "benigni uditori" (56: "well-wishing listeners"), sophisticated individuals who can appreciate the newness ("nuovo caso") of the play, and who form, together with the audience identified in the initial *canzone*, a "dolce compagnia" (55: "sweet company"). With such a "compagnia," Machiavelli can joke in easy familiarity, twitting them for coming only because the performance is free but also offering to buy them wine and join them himself as a boon companion if the play fails to make them laugh (56–57).[9] Machiavelli appeals to this group's sophisticated command of language with his opening pun on "Buezio" and his bawdy double entendre about rising up and falling down in the "Via dello Amore" (56: "Street of Love"). In short, in his prologue Machiavelli clearly satirizes the fools who will not be able to appreciate his play, just as he satirizes Florence and the Florentines during the five acts that follow, while he praises his special audience, which shares his openness and sophistication.

The *Istorie fiorentine* is also a pervasively satirical work, and a bitter one to boot. Rather than write an epic about his native city-state, as both Vergil and Livy did about Rome, Machiavelli presents Florence as a comic inversion, an ironic parody of everything for which he cele-

[9]See Giulio Ferroni, *"Mutazione" e "riscontro" nel teatro di Machiavelli* (Rome: Bulzoni, 1972), p. 37.

brated ancient Rome in the *Discorsi*.[10] Although he sees the early years
of Florentine history as a period of solid growth and even of occasional
heroic accomplishments, the strife between the Guelphs and the Ghibellines, which he dates to 1215, renders the subsequent history of the
city a cruel joke (II, ii, 139–41). All the states of the Italian peninsula,
according to Machiavelli, have participated in this dark and ironic comedy, for all have willingly disarmed themselves so that they must rely on
mercenaries to do their fighting for them, with the result that the
"antica virtú" of their Roman ancestors has disappeared (I, xxxix,
134–36). Thanks to those mercenaries, whom, Machiavelli notes with
disdain, no amount of money can prompt to risk their lives, modern
wars have turned into farces. Describing the battle of Anghiari, he satirically observes that in an engagement that lasted four hours, only one
man died—"il quale non di ferite o d'altro virtuoso colpo, ma caduto
da cavallo e calpesto espirò" (v, xxxiii, 383: "and he [did] not [die] from
wounds or some other blow produced by *virtù*, but fell from his horse
and was trampled to death"). Of course, Machiavelli is twisting historical reality here, but this approach is consistent with the bitterly satirical picture of modern Italian history he wishes to paint. In that history
battles are shameful affairs because their participants lack *virtù* and re-
fuse to face any real danger (VI, xxvii–xxviii, 430–33), and armies are
ridiculous for their lack of energy and bravery (VIII, xxxi, 563–65). The
mere turning of a horse's head, he remarks sharply at one point, suf-
ficed to put thousands of men to flight (VIII, xvi, 537), and he ironically
praises a battle because more than a thousand soldiers died in it (VIII,
xxiii, 552–53). The only people who suffer in these wars are the miser-
able wretches whose homes and villages are sacked by cowardly mercenary armies and the foolish states of Italy that have hopelessly weakened
themselves by wasting their resources on such futile conflicts (VI, i,
387–88). The *Istorie* thus reveal fully the brilliant satirical streak that
runs through all of Machiavelli's works, his capacity for wit, sarcasm,
and bitter irony, which he uses not only to express his disgust with his
contemporaries and with recent Italian history but as one of his chief
weapons in the rhetoric of power on which he relies to intimidate his
audience.

Machiavelli manipulates his audience in a second way by fashioning a
unique and attractive image for himself, a persona with whom they
would wish to identify as an idealized version of themselves. In other

[10]Mark Hulliung, *Citizen Machiavelli* (Princeton: Princeton University Press, 1983),
pp. 61–98.

words, like a good orator, he recognizes the enormous power of the ethical appeal, and he consequently takes great pains to shape his ethos, to make himself consistent, trustworthy, and remarkable. Although this image may constitute a unified whole, for purposes of analysis it will be useful to break it down into its component parts, to investigate how he plays four distinct but closely interconnected roles: the rationalist, the demystifier, the skeptic, and the innovator.

In all of his political works, but especially in *Il principe* and the *Discorsi*, Machiavelli presents himself as a rationalist, as someone who uses reason to eliminate errors, misunderstandings, and delusions and to render the world of history comprehensible. Typically, in *Il principe*, he explains all the mistakes Louis XII made in his Italian campaign and concludes that the king's ultimate failure may be considered "molto ordinario e ragionevole" (III, 25: "very ordinary and reasonable"). Similarly, in response to Francesco Vettori's bafflement about certain political events (see *Let*, #132, 267-70), Machiavelli writes a detailed analysis aimed at explaining them in terms of what is "ragionevole" (*Let*, #135, 278).[11] Moreover, Machiavelli explicitly identifies his goal at the start of the *Discorsi* as a freeing of people from "errore," in this case, from believing the Romans could not be imitated in political and military matters (I, Proemio, 125). In general, he feels that human beings labor under a host of delusions and self-imposed, unexamined errors and assumptions, such as the belief that princes are prudent only if they are surrounded by prudent counselors (*Pr*, XXIII, 96), and it is his task to undeceive them, or to keep them from deceiving themselves by departing from the Roman model he is constructing in his works (*Disc*, I, xxxvi, 214). Machiavelli offers himself as a bringer of light, someone who makes what he analyzes "chiaro piú che la luce" (*Disc*, II, xvii, 327)—or, to be more precise, as someone who causes the sunlight of the Roman Republic to illumine the darkness of the present (*Disc*, II, xxx, 370). As we have seen, he develops this image most extensively in Fabrizio Colonna, in the *Arte della guerra*, but that it clearly fits Machiavelli himself is implied, for instance, not only in the passages cited above but also by his criticisms of human blindness and the references to the darkness of the world which were investigated in Chapter 3.

Machiavelli's rationalism is most evident in his belief that he can formulate general laws about human beings' behavior and the world they live in. In the *Arte della guerra* he insists that "ogni scienza ha le sue

---

[11]For useful comments on this exchange, see Gennaro Sasso, *Niccolò Machiavelli: Storia di suo pensiero politico* (Naples: Istituto italiano per gli studi storici), p. 206.

generalità" (III, 418: "every science has its generalizations"), and in
Il principe he speaks of a "regola generale" (III, 25: "general rule") for
human affairs, though he later admits that he cannot always capture
everything through general rules and must sometimes merely adduce
examples rather than advance arguments (*Pr*, xx, 85). His general conviction that he can usually formulate laws and rules is related to two
underlying assumptions: first, that human nature does not vary (*Disc*,
I, Proemio, 124; II, xxxiii, 377; III, xliii, 496–98); and second, that history repeats itself and that even geography works according to general
rules (*Pr*, III, 23–24; *Disc*, I, Proemio, 124; II, xxxix, 222–23). Hence
Machiavelli is confident that he can learn from the past and that the
audience for whom he writes can use the lives of those good princes he
admires as a mirror ("specchio") for their own (*Disc*, III, v, 389; see also
Pr, xiv, 64).

Machiavelli's belief in laws and rules does not mean that he is the
proto-scientist an entire critical tradition has credited him with being.[12]
After all, he bases his analysis on certain irrational, untested, and un-
testable assumptions about human nature and the world, and that
analysis is dictated and shaped by his overriding political passions, his
dedication to Florence, and his love of ancient Rome. Indeed, as Mark
Hulliung has shown, Machiavelli is a profound mythmaker; he makes
no attempt to demythologize history, as Guicciardini and Polybius did
in their different ways, but operates as a civic activist and shapes a powerful vision of human beings and antiquity in order to transform his
world.[13] Nevertheless, although his ability to concoct such a myth of
power may explain much of his fascination for later generations of readers, it is equally clear that he has also created a compelling image of
himself as a rationalist, an image that all those readers who have celebrated Machiavelli the scientist have obviously accepted at face value.

Machiavelli the rationalist looks at experience without blinders on. He
is not misled by his emotions: unlike most people, he does not praise
Hannibal's success with his army while condemning the cruelty that
caused it (*Pr*, xvii, 71). He is hostile to customary and proverbial wisdom that fails to withstand scrutiny, such as the notions that money is
the nerve of war (*Disc*, II, x, 303), that the good of Italy is owed to the
church (*Disc*, I, xii, 165–66), and that an ideal prince should actually be

[12]For a useful discussion of the notion of Machiavelli as scientist, see the bibliograph-
ical article of Eric W. Cochrane, "Machiavelli, 1940–1960," *Journal of Modern History*
33 (1961): 113–36. See also J. H. Whitfield, *Machiavelli* (1947; rpt. New York: Russell
& Russell, 1965), p. 12, and *Discourses on Machiavelli* (Cambridge: W. Heffer, 1969),
p. 15; and Ezio Raimondi, *Politica e commedia: Dal Beroaldo al Machiavelli* (Bologna:
Mulino, 1972), p. 158.
[13]Hulliung, *Citizen Machiavelli*, pp. 164–67.

virtuous rather than merely seem so (*Pr*, XV-XVIII, 64-74). In other words, Machiavelli as rationalist is free from the blind prejudices of conventional morality and customary ideas which he scornfully ascribes to the *popolo*. Not surprisingly, two of his most characteristic adverbs are the Latin *tamen* and the Italian *nondimanco*, both of which mean "nevertheless"; he uses one or the other after he has stated some commonplace that he is about to refute.

Machiavelli extends his rationalism to the point of insisting that a plan based on a clear analysis of human beings and events must be judged valid even if it fails. Accordingly, he rejects the notion that actions should be judged by their outcomes ("lo evento della cosa"), rather than by the intrinsic merits of the analytical principles on which they were based (*Pr*, XVIII, 74; *Disc*, III, xxxv, 481-82). In one striking passage, for instance, he praises Cleomenes of Sparta for having understood that to reform his city and restore its "antica virtú," he had to bring back the laws of Lycurgus, and to do that he had to have all the Ephors killed (*Disc*, I, ix, 155). Cleomenes carried out part of his plan, and Machiavelli argues that he would have succeeded with the rest of it if the Macedonians had not intervened and conquered his state along with the rest of Greece. Thus Machiavelli concludes that to judge Cleomenes a failure because of the outcome of his actions, as the *vulgo* would, is to be misled by appearances, and that despite Cleomenes' defeat, he may still be used as a model for all those who "desiderassono essere di buone leggi ordinatori" (*Disc*, I, ix, 155: "desire to be the originators of good laws"). Similarly, in the *Arte della guerra* Machiavelli defends one of his own cherished ideas when he has Fabrizio Colonna declare that the defeat of a citizen army does not invalidate the conception of such an army (I, 347). Finally, in analyzing the career of Julius II in *Il principe*, he argues that the pope's constant, uncontrolled impetuosity was a failing, so that even though it allowed him to win victory after victory, it would of necessity have led to his eventual defeat if he had only lived long enough (XXV, 100-101).

As Machiavelli insists that his rational arguments remain valid even though they may seem to be disproved by historical events, one cannot help sensing his personal frustration. Throughout his life, he was never allowed to implement fully his political or military schemes, and he must therefore have felt that his ideas were never really discredited by the failures he experienced, as when the citizen militia he hastily threw together in 1512 was brutally defeated by the professional Spanish army, and when he found in 1526 that he could not drill real soldiers according to the ideal scheme he presented in the *Arte della guerra*.[14] He seems to speak out of that same deep frustration in the *Istorie fiorentine* when once again he defends himself by saying that even the wisest counsel may lead to bad results because of the accidents of history, and goes on to say that those who offer such advice should not be condemned, for otherwise no one would ever be encouraged to offer it (IV, vii, 279).

The image of Machiavelli the rationalist dovetails with that of the demystifier, an opponent of credulity and a facile belief in the miraculous and the marvelous. In the passage concerning Alexander the Great in *Il principe* alluded to earlier (IV, 25-26), he juxtaposes the ideas of the marvelous and the reasonable, suggesting that what common opinion considers inexplicable—the failure of Alexander's conquered states to rebel after his death—will be brought into the province of reason as he explains it. Similarly, he says in the *Discorsi*, if one considers well the differences between the city-states surrounding Venice and those surrounding Florence, one will not wonder ("non si maraviglierà") that his native city has had to fight more wars to acquire territory than the Venetians have (III, xii, 426). Again and again as he constructs his analyses, he indicates that he is stripping away the marvelous and the miraculous: Louis XII's losses in Italy are no "miraculo" (*Pr*, III, 25); anyone who examines Septimus Severus' character closely "non si maraviglierà" that he succeeded (*Pr*, XIX, 81); if you observe the behavior of Ferdinand of Aragon carefully, "voi vi maraviglierete meno" (*Let*, #128, 257: "you will marvel less") about the truce he concluded with France in 1513. In short, Machiavelli's task, as he conceives it, is to remove all mystery from history and thus to free the world from what the credulous naively react to with wonder (*Disc*, II, ii, 284; III, xxi, 446; *Ist*, I, xxviii, 120).

At times, however, Machiavelli embraces two different senses of the marvelous in his works. First, he uses it as a term of outright praise, as when he celebrates the marvelous accomplishments ("maravigliose pruove") of Roman soldiers (*Disc*, III, xiii, 429), or when he declares that the Roman leader Camillus was "maraviglioso" because of his prudence, magnanimity, and discipline (*Disc*, III, xxiii, 454). Both of these examples are found in the third book of the *Discorsi*, in which he celebrates Roman heroes; in his mind, heroism transcends the realm of the ordinary, which is accessible to reason, and thus it legitimately enters the realm of the marvelous. Heroism is again the issue at the end of *Il principe* when he calls on Lorenzo de' Medici to rival the "rari e mara-

[14]On the failure of Machiavelli's militia, see Ridolfi, pp. 127-29; on his inability to drill the soldiers, see pp. 229-30.

vigliosi" men of the past and save Italy (xxvi, 102). Machiavelli uses the notion of the marvelous in a very different way when he says that it is a "cosa miracolosa" if a conspiracy is kept secret for long (*Disc*, iii, vi, 396). Here he is referring to a situation he feels confident will almost never obtain; its very rarity makes it something of a miracle. Although he is skeptical about such things, he does grudgingly acknowledge that some events in the world may indeed occasionally go beyond the bounds of reason. Machiavelli is convinced, however, that most events will not, and he prides himself that he can even explain certain actions of the Roman *plebs*, for instance, at which his admired Livy could only marvel (*Disc*, i, xlvii, 237). Thus in the first case Machiavelli expects his readers to marvel along with him at the exploits of heroes, whereas in the second he wants them to remain skeptical and detached, willing to accept as a miracle the occasional event that truly defies reason, but in general not to marvel ("non si maraviglieranno") at the world, especially as they read the analyses and explanations he provides to dispel its mysteries (*Disc*, i, i, 125).

A rationalist and a demystifier, Machiavelli also presents himself as a skeptic toward authority. He thus freely corrects the proverbial wisdom of his Florentine forefathers about how to keep possession of Pistoia and Pisa (*Pr*, xx, 86), and he declares boldly the superiority of his own reason over received authority in a letter to Francesco Vettori concerned with relations between France and Spain: "Né voglio in queste cose mi muova nessuna autorità sanza ragione" (#128, 253: "In these matters I do not want to be moved by any authority without reason"). Accordingly, throughout the *Discorsi*, which he offers as a commentary on Livy and would thus seem to presuppose his authority, Machiavelli openly disagrees with the ancient author's interpretations of a variety of subjects—the value of the common people, whether fortune or *virtù* was responsible for Rome's grandeur, whether a good leader with a weak army is to be preferred to a weak leader with a good army (i, lviii, 261-62; ii, i, 275; iii, xiii, 429). He consistently distorts Livy's material to suit his own ends, as Leo Strauss and Harvey Mansfeld have shown.[15] And Livy is not the only authority Machiavelli attacks in that work; Plutarch, Caesar, and Tacitus are also subjected to skeptical analysis (*Disc*, i, lv, 255; iii, xiii, 429; iii, xix, 443). Finally, Machiavelli often expresses skepticism toward unnamed authorities, as when he disagrees with cer-

---

[15]Leo Strauss, "Machiavelli and Classical Literature," in *Italy: Machiavelli "500,"* special issue of *Review of National Literatures* 1 (1970): 23-25. See also his *Thoughts on Machiavelli* (Glencoe, Ill.: Free Press, 1958), passim; and Harvey C. Mansfeld, *Machiavelli's New Modes and Orders: A Study of the "Discourses on Livy"* (Ithaca: Cornell University Press, 1979), passim.

tain unidentified figures who condemn the tumults of the Roman Republic (*Disc*, I, iv, 137), and speaks of "scrittori poco considerati" (*Pr*, XVII, 71: "insufficiently thoughtful writers")—he is probably thinking of Livy here, among others—who censure Hannibal for his severity with his troops. Thus as Machiavelli goes through his works rejecting any uncritical submission to authority, he creates a compelling image of himself as a truly free and rational individual, admirably liberated from the unthinking prejudices and narrow allegiances of his fellows.

Still, Machiavelli's skeptical attitude toward Livy is a puzzle, for if he expresses something close to reverence for anything, it is the ancients. And he does generally regard Livy as a source of wisdom, a teacher, as when he cites a passage from the *Ab urbe condita* and then proclaims that those words "insegnano a qualunque come ei debbe procedere a volere tenere il grado del capitano" (*Disc*, III, xxxviii, 490: "teach anyone how he ought to proceed if he wishes to hold the rank of captain"). Moreover, Machiavelli sometimes goes to great lengths to "save" the authority of an ancient author, as when he produces an extremely complex and subtle analysis of the question whether cruelty or mildness is best with a multitude in an attempt to reconcile Livy's opinion on the matter with that of Tacitus (*Disc*, III, xix–xxii, 443–54). At one point, he even admits a "riverenza" toward the ancient historian Herodian, so that although he doubts as unreasonable ("discosto da il ragionevole") Herodian's claim that the same conspirator could have killed two persons at different places at the same time, nevertheless the "autorità" he accords this ancient writer leads him finally to believe the account (*Disc*, III, vi, 405). That Machiavelli reverenced the ancients should come as no surprise, of course, if one recalls the famous letter he wrote from Sant' Andrea in which he describes how he used to put on regal and courtly garments in the evenings to be received into the courts of those revered "antiqui huomini (#140, 304: "ancient men"). Nevertheless, if no surprise, that reverence does create a difficulty for the reader, for it seems to qualify or even deny the skeptical side of Machiavelli's persona in his mature works.

A solution to this problem depends on the way Machiavelli asserts the authority of the ancients. Take, for example, the chapter in the *Discorsi* in which he considers the usefulness of fortresses. Although he begins by saying that the Romans did not depend on them, he spends most of the chapter arguing his case rationally on the grounds of historical probability and human psychology, and he uses modern examples rather than simply relying on ancient authority. Only when he has reached the conclusion of his argument that fortresses are useless does he then, as an added argument, appeal to "l'autorità de' Romani (II, xxiv, 354: "the authority of the Romans"). Similarly, although he argues on the basis of ancient authority for the superiority of infantry to cavalry, he quickly confirms that authority with "ragioni manifeste" (*Disc*, II, xviii, 329: "manifest reasons"). In other words, he virtually never relies on the ancients as authorities by themselves, but always pairs those authorities with his own reasoning. One could thus conclude that he is presenting the ancients as authorities only when, and insofar as, their opinions accord with his.

One might still wonder, however, why Machiavelli needs their authority at all. It may be that he simply shares his contemporaries' uncritical admiration, their almost blind reverence, for practically everything classical. But it is also possible that he does so as part of a conscious rhetorical strategy designed to persuade his audience to share his opinions. After all, his explicitly stated project in the *Arte della guerra* (I, 330–31) and the *Discorsi* (I, Proemio, 123–25), and his implicit goal in virtually all his other works as well, is to persuade his readers to imitate the ancients in military and political matters just as they do in literary and artistic ones. We see, then, that he trades on the authority the ancients already enjoyed in one field and manipulates his audience into transferring it to another. What they are really doing, of course, is transferring it to Machiavelli's myth of antiquity—in a word, to him. As he says in the Proemio to the second book of the *Discorsi*, he wants them to differentiate him from other writers about the ancient world, who evince little more than blind nostalgia for it (271–72), and so to trust him as a guide to that world and to grant his work the status of an authoritative commentary on Livy's "testo" (*Disc*, I, xl, 227; III, xxx, 467). That commentary is worlds apart from those of the Middle Ages which looked up to texts as unimpeachable authorities, and although it shares the skepticism toward authorities and traditions one finds in the commentaries of Lorenzo Valla and Erasmus, it goes well beyond them. For it both undermines the authority of the text it discusses and maneuvers its audience into transferring the general authority it accorded antiquity not to Livy or Plutarch or Tacitus but to Machiavelli and his ideas. Ironically, then, the Machiavelli who poses as a skeptic of authority uses the reverence his audience accorded the ancients to get them to consider him an authority for themselves.

Machiavelli's presentation of himself as a skeptic toward received authority harmonizes perfectly with his conscious assumption of the role of innovator throughout his works. In the prologue to *La mandragola*, for instance, he presents his play as a "nuovo caso" (56: "new [or strange] case"), and in *Il principe*, as he sets out to discuss the all-important subject of the prince's relation to his subjects, he defends himself against the charge that he is presumptuous in departing from the "ordini delli altri" (xv, 65: "arrangements of others [that is, other writers]") by arguing that he pursues the "verità effettuale della cosa" ("actual truth of the matter") rather than its mere image. Machiavelli addresses the issue of innovation most directly, however, in the Proemio to the first book of the *Discorsi*, where he also characteristically divides his audience in two. Innovation in the realm of ideas, he says, like the discovery of new lands, is dangerous because of most human beings' natural tendency to envy others, but he will nevertheless set off upon this untrodden path for the sake of public utility and because he feels he may yet be rewarded at least by those "che umanamente di queste mie fatiche il fine considerassino" (123: "who humanely consider the goal of my labors"). Thus once again Machiavelli manipulates his audience away from criticism of him, lest they appear irrationally envious, like most people, and into a praiseworthy ("umanamente") identification with him, this time in the appealing role of the innovator, the intrepid explorer of the uncharted realm of politics.

As he plays the rationalist and the demystifier, the skeptic of authority and the innovator, Machiavelli fashions an image of himself to which his audience cannot help being attracted. To enhance their identification with him, he characterizes them as individuals very much like himself. They are the "benigni uditori" of the prologue to *La mandragola* (56), sophisticates like the author, who can laugh with pleasure at bawdy innuendo. They are the Lorenzo de' Medici to whom *Il principe* is dedicated, someone who, as the last chapter of the work implies, shares Machiavelli's amoral approach to politics and like him recognizes that the moment is ripe for decisive action. Although Machiavelli mocks the proverbial and traditional wisdom of the supposed "savi" at one point in *Il principe* (xx, 86), he clearly plays the wise man in his texts and identifies the members of his audience in the same way, flattering them in the *Discorsi* on more than one occasion with the label of "savi" (e.g., I, ix, 153, and I, liii, 249) and praising them for their capacity to understand matters "sottilmente" (I, xxviii, 197: "subtly") and "sensatamente" (III, xxx, 468: "sensibly"). In short, by identifying himself and his audience as he does throughout his works, Machiavelli attempts to create an ethical appeal that will be absolutely compelling for those who read them.

Machiavelli also manipulates his audience directly by means of his style. At one extreme, that style is marked by binary oppositions and symmetries.[16] Thus he says in *Il principe* that political troubles are like illnesses, hard to see at first but easy to cure, easy to see later on but then virtually impossible to cure (III, 21). A little later he contrasts France with the Turkish empire, saying that because of the former's independent nobility, it is easy to capture but hard to hold, whereas the latter, because its nobility depends on the ruler, is hard to capture but easy to hold (IV, 26-27). In the *Discorsi* he declares that a leader must be either severe or gentle with his army (III, xix-xxii, 443-54), and he debates whether it is better to have a good captain and a bad army or the reverse (III, xiii, 429-31). More instances of this well-known stylistic habit, which even appears at the level of phrases, could easily be adduced. Its importance lies in its ability to give Machiavelli's audience a feeling of participating in a rational process because of its logical, indeed almost mathematical, mode of proceeding, while at the same time it forces the audience's thought into a narrow channel by eliminating all third possibilities. In other words, it is a stylistic technique that may aim to illuminate the world through analysis but aims also to bring the audience to think in its terms and only in its terms. It is, in short, a powerful tool of coercion.

Machiavelli's style is typically far more complex than such disjunctive structures might suggest. With the exception of the last chapter of *Il principe*, it tends to be deliberative and discursive rather than hortatory, and it does not move, as Gennaro Sasso has remarked, in straight lines, but doubles back on itself to reveal qualifications and express second appraisals.[17] It constantly revises itself, moving toward an extreme of complexity quite the contrary of the simple symmetries with which the first chapter of *Il principe* opens. Indeed, no sooner has that chapter ended than the next one begins by introducing qualifications and formulating additional rules. Machiavelli's basic technique here and elsewhere is to argue for a given position, then to note that an event constitutes an exception or qualification to his rule, and finally to conclude by constructing a new and more complex generalization to account for the exception—a process he sometimes goes through several times in quick succession, as in the famous chapter on conspiracies in the *Discorsi* (III, vi, 390-412) and the equally famous one on hate and

---

[16]On Machiavelli's style, see Federico Chabod, *Scritti su Machiavelli* (Turin: Einaudi, 1964), p. 201; and his *Machiavelli and the Renaissance*, trans. David Moore (New York: Harper & Row, 1958), pp. 127-28.
[17]Sasso, *Niccolò Machiavelli*, p. 77.

fear in *Il principe* (xix, 75-84).[18] This technique can be seen in the complex passage at the start of the *Discorsi* in which Machiavelli first argues that it is best for a people to live in a poor region, then expresses a contrary preference for a rich site, and finally concludes that the rich site is better, but only if good laws and a rigorous education are instituted to counteract the dangers the site poses to its inhabitants (I, i, 127-28). Later in the *Discorsi* he first generalizes that republics are naturally bellicose and seek to expand, then observes that the cantons of Switzerland provide an exception to this rule, and finally explains the exception by noting that all those little republics owe their allegiance to the emperor, whose reputation with them allows him to mediate their difficulties (II, xix, 335-36). Machiavelli then provides a barrage of reasons for the emperor's inability to conquer the Swiss, ranging from their natural bellicosity to the poverty that prevents some German states from aiding the emperor and the envy that makes others unwilling to do so. At times it seems as though Machiavelli has an explanation for everything.

What is striking in all these examples—and many more can be found in all of Machiavelli's mature works—is that whenever he qualifies or admits an exception to the rules he states, he never simply lets that qualification or exception stand as a brute challenge to the rule of reason but finds an explanation for it or incorporates it into a new general proposition. This practice allows his texts constantly to maintain a high level of generality even though they deal with the factual world of history; it is a practice that doubtless was responsible for Guicciardini's feeling that the *Discorsi* ignored the exceptions to its rules.[19] It does not really do so, of course; it simply keeps adding new generalizations to make an increasingly intricate weave of them as it goes along.[20]

One of the most complex instances of this practice occurs in the nineteenth chapter of *Il principe*. Machiavelli notes that the lives of a series of Roman emperors seem to offer "esempli contrarii" (xix, 78:

[18]It is partly true, as Giorgio Barberi-Squarotti says, that Machiavelli's causal sequences follow Machiavelli's will more than their own logic, but there is a logic present, even if it is not necessarily the one indicated by Machiavelli's connectives; see *La forma tragica*, pp. 109-10.

[19]Gilbert, *Machiavelli and Guicciardini*, p. 279.

[20]I disagree with the deconstruction-inspired reading of *Il principe* by Thomas M. Greene, who argues that for Machiavelli the world of facts, of history, finally defeats any attempt to force it into rational schemas, and that that defeat is reflected in the breakdown of such schematizing in the second half of the work and in its escape into pure rhetoric at its close. As my analysis of a long passage in chap. 19 will show, Machiavelli may have a difficult time finding explanatory principles for historical events, but he does find them no matter how complex his analysis becomes. For Greene's explication, see "The End of Discourse in Machiavelli's 'Prince,'" *Yale French Studies* 67 (1984): 57-71.

"counterexamples") to his general rule that a prince who demonstrates *virtù* and is feared and reverenced by his people will be safe from conspiracies, whereas one who appears weak and effeminate and is hated and despised lays himself open to them. He then goes on to say, however, that he will discourse about the emperors' lives precisely to show that the reasons for their ruin only seem not to support his original generalization, although as one reads the remainder of the chapter, one sees that his explanations by no means constitute simple restatements of his original assertion.

Consider, for example, the following passage, which is about as complex an analysis as one may find in Machiavelli. It occurs just after he has finished praising the emperor Septimus Severus as both a lion and a fox.

Ma Antonino suo figliuolo fu ancora lui uomo che aveva parte eccellentissime e che lo facevano maraviglioso nel conspetto de' populi e grato a' soldati; perché era uomo militare, sopportantissimo d'ogni fatica, disprezzatore d'ogni cibo delicato e d'ogni altra mollizie: la qual cosa lo faceva amare da tutti li eserciti. Non di manco la sua ferocia e crudeltà fu tanta e sí inaudita, per avere, dopo infinite occisioni particulari, morto gran parte del populo di Roma, e tutto quello di Alessandria, che diventò odiosissimo a tutto il mondo; e cominciò ad essere temuto etiam da quelli che elli aveva intorno: in modo che fu ammazzato da uno centurione, in mezzo del suo esercito. Dove è da notare che queste simili morti, le quali seguano per deliberazione d'uno animo ostinato, sono da' principi inevitabili, perché ciascuno che non si curi di morire lo può offendere; ma debbe bene el principe temerne meno, perché le sono rarissime. Debbe solo guardarsi di non fare grave iniuria ad alcuno di coloro de' quali si serve e che elli ha d'intorno al servizio del suo principato: come aveva fatto Antonino, il quale aveva morto contumeliosamente uno fratello di quel centurione, e lui ogni giorno minacciava; tamen lo teneva a guardia del corpo suo: il che era partito temerario e da ruinarvi, come li intervenne. [81-82]

But Antoninus his son was also a man of excellent parts that made him admired in the sight of the people and pleasing to the soldiers. For he was a military man, most capable of bearing every fatigue, a despiser of every delicate food and of every other softness, which things made him loved by his entire army. Nonetheless, his fierceness and cruelty were so great and so unheard of, since he had, after the killing of many individuals, put to death a great part of the people of Rome and all those of Alexandria, that he became most hateful to the entire world, and he began to be feared even by those he had around him, so that he was slaughtered by a centurion in the midst of his army. Here it is to be noted that such deaths, which can be traced to the resolve of an obstinate spirit, are not to be avoided by princes, because any man who does not worry about his own death can offend another; but the prince does not have to fear such men much because they are most rare. He must only guard against doing a grave injury to one of those who serve him and whom he has around him in the service of his state, as Antoninus did. He had killed in an outrageous manner a brother of that centurion, and threatened him every day; nevertheless, he kept him in his bodyguard, which was a foolhardy and ruinous decision, as it happened in his case.

This passage begins with praise for Antoninus as a tough and energetic man, clever and respected, like his father. The second sentence, however, changes the evaluation 180 degrees; his toughness is of a piece with his excessive cruelty, which led everyone, including those directly about him, to hate him and hence was responsible for his death. So far, Machiavelli seems indeed merely to have returned to his original assertion at the start of the chapter about the need to avoid hatred, although here he seems to be qualifying it by distinguishing Septimus Severus's ordinary, garden-variety cruelty, which caused manageable amounts of hatred, from Antoninus's excessive cruelty, which led to conspiracies and rebellion. The third sentence ("Dove è da notare"), however, offers a new generalization, or rather, a generalization accompanied by its own qualification; it does not logically depend on the generalization implied by the first two sentences and complicates it considerably as a result. Machiavelli is now saying that a prince like Antoninus will inevitably be assassinated, not merely because of his excessive cruelty but because a determined person, unafraid of death, cannot be stopped from killing someone he hates. Machiavelli ends this third sentence with yet another qualifying generalization—such spirits are rare—a qualification that lessens the force of the generalization in the first part of the sentence. Obviously still brooding on the specific details of Antoninus's life and death, Machiavelli produces a different generalization in the last sentence: the prince has to worry only if he injures persons in his entourage. Since Machiavelli then explains that Antoninus killed a brother of his assassin, the cause of his death finally seems clear: first he awakened general hatred with his excessive cruelty, and then he gravely injured a man in his service who must have been a determined spirit unafraid of death. Yet Machiavelli has still one more qualification to add, a qualification implied by the clause "tamen lo teneva a guardia del corpo suo" ("nevertheless, he kept him in his bodyguard"). Antoninus's problem was not just the hatred he aroused or the existence of a resolute man, but his rashness in keeping that man near him, giving him a good position from which to attack. For if Antoninus had removed the centurion from his bodyguard, Machiavelli seems to imply, he might well have been able to survive. By the time the reader has reached the end of this long passage, Machiavelli has supplemented his original generalization about cruelty and hatred many times over, producing a most complex explanation indeed for the death of Antoninus.

Machiavelli clearly adopts this method of analysis to do justice to a multifaceted, labyrinthine reality but also to maintain a firm rhetorical control over his readers. For what he offers is not a set of simple maxims or abstractions which they can easily recollect and thus feel they can control but a complex play of generalizations, exceptions, and yet more generalizations, the connections among which they must frequently work hard to supply. The movement of Machiavelli's style is deliberately difficult, making large demands on the reader's capacity to reason logically, draw inferences, establish connections, and keep a multitude of elements constantly in play. Although it would be an exaggeration to say, as one critic does, that Machiavelli never explains how he arrives at the judgments he makes, it is true that he forces his readers to adopt a particularly active role in deciphering his texts.[21] Moreover, he keeps them off balance in the sense that he prevents them from feeling that they have ever really mastered his thought, because they can never predict all the exceptions and qualifications he will fish out of the dark mass of history or the new generalizations he will come up with in response to them. Ultimately, however, Machiavelli aims not merely to keep his readers off balance but to alter the way they view the world.[22] Through the complex and demanding movement of his style, he wants to force them, if they are to understand what they read, to see things as he sees them, and the movement of that style simultaneously prevents them from ever second-guessing its creator and arriving at his conclusions before he does. His style thus puts him in the position of leading his readers on a mysterious quest whose endpoint he may envisage, but which they never exactly know in advance and which often turns out to be different from what they anticipated. To get to that desired goal, they have no choice but to place themselves completely in Machiavelli's hands.

Another major trait of Machiavelli's style which deeply affects the response to his writing is his practice of addressing the reader directly as "tu" or "voi," or indirectly as "chi" or "alcuno." Indeed, as Luigi Russo noted long ago, Machiavelli so frequently talks with an imagined inter-

[21]Carlo Pincin, "Osservazioni sul modo di procedere di Machiavelli nei *Discorsi*," in *Renaissance Studies in Honor of Hans Baron*, ed. Anthony Molho and John A. Tedeschi (Dekalb: Northern Illinois University Press, 1971), p. 399.
[22]Mazzeo, "The Poetry of Power," in Machiavelli, *The Prince*, trans. Adams, p. 39.

locutor in his political works that they verge on being dialogues.[23] *Il principe*, for instance, is filled with statements made in the first person (e.g., III, 22; IX, 45; XVII, 68; XIX, 75), with references to "tu" (e.g., III, 17, 24; VIII, 44; XII, 54; XIII, 58), and even an occasional one to "voi" (e.g., IV, 27), which may be read as equivalent in Machiavelli's day to "tu." The presence of dialogue in this work makes sense, of course, because it is addressed to a person Machiavelli hoped would become the prince his text describes. Similarly, the *Discorsi*, as their title suggests, are often spoken in the first person and invoke a "tu" or a "voi" with some frequency (e.g., I, vi, 144; I, ix, 153; I, xliii, 231; II, xvi, 319; III, i, 382). Even the *Istorie fiorentine*, which tend to be a more distanced form of writing, occasionally engage a hypothetical reader directly (I, xxviii, 120–21), and not only is the *Arte della guerra* actually a dialogue in form, but when Fabrizio Colonna speaks of a hypothetical prince who would put his ideas into effect, he addresses that figure as "tu," creating a dialogue within a dialogue (I, 339). Sometimes Machiavelli slips into dialogue in the middle of a discussion—or even of a single sentence—which starts out impersonally (e.g., *Pr*, iii, 17; *Disc*, II, xvii, 325; II, xxiv, 354). When he is not addressing a "tu" or "voi" directly, he invokes other individuals indirectly by using the impersonal pronouns "chi" and "alcuno," both meaning "someone," or the impersonal, reflexive form of a verb, almost always to identify those who are opposed to the views he offers (e.g., *Pr*, III, 24; XII, 54; *Disc*, I, ix, 153; II, xxiv, 354). In all these cases we find a strong oral element, a tendency to engage one or more hypothetical audiences in discussion, which makes Machiavelli's works both vivid and engaging for their real audience as well.

Machiavelli may invoke an audience in his mature works for a number of reasons. First, most of those works grew out of or were refined in actual discussions that took place in the Orti Oricellari. Second, he was already used to engaging friends in the one-sided dialogue of the letter from his years of rustication at Sant' Andrea. Or perhaps his predilection is simply due to his powerfully theatrical imagination, which typically led him to project a speaker behind every text he encountered. Recall the passage in the famous letter to Vettori in which he says that after the close of day at Sant' Andrea, he would don courtly garments and enter the courts—that is, read the works—of the ancients, "dove io non mi vergogno parlare con loro, et domandarli della ragione delle loro actioni" (#140, 304: "where I am not ashamed to speak with them and ask them for some explanation for their actions"). Machiavelli often

<hr>

[23] Luigi Russo, *Machiavelli*, 3d ed. (Bari: Laterza, 1949), p. 156.

seems to launch into dialogue precisely at those moments when he is treating subjects of great importance to him, such as mercenaries or fortresses, subjects about which he differed passionately with many of his contemporaries. Consequently, his imagining an interlocutor seems directly to reflect his own intensified interest at such moments. In short, Machiavelli's proclivity toward dialogue may well be explained as an unconscious habit, a mental trait, a product of passion, or even a quirk of his personality.

It may be as well a conscious rhetorical strategy designed to manipulate the real audience reading his works. His references to "tu" and "voi" are a case in point. Although some of them are fairly neutral in tone, as when he merely offers an imaginary addressee a "for instance" (e.g., *Disc*, I, vi, 144; I, l, 244), the vast majority of them are tendentious. They occur when he is giving a warning, offering counsel, or explaining what a would-be prince or leader or state ought to do. For instance, when he discusses how little faith is to be placed in the promises made by exiles who are desperate to return to their native cities, he invokes a "tu" as their potential victim: "Qualunque volta e' possano per altri mezzi che per gli tuoi rientrare nella patria loro, . . . lasceranno te e accosterannosi a altri" (*Disc*, II, xxxi, 372: "Whenever they can return to their country through means other than yours, . . . they will leave you and approach others"). Similarly, speaking of mercenaries in *Il principe*, he says: "Vogliono bene essere tua soldati mentre che tu non fai guerra; ma, come la guerra viene, o fuggirsi o andarsene" (XII, 54: "They want to be your soldiers while you are not waging war, but when war comes, they flee or run away"; see also *Disc*, I, lxiii, 231). "Tu" also enters the scene when Machiavelli is giving advice. At the start of the sixth chapter of *Il principe*, when he is encouraging imitation of the great men of the past, he speaks of how difficult it is to match the *virtù* "di quelli che tu imiti" (30: "of those you imitate"), and in the *Discorsi*, when he is speaking about a man who could save a state by leading it back to its origins, he says: "Nasce ancora questo ritiramento delle republiche verso il loro principio dalla semplice virtú d'un uomo, sanza dependere da alcuna legge che ti stimoli ad alcuna esecuzione" (III, i, 382: "This returning of states to their beginning arises from the simple *virtù* of a man, without any dependence on a law that impels you to any particular action"). As this last example reveals, when Machiavelli invokes a "tu," he identifies that person repeatedly with his ideal prince, either warning him of possible disasters if he follows a particular course of action or encouraging him to glorious undertakings. He even apostrophizes that princely "tu" when he is discussing fortresses:

O tu, principe, vuoi con queste fortezze tenere in freno il popolo della tua città, o tu, principe o republica, vuoi frenare una città occupata per guerra. Io mi vogli voltare al principe, e gli dico: che tale fortezza per tenere in freno i suoi cittadini non può essere più inutile per le cagioni dette di sopra. [*Disc*, II, xxiv, 351]

Either you, prince, want to hold in check the people of your city with these fortresses, or you, prince or republic, want to control a city taken in war. I want to turn to the prince, and I say to him: that to hold his citizens in check such a fortress can only be useless for the reasons given above.

Machiavelli's imagination here is so excited that he actually imagines his princely audience right in front of him as he urgently insists on his opinion. It is only a moment of direct exhortation, of course, for as the passage continues, Machiavelli reverts to the more impersonal form of the third person which fits the analytical mode of his argument. Nevertheless, for that brief moment, the "tu" has been powerfully addressed — and powerfully united with the ideal prince Machiavelli wishes to create.

Machiavelli's use of such addresses is tendentious, part of a rhetorical strategy designed to invite the audience into his text and into a positive identification with the prince, whether they are being warned against errors or encouraged to perform clever or heroic deeds. This identification of the real audience with the hypothetical one called "tu" or "voi" is enhanced by the presence of a second hypothetical audience, albeit a more distant one, which he also invokes. This is the audience composed of those imaginary individuals whom he summons up through impersonal pronouns and reflexive verbs, individuals with whose opinions he passionately disagrees. In effect, Machiavelli invokes them and their opinions only to refute them, to show up their total insufficiency. These are the misguided souls who believe in using mercenaries, or think fortresses are useful to a prince, or disagree with Machiavelli in evaluating Louis XII's Italian campaigns. He invokes these individuals as negative examples, people with whose wrongheaded ideas no sane person would agree, and in this way he reinforces his readers' identification with the "tu" and the "voi" he warns or praises, and hence with Machiavelli and his ideas. So strong is this identification that at times he directly unites himself with his audience by means of the first person plural pronoun. When he discusses the means the Romans used to expand their empire, for instance, he laments the ignorance of his contemporaries in not following their ancestors' lead: "Standoci con questa ignoranzia, siamo preda di qualunque ha voluto correre questa provincia" (*Disc*, II, iv, 291: "Remaining in this ignorance, we have been the prey of anyone who wants to overrun this country"). Here he binds himself to his readers as suffering Italians, warning them against continuing to follow their disastrous course and forcefully separating himself and them from the ignorance that his analyses have supposedly disspelled. Similarly, he insists that religion should really permit "us" to defend the patria and that "noi l'amiamo ed onoriamo, e prepariamoci a essere tali che noi la possiamo difendere" (*Disc*, II, ii, 283: "we should love and honor it, and prepare ourselves to be such that we can defend it"). Although such uses of the first person plural pronoun are few and far between, they are important as an intensification of what Machiavelli is trying to do when he addresses his readers as "tu" or "voi"; they are designed to bring those readers into an identification with the author which will move them to accept his opinions and act to save Florence and Italy.

Machiavelli's rhetorical technique, it must be stressed, is less an invitation to identification than an attempt to coerce it, to force readers to unite with him by allowing them no viable alternative. Consequently, it is misleading to speak of the dialogue-like character of Machiavelli's works without qualifying that idea. For those works are certainly not dialogues in the way that, say, the dialogues of Petrarch, Alberti, and Castiglione are. That is, they are not dialogues in which two or more separate opinions are expressed in real debates that either leave the issues unresolved or, if they opt for one opinion over the others, do so without denying those others at least partial validity. Such works are genuine dialogues, revelations that some questions do have more than one correct answer and that some writers' minds are deeply divided against themselves, beset with hesitations and doubts. Machiavelli, by contrast, simply drives a steamroller over his opponents; his opinion carries the day in every instance, and there is seldom room for qualifications. His opinion is, of course, qualified by history in the process of generalization-exception-generalization discussed above, but that is not the same thing as allowing another autonomous voice its separate point of view. Machiavelli keeps control over everything in his texts, and he invokes other voices only to silence them or to force them into an identification with his own.

The *Arte della guerra*, the one work that Machiavelli actually wrote as a dialogue, offers an eloquent example of just how undialogic his works are. Like many of Plato's later dialogues as well as Cicero's, this one selects a single character to serve as the spokesman for the author and gives the others minimally important roles: they either play yes-men to the main speaker, feed him questions to enable him to unfold his views, or offer straw-man challenges that he handily demolishes. Plato and Cicero do sometimes offer stretches of real debate before their spokesmen utterly defeat the opposition, but Cosimo Rucellai and his young friends look up to Machiavelli's spokesman, Fabrizio Colonna, with total awe. They seldom challenge his opinions, preferring instead to make humble requests for information and clarification. Symptomatic of their reverence is Rucellai's response when Colonna mildly criticizes the softness of the garden planted by the young man's grandfather; instead of defending it, he not only agrees with Colonna but, to raise his grandfather in the latter's eyes, turns the dead man into a fanatic who out-Colonnas Colonna in his supposed dislike of the softness of the modern world (i, 331-32). This passionate declaration then allows Colonna to suggest that the moderns need not be so extreme and could imitate the ancients in "altri modi piú umani" (i, 332: "other, more humane modes"), a suggestion that gently puts the young Rucellai in his place and provides a pretext for the following seven books, in which Colonna presents, at mind-numbing length, his detailed vision of how the modern world should imitate the ancient one in military matters. The key characteristic that undermines the *Arte*'s dialogic character, then, is the absolute reverence with which the chief speaker is regarded; Colonna preaches to the already converted and merely reconfirms their faith.

In his other works, to be sure, Machiavelli invokes an impersonal "alcuno" who objects to his ideas, thus making a real debate possible, but it is a debate that never occurs because he so completely overwhelms his opponents. As the latter lapse into silence and disappear from the text, they seem to have been either expelled, cast into outer darkness, or converted. Or rather, it is as though those other voices were simply swallowed up in Machiavelli's, their silence not merely giving consent but bespeaking a total identification with him as complete as the one he attempts to achieve with the "tu" he addresses. In other words, Machiavelli establishes a relationship with his hypothetical audiences — and by implication with the real ones beyond them — which parallels that between Colonna and the young men in the Rucellai garden: he is a source of wisdom to be regarded with awe, a figure with whom any real disagreement would be impossible. Thus one may conclude that when he gives his works the impression of dialogue, he is really engaging in a form of deception. He allows other voices to sound as though some real dialogue were going on, but his voice and his alone is the only one he allows to be heard. As he achieves solidarity with his audiences, he is in effect stifling their dissent.

This rhetorical technique of addressing an audience directly to force it to perceive the world the way the author wishes also appears in *La mandragola*. The earlier discussion of the prologue to that play has shown that Machiavelli divides its hypothetical audience into two groups, one admired for its sophisticated wit and the other disdained for its narrow-mindedness, in an effort to make the real spectators identify with the first group and hence with Machiavelli himself. Although the author disappears from the play after the prologue, his voice is hardly silent, for the major traits he manifested there—his witty use of language, his satirical streak, his scorn for fools, and his identification with the intellectually sophisticated—all recur in the play, spread among all those characters who serve as its confidence men. And just like the speaker of the prologue, those characters talk directly to the audience, sometimes in asides but more usually in soliloquies. Of course, the archdupe Nicia also has a pair of soliloquies, but in both of them he is so self-absorbed that he is scarcely aware of the audience. In one he expresses his confusion over the fable Ligurio has concocted to test Frate Timoteo (III.vii.86), and in the other he pours out his misogynistic feelings about Lucrezia and his absurd sense of presumed youthful vitality (IV.viii.100-101). In these speeches, Machiavelli clearly offers up Nicia as food for the audience's laughter, not as a figure with whom to identify, and this intention is underscored in the second instance as Ligurio tells his fellow conspirators just before Nicia's entrance to draw aside and listen with amusement to his rantings (IV.vii.100).

Ligurio's statements here not only unite the three conspirators onstage—himself, Frate Timoteo, and Siro—but they link that trio with the audience, which has been a coconspirator throughout the course of the play, privy to all the plotting and thus vicariously participating in the gulling of Nicia. Ligurio's statements to the other conspirators onstage function at least indirectly to structure the audience's responses as well; in such instances he becomes, at least temporarily, the voice of the author telling the audience what to watch and how to react:

Siro. Tu ridi?
Ligurio. Chi non riderebbe? Egli ha un guarnacchino indosso che non gli cuopre el culo. Che diavolo ha egli in capo? E' mi pare un di questi gufi de' canonici, e uno spadaccino sotto: ah, ah! e' borbotta non so che. Tirianci da parte e udireno qualche sciagura della moglie. [IV.vii.100]

Siro. You're laughing?
Ligurio. Who wouldn't laugh? He has a little cloak on that doesn't even cover his ass. What the devil does he have on his head? He seems to me to have on one of those fur things the canons wear and a little sword underneath: ha, ha! he's mumbling I don't know what. Let's draw apart and listen to his complaints about his wife.

This is not the only time that Ligurio or one of the other confidence men in the play makes statements that directly or indirectly tell the audience how to respond. In the opening acts, both Ligurio and Siro have soliloquies focused on Nicia's stupidity, and in his, Siro uses a rhetorical question to dictate the spectators' reaction: "Ma ecco el dottore che ha un orinale in mano: chi non riderebbe di questo uccellaccio?" (II.iv.73: "But here's the doctor with a chamberpot in his hand: who wouldn't laugh at this gull?").[24] Two of Callimaco's soliloquies tend to resemble Nicia's in making him an object of laughter for the audience, but both are redeemed to some extent by Callimaco's wit: in the first, he suggests that hell would not be so bad because there are so many respectable people there (IV.i.92); and in the second, though he is ready to throw himself in the Arno if his plan fails, he is still capable of making a clever gibe at friars (IV.iv.97–98). Callimaco also has a brief, more confidence-man-like soliloquy in which he confides to the audience his reasons for believing that Siro will serve him faithfully (IV.iii.97)—an explanation obviously intended to impress the audience with his sagacity, to appeal to its own cleverness at the same time, and thus to unite speaker and listeners. Ligurio has relatively few soliloquies or asides after his initial one about Nicia (I.iii.66). One of them tells the spectators again how stupid Nicia is (III.ii.80); the other informs them in a fairly neutral manner of Ligurio's state of mind (IV.ii.93). Frate Timoteo, by contrast, has a fair number of soliloquies, and although in most of them he expresses his thoughts and feelings, paying no particular attention to the audience, in the crucially placed soliloquy at the end of Act IV he does speak directly to his listeners, claiming that they share his prurient feelings about the liaison between Callimaco and Lucrezia.[25] Thus once again one of the play's confidence men speaks to the audience principally to force it into an identification with himself and thereby to shape its response.

In general, the large number of soliloquies and asides establish a strong bond between confidence men and audience as does the fact that the audience is privy to the plotting from the start. The confidence men and the audience share the same mentality: they are amoral, witty, and sophisticated; look down on fools like Nicia; enjoy jokes about friars and religion; and relish the prospect of Callimaco's going to bed with Lucrezia. Such listeners could indeed serve as Machiavelli's drinking companions, as he suggested they might in his prologue. But the soliloquies and asides of Machiavelli's confidence men forcibly move the audience

[24]Ferroni's statement in "Mutazione" e "riscontro," p. 77, that Ligurio does not speak to the spectators is clearly incorrect.
[25]Ferroni stresses Timoteo's closeness to the audience; see ibid., p. 78.

into the conspirators' camp, just as Machiavelli's manipulation of the rhetoric of his political writings aimed to compel his readers to identify with him. Clearly, in all these works produced after the fall of the Florentine Republic and during Machiavelli's exile at Sant' Andrea, he uses every resource of language to force his audiences into his camp not just to persuade them of the rightness of his positions but to regain for himself at least a faint sense of mastery, some substitute for the admittedly qualified political power he once enjoyed. In short, in all of them Machiavelli is rhetorically *prepotente* (overbearing), if only for the sake of once more, somehow being *potente* (powerful).

Machiavelli's rhetorical performance produces a striking picture of him. He forces his audience away from certain opinions by mockery and sarcasm, while manipulating them into an identification with himself by posing as rationalist and demythologizer, skeptic and innovator; he shapes his style to create an illusion of reasonableness through its symmetries and antitheses and to bring his audience to think as he does through a complex play of generalizations and exceptions; and he bonds that audience to him by addressing them directly, warning them against fatal errors, encouraging them to perceive themselves as princes, and telling them generally how to think and feel. All of these tactics parallel the things Machiavelli's confidence men do and thereby identify him as a confidence man himself.[26] Like his princes, Machiavelli the rhetorician continually uses techniques of fraud and force, and like them, he tends to rely more on the latter than on the former as he strives to coerce his readers into accepting his views and seeing the world his way. For Machiavelli knows that only in the ideal world of comedy will fraud alone suffice; in the real world of history, which he and his princes inhabit, fraud must be backed up by — and often yield to — force.

Machiavelli's behavior as prince contradicts the pose he explicitly adopts in most of his mature writing, the pose of adviser or counselor to his readers. Recall the passage in *Il principe* in which he distinguished among three different "cervelli," or minds: one that understands things by itself and is most excellent; a second that understands what others do and is excellent; and a third that understands nothing and is useless (XXII, 94). In the analysis of Chapter 3, the emphasis fell on the distinction between the first and third mentalities, which Machiavelli assigned to his prince and the *popolo*, respectively; the middle one was, for the sake of convenience, lumped together with the first. That middle one,

---

[26]See J. R. Hale, "The Setting of *The Prince*: 1513-1514," in Niccolò Machiavelli, *The Prince*, trans. Adams, p. 150.

however, is really distinct; it is the property of those individuals identified in *Il principe* as advisers to princes, and that is exactly the position Machiavelli adopts in his works. Now, however, it should be clear that his presumably middle position in that three-level hierarchy is a deliberate deception, for as he advises his princely readers, he adopts a superior position with regard to them. In essence, he is the prince himself pretending to be an adviser, a mere "servitore," while effectively placing his princely and upper-class readers in a position well beneath him. As he indicates in the dedication to *Il principe*, for instance, such readers have yet to acquire the knowledge he is imparting to them, whereas he himself has already mastered it through many years of experience, reading, and reflection. It is thus *his* "cervello," not theirs, that is "eccellentissimo," the one on top, the "cervello" of a confidence man of a highest order.

Because he was a political and social inferior in Florence even when he was head of the Second Chancery and Soderini's confidant, Machiavelli was always in the position of playing courtier to those in power as he served and advised them, just as were thousands of others in the Renaissance — merchants turned gentlemen, successful condottieri become dukes, men rising up in ecclesiastical hierarchies, humanists such as Erasmus and artists such as Raphael, and, of course, actual courtiers who flocked to the palaces of the nobility. All of them, Machiavelli included, depended on their manifold talents to win them wealth, status, and power, and all of them had to learn to play the courtier in some measure as well because talent did not guarantee its own reward. Wealth, status, and power all flowed downward in Renaissance society from those individuals placed at the tops of its hierarchies, and they could not be compelled to grant their favors, only cozened to do so.

Machiavelli was, however, a very different sort of courtier from Baldassare Castiglione, who codified for European society the conception of courtiership in his widely read *Libro del Cortegiano*. That book recommended extreme reticence, discretion, and indirection in the courtier's relationship with his prince and his peers, and Castiglione himself, in the very writing of his book, illustrates just what he means. He frames his work as an act of homage to his masters past and present, puts possibly unattractive ideas in secondary and carefully qualified positions, and uses his dialogue form to leave many problematic notions unresolved. Most strikingly, when he has his characters admit the existence of wicked princes and complain about the possibility of unjust treatment at their hands — the chief problem facing everyone who played the courtier in Renaissance society — he has them downplay such matters, leaving them mere hypotheses said to be unlikely to occur and only distantly related to real princes in the real world. Thus, although his book is designed at points to influence the behavior of princes as well as to shape that of courtiers, it does not force its ideas on them; its obliqueness and tactfulness give them freedom of choice. How much more insistent is Machiavelli as he tells an audience of princes what to think and feel, coerces and manipulates them into accepting the ideas he cherishes and rejecting those he does not! In the "Memoriale" written for Raffaello Girolami in 1522, Machiavelli tells the young ambassador that since one's superiors normally dislike to hear an ambassador directly express his own opinions and judgments, it is a good strategy to use indirection and to put those ideas into the mouths of others in diplomatic reports (*SP*, 285). Machiavelli adopted various forms of this strategy himself, doing so fairly consistently in his *Legazioni*, rather transparently in the *Arte della guerra*, and, according to Felix Gilbert, in the *Istorie fiorentine* to some extent as well.[27] But in all these works, and even more strikingly in *Il principe* and the *Discorsi*, he abandons indirection — though not various forms of deception — for a strategy of forcefully attempting to determine his audience's beliefs through rhetorical coercion. Thus, even though he may identify his own role as that of the adviser, the "servitore" — in other words, the courtier — his rhetoric is really a rhetoric of power, not service, and it is designed to make him the true master of those socially and politically superior individuals for whom he writes.

The ambiguity of Machiavelli's position in his mature works — his social inferiority to his readers and his intellectual superiority to them — is revealed most fully when one considers that as adviser, he is really his readers' teacher. He constantly refers to "esempli" (examples) and "precetti" (precepts) throughout his works and presents himself as engaged in rational analysis and intellectual clarification. Just as he sees in Livy a sage and revered teacher — he offers Livy's words as instruction ("insegnano") for a would-be leader (*Disc*, III, xxxviii, 490) — so he himself says that he teaches ("insegna") his readers and encourages them to imitate ("imitar") the ancients he admires (*Disc*, II, Proemio, 274). Recall, moreover, Machiavelli's consistent hostility to what he considered the deficient education of his contemporary world, especially in the *Discorsi* (II, ii, 283; II, xvi, 321; II, xix, 333). By assuming the guise of teacher and attempting to reform that education, Machiavelli offers his readers a service, is their "servitore" in a sense, but the role he plays allows him simultaneously to place himself above them, so that he

---

[27]Felix Gilbert, "Machiavelli's 'Istorie fiorentine': An Essay in Interpretation," in *Studies on Machiavelli*, ed. Myron P. Gilmore (Florence: Sansoni, 1972), pp. 85–86.

remains superior not just to the gray mass of dupes who cannot understand his teaching but also to those who hear and accept it. His adoption of the role of teacher is a shrewd rhetorical strategy, for in effect it
forces his readers to treat Machiavelli as their master.

Machiavelli's strategy of ostensibly providing an instructive commentary on the texts of Greek and Roman writers and his explicit goal of
inducing his readers to imitate the behavior of the ancients seem to move
him into the company of Renaissance humanist educators, who typically taught by commenting on texts and relied on imitation to shape
their pupils' moral character. Like them, Machiavelli is socially ambiguous, superior to his charges in knowledge but inferior to them in
rank and political power. Unlike the humanists, however, he is neither
a sedentary scholar nor a marginal hanger-on at court, a man hired to
teach Latin and Greek and to deliver public orations; he is a man of
action whose past life was absorbed in politics, who had a position of
some real power, and who speaks out of experience as well as from the
wisdom he has acquired through books. Nor is his teaching anything like
the conservative Christian moralism espoused by most humanists. As he
indicates through the deliberate parallelism he constructs in *Il principe*, he sees himself as playing Chiron to the princely Achilles he instructs, and he thereby suggests that he, like that mythical centaur,
possesses in himself the very combination of force and intelligence he
wishes his pupils to imitate (xviii, 72). Ezio Raimondi justly observes
that Machiavelli was a perennially frustrated Chiron, always seeking an
Achilles he could never find, but it is equally true that by assuming such
a role, by using his rhetorical skill to dominate his readers in the very
act of educating them, he also accorded himself a power that served to
compensate in some degree for the frustration he felt.[28] It is instructive
that when he chooses a spokesman for his ideas in the *Arte della guerra*,
he selects a successful man of action, the condottiere Fabrizio Colonna,
and has him play teacher to the young. Obviously priding himself on
his intelligence and the toughness that enabled him to bear up under
torture, Machiavelli revealingly projects himself into a military hero and
figure of power, presenting in this dialogue an idealized version of himself and of the relationship to his readers he wished to establish, in which
he plays the revered sage and they look up to him with total awe.

To say that Machiavelli plays the confidence man–prince in his mature
writings is not to say that he does so in the same way in every one of
them. Indeed, just as his ideal prince is an amalgam of trickster and
epic hero, so Machiavelli and his surrogates appear sometimes heroic,

[28]Raimondi, *Politica e commedia*, p. 286.

princely lions, sometimes clever foxes. As might be expected, he is at his most "epic" when he assumes the identity of Fabrizio Colonna in the *Arte della guerra* and when he speaks in his own person in the brief biography of the heroic Castruccio Castracani. Some deception is going on in both works, of course—the former pretends to be a real dialogue and the latter deliberately reshapes the facts of Castracini's life to make him into an ideal hero—but both works employ a straightforward rhetoric of power, instructing their audiences directly by overwhelming them with technical information in the first case and by creating an unequivocal model to imitate in the second. Both works are essentially displays of epic power.

This epic element appears elsewhere, too, as when Machiavelli characterizes his writing as an alternative to "ozio" (*Arte*, Proemio, 326) or as an "impresa," a heroic quest (*Ist*, Dedication, 67; *Disc*, I, Proemio, 125). Indeed, in the *Istorie fiorentine* he compares the act of writing with entering the field of battle (ibid.: he goes "in campo"), and in *Il principe* he implies that his writing is the intellectual equivalent of a heroic quest into the unknown when he condemns other men for being content to walk along well-worn paths (VI, 30: "camminando li uomini quasi sempre per le vie battute da altri"). The metaphor of writing as heroic journey receives its most striking articulation at the start of the *Discorsi*, when Machiavelli links his enterprise there to the quests of those real-life heroes in the Renaissance, the explorers who sought out "acque e terre incognite" (I, Proemio, 123: "seas and lands unknown"). Here again he insists that he goes along a "via" ("way" or "path") others have not trod, undertaking a journey that will bring him trouble and difficulty. He then concludes on a lofty note:

> E benché questa impresa sia difficile, nondimanco, aiutato da coloro che mi hanno ad entrare sotto questo peso confortato, credo portarlo in modo che ad un altro resterà breve cammino a condurlo a loco destinato. [I, Proemio, 125]

And although this heroic quest may be difficult, nevertheless, aided by those who have supported me in taking up this burden, I believe I can carry it so that another will have only a short road remaining to direct it to its destined place

Machiavelli's metaphor of the quest here connects with a related one he uses on several occasions in the *Discorsi*, that of people's deriving "profit" from or making "capital" out of their reading (I, X, 156–57; II, xxxiii, 376). This metaphor may seem to be merely economic and to have little to do with heroism, but to see the connection, one need only remember the *Istorie*'s denunciation of modern wars that bring no profit (VI, i, 387-88) and the *Discorsi*'s repeated insistence that Rome's heroes enriched its public coffers. Finally, Machiavelli underscores his own "heroic" character in this text subtly and indirectly when he defines the ultimate hero not as a warrior but as an innovator, someone whose wisdom allows his country to take stock of itself so that it can begin a process of renewal, of returning to its origins. He produces a list of such figures from Roman history at the start of the third book (i, 382), and he devotes the last paragraph of the work to Fabius Maximus—indeed, the *Discorsi* end on "Massimo"—a hero who received his title not in recognition of his skill as a warrior but because he reorganized Rome when its institutions were in danger of destruction by a large influx of outsiders (III, xlix, 505-6). To this list of heroes distinguished for their political wisdom the name of Machiavelli must clearly be added.

If the *Arte della guerra*, the *Vita di Castruccio Castracani*, and the *Discorsi* are all marked by a direct assertiveness that constitutes a rhetorical analogue to the heroic side of Machiavelli's prince, other works rely somewhat more on fraud. The *Istorie fiorentine*, for instance, are dedicated to the Medici pope Clement VII by a Machiavelli who poses at the start as his "umile servo" (65) and asserts that his praise of the Medici family is not formulaic but sincere and merited. Machiavelli is being tactful here because he has to be—he depended on the Medici as his patrons—but he also wants to remain his own man. Consequently, he stops his history with the death of Lorenzo, rather than involve himself in charting the rise and fall of the republic in which he played so significant a role. Moreover, he leaves tact well behind and enters into genuine confidence tricks in two distinct ways as he composes the *Istorie*. First, without specifying his point of view, he puts into the mouths of various characters opinions of which he approved and about which the Medici doubtless would have been less than enthusiastic. These include the very radical, demystifying, egalitarian ideas of the plebian who spouts a "Machiavellian" political philosophy during the Ciompi Revolt (III, xiii, 237-38) and the suggestion, which Machiavelli cleverly assigns to Giovanni de' Medici, Cosimo's father, that his son do just the contrary of the Medici's policy and take no greater share in the government of Florence than his countrymen and the laws allow (IV, xvi, 292). Even more subtly, though Machiavelli praises Cosimo and Lorenzo de' Medici—perhaps even with a touch of sincerity here, since they were both confidence men to some extent, and all confidence men found a place in Machiavelli's heart—he structures the entire *Istorie* less to celebrate the rise of their family than to deplore the downfall of Florence and Italy; and since he blames that downfall on factionalism, the astute reader cannot help observing that factionalism was the means by which the Medici achieved and maintained their power.

Il principe, which was written while Machiavelli was at Sant' Andrea, is framed by an even more deferential dedication, this time to Lorenzo de' Medici. Desperate for employment, an exile and outsider, stuck far down on the Florentine social ladder, Machiavelli stresses his lowliness, his *servitù*, and his identity as one of the scorned *popolo*, while he praises the lofty position of Lorenzo, referring four times in three short paragraphs to his dedicatee's "Magnificenzia" (13-14). In the body of the text, though, he adopts his characteristic role of adviser-teacher, manipulating his reader into agreement with his views by means of his style and a very frequent use of *tu* which strikingly replaces the more respectful and courtly *Lei* and *voi* of the dedication. By the end of the work, then, when he is urging Lorenzo to render himself famous and his house illustrious by undertaking the heroic task of redeeming Italy, it is clear that if Lorenzo does so, it will be as Machiavelli's pupil. By the end, in other words, Lorenzo has been brought down from the heights, and Machiavelli, with his larger, clearer vision, has taken his place.

Whereas in *Il principe*, and to a much lesser extent in the *Discorsi*, Machiavelli's addressees are initially accorded superior status, in *La mandragola* they appear in the prologue to be treated more like equals. Nevertheless, even here, by means of several subtle strokes, Machiavelli puts the audience in an inferior position vis-à-vis the confidence men who are his surrogates in the play, so that his presumed equality with them stands revealed as being as much a deception as his supposed inferiority to the Medici was in the *Istorie* and *Il principe*. We have already observed that his confidence men forcefully direct the audience's responses through asides and soliloquies. Moreover, although the audience is privy to the plotting, Ligurio holds information back from them just as he does from Callimaco and the others, making him in effect the master of the audience as well as of all the other characters onstage. More important, Frate Timoteo identifies them with Lucrezia; imagining that Callimaco and Lucrezia will not be sleeping during the night, he says, "perché io so, se io fussi lui, e se voi fussi lei, che noi non dormiremmo" (IV.x.103: "because I know, if I were he, and if you were she, that we would not be sleeping"). In effect, Frate Timoteo establishes an imaginary male-female sexual relationship with the entire audience which underscores and symbolizes the real nature of the power relationship in the play: by being assigned the woman's part, the audience is placed, according to commonplace Renaissance notions, in an inferior position, implicitly looking up to the confidence man–friar, just as

Lucrezia accepts Callimaco as her father, guide, and leader. Once again Machiavelli has shown himself to be the true master of all those he addresses.

It may seem puzzling that Machiavelli plays such a potentially dangerous game, as his audience's discovery that he was deceiving and manipulating them might have alienated the very people he had to depend on for his livelihood and who alone could offer him the only bit of power and status in the social and political world he might ever have. In fact, he seems to go out of his way at moments to suggest that he is deceiving them, just as Callimaco deliberately brings up the idea of deception and charlatans in his first encounter with Nicia (II.ii.71). Recall, for instance, Machiavelli's stress on the undependability of servants in *La mandragola* and his inversion of servant and master roles, after his identification of himself as a servant in the prologue. Recall, too, that having assumed the role of adviser in his political and historical works, he warns that advisers to princes, if they have more intelligence and ability than their masters, will inevitably deceive them and seek ultimately to replace them on their thrones. It is as though Machiavelli were deliberately inviting, indeed daring, his audience to see through his ruse and thus to defeat the elaborate rhetorical strategy he has labored so hard to carry out in his works.

At least three explanations may be offered for his seeming eagerness to flirt with disaster. The first is simple and perfectly consistent with his rhetorical strategy: he suggests deception to increase his audience's confidence in him, on the assumption that humans will tend to interpret any such admission as a sign of sincerity and honesty (if he is willing to bring up the subject, how can he be lying?). Second, Machiavelli plays with fire because doing so increases his pleasure, especially when he is not burned by it. In other words, by telling his readers almost directly that he is deceiving them, he increases the risk and so the excitement, and his final triumph when his ruse succeeds is enormously intense and satisfying. Finally, the various clues Machevelli provides about what he is really doing could suggest, at least to the most perceptive among his audience, that their interaction is a game played out for their mutual enlightenment and pleasure. Ezio Raimondi has remarked that Machiavelli's analytical style is like that of a chess player, and one might do well to extend his metaphor by saying that Machavelli's works are like chess games in which his audience is his chief opponent.[29] They are challenged to a combat of wits which they will always lose because Machiavelli controls the rhetorical situation, but their anger is checked

[29] Ibid., p. 157.

by their reluctance to spoil the play relationship between them and the author; anger would reduce them to the level of peevish spoilsports. From this perspective, then, Machiavelli has done something very clever indeed: he has established a relationship with his readers which permits him to have his cake and eat it too, to enjoy his vicarious power over them while slyly hinting to the wisest among them that this is a most sophisticated game and they should be flattered even as they lose. Thus the servant not only outfoxes his nominal masters but with cunning artistry makes them enjoy it.

In conclusion, let us consider a short work, the "Discursus florentinarum rerum post mortem iunioris Laurentii Medicis" ("Discourse on Florentine affairs after the death of Lorenzo de' Medici the Younger"), written in 1520 and addressed to Pope Leo X, which reveals Machiavelli at his trickiest as a confidence man-prince, but which also reveals the glaring flaw in the rhetorical strategy he implemented with such determination in his works.[30] In the "Discursus" Machiavelli seems at first to be speaking against Medici interests by arguing for a restoration of republican rule in Florence. The Florentines are habituated to political equality and hence to such a form of government, he says, so that they can be content with no other. Moreover, the republic Cosimo and Lorenzo ruled over was imperfect and led eventually to the defeat of the Medici party in both cases. Thus the creation of a true republic is the pope's only practical alternative if he wishes to achieve peace and a stable government in the city (*SP*, 268–73). Machiavelli then adds a very different argument, defending the founding of an enduring state on more idealistic grounds and invoking the revered names of Plato and Aristotle (*SP*, 275–76). It turns out, however, that Machiavelli is not really arguing against the Medici's interests, for he says that the pope can control the republican government he establishes: recreating the Consiglio Grande, which will make everyone feel grateful to him, he will manipulate its voting lists behind the scenes to ensure the dominance of his own party, and he will organize the *popolo* into groups and allow them to be present when decisions are made, so that they seem to have a say in the government although they really have very little (*SP*, 268–73). In essence, then, Machiavelli is advising Leo to play the confidence man, satisfying the Florentines by giving them the appearance of a republic, seeming to allow the city to rule itself but really controlling it himself, slyly keeping watch over it through an eye half-open (*SP*, 276: "la metà di un occhio volto").

[30]For a different view of the "Discursus," see Rodolfo de Mattei, *Dal premachiavellismo all'antimachiavellismo* (Florence: Sansoni, 1969), pp. 81–87.

But if one reads this work more closely still, it turns out to advocate republican rule after all. For although it assures the pope he will essentially rule Florence during his lifetime as a "monarchia" (*SP*, 275), it also acknowledges that both the pope and the other leader of the Medici party, the cardinal Giulio di Giuliano de' Medici, will die, and that after their deaths the state they have established will be stable and powerful because it will be a full-fledged republic. Machiavelli's argument here is based on the assumption — a true enough one, historically — that there were no other leaders for the Medici party except these two men and that neither one could, by virtue of his clerical office, pass on control of the state to his son. The result would be that the pope would create a republic in Florence as a means to bring about internal stability and thus serve his end of ruling the city, but at his death this relationship of means and ends would reverse itself, and he would appear to have ruled the city only to bring about a republican form of government which his party would no longer control because it lacked the support that the power of the papacy could provide. Although Machiavelli encourages Leo to think he plays the confidence man, he will actually be achieving a limited and temporary victory, and Machiavelli, by engineering the creation of a true Florentine republic, will have the last laugh, thus revealing himself as the superior confidence man in the end. His situation here almost perfectly parallels that of Ligurio in *La mandragola*: he is the tricky servant who scripts a scenario in which his master plays the confidence man and satisfies his own ends while making a contented dupe out of his victim; but that tricky servant really acts to serve his own ultimate interests, keeps all the power in his own hands, and will eventually defeat his master. How ironic that Machiavelli, the perfect confidence man here, should have told Pope Leo near the start that he composed his little treatise "per mostrare la fede mia" (*SP*, 264: "to demonstrate my faith"), when the only "faith" Machiavelli really keeps is with himself.

What a clever strategy, but how futile! For the Medici responded to his suggestion with silence; they ignored it, either because they did not believe they could implement it successfully or because they saw through his ruse. Their response — or rather their lack of response — reveals the basic flaw not only in this work but in the rhetorical strategy Machiavelli tried to implement in practically everything he wrote after 1512: although he could coerce hypothetical audiences by his rhetorical power plays, his real readers remained beyond his reach. For the simple truth is that no book or speech or play can coerce its audience to do anything they do not wish to do. They can ignore what they read, misconstrue it in important ways, or misapply it when they attempt to realize it, as the history of the reception of Machiavelli's works in the centuries after his death reveals only too clearly.[31] The choice — and hence the real power — lies in the reader's hands, not the author's.

Although Machiavelli may fantasize that he, like Fabrizio Colonna in the *Arte della guerra*, is a revered sage whose words are taken as gospel by his readers and listeners if only because he has maneuvered them through his rhetoric into seeing them so, the truth is, of course, that he has no way of ensuring that they will react as he wants them to, or even that they will react at all. In a sense, the clever game he plays with them is one he may always win hypothetically but all too often loses in actuality; if his rhetoric of power reveals at times the immense power of rhetoric, it reveals equally just how powerless rhetoric can be. For every Charles V who kept *Il principe* by his bedside, for every Francis Bacon who admired Machiavelli's insights into politics, there were thousands of Innocent Gentillets and Reginald Poles who condemned him as the devil incarnate, thousands of theatergoers who hissed at the villainous Machiavels paraded before them. By playing the consummate confidence man-prince in his works, Machiavelli wanted to affirm for himself that in some way knowledge could confer power. Unfortunately, although it could do so from time to time, it could not do so absolutely and consistently, as Machiavelli knew only too well from bitter experience. That realization never made him change his approach, however, as he carried out various forms of the same strategy in work after work between 1512 and his death in 1527, perhaps because the rhetorical power he could wield over a hypothetical audience was too strong a lure to resist, or perhaps simply because, after the death of the republic, real social and political power was scarcely ever available to him. Through his writing, then, he could at least confirm his own value, could prove to himself what he says to Zanobi Buondelmonte and Cosimo Rucellai in the dedication of the *Discorsi*: those individuals who know how to rule but lack kingdoms are truly more estimable than those who have kingdoms but do not know how to rule them.

[31]For the history of the reception of Machiavelli's works, see de Mattei, *Dal premachiavellismo all'antimachiavellismo*; Franco Fido, *Machiavelli* (Palermo: Palumbo, 1965); and Felix Raab, *The English Face of Machiavelli: A Changing Interpretation, 1500–1700* (London: Routledge & Kegan Paul, 1964).

6

Confidence Games in the
Republic of Wooden Clogs

In May 1521, Machiavelli was sent to the Chapter General of the Minorite Friars at Carpi, and he recorded his activities there in a series of letters to Francesco Guicciardini, then governor of the Papal States in the Romagna. We have already examined those letters briefly at the start of Chapter 1.[1] Machiavelli's task at Carpi was twofold: first, on behalf of the Signoria and the cardinal Giulio de' Medici, he was to secure the separation of the minorite convents in Florentine territory from the rest of those in Tuscany; and second, the Arte della lana (the Wool Guild) had asked him to arrange for a noted preacher, a certain fra Giovanni Gualberto da Firenze, to come to Florence and preach there during Lent. Neither task apparently occupied much of his time, especially since the first had to wait until the Chapter General convened. As a result, Machiavelli was left idle (*Let, #184, 404: "ozioso"*) in the midst of a group of friars whom both he and Guicciardini despised with a typical Italian anticlericalism and satirically dubbed "la Repubblica de' Zoccholi" (#186, 407 and #188, 412: "the Republic of Wooden Clogs"). To pass the time, Machiavelli devised an immense practical joke, a "scherzo," to play on the poor frati and the people of the town (#188, 412). This joke springs from the very core of Machiavelli's personality and shows how deeply the model of the confidence man influenced his conceptions of his own activity and of the world about him. It also shows just how powerful the dialectic of confidence man and dupe was for him and how intimately he experienced—and thus came to recognize fully— the limits of the confidence games he played. Finally, Machiavelli's letters from Carpi reveal that if he could never escape from the dialectic

---

[1]For a detailed narrative based on these letters, see Roberto Ridolfi, *The Life of Niccolò Machiavelli*, trans. Cecil Grayson (Chicago: University of Chicago Press, 1963), pp. 186–94.

of confidence man and dupe no matter what strategy he adopted, his irony and self-reflexive laughter at least enabled him to live with it and with the degradation to which it seemed inevitably to lead.

In one of the pair's first exchanges, Machiavelli writes Guicciardini that when the latter's messenger arrived bearing a letter, bowed low in public, and declared that he had been sent in haste, Machiavelli was suddenly treated as though he were a very important individual: "Ognuno si rizzò con tante riverenze et tanti romori, che gli andò sotto-sopra ogni cosa, et fui domandato da parecchi delle nuove" (#184, 404: "Everyone stood up with such bowing and such noise that everything was turned topsy-turvy, and I was asked by several of them for news"). Rather than tell the truth, that he and Guicciardini were merely engaged in a largely personal correspondence, Machiavelli allowed the false impression created by the messenger to continue. He improvised for the friars and the other Carpigiani about him a bogus news report concerned with the doings of the emperor, the Swiss, the French king, and so forth. His performance had the desired—and marvelously comic—effect, for he records that "tutti stavano a bocca aperta et con la berretta in mano" (ibid.: "all stood there with their mouths agape and their hats in their hands"). Consequently, he was led to embroider his performance even further, and he reports to Guicciardini.

Mentre che io scrivo ne ho un cerchio d'intorno, et veggendomi scrivere a lungo si maravigliano, et guardonmi per spiritato; et io, per farli mara-vigliare piú, sto alle volte fermo su la penna, et gonfio, et allota egli sbavigliano. [Ibid.]

While I am writing, I have a circle of them about me, and seeing me write at length, they all marvel and think I am possessed; and I, to make them marvel all the more, sometimes stop writing and hold my breath, and then they gape.

Since Machiavelli relished the duping of the friars, the Carpigiani, and his host, Sigismondo Santi—the chancellor of Alberto Pio, who was then lord of the city—he asked Guicciardini to help him elaborate the joke, either by coming there in person or at least by sending frequent messengers carrying "important" letters for him. Guicciardini, who ap-parently derived almost as much pleasure from this joke as did Machia-velli, complied willingly and sent messengers posthaste with large packets of dispatches so that everyone around Machiavelli would indeed be deceived into thinking he was a "gran personaggio" (#185, 406) whose affairs concerned more than mere friars.

This episode is a classic example of the art of the confidence man. It divides the world into dupes and sharpers, the former gloriously stupid as they stand about in open-mouthed amazement, the latter relying on their "cervello" (#184, 404: "brains") to pull the wool over their victims' eyes. From Boccaccio's Frate Cipolla on, this division is typically that between country bumpkins and a fast-talking city slicker, an opposition Machiavelli evokes when he explains how difficult it was to persuade the friar-preacher at Carpi to come to Florence for Lent. The preacher's sister, reports Machiavelli, warned the man that the whores in Florence had stopped wearing the yellow veils he once prescribed for them and that they now moved freely about the city. To calm the fears of this small-town moralist, Machiavelli, the big-city man, told him:

> ché gli era usanza delle città grandi non star ferme molto in un proposito, et di fare hoggi una cosa et domani disfarla; et gli allegai Roma et Athene, tale che si racconsolò tutto, et hammi quasi promesso. [#187, 410]

> that it was the custom of great cities not to stick much to one arrangement, and to do one thing today and undo it tomorrow; and I cited for him Rome and Athens, so that he was entirely reconciled and almost promised [to come].

Though Machiavelli's lying and deceiving, like the confidence man's, might be considered morally reprehensible, they evade straitlaced condemnation here for several reasons: no real harm is done to anyone; the friars are themselves repeatedly criticized as liars and hypocrites (see #183, 402, and #184, 405), so that to deceive them is to give them their just desserts; and finally, the trick is a matter of exuberance and delight, not mean-spirited nastiness or malice, so that one can hardly take offense at it.[2] In fact, one has to admire Machiavelli's cleverness, energy, and inventiveness, the sheer histrionic genius involved in the little drama he has acted out to amuse himself at a time of enforced idleness.

The exuberance, joy, and pleasure involved in Machiavelli's trick make him a very different sort of confidence man from his princes. As he characterizes himself in his letters from Carpi, he is a fully carnivalesque figure, and the role of confidence man he plays has many of the festive characteristics it traditionally had in literature. First, it involves turning the world upside down as Machiavelli engages in anticonventional and even nonsensical behavior. He rejoices, for instance, when

---

[2] Machiavelli's exuberance is evident at the start of #187, 409. For a discussion of how a writer blunts criticism of the confidence man's amoral, if not immoral, actions, see Orin E. Klapp, "The Clever Hero," *Journal of American Folklore* 67 (1954): 21–34.

Guicciardini's messenger causes so much excitement that everything is turned "sottosopra," and he reports that he went about thinking up other ways he might create some great "scandolo" among the Carpigiani (#184, 404). And he is consistent in his topsy-turviness; he is as "contrario" to the common opinions held by Florentines as to those of the yokels (#184, 403). Finally, when his trick is later being sniffed out by his host, Sigismondo Santi, Machiavelli puts him off with "a few confusing words" ("poche parole et mal conposte") on such things as the flood to come, the passage of the Turks, and a new crusade (#187, 409). In other words, he speaks both in a nonsensical, upside-down manner and of matters that would indeed turn the world topsy-turvy if they occurred.

Also carnivalesque is Machiavelli and Guicciardini's satire on the elevated subjects of politics and religion. Both writers parody the idea of serious diplomatic missions when they call Machiavelli an "oratore" to the Frati Minori and speak of the "Repubblica de' Zoccholi."[3] Machiavelli can also, with exquisite irony, insist that he is doing his "patriotic" duty in seeking a preacher to come to Florence,[4] even though the preacher he would choose would hardly be to his fellow citizens' liking and the task is something less than a serious diplomatic endeavor. Moreover, both Guicciardini and Machiavelli are generally irreverent in these letters, mocking the friars for lying and stupidity, and even parodying religious language at times, as when Machiavelli identifies Guicciardini as his "Signoria, *quae vivat et regnet in saecula saeculorum*" (#187, 411: "Lord, *who should live and reign forever and ever*"), and reports Sigismondo's doubts that Guicciardini would really write "sí lunghe bibbie in questi deserti d'Arabia" (#187, 409: "such long Bibles in these Arabian deserts").[5] This religious satire is announced in the first letter preserved from the pair's exchanges, in which Guicciardini proclaims with mock seriousness that sending Machiavelli to seek a preacher is like sending Pacchierotto or Ser Sano, two notorious sodomites, to seek a beautiful wife for a friend (#183, 401). Embracing fully the role of one who turns the world upside down, Machiavelli replies that he will indeed find a preacher to his liking, one who teaches the Florentines the way

---

[3]Machiavelli was, technically speaking, an *oratore*, although his mission to Carpi was not very important in a diplomatic sense. See the subscriptions to his letters #184, 405 and #187, 411, as well as the meditation at the opening of Guicciardini's letter #186, 407.

[4]#184, 403: "Et perché io non mancai mai a quella repubblica, dove io ho possuto giovarle, . . . io non intendo mancarle anco in questo" ("And because I never failed that republic where I was able to aid it, . . . I don't intend to fail it in this either").

[5]Machiavelli also uses the word *bibbie* ironically in an early letter to Giovanni Ridolfi; see #74, 156.

not to paradise but to the devil's house, one who is not prudent and noble but "piú pazzo che il Ponzo, piú versuto che fra Girolamo, piú ippocrito che frate Alberto" (#184, 403: "madder than il Ponzo [one of Savonarola's opponents], wilier than fra Girolamo [Savonarola], more hypocritical than frate Alberto"). Fittingly, although Machiavelli goes on to denounce the false religious—he laments "quanto credito ha un tristo che sotto il mantello della religione si nasconda" (ibid.: "how much credit a wicked man has who hides under the cloak of religion")—he nevertheless celebrates as his sort of preacher a set of charlatans and confidence men.

If carnival involves criticism and satire, it also involves a basic affirmation of life, of the body and pleasure, and Machiavelli's letters from Carpi testify fully to the enthusiasm with which he embraces this side of it. Although his *ozio* leads him to let out his frustration by playing confidence games on the friars, here he does not reject it as he does for his prince in his political and historical works. *Ozio* now possesses positive attractions, being associated with such bodily pleasures as eating and drinking, which are described in Rabelaisian terms and which affirm the animal nature of human beings. Sigismondo Santi, writes Machiavelli, offers him "i pasti golfi" ("immense meals"), to which he responds by eating voraciously: "io pappo per sei cani et tre lupi" (#187, 410: "I wolf down enough for six dogs and three wolves"). His idleness also gives Machiavelli the chance to sleep and read (#187, 409), and he tells Guicciardini that he hopes his "scherzo" will not take away the sensual benefits he has been enjoying: "pasti gagliardi, letti gloriosi, et simili cose, dove io mi sono già tre dí rinfantocciato" (#188, 412: "grand meals, glorious beds, and such things, where I have been truly rejuvenated the last three days"). "Rinfantocciato" needs to be taken seriously, for Machiavelli's experience—the combination of tricking others and satisfying one's appetites—is very much the carnivalesque experience of rejuvenation. It is not the premature senility, the return to second childhood, for which Guicciardini says men would denounce Machiavelli if he suddenly gave up his profession of impiety and became seriously religious (#183, 402: "sarebbe attribuito piuttosto al rimbambito che al buono"). Rather, it is a reprise of youthful strength and vital energy, qualities especially valuable to the fifty-two-year-old Machiavelli.

The letters from Carpi affirm the full range of bodily experience, including sexuality (see his false Latinism "Cazzus" in #188, 411) and even defecation, as when he reports that he is reading Guicciardini's letter in the privy:

Magnifice vir, major observandissime. Io ero in sul cesso quando arrivò il vostro messo, et appunto pensavo alle stravaganze di questo mondo, et tutto ero volto a figurarmi un predicatore a mio modo per a Firenze, et fosse tale quale piacesse a me, perché in questo voglio essere caparbio come nelle altre oppinioni mie. [#184, 402-3]

Magnifice vir, major observandissime. I was on the toilet when your messenger arrived, and I was just thinking of the absurdities of this world, and I was entirely absorbed in imagining a preacher of my sort for Florence, the kind that would please me, because in this I want to be as pigheaded as in my other opinions.

Note here the wonderful juxtaposition of the fulsome and elevated Latin titles given Guicciardini and the unsavory location from which Machiavelli delivers his response. The privy serves to bring down to the lowest bodily level all the pretension involved in titles and political hierarchies. It does not, however, as it did for Martin Luther and the Protestants, serve as a symbolic locus for attacks by and on the devil, a place in which to be inspired with divine knowledge or to acquire insight into the doctrine of justification by faith.[6] For the secular Machiavelli, the privy is associated with the pleasures, the egocentric focus, and the solidity of the flesh, from which all the hierarchies of this world are judged absurd, all matters spiritual dismissed through parody.

The letters from Carpi show that playing the confidence man is not merely a carnivalesque experience but one that requires skill as an actor-director-scriptwriter, a skill Machiavelli possessed in abundance. He had what Ezio Raimondi has called "histrionic sensibility,"[7] an extraordinarily theatrical intelligence that allowed him to insert himself into his characters, as he does throughout the *Istorie fiorentine* and, of course, in "Belfagor" and his plays. His analyses of political situations and his diplomatic negotiations also required an ability to project himself into the minds and characters of others. As he tells Francesco Vettori, in order to analyze the pope's political situation, "mi son messo nella persona del papa" (#129, 259: "I have put myself in the position [the role or mask] of the pope"). And in two of his most famous letters, both addressed to Vettori, Machiavelli underscores his ability to play a wide variety of roles. In one he describes his life at Sant' Andrea: he rises and goes hunting; tends to the business of the farm; reads love poetry and reflects on his own love affair; dines with his "brigata"; then plays

---

[6]See Norman O. Brown, *Life against Death* (New York: Random House, 1959), pp. 206-10.
[7]Ezio Raimondi, "Machiavelli and the Rhetoric of the Warrior," *MLN* 92 (1977), 12.

cards with local farmers and tradesmen at the inn; and finally, in the evening, takes off his dirty, workaday clothes and dresses in regal garments before he converses, through reading, with the ancients (#140, 302-4). His life is thus a series of discrete roles played on a daily basis; he transfers himself, as he says, from one scene to another, each with its own language, costume, and gestures. The transfer is sometimes physical (303: "Trasferiscomi poi in su la strada nell'hosteria") and sometimes mental (304: "tucto mi transferisco in loro [the ancients]"). In the second letter to Vettori, Machiavelli notes in passing the way the two of them change their roles from letter to letter, page to page, now being men who are "gravi" and then "leggieri, incostanti, lascivi, volti a cose vane" (#163, 374: "light, inconstant, lascivious, devoted to vain matters"). Finally, matching this skill as an actor, Machiavelli is capable of projecting or creating dramatic scenes, as he does in his dramatic works and in the *Istorie*. He does so in his letters as well: he imagines a scene in Vettori's Roman residence, which he has never seen and about which he has only Vettori's incomplete reports (see #145, 320-23); he details his encounter with an ugly old prostitute in Verona in one of his most memorable if repulsive narratives (#108, 204-6); and of course he describes fulsomely his comic experiences at Carpi.[8] As Raimondi has noted, Machiavelli has an instinctive sense of the world as theater, as a stage on which the action is always ready to explode.[9]

Machiavelli's letters about his experiences in Carpi document the firm connection the role of confidence man had with his sense of personal integrity and dignity. For a man who had once been sent on diplomatic missions to the greatest rulers of Europe, his reduction to the paltry concerns of this mission was, to say the least, shameful and degrading.[10] Although Machiavelli does not brood on his humiliation, Guicciardini brings the matter up in one of his letters, comparing his "Machiavello carissimo" to the great Spartan general Lysandros, who, after many victories and trophies, was given the petty task of distributing meat to the very soldiers he had once gloriously commanded (#186, 407). Perhaps Guicciardini intends to console his friend by this comparison as well as by referring, later in the same letter, to Machiavelli's cherished theory of historical repetition. Still, the contrast of Machiavelli's former glory as an *oratore* to great princes and states and his present engage-

---

[8]See Luigi Russo's comment on Machiavelli's dramatic genius in *Machiavelli*, 3d ed. (Bari: Laterza, 1949), p. 160.

[9]Ezio Raimondi, *Politica e commedia: Dal Beroaldo al Machiavelli* (Bologna: Mulino, 1972), pp. 144-45.

[10]See Ridolfi's excellent analysis in *Machiavelli*, pp. 186-87. See also Gennaro Sasso, *Niccolò Machiavelli: Storia del suo pensiero politico* (Naples: Istituto italiano per gli studi storici, 1958), pp. 485-86.

ment in trivialities could not fail to strike a live nerve in a man who had spent years in exile on his farm at Sant' Andrea and had been reduced to begging the Medici for employment. Aware of Machiavelli's feelings, Guicciardini launches into a satire on the illogical reasoning of friars about matters historical, thus encouraging Machiavelli to direct his frustration and anger not at his Medici masters but at the less powerful *frati*. Similarly, one might interpret Machiavelli's decision to play his confidence game with the Carpigiani not simply as a playful reaction to boredom but as a deeply troubled response to the humiliating nature of his mission. Machiavelli's self-proclaimed motive for his trick is his desire to enhance his standing with the Carpigiani.[11] How he wants to be marveled at, and how he must have reveled in Guicciardini's comically exaggerated praise of his trick as "la piú egregia opera che mai facessi" (#185, 406: "the most outstanding work you have ever done")!

If Machiavelli's letters reveal him as a high-spirited, carnivalesque confidence man, they also expose the risks involved in such a mode of existence.[12] For every confidence game is just that—a game—and it can be played only at the risk of failure, the risk that the trick will be discovered by the other players, who are one's opponents. Of course, the risk entailed offers a distinct benefit to the participant, for it increases the basic excitement of the game—after all, nothing is more boring than gambling without using money—but as most gamblers know, the pain of losing is a far more frequent experience than the exultation of winning. Machiavelli's letters reveal that his trick was indeed at least partially exposed. Although the hapless *frati* seem never to have doubted the veracity of his performance,[13] his host was considerably sharper, and Machiavelli records that Sigismondo worried that Guicciardini, who had written on behalf of Machiavelli, might be taking him in. Machiavelli reproduces Sigismondo's line of reasoning (#187,

---

[11] Machiavelli writes Guicciardini that he will achieve two good ends by sending letters: "l'uno che voi mi alluminerete di qualche cosa a proposito, l'altro che voi mi farete piú stimare da questi di casa, veggendo spesseggiare gli avvisi" (#184, 404: "first, that you'll enlighten me with something appropriate, and second, that you'll make me more esteemed by those here, seeing the messages come thick and fast"). A little later he explains that he spoke of the emperor and other important matters, "perché la riputatione crescesse" (ibid.: "so that my reputation would grow").

[12] Russo's assertion that these letters show Machiavelli's natural joy in the artful, the fictive, and the active is true enough, but too simple. See his *Machiavelli*, p. 168.

[13] Machiavelli tells Guicciardini: "Vostra Signoria sa che questi frati dicono, che quando uno è confermato in gratia, il diavolo non ha piú potentia di tentarlo. Cosí io non ho paura che questi frati mi appicchino lo ippocrito, perché io credo essere assai ben confermato" (#184, 404: "Your Lordship knows that these friars say that when one is confirmed in grace, the devil no longer has the power to tempt him. Thus I don't fear that these friars will stick 'hypocrite' on me, because I think I'm already well confirmed"). Note the religious language of this passage that Machiavelli is parodying.

409) and recounts how he put him off with vague replies and absurd prophecies. It is a clear battle of wits in which Machiavelli sees that Sigismondo realizes, or at least glimpses, that this is all a "giuoco" (#187, 410). Finally, in the last letter to Guicciardini, Machiavelli reports that Sigismondo has indeed concluded that theirs is no serious diplomatic correspondence, and Machiavelli was forced to concoct a new explanation for the letters, to concede that they concerned merely private, though serious, business. Moreover, he writes that the preacher continued to express grave reluctance to come to Florence, so that Machiavelli feared he would be shamed, especially with his good friends Francesco Vettori and Filippo Strozzi, who were expecting the preacher and whom he says he failed in a similar mission once before (#188, 411-12). After his triumphant performance as confidence man at Carpi, what a painful descent in the end!

Machiavelli pays for his failure primarily in shame and humiliation, for although he stands to forfeit the physical comforts that were so important to him, the real issue is his own ridiculousness and sense of degradation. He tells Guicciardini: "Il culo mi fa lappe lappe, ché io ho paura tuttavia che non pigli una granata et rimandimi alla hosteria" (#188, 411: "My ass is going smack-smack, and I am really afraid he'll make a clean sweep of it and send me to the inn"). Machiavelli's reference here to the ridiculous, fearful shaking of his posterior and his use of the onomatopoetic "lappe lappe" suggest a childish helplessness. Moreover, as he contemplates being forced away to the inn, it is the idea of being swept out like so much dirt or litter that seems to bother him. Thus in the course of his stay in Carpi, Machiavelli has fallen indeed. The clever and powerful confidence man, rejuvenated by his successful duping of others, has become an inconsequential, ridiculous dupe, rejuvenated now as a child, the victim of his own game.[14] Once the focus of everyone's attention, he is threatened with expulsion to the inn, being swept out to the periphery of Carpi's social life. Machiavelli has thus experienced both sides of the confidence man-dupe relationship—both power and powerlessness, adulthood and childishness, madcap energy and foolish fear, centrality and marginality—and his experience cannot help sharpening his sense of the irony and paradox of life, just as it creates serious problems for his sense of personal integrity and dignity, which were so heavily involved in the confidence-man role he played.

[14]Mireille Celse has remarked that in Machiavelli's universe it is possible for anyone to be tricked at any time; being a successful confidence man is a matter of relative position and luck more than of one's essential nature. See "La *beffa* chez Machiavel, dramaturge et conteur," in *Formes et significations de la "beffa" dans la littérature italienne de la Renaissance*, ed. André Rochon (Paris: Université de la Sorbonne nouvelle, 1972), p. 102.

To understand Machiavelli's profound experience of degradation in Carpi, it is essential to remember how rigorously and relentlessly he divides the world into confidence men and dupes, and how he condemns the shrewdest tricksters once they suffer a defeat, no matter the reason. Consider, for instance, his response to Piero Soderini, whom he served throughout the years of the Florentine Republic: once the republic has fallen and Soderini is driven into exile, Machiavelli condemns him repeatedly for insufficient toughness and ruthlessness, for his failure to kill "the sons of Brutus," for lack of flexibility or clear-sightedness in the face of political realities (*Disc,* I, lii, 247; III, iii, 386–87; ix, 418; xxx, 468; cf. *Let,* #118, 225–26). Even though Machiavelli continued to communicate with his former master after the fall of the republic and even to praise him for his prudence (*Let,* #119, 228–31), his general attitude was condemnatory, and it erupted as open contempt in the famous epigram written after Soderini's death, which mocks him mercilessly as a hapless baby who belongs not in hell with great, heroic figures of evil, but in limbo, a gray and ambiguous location perfectly fitting for a person Machiavelli consistently faulted for procrastination and indecisiveness (*SL,* 365). Thus the Soderini Machiavelli advised and faithfully served during the years of the republic becomes a pathetic dupe once he has failed and his state has fallen, and Machiavelli, casting aside all residual loyalty and gratitude, finally unlooses the most withering scorn at him. Once the confidence man loses, Machiavelli's ruthless dialectic takes over, and he inevitably refashions that individual as a ridiculous and contemptible dupe.

Such a process of recharacterization occurs most dramatically in Machiavelli's writings in connection with Cesare Borgia. Borgia is, of course, the one contemporary figure Machiavelli celebrates as something close to an ideal prince in *Il principe.* He had met Borgia well before he wrote his little treatise, having been sent to him on several diplomatic missions in 1502 and 1503, and he wrote about Borgia both in diplomatic reports (*Legazioni*) and in a few minor works completed in 1503 and 1504.[15] In these early writings, Machiavelli marvels with his contemporaries at Borgia's political astuteness, resolution, and boldness; characteristically, he admires Borgia just as he admires all clever confidence men, even though Borgia, like many of those other tricksters, posed a grave danger to Florentine independence.[16] Thus in his early "Descrizione del modo tenuto dal duca Valentino nello ammazzare

---

[15] For a comprehensive account of Machiavelli's responses to Cesare Borgia throughout his life and works, see Gennaro Sasso, *Machiavelli e Cesare Borgia: Storia di un giudizio* (Rome: Ateneo, 1966).

[16] Ibid., p. 4.

Vitellozzo Vitelli, Oliverotto da Fermo, il signor Pagolo e il duca di Gravina Orsini" ("Description of the manner in which Duke Valentino [Cesare Borgia] massacred Vitellozzo Vitelli, Oliverotto da Fermo, Signor Pagolo [Orsini], and the Duke of Gravina Orsini"), Machiavelli idealizes Cesare Borgia, celebrating the "grandezza" of his spirit, the cleverness with which he outwitted his opponents, and his ability to put on a "buono volto" ("good face") and play the role of trusted ally (*SP*, 47). Complementing this positive evaluation, Machiavelli heaps scorn on Borgia's opponents, emphasizing the folly of the Duke of Gravina Orsini in trusting his family's enemy, the fatalism and helplessness of Vitellozzo Vitelli as he approached his final meeting with Borgia, and the weakness and unworthiness of Vitellozzo and Oliverotto da Fermo in the hour of their deaths (45, 47-48). Machiavelli does characterize Borgia as feeling fear and dejection at Imola when his soldiers suddenly turned against him and his enemies surrounded him, but the timely aid of Florence allowed him to master his fear and regain possession of himself (43: "ripreso animo"), so that his fear becomes merely a minor flaw in a character who emerges otherwise in the "Descrizione" as a proto-prince.[17] After the early months of 1503, when the "Descrizione" was composed, however, Machiavelli's contacts led him to see a now less successful Borgia as being plagued by all too human weaknesses, and the subsequent *Legazioni* characterize the condottiere as childish, undignified, and irresolute. Ultimately, as one might expect, they come to mock Borgia, scorning him for losing the battle to control the election of the pope and thus becoming nothing less than the dupe of Julius II.[18]

When Machiavelli composed *Il principe*, years after Borgia's death, he apparently decided to use him as an exemplum of princely conduct, a model of *virtù* struggling against a hostile Fortuna so that he consciously suppressed his earlier, negative judgment and omitted most of the unattractive features he had observed in the man. Nevertheless, even in *Il principe*, Machiavelli vacillates in judging Borgia's final actions, alternately condemning him for failing to influence the election of the pope and declaring that he failed only because his illness at the time of his father's death was an untimely blow from Fortune for which he could not be held responsible (VII, 39-40). In other words, although Machiavelli wants to present Borgia as an unabashed hero and consciously characterizes his defeat as being ultimately beyond his control and therefore excusable, the trickster-dupe dialectic dominating Machia-

[17]Ibid., p. 59.
[18]Ibid., pp. 109-19.

velli's thought leads him to contradict himself and condemn the man as well.

If the failures of Piero Soderini and Cesare Borgia provoke Machiavelli's scorn, his own failure at Carpi is a considerably larger problem for him, especially since his brief rise and fall there duplicate the trajectory of his entire political career. Although never a prince, Machiavelli did, during the years of the republic, rub shoulders with members of the ruling class, and although he scarcely had his own way in Florence and continually complained about the city's unwillingness to implement his plans, he did enjoy real, if limited, power, in part because of his office but also because of his genuine ability to manipulate others both above and below him — because of his ability to play the confidence man with them. Then, after having helped rule Florence for over a decade, Machiavelli was suddenly thrust from power when the Medici regained control in 1512. Subjected to torture and forced into exile at his country estate, for eight years he was essentially in the position of the dupe, the *beffato*.[19] That he keenly felt his humiliation and degradation can be seen in his desperate attempts to curry favor with the powerful, in his frantic worry at one point that he may even have lost Francesco Vettori's help when the latter, for a brief period, failed to write to him from Rome (*Let*, #140, 301), in his hatred of being reduced to occupying himself with trivial domestic affairs, and in his contempt for the country folk, the "pidocchi" ("lice"), in whose midst he had to live (*Let*, #140, 303 and #152, 343). Machiavelli never regained the power he once exercised under the republic, and his life after 1512 always contained a large measure of degradation in the root sense of the word: a loss of position, of grade or degree, in the social and political hierarchy. Since for Machiavelli one was either a manipulator or a dupe, either praiseworthy or contemptible, and since after 1512 Machiavelli must have felt continually that he fell into the second category, it should be easy to understand why he would be so profoundly attracted to the figure of the confidence man throughout his major political and literary writings, why he would amalgamate that figure with the hero, why he would play the role of confidence man himself with his readers, and why he would embrace it so willingly among the Carpigiani. To play that role in the Republic of Wooden Clogs freed him, at least temporarily, from the most withering self-contempt.

To play the confidence man, however, is, as the letters from Carpi show, to embark on a perilous course, exposing oneself to the real pos-

---

[19]For Machiavelli's feelings of powerlessness and humiliation, see Ridolfi, *Machiavelli*, pp. 136-64.

sibility of failure and hence even further degradation. Indeed, one might almost say, to judge from Machiavelli's writings, that he saw defeat and humiliation as being virtually entailed in the playing of that role. There is no enduringly successful princely figure in all of Machiavelli's works, no one who does not at some time and in some way come a cropper and wind up the dupe. Cesare Borgia, even in *Il principe*, is faulted for failing to control the election of the pope and even for dying prematurely. Castruccio Castracani dies because he recklessly exposes himself to a disease-bearing wind and condemns himself on his deathbed for his failure to establish a secure, lasting realm for his successor. And most of the rest of Machiavelli's confidence man–princes either fail or play the role only intermittently and in limited ways, as do the Roman generals and statesmen celebrated in the *Discorsi*. Even Rome, Machiavelli's grandest example of confidence trickery in action, ultimately succumbs to decadence and tyranny. Characteristically, instinctively, when Machiavelli is brooding in his privy at Carpi on the selection of a Lenten preacher for Florence, his meditation leads him to the figures of il Ponzo, Savonarola, and Frate Alberto, clowns and confidence men, and each in his own way a magnificent failure. In essence, the confidence man for Machiavelli is a gambler in a high-risk game he will ultimately lose; he is virtually programmed for failure. And this truth, the letters from Carpi reveal, Machiavelli knew intimately, and he was periodically forced to relearn it through the most degrading personal experiences.

As we have seen, Machiavelli developed a particular rhetorical strategy in his writings to deal with the personal sense of powerlessness and degradation that descended on him after 1512. We have also seen that his strategy of manipulating his audience while seeming to place it in a superior position was most imperfect and unsatisfying; he had to repeat it incessantly in work after work because it could supply only an illusion of power and could never compel his audience to behave as he wished. That strategy was not, however, the only means at his disposal to deal with his continual frustration at playing the dupe. He had at least four other options, four other roles or stances, which he adopted from time to time and which allowed him to cope with his condition admittedly in very imperfect and, except perhaps in the last instance, ultimately unsatisfying ways. Those four options or strategies are heroic stoicism, aggression, separation, and irony. Let us review them in order.

Francesco Vettori, in a letter he wrote to Machiavelli in 1514, implies that his rusticated friend was adopting the first option, heroic stoicism. Referring to Giovanni Pontano's *De fortuna*, Vettori consoles Machiavelli by stressing the immense power of Fortune, which no virtue or prudence can resist and which has raised up the unworthy, especially in the Rome of the present. Vettori then continues: *"Tamen acquies-cendum est; et presertim tu hoc facere debes, qui malorum non es ignarus, et qui graviora passus es. Dabit Deus his quoque finem"* (#158, 362: *"Nevertheless you must acquiesce; and you especially must do so, you who are not ignorant of evils and who have suffered worse things. God will put an end to these too"*). Vettori is here encouraging a stoic endurance of hardships and a cautious hope for better days to come. Vettori's last sentence repeats a line from the *Aeneid* (1, 199) in which Aeneas is cheering up his storm-battered followers, and it thus identifies Machiavelli directly with that ancient Roman hero, putting him in a role that Machiavelli assigned to his prince. Nevertheless, although Machiavelli prided himself on heroic ability to endure hardship and even torture, the role of stoic hero was too limited to satisfy him as a response to his very real feelings of degradation. For it could not finally give him what he also saw that his prince needed: if it allowed for independence and self-mastery, it could not give real power over others in the world, and hence it could only most imperfectly grant one a sense of dignity and value.

The limits of the role of heroic stoicism are revealed by one of Machiavelli's most memorable poems, "Io ho, Giuliano, in gamba un paio di geti," in which he asked Giuliano de' Medici to free him from prison, where he had been placed after his name was found on a list possessed by conspirators against Medici rule. Here Machiavelli plays the hero by making light of the six "tratti di fune" (*SL*, 362) he endured (this was a form of torture in which the prisoner had his hands tied behind his back, was hauled up by them, and was released and then suddenly jerked to a stop while still in the air). He also jokes about the lice, the stench, and the deafening noises and screams of his "delicato ostello" ("delicate inn"), and at the end he execrates the conspirators who were responsible for having him placed in such a situation. If there is indeed something heroically stoic about Machiavelli's ability to laugh at his discomfort, to smile his way through squalor and torture, the poem is nevertheless hardly an unqualified celebration of heroic selfhood. Indeed, Machiavelli's heroism is presented as much less than complete and perfect, especially since he stresses his fear when he hears the priests chanting for the condemned conspirators one morning: "Quel che mi fe' più guerra / fu che dormendo presso a la aurora / cantando sentii dire: 'Per voi s'òra'" (*SL*, 362: "What disturbed me most / was that while sleeping near dawn one morning / I heard them chant: 'The hour has come for you'"). Machiavelli's joking and cursing, combined with the revelation of his fear, could be read as a form of a clowning: he transforms himself into a farcical spectacle meant to amuse the all-powerful Giuliano, his "buon padre" (*SL*, 363: "good father"), on whose favor Machiavelli's release depended. Thus Machiavelli makes his experience a farce less to demonstrate stoic freedom and distance from it than to cajole Giuliano into releasing him; what starts out as a seeming expression of heroism turns into an exercise in self-degradation.

Machiavelli's adoption of the clown's role in his poem to Giuliano may be considered merely a tactic designed to win his release, but it also dramatizes the essential weakness of the strategy of heroic stoicism: to adopt such a strategy is essentially to accept one's degraded condition, so that what seems like toughness and stoic independence at first glance turns out to look like the degradation it really is. In other words, as long as Machiavelli's basic condition remained one of exclusion, powerlessness, and dependence, all the heroic self-possession he could muster could not save him from himself; his basic feeling of degradation persisted, and ultimately, inevitably announced its presence through gestures of self-inflicted humiliation. It is consequently not surprising that Machiavelli chose to represent himself, admittedly at some remove, as the hapless Nicomaco in *Clizia* and to revel in the humiliation and physical embarrassment of his alter ego. For Machiavelli, the option of heroic stoicism was clearly no option at all.

A second option, aggression, was unfortunately as qualified as the first. As a model of this response, consider the famous encounter with an old prostitute in Verona which Machiavelli describes in a letter to Luigi Guicciardini, an encounter that occurred not after Machiavelli's rustication in Sant' Andrea but when he was still at the height of his admittedly qualified power and prosperity in 1509. Machiavelli centers on the degradation involved in the incident, which he links to his "disperata foia" (#108, 205), his uncontrollable sexual desire and weakness for women. Framing the incident, he characterizes himself near the start as a "nuovo cazzo" (204: "innocent [or strange] prick"), thus reducing himself to his sexual apparatus and seeing himself as an innocent in the worst sense of the word, that is, a simpleton and a dupe. He tells in vivid detail how the old woman's accomplice, his laundress, offered to sell him a "shirt" and literally led him by the hand like a child to the old woman (204: "Questa vechia ribalda mi prese per mano et menatomi ad colei"). Machiavelli describes the woman's room (it was appropriately dark), his confusion (205: "mi sbigottí tucto"), and the desperate lust that drove him to an act that obviously disgusted him even while he was engaged in it. Ironically, although Machiavelli presents the sexual act essentially as an assault, a blow (205: "la fotte' un colpo"), and reduces it to a commercial exchange — the woman is a "camicia" and a "mercatantia" (205:

"shirt," "merchandise")—he cannot distance himself from it through his metaphors or experience it as a victory, but only as humiliation and degradation. His sexual encounter is the reverse of Castruccio Castracani's: when Machiavelli "takes" the woman, he feels he is really being taken or had by her.[20]

And Machiavelli went out of his way to make the degradation even worse. When he felt the old woman's thighs to be withered and smelled her stinking breath, Machiavelli did not simply leave the scene in its original darkness and thereby preserve a measure of self-protecting ignorance. Perhaps because part of him wished to wallow in the experience of degradation, he fetched a torch so he could examine her. What he saw was not merely an old woman but one whose ugliness he describes in such hyperbolic terms that she becomes a loathsome "mostro" (205: "monster"). Her lice, distorted features, diseases, and reddened face (which he associates with the butchering of animals) all link her to the lower classes, thus giving Machiavelli's experience of degradation a social as well as a sexual dimension. He observes that the woman's mouth seemed to resemble that of Lorenzo de' Medici, his and the republic's enemy. The observation is double-edged, satirizing Lorenzo by associating him with the prostitute but ridiculing Machiavelli as well by making him symbolically Lorenzo's victim and thereby adding political insult to the physical injury he felt he had already suffered from the old woman. Significantly, at the beginning of the letter, when he praises Luigi Guicciardini for his sexual prowess, Machiavelli uses an ambiguous feminine pronoun that logically identifies some unnamed woman whose favors Guicciardini enjoyed but grammatically refers back to "la fortuna" (204).[21] Thus Machiavelli presents his friend as a master of Fortuna, identifying that mastery with the sexual dominance of a woman, and implying, as he goes on to describe his degrading experience, that his own situation is just the reverse.

In the last lines of the letter, however, Machiavelli recounts how he, perhaps unconsciously, contrived a response to this experience of degradation: he vomited in disgust all over the woman. This unattractive gesture is an act of personal purgation, and in keeping with it, Machia-

[20]See the discussion of Castruccio Castracani's sexual aggressiveness in chap. 4. For the notion of his "taking" a woman rather than being taken by her, see the remark attributed to him in *CC*, 37.

[21]#108, 204: "Affogaggine, Luigi; et guarda quanto la fortuna in una medesima faccenda dà ad li huomini diversi fini. Voi, fottuto che voi havesti colei, vi è venuta voglia di fotterla et ne volete un'altra presa" ("Damn, Luigi! Look how fortune gives men different outcomes in the same business. You, once you fucked her once, felt the desire to fuck her again, and you wanted another go at it"). The word "colei" in this sentence, which may refer to an unnamed woman or to "la fortuna," is ambiguous.

velli closes the letter by interpreting his experience, ironically, as a grotesque parody of a cure for lust, wittily thanking God that he would not have to displease Him any longer — at least while he is in Lombardy (206). But the act is also a spontaneous expression of revulsion, an act of aggression and intended dominance paralleling the sexual act but going beyond it by eliminating the motive of pleasure, by dehumanizing the old woman, and, most important, by removing any possible dependence on her and thereby giving the aggression a pure, unqualified form. It may be read as a doubly symbolic act: a projection of Machiavelli's disgust with himself and his weakness and dependence onto the old woman, who becomes a scapegoat as a result; and an attempt to cancel his feeling of degradation by expelling it outward upon her, by literally almost covering over and obliterating her. Thus it enables him to end the letter on a note of triumph as he seems successfully to reassert his personal power and reestablish his dignity in this encounter. This triumph is, however, very limited and imperfect, for the social and political dimensions of the degradation which figure in Machiavelli's experience were in no way affected by his final treatment of the old woman. No matter what he did to her, he still had to return from Verona to Florence, still had to bend to the wishes of the Florentine magnates whose interests he served, still had to endure his subservient position in the social and political order. And later, after the fall of the republic, his options for aggressive action became even fewer; the best he could manage was to threaten the critics in the audience of *La mandragola* that he would speak evil of them if they did not like his play. More characteristic is the poem to Giuliano de' Medici cited earlier: there Machiavelli execrates the conspirators who caused his arrest but does not attack Giuliano and the Medici, who were responsible for his imprisonment and torture. Aggression directed at various scapegoat figures thus could continue to serve Machiavelli as a useful release, but it was always imperfectly satisfying because he could never direct it at the true sources of the social and political degradation he experienced continually.

Machiavelli's third mode of dealing with his sense of degradation is related to the second and is just as unsatisfactory. Rather than attack a scapegoat, he simply attempts to maintain his distance from the source of his degradation. The most notable instance of this strategy occurs in the famous letter to Francesco Vettori in which Machiavelli recounts his daily routine at Sant' Andrea (#140, 301-6). What he recounts in that letter is initially presented almost consistently as degrading for him. Thus he speaks of the difficulties he has with the petty complaints of his woodcutters and of unpleasant negotiations over firewood involving trivial sums of money. He stresses the poor fare he has to eat with his family and the wasted afternoons of games and squabbling with the locals at the inn. All of these activities he sees as being beneath him, the sort of thing one might expect of a servant. When he speaks of hunting for thrushes, an activity that could be considered noble, it is not by accident that he describes himself as looking like a comically burdened Geta, a servant made famous by the quattrocento story "Geta e Birria," based on Plautus's *Amphitruo*. To go hunting or to manage the affairs of his estate is, for Machiavelli, essentially a loss of rank, a lowering to the level of servants and peasants, which is then repeated in his association with common people at the inn, whom he labels contemptuously "pidocchi" (303: "lice"; cf. #152, 343). With them he sees himself becoming what his exile to Sant' Andrea forced him to become economically, socially, and politically—a "gaglioffo," a "beggar," and, by extension, a rogue or knave: "Con questi io m'ingaglioffo per tutto dì" (303: "With these I become a knave the entire day").[22] Machiavelli concludes this section of his letter by saying that he associates with these people in order to unburden himself (303: "sfogo"), to gain release by squabbling with them as he waits to see if his fate (303: "questa mia sorta") will ever be ashamed of persecuting him thus. It is clear, of course, that the shame he transfers to fate is a shame he feels about himself and his position.

Consequently, Machiavelli goes on to describe how, once evening has come, he separates himself from the "pidocchi," strips off his daytime clothes, which are literally and symbolically "piena di fango e di loto" (304: "full of mud and filth"), and becomes a new man by putting on "panni reali et curiali" ("regal and courtly garb"). Segregating himself from the degrading world of everyday reality, Machiavelli replaces every aspect of it with the world of the ancients: he enters "antique corti," eats that food "che *solum* è mio" ("which alone is mine"), and associates with men who receive him "amorevolmente" and, as they converse with him, treat him with "humanità." In other words, in place of his meals with his family and the rowdy celebrations at the local inn, Machiavelli

---

[22] According to the *Dizionario etimologico italiano*, ed. Carlo Battisti and Giovanni Alessio (Florence: G. Barbera, 1952), many of the fourteenth- and fifteenth-century meanings of *gaglioffo* point to lower-class status or to the status of a beggar: "pezzente, mendico; buono a nulla, malaccorto, sciocco; villano, contadino." In the same dictionary, *gaglioffare* is identified as a synonym for begging in Pulci's *Morgante Maggiore*, 6, 188, and *gaglioffería* is defined as a "stato miserabile, povertà." According to the *Dizionario etimologico della lingua italiana*, ed. Manlio Cortelazzo and Paolo Zolli (Bologna: Zanichelli, 1980), the earliest meanings associated with *gaglioffo* involve beggars and people so wretched that they were considered unfit to be given lodging by innkeepers.

becomes a participant in a stately symposium or convivium with the ancients, an ideally refined and fulfilling experience, which allows him, he claims, to forget for as much as four hours his troubles, his poverty, and even his fear of death as he becomes one with them: "tucto mi transferisco in loro" (304: "I entirely transfer myself into them"). This, Machiavelli insists, is his true life, and out of it, out of his conversations with Livy and Cicero and Tacitus, he tells Vettori, he has completed his little work *De principatibus*, that is, *Il principe*. Unfortunately, of course, this "real" life is mere play-acting, a fantasy experience that reveals its insubstantiality even as he describes it, for when he declares that it allows him to forget trouble, poverty, and death, he reminds his reader of the realities he is attempting to evade, and when he says he escapes them for four hours at a time, he likewise reminds the reader of the other twenty hours in each day when realities must be faced. In essence, then, although Machiavelli manages a fitful escape from the lice of reality and the degradation he feels, his escape can be only what he admits it is: imaginary and temporary.

Machiavelli's letters from Carpi reveal that he has one final strategy for dealing with his humiliation, powerlessness, failure, and degradation. This strategy does not permit him to snatch triumph from the jaws of defeat or otherwise step outside the dialectic of confidence man and dupe by means of which he made his life and his world comprehensible. But it does allow him to live with that dialectic and with the experience of defeat and degradation it so frequently entails. Essentially, that strategy amounts to his adoption of the role of ironist, a role that allows him to maintain a self-preserving distance from his experiences and to view them through the lens of satire, so that he can laugh knowingly, freely, and securely at himself and at the comic spectacle his life has become in defeat. At the same time, that role allows him to accept all aspects of his life, and especially to embrace the reality of his body, with its pleasures, imperfections, and excesses, as well as his need for festive release. Such an acceptance was not possible for Machiavelli when he adopted his other strategies, for some denial of the body and of festive pleasure was inevitably involved when he identified himself with the stoic hero, rejected sexual dependence through acts of aggression, or attempted to segregate himself from real banquets shared with the "lice" of ordinary experience by escaping into an imaginary symposium among the books of the ancients. By playing the ironist, then, he gains a measure of control over his life even at its nadir, placing himself beyond others' judgments and embracing his existence in the most intimate, intense, and complete manner.

In the letters from Carpi, Machiavelli shows himself the consummate ironist not only in his general treatment of the hapless friars but especially at the end, in his final response to his obvious feelings of degradation over being sent on such a mission and over his failure when his trick has been discovered. His last letter is a response to one in which Guicciardini referred in passing to Machiavelli's favorite theories about the nature of history and offered the consoling thought that every experience, even the degrading one of being sent to Carpi, could provide food for analysis to a mind as subtle as his. Machiavelli writes:

> Circa alle *Storie* et la repubblica de' zoccoli, io non credo di questa venuta havere perduto nulla, perché io ho inteso molte constitutioni et ordini loro che hanno del buono, in modo che io me ne credo valere a qualche proposito, maxime nelle comparationi, perché dove io habbia a ragionare del silentio, io potrò dire: "Gli stavano piú cheti che i frati quando mangiono"; et cosí si potrà per me addurre molte altre cose in mezzo, che mi ha insegnato questo poco della esperienza. [#188, 412-13]

> About the *Histories* and the Republic of Wooden Clogs: I don't believe I've lost anything by this trip, because I've understood much about their constitution and organization, which have some good in them, so that I believe they will be of use to me, especially in comparisons. When I have to speak of silence, I will be able to say: "They were quieter than the friars when they eat"; and thus many other things could be adduced by me which this little bit of experience has taught me.

Although Machiavelli seems to affirm in a straightforward manner the usefulness of even such a trivial experience as this one to a wide-ranging, analytical mind like his own, the one comparison he offers is strictly the stuff of folk sayings, not the profound insight of a political analyst.[23] Although this passage begins in an apparently unambiguous manner, by the time one has finished it, one does not know just how to take Machiavelli — and that, of course, is the point. By preventing his readers from reaching any easy judgment about meaning, by keeping us off balance, Machiavelli maintains control. Moreover, it is noteworthy that the passage — and the letter — ends with a final jibe at the friars, a final bit of high-spirited humor at the expense of the inhabitants of the Republic of Wooden Clogs. Thus Machiavelli deals with a world full of disappointment, humiliation, and cruelty not by indulging in pathos or trag-

---

[23] Ridolfi takes this straight and misses Machiavelli's irony; see his *Machiavelli*, p. 193.

edy or self-pity but by seeking release through self-reflexive, ironic laughter.[24]

Machiavelli's ability to laugh at himself and the world separates him from his unrelievedly serious confidence man–prince, who sees the body strictly as an instrument of politics and can never enjoy festive release. Although Machiavelli was equally obsessed with power, his letters from Carpi reveal that he is a different sort of man altogether. First, he plays his confidence game with more gusto and sheer pleasure than his ideal prince ever could; indeed, it is precisely that—a game—for him, although a serious one, whereas for his prince there was nothing playful about life. Second, whereas the prince rejects carnival and its festive pleasures, Machiavelli delights in them. Finally, the letters reveal that Machiavelli, unlike the prince, could laugh at himself in defeat. He makes himself into a comic spectacle for Guicciardini without sacrificing his personal dignity by presenting his humiliating experiences with self-conscious irony. To be sure, Machiavelli's princes play for higher stakes than he does, but the texts that focus on them spare them the problem of living with humiliation; once defeated, they simply vanish, either through death, like Niccolò Piccinino in the *Istorie fiorentine*, or through authorial omission, like Cesare Borgia in *Il principe*. Machiavelli has no such option; he must deal with a humiliation and sense of degradation which his prince never has to face. In the prince's world, shame and embarrassment either do not exist or are simply fatal; Machiavelli has to live with those feelings day after day.

At Carpi Machiavelli manages to live with his confidence man–dupe dialectic and maintain his personal integrity by transforming the most humiliating experience into the stuff of art. The image he creates of himself and of his "culo" going "lappe lappe" is brilliant farce, brilliant irony. In such passages Machiavelli successfully distances himself from his experience and turns it into art. In the course of his letters from Carpi, Marchiavelli thus participates in the full ambivalence of carnival. He starts out being the center of an absurd world whose hypocrisy, status-mongering, and exaggerated forms of deference he mocks through the witty confidence game he plays; and he ends up being one with those he satirizes, a carnival clown like all the rest. Or perhaps not

[24] I agree with the analysis of those scholars who stress the chasm between Machiavelli's ideals and aspirations and his awareness of historical realities, but I would rather not describe it with the honorific term *tragedy* as Giorgio Barberi-Squarotti does in *La forma tragica del "Principe" e altri saggi sul Machiavelli* (Florence: Olschki, 1966), pp. 6–15, 25–26, and passim. I also agree with Peter Bondanella, who follows Ridolfi and sees Machiavelli as using "laughter as a defense against a cruel world, turning misfortune into comedy"; see his *Machiavelli and the Art of Renaissance History* (Detroit: Wayne State University Press, 1973), p. 143.

quite like all the rest. For Machiavelli remains the satirist to the end, and unlike the Carpigiani, he plays the role of clown self-consciously, knowingly making a spectacle of himself for his own and his correspondent's delight. Like Shakespeare's Falstaff, whose masterly defense of his cowardice at Gadshill before Prince Hal is a self-conscious parody of confession and a bravura piece of comic self-display, Machiavelli presents his humiliation with a knowing wink clearly visible in the comic exaggeration of his description. He salvages his dignity here, as he must have done at other times throughout is life, not by simply accepting the role of clown but by ironizing it. He does not attempt to escape the role of dupe, which failure inevitably thrusts upon him, but takes a stance that makes him both dupe and nondupe all at once, so that the joke, however painful, can never be played at his expense. In the letters from Carpi Machiavelli thus demonstrates that escape from the confidence man–dupe dialectic is not only not possible but, in a sense, not even necessary, at least for one who possesses the supreme strength of the ironist, the knowledge that whoever laughs at himself in a knowing way could scarcely become the victim of another's laughter. Never really able to play the princely lion and repeatedly a failure as a crafty fox, Machiavelli played his last, best role here at Carpi. He played the ironic clown and thereby, through a self-conscious artistic transformation of his humiliation and degradation, defended himself brilliantly both against the lions of his world, who would have gladly eaten him alive if he had appeared threatening to them, and against the foxes, who would have gloated and smirked over his defeat.

Bibliography

Abrams, David M., and Brian Sutton-Smith. "The Development of the Trickster in Children's Narrative." *Journal of American Folklore* 90 (1977): 29-47.

Alberti, Leon Battista. *I Libri della famiglia.* Ed. Ruggiero Romano and Alberto Tenenti. Turin: Einaudi, 1969.

Aquilechia, Giovanni. "La favola *Mandragola* si chiama." In *Collected Essays on Italian Language and Literature Presented to Kathleen Speight,* ed. Giovanni Aquilecchia, Stephen N. Cristea, and Sheila Ralphs, pp. 73-100. Manchester: Manchester University Press, 1971.

Archambault, Paul. "The Analogy of the 'Body' in Renaissance Political Literature." *Bibliothèque d'Humanisme et Renaissance* 29 (1967): 32-53.

Arden, Heather. *Fools' Plays: A Study of Satire in the "Sottie."* Cambridge: Cambridge University Press, 1980.

Ariès, Philippe. *Centuries of Childhood: A Social History of Family Life.* Trans. Robert Baldick. New York: Random House, 1962.

Ariosto, Ludovico. *Orlando furioso.* Ed. Remo Ceserani. 2 vols. Turin: Unione Tipografico-Editrice Torinese, 1962.

Babcock (Babcock-Abrahams), Barbara. "'A Tolerated Margin of Mess': The Trickster and His Tales Reconsidered." *Journal of the Folklore Institute* 11 (1975): 147-86.

———, ed. *The Reversible World: Symbolic Inversion in Art and Society.* Ithaca: Cornell University Press, 1978.

Bakhtin, Mikhail. *Rabelais and His World.* Trans. Hélène Iswolsky. Cambridge: M.I.T. Press, 1968.

Barberi-Squarotti, Giorgio. *La forma tragica del "Principe" e altri saggi sul Machiavelli.* Florence: Olschki, 1966.

Barish, Jonas. *The Antitheatrical Prejudice.* Berkeley: University of California Press, 1981.

Barroll, J. Leeds. "Antony and Pleasure." *Journal of English and Germanic Philology* 57 (1958): 708-20.

———. "Enobarbus' Description of Cleopatra." *Texas Studies in English* 37 (1958): 61-78.

Bergmann, Johannes D. "The Original Confidence Man." *American Quarterly* 21(1969): 560-77.

Blair, John G. *The Confidence Man in Modern Fiction.* New York: Barnes & Noble, 1979.

Boccaccio, Giovanni. *Il Decameron.* Ed. Carlo Salinari. 2 vols. Bari: Laterza, 1966.

Bonadeo, Alfredo. *Corruption, Conflict, and Power in the Works and Times of Niccolò Machiavelli.* University of California Publications in Modern Philology, 108. Berkeley: University of California Press, 1973.

——. "The Role of the 'Grandi' in the Political World of Machiavelli." *Studies in the Renaissance* 16 (1969): 9-30.

——. "The Role of the People in the Works and Times of Machiavelli." *Bibliothèque d'Humanisme et Renaissance* 32 (1970): 351-77.

Bondanella, Peter E. *Machiavelli and the Art of Renaissance History.* Detroit: Wayne State University Press, 1973.

Borsellino, Nino. *Niccolò Machiavelli.* Rome: Laterza, 1973.

Braudel, Fernand. *Civilisation matérielle, économie, et capitalisme, XVe-XVIIIe siècle.* Paris: Armand Colin, 1979. Vol. 2: *Les Jeux de l'échange.*

Brown, Norman O. *Life against Death.* New York: Random House, 1959.

Burke, Peter. *Popular Culture in Early Modern Europe.* New York: Harper & Row, 1978.

Butterfield, Herbert. *The Statecraft of Machiavelli.* London: G. Bell & Sons, 1940.

Caspari, Fritz. *Humanism and the Social Order in Tudor England.* New York: Teachers College Press, 1954.

Cassirer, Ernst. *The Myth of the State.* New Haven: Yale University press, 1946.

——, Paul Oskar Kristeller, and John H. Randall, Jr., eds. *The Renaissance Philosophy of Man.* Chicago: University of Chicago Press, 1948.

Castiglione, Baldesar. *Il libro del Cortegiano.* Ed. Bruno Maier. 2d ed. Turin: Unione Tipografico-Editrice Torinese, 1964.

Catalogue général des livres imprimés de la Bibliothéque Nationale, Auteurs. Paris: Imprimerie nationale, 1920. Vols. 73 and 139.

Cavallini, Giorgio. *Interpretazioni della "Mandragola."* Milan: Marzorati, 1973.

Chabod, Federico. *Machiavelli and the Renaissance.* Trans. David Moore. New York: Harper & Row, 1958.

——. *Scritti su Machiavelli.* Turin: Einaudi, 1964.

Chiappelli, Fredi. "Machiavelli as Secretary." *Italian Quarterly* 13 (1970): 27-44.

——. *Nuovi studi sul linguaggio del Machiavelli.* Florence: Le Mounier, 1969.

Chiarini, Gioachino, ed. *Novelle italiane: Il Quattrocento.* Milan: Garzanti, 1982.

Cicero, Marcus Tullius. *De Officiis.* Ed. Walter Miller. Cambridge: Harvard University Press, 1961.

Clough, Cecil. "Machiavelli Researches." *Annali, Istituto Universitario Orientale-Napoli, Sezione Romanza* 9 (1967): 21-129.
Cochrane, Eric W. "Machiavelli, 1940-1960." *Journal of Modern History* 33 (1961): 113-36.
Colie, Rosalie. *Paradoxia Epidemica*. Princeton: Princeton University Press, 1966.
——. *The Resources of Kind: Genre-Theory in the Renaissance*. Ed. Barbara K. Lewalski. Berkeley: University of California Press, 1973.
Cullen, Patrick. *Spenser, Marvell, and Renaissance Pastoral*. Cambridge: Harvard University Press, 1970.
D'Amico, Jack. "Three Forms of Character: *Virtù, Ordini*, and *Materia* in Machiavelli's *Discorsi*." *Italian Quarterly* 22 (1981): 5-13.
Davis, Natalie Z. *Society and Culture in Early Modern France*. Stanford: Stanford University Press, 1975.
Defaux, Gérard. *Le Curieux, le glorieux et la sagesse du monde dans la première moitié du XVIe siécle: L'Exemple de Panurge (Ulysse, Démosthène, Empédocle)*. Lexington, Ky.: French Forum, 1982.
Della Terza, Dante. "The Most Recent Image of Machiavelli: The Contribution of the Linguist and the Literary Historian." *Italian Quarterly* 13 (1970): 91-113.
Dionisotti, Carlo. "Appunti su capitoli di Machiavelli." In *Collected Essays on Italian Language and Literature Presented to Kathleen Speight*, ed. Giovanni Aquilecchia, Stephen N. Cristea, and Sheila Ralphs, pp. 55-71. Manchester: Manchester University Press, 1971.
Dizionario etimologico della lingua italiana. Ed. Manlio Cortelazzo and Paolo Zolli. Bologna: Zanichelli, 1980.
Dizionario etimologico italiano. Ed. Carlo Battisti and Giovanni Alessio. Florence: G. Barbera, 1952.
Douglas, Mary. *Purity and Danger: An Analysis of the Concepts of Pollution and Taboo*. Harmondsworth: Penguin, 1966.
Duckworth, George E. *The Nature of Roman Comedy: A Study in Popular Entertainment*. Princeton: Princeton University Press, 1952.
Eisenstein, Elizabeth L. *The Printing Press as an Agent of Change*. Cambridge: Cambridge University Press, 1979.
Elliott, Robert C. *The Power of Satire: Magic, Ritual, Art*. Princeton: Princeton University Press, 1960.
Erasmus, Desiderius. *Declamatio de pueris statim ac liberaliter instituendis*. Ed. Jean-Claude Margolin. Geneva: Droz, 1966.
Ferguson, Wallace K. *Europe in Transition, 1300-1520*. Boston: Houghton Mifflin, 1962.
Ferroni, Giulio. *"Mutazione" e "riscontro" nel teatro di Machiavelli, e altri saggi sulla commedia del Cinquecento*. Rome: Bulzoni, 1972.
Fido, Franco. "L'esule e il centauro: Emblemi e memoria in Machiavelli." In *La metamorfosi del centauro: Studi e letture da Boccaccio a Pirandello*, pp. 109-22. Rome: Bulzoni, 1977.

——. *Machiavelli*. Palermo: Palumbo, 1965.
——. "Machiavelli in His Time and Ours." *Italian Quarterly* 13 (1970): 3–21.
——. "Machiavelli, 1469–1969: Politica e teatro nel badalucco di Messer Nicia." *Italica* 46 (1969): 359–75.
Fleisher, Martin. "Trust and Deceit in Machiavelli's Comedies." *Journal of the History of Ideas* 27 (1966): 365–80.
——, ed. *Machiavelli and the Nature of Political Thought*. New York: Atheneum, 1972.
Foucault, Michel. *Discipline and Punish: The Birth of the Prison*. Trans. Alan Sheridan. New York: Random House, 1977.
Freeman, Rosemary. *English Emblem Books*. London: Chatto & Windus, 1948.
Garin, Eugenio. *L'educazione in Europa: 1400–1600*. Bari: Laterza, 1957.
——. *L'umanesimo italiano*. Bari: Laterza, 1965.
Garosci, Aldo. *Le "Istorie fiorentine" del Machiavelli*. Turin: Giappichelli, 1973.
Geerken, John H. "Homer's Image of the Hero in Machiavelli: A Comparison of Arêtê and Virtù." *Italian Quarterly* 14 (1970): 45–90.
——. "Machiavelli Studies since 1969." *Journal of the History of Ideas* 37 (1976): 351–68.
Geertz, Clifford. *The Interpretation of Cultures*. New York: Basic Books, 1973.
Gerhardt, Mia I. *La Pastorale*. Assen: Van Gorcum, 1950.
Giamatti, A. Bartlett. "Proteus Unbound: Some Versions of the Sea God in the Renaissance." In *The Disciplines of Criticism: Essays in Literary Theory, Interpretation, and History Honoring René Wellek on the Occasion of His Sixty-fifth Birthday*, ed. Peter Demetz, Thomas M. Greene, and Lowry Nelson, Jr., pp. 437–75. New Haven: Yale University Press, 1968.
Gilbert, Allan H. *Machiavelli's "Prince" and Its Forerunners: "The Prince" as a Typical Book "de Regimine Principum."* Durham, N.C.: Duke University Press, 1938.
Gilbert, Felix. "The Concept of Nationalism in Machiavelli's *Prince*." *Studies in the Renaissance* 1 (1954): 38–48.
——. *Machiavelli and Guicciardini: Politics and History in Sixteenth-Century Florence*. Princeton: Princeton University Press, 1965.
——. "Machiavelli in Modern Historical Scholarship." *Italian Quarterly* 13 (1970): 9–26.
Gilmore, Myron P., ed. *Studies on Machiavelli*. Florence: Sansoni, 1972.
Grande dizionario della lingua italiana. Ed. Salvatore Battaglia. Turin: Unione Tipografico-Editrice Torinese, n.d.
Greenblatt, Stephen. *Renaissance Self-Fashioning: From More to Shakespeare*. Chicago: University of Chicago Press, 1980.
Greene, Thomas M. "Ben Jonson and the Centered Self." *Studies in English Literature, 1500–1900* 10 (1970): 325–48.
——. "The End of Discourse in Machiavelli's 'Prince.'" *Yale French Studies* 67 (1984): 57–71.

———. "The Flexibility of the Self in Renaissance Literature." In *The Disciplines of Criticism: Essays in Literary Theory, Interpretation, and History Honoring René Wellek on the Occasion of His Sixty-fifth Birthday*, ed. Peter Demetz, Thomas M. Greene, and Lowry Nelson, Jr., pp. 241–64. New Haven: Yale University Press, 1968.

———. *The Light in Troy: Imitation and Discovery in Renaissance Poetry*. New Haven: Yale University Press, 1982.

Guillemain, Bernard. *Machiavel: L'Anthropologie politique*. Geneva: Droz, 1977.

Hale, J. R. *Machiavelli and Renaissance Italy*. New York: Collier, 1963.

———. *Renaissance Europe: Individual and Society, 1480–1520*. Berkeley: University of California Press, 1971.

Herrero, Javier. "Renaissance Poverty and Lazarillo's Family: The Birth of the Picaresque Genre." *PMLA* 94 (1979): 876–86.

Hexter, Jack H. "The Education of the Aristocracy in the Renaissance." In *Reappraisals in History*, pp. 45–70. 1961; rpt. New York: Harper & Row, 1963.

———. "The Loom of Language and the Fabric of Imperatives: The Case of *Il Principe* and *Utopia*." *American Historical Review* 69 (1964): 945–68.

Hulliung, Mark. *Citizen Machiavelli*. Princeton: Princeton University Press, 1983.

Italy: Machiavelli "500." Special issue, *Review of National Literatures* 1 (1970).

Jonson, Ben. *Volpone*. Ed. Alvin B. Kernan. New Haven: Yale University Press, 1962.

Klapp, Orin E. "The Clever Hero." *Journal of American Folklore* 67 (1954): 21–34.

Kuhlmann, Susan. *Knave, Fool, and Genius: The Confidence Man as He Appears in Nineteenth-Century American Fiction*. Chapel Hill: University of North Carolina Press, 1973.

Landucci, Luca. *A Florentine Diary from 1450 to 1516 Continued by an Anonymous Writer Till 1542 with Notes by Iodoco del Badia*. Trans. Alice de Rosen Jervis. London: J.M. Dent, 1927.

Lerner, Daniel. *The Passing of Traditional Society: Modernizing the Middle East*. Rev. ed. New York: Free Press, 1964.

Lovejoy, A. O., and George Boas. *Contributions to the History of Primitivism: Primitivism and Related Ideas in Antiquity*. Baltimore: Johns Hopkins University Press, 1935.

McCanles, Michael. "Machiavelli's *Principe* and the Textualization of History." *Modern Language Notes* 97 (1982): 1–18.

McCutcheon, Elizabeth. "Thomas More, Raphael Hythlodaeus, and the Angel Raphael." *Studies in English Literature, 1500–1900* 9 (1969): 21–38.

Machiavelli, Niccolò. *Arte della guerra e scritti politici minori*. Ed. Sergio Bertelli. Milan: Feltrinelli, 1961.

———. *The Chief Works and Others*. Trans. Allan Gilbert. Durham, N.C.: Duke University Press, 1965.

———. *Istorie fiorentine.* Ed. Franco Gaeta. Milan: Feltrinelli, 1962.
———. *Legazioni, Commissarie, Scritti di governo.* Ed. Fredi Chiappelli. Rome: Laterza, 1973. Vol. 2 (1501-1503).
———. *Lettere.* Ed. Franco Gaeta. 2d ed. Milan: Feltrinelli, 1981.
———. *La mandragola.* Ed. Roberto Ridolfi. Florence: Olschki, 1965.
———. *The Prince.* Ed. and trans. Robert M. Adams. New York: Norton, 1977.
———. *Il principe e Discorsi sopra la prima deca di Tito Livio.* Ed. Sergio Bertelli. Milan: Feltrinelli, 1960.
———. *Il teatro e tutti gli scritti letterari.* Ed. Franco Gaeta. Milan: Feltrinelli, 1965.
Makarius, Laura. "Le Mythe du 'Trickster.'" *Revue de l'histoire des religions* 175 (1969): 17-46.
———. "Ritual Clowns and Symbolic Behaviour." *Diogenes* 69 (1970): 44-73.
Mallett, Phillip. "Shakespeare's Trickster-Kings: Richard III and Henry V." In *The Fool and the Trickster: Studies in Honour of Enid Welsford*, ed. Paul V. A. Williams, pp. 64-82. Cambridge: D.S. Brewer, 1979.
Mansfeld, Harvey C. *Machiavelli's New Modes and Orders: A Study of the "Discourses on Livy."* Ithaca: Cornell University Press, 1979.
———. "Machiavelli's New Regime." *Italian Quarterly* 13 (1970): 63-95.
Marcus, Millicent. *An Allegory of Form: Literary Self-Consciousness in the "Decameron."* Stanford French and Italian Studies, 18. Saratoga, Calif.: Amna Libri, 1979.
Martines, Lauro, ed. *Violence and Civil Disorder in Italian Cities, 1200-1500.* Berkeley: University of California Press, 1972.
Mattei, Rodolfo de. *Dal premachiavellismo all'antimachiavellismo.* Florence: Sansoni, 1969.
Mazzeo, Joseph A. *Renaissance and Revolution: Backgrounds to Seventeenth-Century English Literature.* New York: Random House, 1965, 1967.
Minogue, K. R. "Theatricality and Politics: Machiavelli's Concept of Fantasia." In *The Morality of Politics*, ed. Bhikha Parekh and R. N. Becki, pp. 148-62. London: George Allen & Unwin, 1972.
Mirollo, James V. *The Poet of the Marvelous: Giambattista Marino.* New York: Columbia University Press, 1963.
Najemy, John M. "Machiavelli and the Medici: The Lessons of Florentine History." *Renaissance Quarterly* 35 (1982): 551-76.
Ohly, Friedrich. *Hohelied-Studien: Grundzüge einer Geschichte der Hohelied-auslegung des Abendlandes bis zum 1200.* Schriften der Wissenschaftlichen Gesellschaft an der Johann Wolfgang Goethe-Universität, Geisteswissenschaftliche Reihe, 1. Frankfurt am Main, 1958.
Olivieri, Mario. "La tecnica politica nel 'Principe' di Niccolò Machiavelli." *Filosofia* 20 (1969): 565-78.
O'Loughlin, Michael. *The Garlands of Repose: The Literary Celebration of Civic and Retired Leisure.* Chicago: University of Chicago Press, 1978.
Olschki, Leonard. *Machiavelli the Scientist.* Berkeley: University of California Press, 1945.

Orgel, Stephen. "Shakespeare and the Kinds of Drama." *Critical Inquiry* 6 (1979): 107-33.

Parel, Anthony, ed. *The Political Calculus: Essays on Machiavelli's Philosophy.* Toronto: University of Toronto Press, 1972.

Parronchi, Antonio. "La prima rappresentazione della *Mandragola*. Il modello dell'apparato, L'allegoria." *La Bibliofilia* 64 (1962): 59-69.

Patch, Howard R. *The Goddess Fortuna in Mediaeval Literature.* 1927; rpt. New York: Octagon Books, 1974.

Pennington, D. H. *Seventeenth Century Europe.* London: Longman, 1970.

Piccolomini, Aeneas Silvius. *De liberorum educatione.* Ed. J. S. Nelson. Studies in Medieval and Renaissance Latin Language and Literature, 12. Washington, D.C.: Catholic University of America Press, 1940.

Picot, Emile, ed. *Recueil général des Sotties.* Société des anciens textes français. Paris: Firmin Didot, 1902. Vol. 1.

Pincin, Carlo. "Osservazioni sul modo di procedere di Machiavelli nei *Discorsi*." In *Renaissance Studies in Honor of Hans Baron*, ed. Anthony Molho and John A. Tedeschi, pp. 385-408. Dekalb: Northern Illinois University Press, 1971.

Pitkin, Hanna F. *Fortune Is a Woman: Gender and Politics in the Thought of Niccolò Machiavelli.* Berkeley and Los Angeles: University of California Press, 1984.

Pocock, J. G. A. *The Machiavellian Moment: Florentine Political Thought and the Atlantic Republican Tradition.* Princeton: Princeton University Press, 1975.

——. "Machiavelli in the Liberal Cosmos." *Political Theory* 13 (1985): 559-74.

Poggiolo, Renato. "The Oaten Flute." *Harvard Library Bulletin* 11 (1957): 147-84.

Praz, Mario. *Studi sul concettismo.* Florence: Sansoni, 1934.

Preuss, J. Samuel. "Machiavelli's Functional Analysis of Religion." *Journal of the History of Ideas* 40 (1979): 171-90.

Price, Russell. "The Senses of *Virtù* in Machiavelli." *European Studies Review* 3 (1973): 315-45.

——. "The Theme of *Gloria* in Machiavelli." *Renaissance Quarterly* 30 (1977): 588-631.

Raab, Felix. *The English Face of Machiavelli A Changing Interpretation, 1500–1700.* London: Routledge & Kegan Paul, 1964.

Radcliff-Umstead, Douglas. *The Birth of Modern Comedy in Renaissance Italy.* Chicago: University of Chicago Press, 1969.

Radin, Paul. *The Trickster: A Study in American Indian Mythology.* 1956; rpt. New York: Schocken, 1972.

Raimondi, Ezio. "Machiavelli and the Rhetoric of the Warrior." *Modern Language Notes* 92 (1977): 1-16.

——. *Politica e commedia: Dal Beroaldo al Machiavelli.* Bologna: Mulino, 1972.

Rebhorn, Wayne A. *Courtly Performances: Masking and Festivity in Ca-stiglione's "Book of the Courtier."* Detroit: Wayne State University Press, 1978.

———. "Machiavelli at Carpi: Confidence Games in the Republic of Wooden Clogs." *Italian Quarterly* 24 (1983): 27–40.

Ridolfi, Roberto. *The Life of Niccolò Machiavelli.* Trans. Cecil Grayson. Chicago: University of Chicago Press, 1963.

Rochon, André, ed. *Formes et significations de la "beffa" dans la littérature italienne de la Renaissance.* Publication du Centre de Recherche sur la Renaissance italienne. Paris: Université de la Sorbonne nouvelle, 1972.

Rosenmeyer, Thomas G. *The Green Cabinet: Theocritus and the European Pastoral.* Berkeley: University of California Press, 1969.

Ruffo-Fiore, Silvia. *Niccolò Machiavelli.* Boston: Twayne, 1982.

Ruggiero, Guido. *Violence in Early Renaissance Venice.* New Brunswick: Rutgers University Press, 1980.

Russo, Luigi. *Machiavelli.* 3d ed. Bari: Laterza, 1949.

Sasso, Gennaro. *Machiavelli e Cesare Borgia: Storia di un giudizio.* Rome: Ateneo, 1966.

———. *Niccolò Machiavelli: Storia del suo pensiero politico.* Naples: Istituto italiano per gli studi storici, 1958.

———. *Studi su Machiavelli.* Naples: Morano, 1967.

Segal, Erich. *Roman Laughter: The Comedy of Plautus.* Cambridge: Harvard University Press, 1968.

Shakespeare, William. *The Complete Works.* Ed. Alfred Harbage. New York: Viking Press, 1969.

Siegel, J. E. "Violence and Order in Machiavelli." In *Violence and Aggression in the History of Ideas*, ed. Philip P. Wiener and John Fisher, pp. 49–64. New Brunswick: Rutgers University Press, 1974.

Skinner, Quentin. *Machiavelli.* New York: Hill & Wang, 1981.

Spirito, Ugo. *Machiavelli e Guicciardini.* 4th ed. Florence: Sansoni, 1970.

Spivack, Bernard. *Shakespeare and the Allegory of Evil.* New York: Columbia University Press, 1958.

Stanford, W. B. *The Ulysses Theme: A Study in the Adaptability of a Traditional Hero.* 2d ed. Ann Arbor: University of Michigan Press, 1963.

Stone, Lawrence. "Social Mobility in England, 1500–1700." *Past and Present* 33 (1966): 17–55.

Strauss, Leo. *Thoughts on Machiavelli.* Glencoe, Ill.: Free Press, 1958.

Sumberg, Theodore A. "*La mandragola*: An Interpretation." *Journal of Politics* 2 (1940): 320–40.

Toliver, Harold E. *Pastoral Forms and Attitudes.* Berkeley: University of California Press, 1971.

Turner, Victor. *Dramas, Fields, and Metaphors: Symbolic Action in Human Society.* Ithaca: Cornell University Press, 1974.

Vanossi, Luigi. "Situazione e sviluppo del teatro machiavelliano." In *Lingua e strutture del teatro italiano del Rinascimento: Machiavelli, Ruzzante,*

Aretino, Guarini, Commedia dell'arte, ed. G. Folena, pp. 3-108. Padua: Liviana, 1970.

Wadlington, Warwick. *The Confidence Game in American Literature*. Princeton: Princeton University Press, 1975.

Waley, Daniel. "The Primitivist Element in Machiavelli's Thought." *Journal of the History of Ideas* 31 (1971): 91-98.

Whigham, Frank. *Ambition and Privilege: The Social Tropes of Elizabethan Courtesy Theory*. Berkeley: University of California Press, 1984.

Whitfield, J.H. "The Anatomy of Virtue." *Modern Language Review* 38 (1943): 222-25.

——. *Discourses on Machiavelli*. Cambridge: W. Heffer, 1969.

——. *Machiavelli*. 1947; rpt. New York: Russell & Russell, 1965.

Wilcox, Donald J. "The Sense of Time in Historical Narratives from Eusebius to Machiavelli." In *Classical Rhetoric and Medieval Historiography*, ed. Ernst Breisach, pp. 167-237. Studies in Medieval Culture, 19. Kalamazoo: Medieval Institute Publications, 1985.

Wood, Neal. "Machiavelli's Concept of *Virtù* Reconsidered." *Political Studies* 15 (1967): 160-72.

Woodward, William H., trans. *Vittorino da Feltre and Other Humanist Educators*. 1897; rpt. New York: Teachers College Press, 1963.

Index

Library of Congress Cataloging-in-Publication Data

Rebhorn, Wayne A., 1943–
  Foxes and lions.
  Bibliography: p. 251
  Includes index.
    1. Machiavelli, Niccolò, 1469-1527—Criticism and interpretation. 2. European
literature—Renaissance, 1450-1600—History and criticism. 3. Trickster in literature.
I. Title
PQ4627.M2Z784 1988   858'.309   87-47824
ISBN 0-8014-2095-4 (alk. paper)